LUSTMORD

The Writings and Artifacts of Murderers

edited by Brian King

BLOAT, a publishing company

a Bloat book

ISBN 0-9650324-0-X

Book design: Tom Dolan. Cover design: Bloat.

Bloat
P. O. Box 254
Burbank, California 91503
email bloat@cinenet.net
phone 818 759 6460

TABLE OF CONTENTS

INTRODUCTION

> *Art of the ugly soul.* One is limiting art much too severely when one demands that only the composed soul, suspended in moral balance, may express itself there. As in the plastic arts, there is in music and poetry an art of the ugly soul, as well as an art of the beautiful soul; and in achieving art's mightiest effects – breaking souls, moving stones, and humanizing animals – perhaps that very art has been most successful.
>
> – *Human, All Too Human*, Friedrich Nietzsche

> I sat in silence as my heart was pounding against my breast as it was rising involuntarily in an occasional deep reminiscent sob, than [sic] my deformity compelled, by heart became a grimace of hatred, crimson, and than my heart as though to have matirialized out of the atmosphere a wildcatten hatred burned into it, and it seem as though I could see my heart before my eyes, turning dark black with hate of rages, of harhequinade, stripped from that of munner life leaving only naked being-hate.
>
> – from the writings of Charles Starkweather, murderer

Obsessive, dedicated, alienated, neurotic, rebellious, inspired. Classic qualities of a writer, an artist: a creative person. But what if this creative person is a rapist, mutilator, torturer, murderer? A person who does not kill for money, does not kill a loved one in a moment of anger, does not kill an enemy in the field of combat, does not kill in self-defense, does not kill to exact revenge, does not kill for political gain? A person who takes pleasure in the act of murder, who kills for the simple delight of seeing another die?

A murderer – a person compelled to kill – does not, however, usually create with the intention of an artist. The substance of a murderer's creativity lies in how it is viewed. As viewed by a criminologist, it can be evidence of guilt; by a psychologist, evidence of psychosis; by a sociologist, evidence of class or cultural conflict. The phenomena surrounding the act of murder, however – letters, diaries, photographs, memoirs, essays, drawings, notes, poems – can also be viewed and evaluated as objects of unschooled creative expression.

The murderers in this volume lack a singularity of purpose save one: the need to express themselves through an outlet *other than murder.* They have attempted to decipher their psychopathic actions; their writings and artifacts are genuine human documents of sadism, guilt, delusion and madness, filtered through various forms of expiation, fabrication and exculpation. Some had such a need to express themselves that their words and images led to their capture, conviction and execution.

Novelists have long been entranced and captivated by the workings of the criminal mind, what Joseph Conrad called the "fascination of the abomination." The machinations of the diseased psyche have been insightfully displayed and examined by such authors as Fyodor Dostoevsky, Jim Thompson and Patricia Highsmith, and cynically exploited by such authors as James Ellroy and Bret Easton Ellis. Some literary figures have killed, or have attempted to kill, such as William S. Burroughs and Norman Mailer. But even the most imaginative writers of fiction cannot equal the stark intensity and demented enthusiasm evident in the authentic writings of murderers. These writings are an aesthetic testimony to the sickness and depravity, the emotion and logic, of a murderer's thoughts, a mind filled with terror and hatred, absurdity and horror, pathos and iniquity.

> Once we recognize the peculiar inception of the word *aesthetic* in the English language, and begin to appreciate the problematic role that aesthetics has come to play in Western philosophy and culture in general, we may begin to sense – although not without resistance – the extent to which our customary experience of murder and other forms of violence is primarily aesthetic, rather than moral, physical, natural, or whatever term we choose as a synonym for the word *real.* Only the victim knows the brutal "reality" of murder; the rest of us view it at a distance, often as rapt onlookers who regard its "reality" as a peak aesthetic experience.
>
> – *The Aesthetics of Murder,* Joel Black

> I would like to be able to free myself from this world, because it inhibits my creative ability. My mind cannot function properly when it is preoccupied with averting a social calamity and a personal tragedy. It is trying to fight the urge to relieve these terrible cravings. I am sure that there must be an answer somewhere, and some day I will be cured.
>
> – from the writings of Gerard Schaefer Jr., murderer

There is no glamour in the reality of murder; there is no glamour in the reality of death. It is the writer and artist who does *not* kill who usually attaches the sensibility of glamour to murder and death. These killers have no notion or pretension of murder as a surrealistic act – their murders were not enacted as performance art and their confessions were not recited as coffeehouse poetry. Their words are not merely modernist hieroglyphics; their writings retain their power only in the narrative of their murders. They have in common the knowledge that someone has died at their hands. They have crossed the line most of us would not care to cross.

It would be an injustice, to the murderers and their victims, to simply elevate these artifacts to the level of "art"; these men and women are killers first and artists second. As sociopaths, they have *really* given up being accepted as part of society; their alienation is not a pose to sell books and paintings. They have destroyed, and therein lies the fascination. Uninhibited and malicious, they have succumbed to the basest desires and taboos known to civilization: sexual murder, wholesale slaughter, necrophilia, cannibalism.

Most acts of murder are distinctively mundane. According to criminologist Marvin E. Wolfgang, "homicides are principally . . . violent slayings that are not premeditated or psychotic manifestations." A husband beats his wife in a jealous frenzy, a drunk stabs another inebriate outside a bar, an employee shoots his boss after being fired, a gang member shoots his enemies over turf. Unfortunately, the same lack of thought that results in these killers' imprisonment or death is also apparent in their words and imagery. Havelock Ellis noted in his pioneering book *The Criminal* that in the artwork of prisoners, "the design is pathetically commonplace; it is naturalistic in the lowest sense of the word, adding nothing, suppressing nothing."

Usually in conjunction with this typical kind of murderer is the notion of rehabilitation through expression; if these misguided souls can just *write* or *draw* away their rage, the catharsis can result in their being useful members of society. Writers' workshops in prisons across the country help prisoners with their writing skills, but this intervention usually removes them from the context of their own lives and reconditions them into a morass of Hemingway and Mailer clones. Most of the writing is also reflective of their circumstances; faced with prison for a substantial part of their lives, their words are used, as noted by one prison writer, "primarily as weapons of psychic survival and only incidentally as good literature."

The murderers in this book are societally in the minority: they are *Lustmörders*, or pleasure-killers. (The word *Lust* in the German language is defined as "joy, delight, desire"; when combined with other words, "comedy" [*Lustspiel*], "venereal disease" [*Lustseuche*], or "lustful murder" [*Lustmord*].) They can, through their forms of expression, be amazingly lucid and intelligent, sexually pornographic and cruel, amusingly self-serving and fantastic, disturbingly naive and unrepentant. They were chosen for this book on the basis of creative expression in relation to their crimes; their works were, in most cases, not muddied by prison workshops. Some are well-educated and write on a professional level, some are nearly illiterate. Their works were mostly created while in the arena of their crimes: before, during, or immediately after their moments of destruction.

The style and substance of the murderers' words and images vary as much as their origins and methods of violence. William Bonin, who was abused as a child, murdered twenty-one teenage boys and young men. An element of his writing is his role displacement of the adolescent as waif-like victim; he writes disturbingly from the point of view of the teenagers he tortured, raped and murdered. Jeannace Freeman mutilated and killed two of her lesbian lover's children. She attempts to convince the reader, in a bathetic, self-serving plea, that she is misunderstood, that she really tried to kill her manipulative lover, but the children tragically got in the way. Herbert Mullin shot and stabbed thirteen people to death. His poetry, notes and essays are rife with paranoia and madness, yet there is also an unconscious underlying tone of humor and sadness. Edgar Smith sexually assaulted and bludgeoned to death a teenage girl. In a chapter of his best-selling book Smith self-righteously proclaims his innocence while cruelly enumerating the details of his crime and libeling his victim and her family. Harvey Glatman raped and murdered three women after he photographed them in various forms of bondage. What would perhaps be cliché sadomasochistic pornography became, to Glatman, masturbatory relics documenting his ritual of murder.

As shown by Elliott Leyton in his book *Compulsive Killers*, the pleasure-killer of today "can only be accurately and objectively perceived as prime embodiment of [his] civilization [who] nets . . . a substantial social profit of revenge, celebrity, identity, and sexual relief." It is possible, based on this observation, to posit that the motivation to murder for pleasure is increasing due to the escalating oppressive hyperreality of our present world. In this context, Leyton sees these murderers as enacting "a kind of primitive rebellion against the social order . . ." He also notes, however, that "this fundamentally rebellious, not revolutionary, nature of their protest is undoubtedly why so few government and police resources are allocated to the capture of these killers (compared, say, to the huge police apparatus that monitors political dissidents), for they pose no threat to the established order – neither in their ideology nor in their acts."

> What we call evil in this world, moral as well as natural, is the grand principle that makes us sociable creatures, the solid basis, the life and support of all trades and employments without exception; that there we must look for the true origin of all arts and sciences, and that the moment evil ceases, the society must be spoiled, if not totally dissolved.
>
> – *The Fable of the Bees*, Bernard Mandeville

> Men have made a study of crime
> its cause, effect and the remedy.
> Many men know the effect.
> Many men know the cause.
> I know the remedy.
> The answer is. Truth.
>
> – from the writings of Carl Panzram, murderer

This is, by necessity, a morbid work. It is not, however, intended as a work of nihilism, although these writings and artifacts were chosen with darkness, absurdity and horror as the primary criteria. Perhaps when one acknowledges that evil is compelling and that we, as an audience, carry our own ideas of prurience and morality, one can enter this world with a clearer understanding of our vacillation between attraction and repulsion when the subject is murder.

ACKNOWLEDGMENTS

I would like to thank the following people for their valuable contributions and assistance: Deborah Eaglebarger and William Bonin; Richard Reynolds, author of *Cry for War*, for a copy of the Carsons' manuscript; Morgan Broadley and Andrew Codding for their library research relating to Jeannace Freeman; Janet Toal and Joseph Kallinger; Herbert Mullin for his preface and writings; the late Henry Lesser, who donated the Carl Panzram Papers to San Diego State University, and the staff of the University's Special Collections (Jenny Caguimbal, Martha McPhail, Ruth Leerhoff and Lynn Olsen); Bruce Yonemoto, for bringing Issei Sagawa to my attention, and Sumie Nobuhara, for her excellent translation of Sagawa's writings; and Richard R. Davison, for his generous contribution of research and writings relating to Charles Schmid.

I am also indebted to Tony Mostrom, who, at the beginning of this project, was extremely helpful with his research, especially relating to the writings of John George Haigh, William Edward Hickman, Carl Panzram and Pauline Parker.

I would also like to note my gratitude to the following people for their various observations, assistance and support: Barbara Bestor, Eli Bonerz, Eric Bonerz, Susan Bradley, Craig and Claudia Broadley, Michael Curtis, Tom Dolan, Lisa Fredriksen, Gary Ichihara, Tracy James, Yoko Kanayama, Jay and Virginie King, Susan King and Rob Pingel, Steve Knezevich, Sarah Koplin, Mariska Leyssius, Rachel Loeb, John and Gloria Panosian, Adam Silverman, Leonard and Suzanne Sklar, Gregory Walker and Jennifer Shortt, and Julie Weiss.

PREFACE

Herbert Mullin, author of the preface below, killed thirteen people between October 1972 and February 1973. Hearing voices and exhibiting other symptoms of paranoid schizophrenia, he believed he was saving mankind from a series of cataclysmic natural disasters with his murders. He is now serving a life sentence at the California Men's Colony in San Luis Obispo.

The clerical historians and accountants that accompanied Cortez on his journeys through Central and North America during the 16th century reported that there were approximately 10,000 human sacrifices every year in the new world that they explored. The theocracies of Middle America used human sacrifice to appease, placate, and petition the gods and goddesses of their theocracy.

The fatalities of war during the 17th, 18th, and 19th centuries here on Planet Earth clearly show that mankind's penchant for extreme violence is progressing with time.

Even in this, the 20th century, we find the numerical atrocities of World War I and World War II to be staggering and horrible.

One of the major themes of the New Testament of the Holy Bible is that Jesus Christ is the only Son of God, and that He came to Earth and became a man, was crucified to death, sacrificed so that mankind's sins could and would be forgiven, thus making it possible for all of us humans, even afterwards, to enter into a state of eternal life in the perfect kingdom of Heaven.

In the past 500 years approximately 30 million Native Americans have met with death because of the pressures of violence and imperialism.

Definitely the social, economic, political, and spiritual struggles of mankind sometimes result in violence, murder and killing. It is a historically proven fact.

Lustmord is a compilation of the writings and artworks of individuals from our Western civilization's culture that for some reason or another committed horrible and heinous crimes of violence and murder.

Brian King compiled these writings and arranged them in their present order in an attempt to illustrate the bizarre logic that surfaces in people who are driven into the territory of the criminally insane. He shows with comments and sequence the human delusions and viewpoints that preoccupied the minds of the individuals before, during and after the illegal, cruel, and terrible violent crimes.

The United States has a very violent problem. Statistics show that on the average 67 people are shot to death every day, 57 people are stabbed to death every day, and 57 children are beaten to death every day. The United States is eleven times more violent in these areas than any other country in the industrially developed nations.

One of the modern reasons for our society's penchant for violence lies in our entertainment. Television violence, movie violence, and musical lyric violence all have created a subconscious psychological atmosphere that develops in the viewer, a propensity for violence. Everett Koop, former Surgeon General of the U.S.A., made a similar finding in his report to Congress of the effects of television and movie violence here in America.

The U.S.A. National Institute of Mental Health and the American Mental Health Association have cooperated with the President's Council on Physical and Mental Health to create guidelines for the development, preservation and maintenance of mental and physical health. It would be a very good thing if those guidelines would be taught in our nation's classrooms, homes, and churches.

Lustmord explores some of the individual writings of a few people. Perhaps it will give you, the reader, a chance to see for yourself the necessity of avoiding crime and unhealthy psychological atmospheres.

Herbert Wm. Mullin
— Saturday —

Concerning Herbert Wm. Mullin on the day he wrote the preface to **Lustmord** ——

I am 44 yrs. old —. 1/2 Irish, 1/4 English & 1/4 Norse-Scandanavian —. I have been behind prison bars for 18 yrs. 7 months 21 days —. I have never been married and I have no children —. I would love to sire children, get married, and experience the love and happiness of my family —. I enjoy poetry, natural beauty, birds and bees, flowers and trees, clouds and wind, earth and sky —.

The majority of the state psychiatrists and psychologists have concidered me a paranoid schitzophrenic, guilty and responsible for the crimes I am convicted of committing —.

One of them told me in a private conversation that he knows that my family and friends caused me to committ the crimes —. He said that he knows that the other psychs know that I was forced by my family and friends to committ the crimes —. He said that there is no way of proving it in court —. So, this is the way California traditionally deals with such a case —. He said that Society will slowly punish my family and friends in the Social and Ecconomic AREANAS —. Meanwhile I will be treated as a paranoid schitzophrenic, guilty and responsible for the crimes —.

With all these legal psychological problems, I am having a hard time finding a young woman who is like me physically and mentally, spiritually and socially — I really need a woman, a wife — I hope someone who reads this will find me worthwhile enough to sponsor in my search for a wife, and then children!!

LUSTMORD

The Writings and Artifacts of Murderers

GERTRUDE **BANISZEWSKI**

In the summer of 1965, 16-year-old Sylvia Likens and her younger sister Jenny were taken as boarders by Gertrude Baniszewski, a 37-year-old divorced housewife living in Indianapolis, while their parents worked in a travelling fair. During the following weeks until her murder on October 26, 1965, Sylvia was imprisoned and tortured by Baniszewski and four accomplices: Baniszewski's two children, Paula and John, and two neighborhood teenagers, Coy Hubbard and Richard "Rickie" Hobbs. Tied up in the basement of the Baniszewski house, Sylvia Likens was burned with cigarettes and matches, starved, beaten, mutilated and sexually assaulted. Her death resulted from a heavy blow to the head by Baniszewski. The murder instrument: a book.

Baniszewski's youthful accomplices served short prison sentences, while Baniszewski was sentenced to life in prison. She was released over twenty years later.

Sometime before her death, Sylvia Likens was forced to write the following note – dictated by Baniszewski – to her mother and father:

Dear Mom and Dad,
I am writing to tell you what I've done for the last two weeks. I went to school and took a gym suit out of the girls gym locker.
I went to the park and was going to take some cokes out of a coke machine.
I let Ronnie and Donnie Simpson have intercorse with me. Danny and Jenny knows about it.
In California I was under the covers with Mike Erson. Jenny & Benny seen Mike's pants down.
I was trying to get Jenny in trouble with me.
I told lies on Mommie to Grandma Martin.
I hit a three year old kid in the face and spanked it on the butt.
At the house out on Post Road.
I stole things in California when we lived out there.
The reason why I got fired from that job in Post Road is because I hit the boy in the face.
I done things that could cause alot of trouble.
I always want Mommy and Daddy to break up so I could get my way when I live with Mommie.
I went out with a married man driving around in a convertible.
I took ten dollars from Gertie Wright [Baniszewski].

I knocked Jimmy B. off my back.
I hit Shirley B. for no reason.
This is all the truth.
Jenny has been behaving herself.
Sylvia Likens

When Sylvia Likens was near death, Baniszewski and Rickie Hobbs used a white-hot needle to brand the following statement on Likens' stomach:

I am a prostitute and proud of it

Following this torture, Baniszewski made Likens write the following note:

To Mr and Mrs Likens,

I went with a gang of boys in the middle of the night and they said that they would pay me if I would give them something so I got in the car and they all got what they wanted and they did and when they finished they beat me up and left sores on my face and all over my body.

And they also put on my stomach, I am a prostitute and proud of it. I have done just about everything that I could do just to make Gertie mad and cost Gertie more money than she's got. I've tore up a new mattress and peaed on it. I have also cost Gertie doctor bills that she really can't pay and made Gertie a nervous wreck. I have broken another kitchen chair. I have been making Gertie a nervous wreck and all her kids. I cost her $35.00 for a hospital in one day and I wouldn't do nothing around the house. I have done any thing to do things to make things out of the way to make things worse for them.

MARY BELL

Eleven-year-old Mary Bell murdered two young boys from Newcastle, England, in the early summer of 1968. With her friend Norma Bell (no relation) present, she strangled 4-year-old Martin Brown on May 25 and 3-year-old Brian Howe on July 31; she also mutilated Howe's body with a pair of scissors and a razor, carving the letter "M" on his stomach. Four days after Brown's body was found, Mary Bell asked his mother if she could see him. When Mrs. Brown told her that her son was dead, Mary replied with a grin, "Oh, I know he's dead. I wanted to see him in his coffin."

Brian Howe was buried on August 7, a week after his murder. Chief-Inspector James Dobson later recounted to Gitta Sereny, author of *The Case of Mary Bell*, what he observed the morning of the funeral:

> Mary Bell was standing in front of the Howes' house when the coffin was brought out. I was, of course, watching her. And it was when I saw her there that I knew I did not dare risk another day. She stood there, laughing. Laughing and rubbing her hands. I thought, My God, I've got to bring her in, she'll do another one.

Dobson had Mary and Norma arrested that afternoon. Both girls accused the other of the murders; tried in court, Norma was acquitted, and Mary was found guilty of manslaughter. Sentenced to serve time in an institution where she was the only girl among twenty-two older boys, she escaped in 1977 at the age of twenty and lost her virginity during her three days of freedom. When she was later released, Mary Bell was described as "an attractive woman" who "expressed the wish to live near her mother."

The following is Mary's oral statement, taken by police after her arrest on August 7, 1968. Feigning innocence, she unsuccessfully attempted to frame her friend Norma Bell for the murder of Brian Howe:

> I, Mary Flora Bell wish to make a statement. I want someone to write down what I have to say. I have been told that I need not say anything unless I wish to do so, but that whatever I say may be given in evidence.
>
> Signed: Mary F. Bell

Brian was in his front street and me and Norma were walking along towards him. We walked past him and Norma says, "are you coming to the shop Brian" and I says, "Norma, you've got no money, how can you go to the shop. Where are you getting it from?" She says, "nebby" (Keep your nose clean). Little Brian followed and Norma says, "walk up in front." I wanted Brian to go home, but Norma kept coughing so Brian wouldn't hear us. We went down Crosshill Road with Brian still in front of us. There was this coloured boy and Norma tried to start a fight with him. She said, "Darkie, whitewash, it's time you got washed." The big brother came out and hit her. She shouted, "Howay, put your dukes up." The lad walked away and looked at her as though she was daft. We went beside Dixon's shop and climbed over the railings, I mean through a hole and over the railway. Then I said, "Norma, where are you going?" and Norma said, "Do you know that little pool where the tadpoles are?" When we got there, there was a big, long tank with a big, round hole with little holes round it. Norma says to Brian, "Are you coming in here because there's a lady coming on the Number 82 and she's got boxes of sweets and that." We all got inside, then Brian started to cry and Norma asked him if he had a sore throat. She started to squeeze his throat and he started to cry. She said, "This isn't where the lady comes, it's over there, by them big blocks." We went over to the blocks and she says, "Ar – you'll have to lie down" and he lay down beside the blocks where he was found. Norma says, "Put your neck up" and he did. Then she got hold of his neck and said "Put it down." She started to feel up and down his neck. She squeezed it hard, you could tell it was hard because her finger tips were going white. Brian was struggling, and I was pulling her shoulders but she went mad. I was pulling her chin up but she screamed at me. By this time she had banged Brian's head on some wood or corner of wood and Brian was lying senseless. His face was all white and bluey, and his eyes were open. His lips were purplish and had all like slaver on, it turned into something like fluff. Norma covered him up and I said, "Norma, I've got nothing to do with this, I should tell on you, but I'll not." Little Lassie was there it was crying and she said, "Don't you start or I'll do the same to you." It still cried and she went to get hold of its throat but it growled at her. She said, "Now now, don't be hasty." We went home and I took little Lassie home an all. Norma was acting kind of funny and making twitchy faces and spreading her fingers out. She said, "This is the first but it'll not be the last." I was frightened then. I carried Lassie and put her down over the railway and we went up Crosswood Road way. Norma went into the house and she got a pair of scissors and she put them down her pants. She says, "go and get a pen." I said "No, what for." She says, "To write a note on his stomach," and I wouldn't get the pen. She had a Gillette razor blade. It had Gillette on. We went back to the blocks and Norma cut his hair. She tried to cut his leg and his ear with the blade. She tried to show me it was sharp, she took the top of her dress where it was raggie and cut it, it made a slit. A man come down the railway bank with a little girl with long, blonde hair, he had a red checked shirt on and blue denim jeans. I walked away. She hid the razor blade under a big, square concrete block. She left the scissors beside him. She got out before me over the grass on to Scotswood Road. I couldn't run on the grass cos I just had my black slippers on. When we got along a bit she says, "May, you shouldn't have done cos you'll get into trouble" and I hadn't done nothing I haven't got the guts. I couldn't kill a bird by the neck or throat or anything, it's horrible that. We went up the steps and went home, I was nearly crying. I said, if Pat finds out she'll kill you, never mind killing Brian cos Pat's more like a tomboy. She's always climbing in the old buildings and that. Later on I was helping to

look for Brian and I was trying to let on to Pat that I knew where he was on the blocks, but Norma said, "he'll not be over there, he never goes there," and she convinced Pat he wasn't there. I got shouted in about half past seven and I stayed in. I got woke up about half past eleven and we stood at the door as Brian had been found: The other day Norma wanted to get put in a home. She says will you run away with us and I said no. She said if you get put in a home and you feed the little ones and murder them then run away again.
I have read the above statement and I have been told that I can correct, alter or add anything I wish, this statement is true. I have made it of my own free will.

Mary Flora Bell

On May 26, 1968, the day after Martin Brown was murdered, Mary Bell broke into and vandalized the Day Nursery School. Police found in the debris four notes that were later proven to be Mary's:

The first note:

I murder
SO That
I may come
back

The second note:

fuch of
we murder
watch out
Fanny
and Faggot

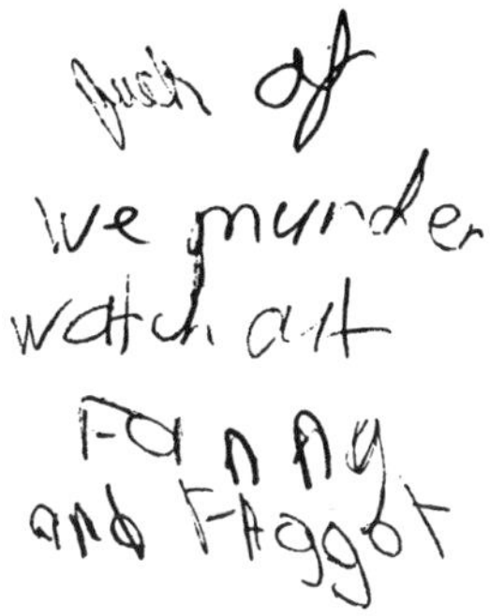

The third note:

WE did
murder
martain
brown
Fuckof
you Bastard

The fourth note:

You ArE micey
y BECUASE
WE murderd
MArtain GO
Brown you BEttEr
Look out THErE
are MurdErs aBout
By FAnny AnD
and auld Faggot
you Srcews

The day after vandalizing the nursery school, Mary wrote the following entry in her school "Newsbook"; there was also an illustration at the bottom of the entry where she crudely reproduced the crime scene and position of Martin Brown's body. (The word "TABLEt" in the illustration refers to a bottle of pills that were found near the body; the pills were initially thought by police to be the cause of his death.)

On saturday I was in the house. and my mam sent Me to ask Norma if she Would come up the top with me? we went up and we came down at Magrets Road and there were crowds of people beside an old house. I asked what was the matter. there has been a boy who Just lay down and Died.

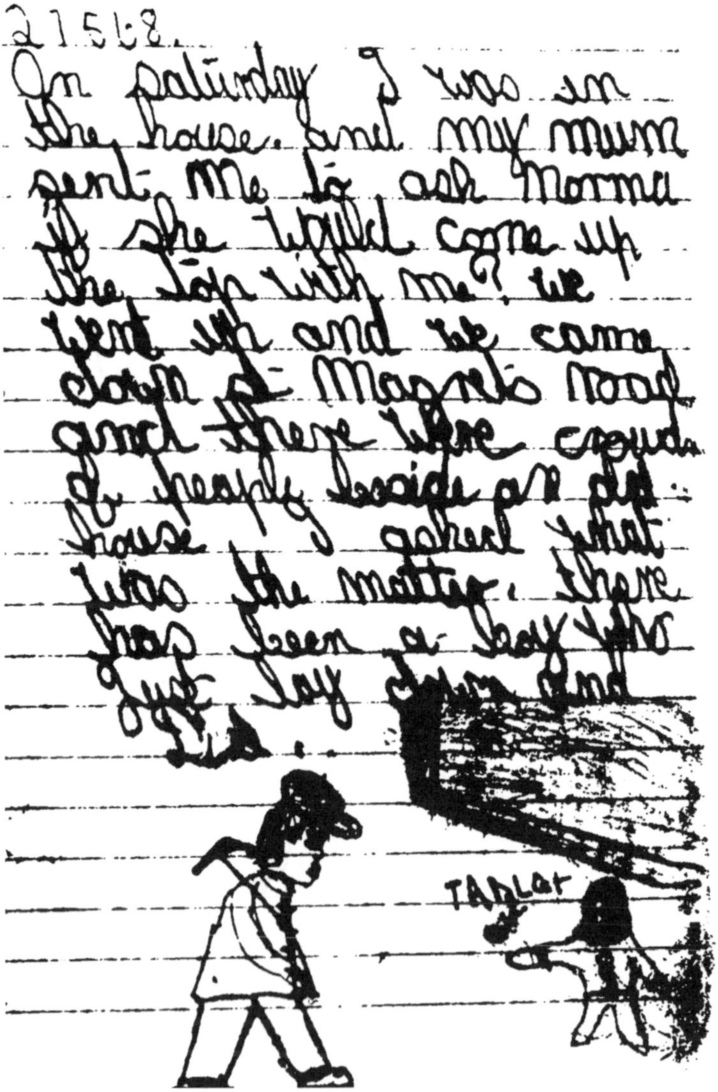

Poem sent to a policewoman after her trial:

A Christmas poem

I looked out the window one night
Oh what a beautiful sight —
There was a shrill call, it was
from the wall. Help! Help! Please
let me out a squicky voice
began to shout. I've ate an
hamburger. But you'll commite
Murder if you don't let me
out.

Letter/poem sent to her mother in the spring of 1970:

MAM

I know that in my heart
From you once was not apart
My love for you grows
More each day
When you visit me mam
I'd weep once your away
I look into your eyes, so blue and
they're very sad. you try to be very
cheery. But I know you think IM Bad so Bad
though I really dont know If you
feel the same,
and treat it as a silly game
a child who has made criminal fame
Please mam put my tiny mind at ease
tell Judge and Jury on your knees
they will LISTEN to your cry of PLEAS
THE GUILTY ONE IS you not me
I sorry it HAS to BE this way
We'll both cry and you will go away
to other gates were you are free
locked up in prison cells.
Your famley are wee,
these last words I speak, on behalf
of dad . . . and me
tell them you are guilty
Please, so then mam, Ill be free, Daughter
May

DAVID BERKOWITZ

For a period of one year – from July 29, 1976 to July 31, 1977 – 24-year-old postal worker David Berkowitz shot to death five women and one man, and seriously wounded another four men and three women. Prowling the New York boroughs of Queens, Brooklyn, and the Bronx in his 1970 cream-colored Ford Galaxie, he targeted mostly young couples necking in their cars after an evening at the discos or the movies. By the late spring and early summer of 1977 the people of New York were in a frenzied state of panic, fed in part by blaring headlines trumpeting the ".44 Caliber Killer" and – after his letters to the police and the *Daily News* were released – the "Son of Sam." A parking ticket received while he was shooting his last victims led to his arrest on August 10, 1977. In his confessions to police, Berkowitz stated that voices of demons commanded him to kill, and named his 64-year-old neighbor Sam Carr, a retired city of Yonkers employee, as his main tormentor (thus the moniker, "Son of Sam"). Berkowitz told police Carr was actually 6,000 years old and spoke to him through Harvey, Carr's black Labrador retriever. (He attempted to silence the canine "demon" by shooting him in the leg on April 27, 1977, but the dog survived.)

He was, however, judged sane enough to be prosecuted for his crimes. Dr. David Abrahamsen, a psychiatrist for the prosecution who interviewed Berkowitz extensively, stated somewhat ambivalently:

> David feels that his distorted beliefs are of such importance that all other topics should be relegated to the sidelines. Thus, the defendant's main excuse for committing the crimes is his delusions. It is also noteworthy that the delusions the defendant states he has, seem to be more transitory and situational, rather than constant. They may, in fact, be exaggerated by him. . . . While the defendant shows paranoid traits, they do not interfere with his fitness to stand trial.

Berkowitz immediately pleaded guilty to second-degree murder and was sentenced to serve 365 consecutive years in prison. Residing as Prisoner #78-A-1976 at Attica Correctional Facility, he will be eligible for parole in 1999.

Letter of April 17, 1977; addressed to a Queens police detective, Captain Joseph Borrelli, it was found on the street at the Bronx murder scene of Valentina Suriani and Alexander Esau:

I AM DEEPLY HURT BY YOUR CALLING
ME A WEMON HATER. I AM NOT.
BUT I AM A MONSTER.
I AM THE "SON OF SAM." I AM A LITTLE
"BRAT."

WHEN FATHER SAM GETS DRUNK
HE GETS MEAN. HE BEATS HIS
FAMILY. SOMETIMES HE TIES ME
UP TO THE BACK OF THE HOUSE.
OTHER TIMES HE LOCKS ME
IN THE GARAGE. SAM LOVES TO
DRINK BLOOD.

"GO OUT AND KILL" COMMANDS
FATHER SAM.

BEHIND OUR HOUSE SOME
REST. MOSTLY YOUNG – RAPED
AND SLAUGHTERED – THEIR
BLOOD DRAINED – JUST BONES
NOW

PAPA SAM KEEPS ME LOCKED
IN THE ATTIC, TOO. I CAN'T
GET OUT BUT I LOOK OUT THE
ATTIC WINDOW AND WATCH
THE WORLD GO BY.

I FEEL LIKE AN OUTSIDER.
I AM ON A DIFFERENT WAVE
LENGTH THEN EVERYBODY
ELSE – PROGRAMMED TOO
KILL.

HOWEVER, TO STOP ME YOU
MUST KILL ME. ATTENTION
ALL POLICE: SHOOT ME FIRST –
SHOOT TO KILL OR ELSE.
KEEP OUT OF MY WAY OR
YOU WILL DIE!

PAPA SAM IS OLD NOW.
HE NEEDS SOME BLOOD TO
PRESERVE HIS YOUTH.
HE HAS HAD TOO MANY
HEART ATTACKS. TOO MANY
HEART ATTACKS. "UGH ME
HOOT IT URTS SONNY BOY."

I MISS MY PRETTY
PRINCESS MOST OF ALL.
SHE'S RESTING IN
OUR LADIES HOUSE
BUT I'LL SHE HER SOON.

I AM THE "MONSTER" –
"BEELZEBUB" – THE
"CHUBBY BEHEMOUTH."

I AM DEEPLY HURT BY YOUR CALLING
ME A WEMON HATER. I AM NOT.
BUT I AM A MONSTER.
I AM THE "SON OF SAM." I AM A LITLE
"BRAT."
WHEN FATHER SAM GETS DRUNK
HE GETS MEAN. HE BEATS HIS
FAMILY. SOMETIMES HE TIES ME
UP TO THE BACK OF THE HOUSE.
OTHER TIMES HE LOCKS ME
IN THE GARAGE. SAM LOVES TO
DRINK BLOOD.
"GO OUT AND KILL" COMMANDS
FATHER SAM.
BEHIND OUR HOUSE SOME
REST. MOSTLY YOUNG – RAPED
AND SLAUGHTERED – THEIR
BLOOD DRAINED – JUST BONES
NOW
PAPA SAM KEEPS ME LOCKED
IN THE ATTIC, TOO. I CAN'T
GET OUT BUT I LOOK OUT THE
ATTIC WINDOW AND WATCH
THE WORLD GO BY.
I FEEL LIKE AN OUTSIDER.
I AM ON A DIFFERENT WAVE
LENGTH THEN EVERYBODY

ELSE – PROGRAMMED TOO
KILL.
HOWEVER, TO STOP ME YOU
MUST KILL ME. ATTENTION
ALL POLICE: SHOOT ME FIRST –
SHOOT TO KILL OR ELSE.
KEEP OUT OF MY WAY OR
YOU WILL DIE!

PAPA SAM IS OLD NOW.
HE NEEDS SOME BLOOD TO
PRESERVE HIS YOUTH.
HE HAS HAD TOO MANY
HEART ATTACKS. TOO MANY
HEART ATTACKS. "UGH ME
HOOT IT URTS SONNY BOY."

I MISS MY PRETTY
PRINCESS MOST OF ALL.
SHE'S RESTING IN
OUR LADIES HOUSE
BUT I'LL SHE HER SOON.

I AM THE "MONSTER" –
"BEELZEBUB" – THE
"CHUBBY BEHEMOUTH."

I LOVE TO HUNT. PROWLING
THE STREETS LOOKING FOR
FAIR GAME – TASTY MEAT. THE
WEMON OF QUEENS ARE Z
PRETTYIST OF ALL. I MUST
BE THE WATER THEY DRINK.
I LIVE FOR THE HUNT – MY LIFE.
BLOOD FOR PAPA.

MR. BORELLI, SIR,
I DONT WANT TO KILL ANYMORE
NO SIR, NO MORE BUT I
MUST, "HONOUR THY FATHER."

I WANT TO MAKE LOVE TO THE
WORLD. I LOVE PEOPLE.
I DON'T BELONG ON EARTH.
RETURN ME TO YAHOOS.

TO THE PEOPLE OF QUEENS,
I LOVE YOU. AND I
WANT TO WISH ALL OF
YOU A HAPPY EASTER.
MAY GOD BLESS YOU
IN THIS LIFE AND IN
THE NEXT AND FOR NOW
I SAY GOODBYE AND
GOODNIGHT.

POLICE – LET ME
HAUNT YOU WITH THESE
WORDS;

I'LL BE BACK!

I'LL BE BACK!

TO BE INTERRPRETED
AS – BANG, BANG, BANG,
BANK, BANG – UGH!!

YOURS IN
MURDER

MR. MONSTER

Letter of May 30, 1977, addressed to New York *Daily News* columnist Jimmy Breslin:

HELLO FROM THE GUTTERS OF N.Y.C.,
WHICH ARE FILLED WITH DOG MANURE,
VOMIT, STALE WINE, URINE, AND BLOOD.
HELLO FROM THE SEWERS OF N.Y.C. WHICH
SWALLOW UP THESE DELICACIES WHEN
THEY ARE WASHED AWAY BY THE SWEEPER
TRUCKS. HELLO FROM THE CRACKS IN THE
SIDEWALKS OF N.Y.C. AND FROM THE
ANTS THAT DWELL IN THESE CRACKS
AND FEED ON THE DRIED BLOOD OF THE
DEAD THAT HAS SEEPED INTO THESE CRACKS.
J.B., I'M JUST DROPPING YOU A LINE
TO LET YOU KNOW THAT I APPRECIATE
YOUR INTEREST IN THOSE RECENT AND
HORRENDOUS .44 KILLINGS. I ALSO
WANT TO TELL YOU THAT I READ YOUR
COLUMN DAILY AND I FIND IT QUITE
INFORMATIVE.
TELL ME JIM, WHAT WILL YOU
HAVE FOR JULY TWENTY-NINTH?
YOU CAN FORGET ABOUT ME IF YOU
LIKE BECAUSE I DON'T CARE FOR
PUBLICITY. HOWEVER YOU MUST
NOT FORGET DONNA LAURIA AND
YOU CANNOT LET THE PEOPLE FORGET
HER EITHER. SHE WAS A VERY,
VERY SWEET GIRL BUT SAM'S A
THIRSTY LAD AND HE WON'T LET ME
STOP KILLING UNTIL HE GETS HIS
FILL OF BLOOD.

MR. BRESLIN, SIR, DON'T THINK
THAT BECAUSE YOU HAVEN'T HEARD FROM
FOR A WHILE THAT I WENT TO SLEEP.
NO, RATHER, I AM STILL HERE. LIKE
A SPIRIT ROAMING THE NIGHT.
THIRSTY, HUNGRY, SELDOM STOPPING
TO REST; ANXIOUS TO PLEASE SAM.
I LOVE MY WORK. NOW, THE VOID
HAS BEEN FILLED.

PERHAPS WE SHALL MEET FACE TO
FACE SOMEDAY OR PERHAPS I WILL
BE BLOWN AWAY BY COPS WITH
SMOKING .38'S. WHATEVER, IF I
SHALL BE FORTUNATE ENOUGH TO
MEET YOU I WILL TELL YOU ALL ABOUT
SAM IF YOU LIKE AND I WILL
INTRODUCE YOU TO HIM. HIS NAME
IS "SAM THE TERRIBLE."

NOT KNOWING WHAT THE FUTURE
HOLDS I SHALL SAY FAREWELL AND
I WILL SEE YOU AT THE NEXT JOB.
OR SHOULD I SAY YOU WILL SEE
MY HANDIWORK AT THE NEXT JOB?
REMEMBER MS. LAURIA. THANK YOU.
IN THEIR BLOOD
AND
FROM THE GUTTER
"SAM'S CREATION" .44
HERE ARE SOME NAMES TO HELP YOU ALONG.
FORWARD THEM TO THE INSPECTOR FOR
USE BY N.C.I.C.:
"THE DUKE OF DEATH"
"THE WICKED KING WICKER"
"THE TWENTY TWO DISCIPLES OF HELL"
"JOHN 'WHEATIES' — RAPIST AND SUFF-
OCATER OF YOUNG GIRLS."

PS: J.B. PLEASE INFORM ALL THE
DETECTIVES WORKING THE
SLAYING TO REMAIN.

P.S: JB, PLEASE INFORM ALL THE
DETECTIVES WORKING THE
CASE THAT I WISH THEM THE BEST
OF LUCK. "KEEP 'EM
DIGGING, DRIVE ON, THINK
POSITIVE, GET OFF YOUR
BUTTS, KNOCK ON COFFINS, ETC."

UPON MY CAPTURE I PROMISE TO
BUY ALL THE GUYS WORKING
ON THE CASE A NEW PAIR OF
SHOES IF I CAN GET UP THE
MONEY.
SON OF SAM

Written on the back of the envelope:

BLOOD AND FAMILY
DARKNESS AND DEATH
ABSOLUTE DEPRAVITY
.44

In March of 1977, 26-year-old Craig Glassman separated from his wife and moved into apartment 6E of the Pineview Towers at 35 (since changed to 42 by the owner) Pine Street in Yonkers, New York. Employed as a registered nurse at Montefiore Hospital in the Bronx, he was also a part-time volunteer deputy sheriff in the Emergency Services Unit of the Westchester County Sheriff's office; as such, he sometimes came home late at night wearing his sheriff's uniform and carrying a licensed gun in his holster. Unfortunately, Glassman's upstairs neighbor in apartment 7E was the "Son of Sam." Berkowitz, observing his neighbor from a distance, thought the police had sent a spy. Interviewed by Lawrence Klausner for his book *Son of Sam*, Berkowitz recounted his conviction that the burly Glassman was evil personified:

> He just came – he just appeared one day – this Craig. He remained hidden in the walls and in the floor. He made funny screams all night long. I used to beg him to stop yelling and screaming, but he'd never listen. His real name was Gregunto Lacinto. He was one of *them*. He's got power to go into my mind. There was no doubt about who he was.

Towards the end of his murder spree, Berkowitz sent a total of five letters to Glassman. The first letter was postmarked June 7, 1977:

Craig Glassman,

You have been chosen. You have been chosen
to die.
Craig I curse your mothers grave. I curse
your mothers grave. I am pissing on her
Craig. urinating on her head
Your mouth is filled with cum. you
blood is sour.
You, Craig Glassman, are truly Satan's
child, and now, he wants you by his side.
Come join him in death little ones
Master Glassman, you are a man with
power (the power of darkness). You are hereby
ordered to onleash your terror upon the
people. "Destroy all good and ruin peoples'
lives. Begin immediately!"
Mighty Craig, where is your weapon.
If you don't obey thes commands, the
commands of you father then you will
be punished. I swear, Glassman, your life will
be pure Hell.
We will kill you. We will murder you.
Remember, Craig that your mother the harlot
the lesbian whore wants to love your
so make her happy – kill some your child.
Remember if you dont do as we say you
will surely die a premature death.

Your brothers & sisters
Craig darling

Craig Glassman the cruelest sickest man
on earth.
cruel Glassman, cruel Glassman,
mean, terrible, cruel, hateful Craig Glassman,
Die Craig Die

The return address on the envelope read:

Mother, The Cemetery
174 Coligni Avenue
New Rochelle, New York 10801

The second letter, postmarked July 13, 1977:

My Superior: Craig Glassman

Sergeont Glassman,

I know how successful you have been with your assignment, forcing me out into the street for Mr. Carr, however, the dead are crying in their graves for justice and God has promised it to them.

I myself realize that I am beyond hope and redemption because I have succumbed to the powers' of your commander, Mister Carr. I obey all my orders as you well know and I carry them out dutifully. But we must face the fact that our deaths will come one day. Then there shall be the Judgement! Since you are a fallen angel and have been condemned it the eternal fire before the earth was created, still, God will be more merciful to you if you rebel against General Cosmo and his horde of demons.

There is at this time little for you to gain by loyal service. I believe the end of the "Reign of Terror" is near and the authorities will be dealing with you in their own way.

I guess I'm foolish to plead with you to surrender and turn to God because I know that your soul is evil and that you have no heart. Therefore, you will have to spend eternity in the lowest depths of Hell. Don't fear because Captain Carr and his family, and me will be at your side.

You have done well in your 6,000 plus years of service. You have taken over my soul despite my early resistance and

my denials and protests. Go ahead
if you must and continue to torture
the people of earth. Don't stop
issuing Captain Carr's wrath upon the
world at my plea's. Just go ahead
you cruel monster and continue
your torments. You will stand naked
at the Judgement seat of Christ.

Deso

Your Brother Demesmutz

The return address read:

Bro. Demesmutz
Command Post 316
Gibor Merritt Aves
Bronx 10475

"Bro. Demesmutz" loosely translates as "Brother Little Shit" in Yiddish.

The third letter, postmarked August 6, 1977. Berkowitz mailed this letter after setting fire to some rubbish he deposited in front of Glassman's metal apartment door; he also threw approximately twenty .22-caliber long-rifle bullets into the fire, but Glassman doused the fire before they could explode:

My Master;

Craig, you will be punished!
Craig, how dare you force
me into the night to do
your bidding!
I promise you Craig
that the world shall spit
on you and your mother.

I know Master that I am
doomed but do not think
that I will not tell the
authorities of you.
True, I am the killer
but Craig, the killings are
your commands.

I shall see you standing
naked at the Judgement
seat. Upon your condemnation
the world shall rise in
jubulation. "The Terrible, Wicked
Craig is dead" they shall shout.

The streets have been filled
with blood Glassman, per
your request.

Your Brother

The fourth letter, postmarked the same day as the third:

So In the morning the streets of
White Plains, N.Y. have been covered with
blood, as per, the request of **Craig**.

As your servant shall serve you until
the end — but it shall come quickly.

Cruel, Crazy Craig says "the streets
shall be run with blood."

So Craig, in your honour
I present you with many corpses
so that you should have plenty
of meat in the off season.

Your Brother

White Plains N.Y.
God help and keep
the dead

Berkowitz sent the fifth and last letter, postmarked September 20, 1977, to Glassman from Attica after being sentenced:

My Brother and my Lord,

Lord Craig forgive me
for my failings and disruptions
to your cause.
I see now how wise the
Master as been in these
last few weeks. For trully
what you've said has come
true – That I would be
standing naked at the
end of my life.
You and Papa have done
well in concealing your
true identities to earth.
Their are many of you, in-
vaders, in high places
of government awaiting the

orders to destroy Good.
But I, God willing, am
ready to tell the world
about you. I am not
afraid of your Magic Box
nor your death rays.
I tried to kill you,
like a fool. I know
that you can never
die but what could
I do.
I shall attempt to tell
the world of your real
existense and mission.
Judging from your
silence, one could
anticipate my folly.
However, my words
shall be realeased
to the people of the earth.
I pray to God for
your destruction.
Your Brother and slave
Demesmutz

When Berkowitz was captured and searched, police found a poem addressed to Glassman in his wallet:

BECAUSE CRAIG IS CRAIG
SO MUST THE STREETS
BE FILLED WITH CRAIG (DEATH)

AND HUGE DROPS OF LEAD
POURED DOWN UPON HER HEAD
UNTIL SHE WAS DEAD
YET, THE CATS STILL COME OUT
AT NIGHT TO MATE
AND THE SPARROWS STILL
SING IN THE MORNING

In his apartment, Berkowitz wrote the following graffiti on his walls:

God Save
Us From
Craig Glassman

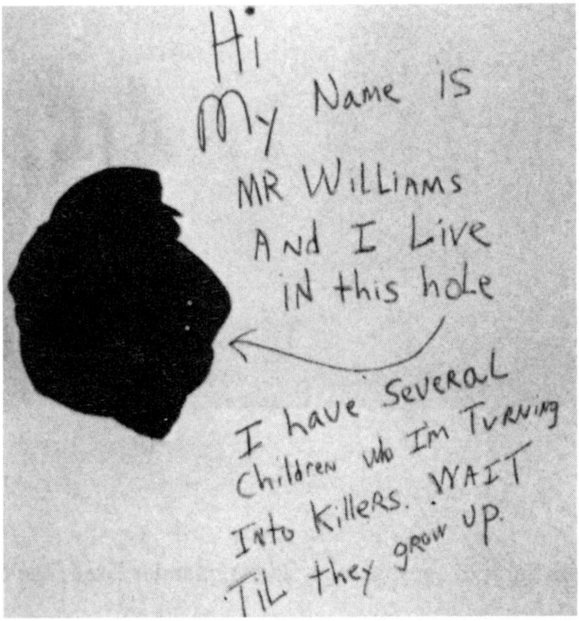

My Name is
Craig Glassman
And I Shall Never
let a soul rest

CRAIG
GLASSMAN
WORSHIPS
THE
DEVIL AND
HAS POWER
OVER ME

KILL
FOR
SAM
CARR

SAM
CARR
MY MASTER
X

Hi
My Name is
MR Williams
And I Live
in this hole
[an arrow pointed towards a hole in the wall]

I have several
children who I'm Turning
Into Killers. WAIT
TIL they grow up

WILLIAM **BONIN**

In the 1970s and early '80s, Southern California became a dumping ground for the bodies of murdered teenage boys and young men. They were runaways, hustlers, servicemen, hitchhikers; most of their bodies – numbering over one hundred – were found near the freeways, and all of them had been sexually assaulted and mutilated in some manner. The news media proclaimed that a lone "Freeway Killer" was at work, but the courts eventually tried and convicted three South Bay residents as the main offenders: Randy Kraft, a computer programmer from Long Beach, with a total of sixty-seven victims between 1972 and 1983; Patrick Kearney, a Hughes Aircraft engineer from Redondo Beach, with a total of twenty-eight victims between 1966 and 1977; and William Bonin, a truck driver from Downey, with a total of twenty-one murders between 1978 and 1980. Bonin's murderous scorecard could have easily surpassed the other two if his "career" hadn't been cut short by his arrest on June 11, 1980.

Bonin's father, an alcoholic and gambler who routinely abused his wife and sons, died from cirrhosis of the liver when Bonin was a child. Bonin was arrested at the age of ten, and while serving in a detention center he was molested by a counselor. Thereafter, according to Dennis McDougal in his book *Angel of Darkness*, Bonin developed an "unstinting, often schizophrenic, interest in pedophilia." In 1969 – after a brief marriage and a tour of duty in Vietnam – he was arrested again after Torrance police found him attempting to sodomize a handcuffed 16-year-old in his car. After a five-year imprisonment in Atascadero State Hospital he was released on May 20, 1974. Sixteen months later he was arrested for raping a 14-year-old boy at gunpoint, for which he served three more years. He was paroled on October 11, 1978; ten months later, Orange County deputies found him molesting a 17-year-old in Dana Point. Even though he was still on parole, Bonin was mistakenly released by police. He told a friend who gave him a ride home that "no one's going to testify again. This is never going to happen to me again."

He began roaming the streets in his light-green Chevy van, often with one of his four buddies along "for the ride." The most notable member of this ragtag bunch was Vernon Butts, a 23-year-old sales clerk at the Knott's Berry Farm magic store; a fan of the game "Dungeons and Dragons" and heavy metal music, he decorated his apartment with strobe lights and rubber spiders, had two coffins serve as a phone booth and a coffee table, and wore a Darth Vader cloak and laser sword as part of his wardrobe. He hanged himself in prison soon after his arrest. Bonin would usually pick up his young victims hitchhiking, drive to a secluded area, and sodomize and murder them in the back of his van. Most were killed by strangulation – Bonin preferred to use a T-shirt and tire iron as his method of killing – but others died more slowly, enduring such tortures as having pieces of their flesh sliced off, ice picks jammed into their ears, acid poured down their throats, and coat hangers shoved into their rectums.

In 1982 Bonin was judged guilty on fourteen counts of murder and sentenced to death. With his appeals slowly running out, he spent most of his time in San Quentin writing, painting and playing bridge with three other Death Row prisoners: "Sunset Strip Killer" Douglas Clark, rapist/torturer/murderer Lawrence "Pliers" Bittaker, and fellow "Freeway Killer" Randy Kraft. Shortly after midnight on February 23, 1996, Bonin became the first California inmate executed by lethal injection. His last meal: two large sausage and pepperoni pizzas, three pints of coffee ice cream, and three six-packs of Coca-Cola.

Two short stories from Bonin's book *Doing Time: Stories from the Mind of a Death Row Prisoner,* a chapbook published in 1991 and sold mainly through the San Quentin prison giftshop:

A DAY IN A 12-YEAR-OLD'S LIFE

(This story is the first that I wrote in short form. It is derived from things that happened to me during the time I was that age. There are some things that are exaggerated in order to make for a better story. There are things that may sound very unbelievable, yet really happened. There is a message at the end of this story that I hope can be heard loud and clear — a message to hear and put into practice. It would definitely make the world a better place. I hope that all parents will listen to their children. There are times when what they say could be quite important. Children have thoughts and ideas too. Let them be heard, if not by others, then by the people who love them the most, their parents.)

Saturday morning. Great! No school today! Even though it's 7:00 I'm up, dressed, and have eaten breakfast — my turn to do the dishes. God, how I hate to do girl's work — sure wish I had a sister. There goes Mom. She got a call about an hour ago from her boss. He wanted to know if she could come in today. Even though it's her day off she went in. She said something about needing the work. Why anyone needs work is way beyond me. I guess some people need work like I need Saturdays. I think when I get older I'll stick to needing Saturdays rather than needing work.

Now to the dishes . . . Hey, did you see that? I mean, what was it!? I'd better open that door underneath the sink real careful like. Yeah, real careful. Wow! I mean, like real wow! My Gramps told me about these things, but I never thought I'd ever come face to face with one. I'd better get something to kill it before it kills me. Gramps told me that these water rats go straight for the throat. Where's my turtleneck? Gee, will that be enough? Hey, the poker! Yeah! That'll do the trick. It's sharp and pointy and I can keep far away from that rat. Can't go opening that door too wide, I won't have a throat left.

I opened the door and it creaked, giving me goose bumps. In goes the poker. There, take that you dirty rat! . . . It sure isn't trying to avoid my jabs. I wonder what's wrong . . . Wait a minute. I know now. I remember. My dad put poison underneath the sink and in the attic. That must have been what happened. The dirty rat ate some of that poison. That's why he's just lying there, in the plastic wash basin to boot. Can't do the dishes until I get rid of that rat. . . .

Yeah, I'm scared! Wouldn't you be? Like you only have one throat and I sure do want to keep it. Well, here goes. I'll open the door real slow and see if he moves. Say, how do I know if he is a he? He could be a she. I wonder how you tell the difference. Guess it doesn't matter though. Got to get rid of that rat and the sooner the better.

Wait a minute. I know what I'll do. I'll put a board over the top of the wash basin. Then I can carry the pan, rat and all, out. I can leave it in the basin. No, I need the basin to do the dishes. God, what a predicament to be in. Well, first things first. Let's get the rat out of the house. . . .

This board should work fine. Now to slide it in so it stays between me and him. Her? What the heck. There go the creaks again. Now, easy does it Ricky Boy . . . slow . . . slow . . . there. Now, let's get this varmint outside and far away . . .

All right! That's the answer! I'll just put the rat, board and all, into the barrel we burn our paper trash in. Put the lid on tight and everything's A-OK. . . .

Oops! Darn! Why do I have to be so clumsy!? And at a time like this! Any time but now would have been much better! Okay Ricky, keep your cool. This isn't a time to get scatter-brained. So the rat is lying on the ground uncovered and you're standing in front of him petrified. We sure must be a sight. Both of us staring at each other, me scared to move and him either not able to move or playing possum. At least I still have this board to defend myself with. I think I'll just sort of ease back a bit until I'm a safe distance away — like with the house between him and me!

Lord, I ain't never been so scared in all my life. Well, I sure can't leave him there. What if he gets away and recovers? He might get me some other day! Maybe while I'm down by the river. He could all of a sudden jump up at me as if to say, "I've got you now!"

Let's see, there's the hose, shovel, rake, pitchfork, wheelbarrow. Pitchfork? Sure, just the thing I need. Drill him good. No, wait! Of course, my older brother's bow and arrows. Sure! It shouldn't be hard at all — just aim and let go. It's not like I never shot an arrow. I may not be an expert, but I'll get that rat. . . .

Now, I'll take this bow and these arrows and just mosey on up in this pear tree and have aim. . . . That wasn't bad at all. I'd say five feet or so off target. Could be worse. I'll just have to aim better. Let's see what happens this time. . . . Did I hit him? Nope. But that's darn close without hitting him.

Well, here goes the last arrow. . . . Darn, still no hit. I'd of thought that there would have been at least one hit out of twenty-five tries! Guess this calls for more drastic action — the pitchfork!

Here goes. I'll come up from the back side . . . got to get close . . . just a little closer . . . whoa! Now that's what I call close! Didn't know a dying rat could turn so fast. Or is he really playing possum?

Where'd you come from? Hey, stay away from that rat! Shoo, go away! You trying to get killed!? Get a . . . what? Will you look at that. The rat is paying more attention to my next door neighbor's dog than to me. Maybe now's my chance. Keep it up, Skip, I'm almost close enough. Whoa there! Good thing I was in a downward swing when he turned this time. In the barrel you go, with the lid on tight. . . .

Whew. Thank heaven that's done. I'll light a fire later and make sure he's dead. But I reckon he should be dead from the poison before the day is over, and if not from the poison, then the wounds from the pitchfork will surely have done the job. So, it won't be like I'm burning a live rat. It'll be more like cremation. I hear they do that to people sometimes. If it's humane enough to do that to people then there shouldn't be anything wrong with doing it to a rat. A rat that would have torn open my throat if he had been given the chance to do so. . . .

Time sure is going slow. Here it is only 8:00. The rat's taken care of and the dishes are all done. Guess I'll take a walk in the woods. There's always something to do there. I know . . . yeah . . . I have plenty of time. They don't start work until 10:00 . . . always did like to drive, even if it is a tractor. It's easy to get there through the woods. Just walk up the path and into the woods a little and down the slope that I ride my sled down in the winter in the snow. The road entrance to the sand bank is just down the highway from my house. . . .

There she is. Yellow, cold, and ready for immediate action. Yeah, I know what you're thinking: how do I know it's a she? Well, it's just a figure of speech. At least that's what I'm told. And who am I to argue with Gramps? Isn't he the one that told me what a rat would do if given the chance?

I usually don't have this much trouble getting her started. All right! It's about time, sweetheart. . . . Now where is that . . . used to be . . . road I found a while back? . . . There! Almost missed it. Not that it would have mattered, I could always make my own road.

I'm going to drive this yellow hunk of metal through the woods to the sand bank that's over by Pleasant Road. I'll leave it there and then take the tractor from that sand bank and drive it back through the woods to the sand bank where I got this one from. I can't be expected to walk back when there is a perfectly good tractor to drive. And anyways, it wouldn't be right to leave one bank without a tractor. Besides, come 10:00 it'll be fun watching the workmen pass my house when they take their tractors back to their own bank. Why they don't use the makeshift road through the woods is beyond me. Maybe they feel closed in.

You know, these tractors come in handy for protection, too. Once, these two guys were picking on my kid brother. He's eight, almost nine. We were in the woods — actually he was in the woods and I was sitting on a pile of sand next to the tractor at the sand bank. He suddenly came running down the road and told me about two boys that were picking on him. I swung into action.

I got that yellow beast fired up, put it into high gear and down the road I flew — all of 5 miles per hour — but a power-packed 5 miles per hour. I saw the two boys. I knew one — Danny Brunster. They couldn't believe their eyes when they saw me coming at them. Off they went. I was knocking down small trees in pursuit of them. They got away, but let me tell you this: I heard that Danny's mom wanted to know why he smelled when he got home. He said he fell into some cow manure. I mean, like really, moms will believe anything. It would have been understandable if there were cows around to leave the manure for Danny to fall into, but the closest thing to cow manure would be something a dog might leave. It's the only animal I've ever seen in my woods capable of leaving something like that — never did see a cow. But I'll tell you this: I bet Danny washed his own drawers that night! 'Cause I know I scared something out of him, and I'm not talking about air! No other explanation for him smelling such. . . .

Ah, look at all those trees — they're just begging to be knocked down. Guess it'll just have to wait for another day. Only have a short time . . . Hey! What the heck!? I'm going over ! . . . Hey, stop tumbling! . . . Stop! . . . STOP! . . . What the . . . Oh, wow . . . anything broken? . . . Wow! . . . I could have killed myself! I'm sure glad this thing is built like it is. Sure am lucky, didn't even get a single scratch.

Oh boy, I can't leave this tractor on its side. How the heck am I going to . . . of course, just use the other tractor to turn in over with. That scoop on the front should be good for more than shoveling sand and dumping it into a truck. . . .

A little to the right . . . oops, too much . . . A little left . . . lift . . . forward . . . lift . . . forward . . . almost there . . . lift . . . there she goes. . . . Sure does make a lot of noise landing. Better check it out for damage. . . . Nope, looks okay. Starts up okay, too. Well, better get this other one and get out of here. . . . Yeah, I was lucky. Talk about Danny smelling. I'd better keep this to myself. . . .

Back home again. I'd better change these drawers before anything. Yeah, you guessed it, I'll be washing them myself. Sure is good to be home, especially after that near-death experience. It seems like no matter where you go or for how long, you can always count on one thing, you'll end up back at home somewhere along the line. I'd hate to think what life would be like not having a home to come back to. I heard on TV last night that there were lots of people who didn't have a home though. Time to think about happier things. Saturday isn't a time to be sad; at least not for me, that is. . . .

Right on time. I can hear the tractor coming down the road now. He sure doesn't look too happy. Can't for the life of me understand why. After all, it's fun driving that tractor and I've given him the opportunity to drive it on the road instead of back and forth putting sand in dump trucks. . . . He isn't waving back. . . . Sure is giving me a dirty look. Think maybe he knows it's me who's switching the tractors? . . .

So much for the big moment. Wasn't as exciting as I expected. Guess I'll make some sandwiches and go fishing. I'm not too bad a fisherman either. Catch something every time. I have a favorite spot: I go under the train trestle just this side of Pleasant Road. It's close to the sand bank where I had the accidents. The one with the tractor and the personal one.

You know what bothers me though? It's how the fish can find that small hook dangling under that swift moving river. After all, they're going along with the current and only have one chance of grabbing onto that hook. But somehow they always seem to find the hook.

I catch catfish mostly. Before I caught one I wondered how in the world a catfish could stand water. I visualized a cat with paws swimming under the water using his paws to grab onto the hook and put it in its mouth. And cat's don't even like water. I heard once that they couldn't even swim. You can understand my surprise when my dad told me that I had caught a catfish. . . .

I always go through the woods, across a small swampy patch, then onto the railroad tracks that lead down to the trestle. It's easier than walking down the highway with all those speeding cars. A fast-moving river with fish is one thing, but fast cars is something I can do without; especially when someone else is driving and I'm on the outside watching. . . .

Hey, check out those squirrels. It always cracks me up to watch them fight over who gets what nut or anything else they fight over. It's all in fun, I'm sure. . . . This swampy area always is the pits. I used to get soaked every time until I got smart and started taking my shoes and socks off and rolling up my pants legs. The towel I bring along to dry my feet also helps. The Boy Scouts have taught me something I try always to remember: be prepared. . . .

Walking down these tracks is the boring part. These big pieces of wood that hold the rails in place tend to call my feet to land on each and every one of them. It's almost hypnotic. . . . There's the trestle. I always go under it at the far end. The only way anyone knows you're there is if they go under the trestle and look in. Never happened yet while I was there. . . .

Ah! Got one! That was sure quick. This is gonna be a good day. I'd like to catch five fish. That way my mom, dad, my two brothers, and me could have fried fish tonight. . . .

There's number two. Great! Two in one hour. At this rate I'll be home by one or two o'clock. . . .

Number three coming up. I guess the fish are getting wise. It took over an hour to get this one. I'll just put it on the stick with the others. . . . Cast off. . . . Number four coming up soon. Guess it's time to eat one of these sandwiches. . . .

Get away you darn pest! These sewing needles (dragonflies) always seem to come around when they're not wanted. Come to think of it, when are they wanted? By the way, don't ever cuss when there's a sewing needle around. Gramps told me that if you do that this flying critter will sew your lips together. . . .

Darn it, get away, get a . . . whooo . . . Now doesn't that beat all. I'm supposed to be fishing not swimming! Got to make that shore. This river sure moves fast. Thank heaven I'm close to shore. It moves slower than out in the middle. Swimming with a fishing pole in one hand isn't the easiest thing I ever did. . . .

Look at me, I'm drenched! At least I have a dry towel to wipe off with. No way am I going to walk all the way home soaked. At least I didn't lose my rod! That's the end of this fishing day. Three fish will just have to suffice. I'll try again tomorrow for two more. . . .

Oh heck, I guess it won't hurt to at least put my pants on. It's about the same as walking around in wet swimming trunks, which is something I do all the time. Going barefoot won't hurt in the least. To tell you the truth, I'd rather go barefoot. It's more natural in this neck of the woods. I sound like Tom Sawyer don't I? Right now I feel like him too! . . .

Back home again. I'll clean these catfish and put them in the freezer. Couldn't ever figure out why they call it a freezer. I always thought that a freezer was a big cold room that you could walk into. Yes, I realize that the compartment at the top of the ice box is cold enough. You'd better believe it. I was getting some ice out once and my hand stuck to the ice tray. My dad told me that there wasn't anything to worry about. He said that the ice didn't get dry enough to burn me. Burn me? Now who ever heard of ice burning? But he told me it was called dry ice. Isn't that the most ridiculous thing you ever heard? Ice, dry ice, burning you? Did you ever hear of something getting so hot that it would freeze you? Sometimes I wonder if my dad thinks I'll believe anything he says. But I will respect ice that is smoking. Who knows, maybe my dad knows something I don't.

By the way, if you hear me using some words that a 12-year-old normally wouldn't use, let it be known that I've had some help: my friend Webster, Webster's Dictionary, that is. You'd be amazed what I found in there.

Once I heard my mom ask my dad how he saw the future. He answered, "optimistic." I thought it had something to do with the eyes, until I look it up in Webster's. From that day on I'd look up any word I heard and didn't understand. That's how I found words I never knew existed. . . .

Here it is 3:00. Time sure did pass by after I started doing things. Mom should be home in a while. John, my kid brother, is spending the day with Gramps and Granny. My older brother, Don Jr., is at his girlfriend's learning some new dance steps for tonight. There's a dance every Saturday night with a prize for the best dance couple. Some day the people that put on the dance are going to stop him from competing — he usually wins. They should have him judge the couples competing for the prizes. Dad's off somewhere in town watching a football game or something. He goes into town twice a month to be with his buddies. The rest of the time he spends with John, Don Jr., and me. That's how I learned most of the things I know about like how to fish and other things. No, I didn't learn how to do the tractor bit from Dad. If he knew about it I'd probably have a hard time sitting for a while. Can you imagine having to stand up in the back of the class because it's too painful to sit? But it's a calculated risk I'm taking. Calculated — thanks Webster, I really needed that. . . .

10:00 P.M. You must be wondering what happened between the time I got back from fishing and now. Well, not much really. The first thing I did was change into warm clothes. The trip back from the river was a chilling experience. After that, I made myself some hot chocolate. It sure did taste good. Warmed me all over.

Mom came home around 3:30. My dad got home about a half-hour before we ate supper. On the east coast we call the late meal supper; on the west coast they call it dinner. After supper I spent some time working on a model of the USS Enterprise that was given to me on my last birthday. My Gramps always gives me model kits on my birthday and Christmas. Sometimes he gives me a model just to give it to me. I have models all over my room — planes, ships, cars, even houses — no doll houses though, that's for girls — mine are log cabins and space stations and things like that.

There was a movie on TV that I wanted to watch. It was dealing with outer space. Couldn't miss that now could I? It was all about these aliens from another planet landing on earth and taking over the bodies of humans. Their plan was to take over the world. Naturally, we humans defeated the aliens — one got away though. He must have warned the others that we were too tough, as neither he nor any of the rest of his kind ever returned. At least that's the way the movie ended.

Since it's 10:00 you might think it's time for bed, right? Wrong! Hey, I'm a growing boy. I don't need all that sleep that the old folks need. I'll get where they're at soon enough. Right now I'm going to check out the sky. I really have a spectacular view of the northern sky. There is this wide open field that gives me access to a stunning view of the heavens. All I can see to the east, west, and south are trees. At night, after the traffic dies down, I can get out my telescope and bring the stars and planets into focus and watch without interruption all the beauty that's up there. . . .

There's the moon. It's really a beautiful thing to look at on a clear night like tonight. Looking at it is what I like doing the most. There's so much of it to look at, not to mention all those craters.

The reason I like looking at the moon so much is that going there is a reality. Who knows, when I grow up I just might be able to visit the moon. The way things are progressing these days, there will probably be people living on the moon in the next ten years or so. Don't think that that isn't possible either. Remember, there was a time when people thought that the telephone, radio, TV, and even flying were just dreams. They also thought that going into outer space was unrealistic. Back in the 1800s if you would have told anyone that we'd have people flying around in outer space and actually walking on the moon they'd have thought you were totally insane.

Anyways, tonight I can see the moon in all its splendor. There are nights that are so clear that the stars turn color and dance for me. In the winter time, on a lucky night, I can see the aurora borealis (northern lights). Wow! What a sight! It's like a painting I once saw in a museum I went to with my sixth grade class to Boston. Now that was something I'll always remember. We took a bus to the train station in New London and then up to Boston.

The teacher warned us about pickpockets so I had my wallet in my front pocket and my hand stayed in my pocket holding onto it all day. After all, I had ten dollars, and that isn't peanuts. It was all cold, hard cash. You know, come to think of it, maybe there is something to dry ice burning. The cold cash was sure burning a hole in my pocket. So much that I was itching to spend it. . . .

Well, there you are, one day in a 12-year-old's life. I hope you were listening. Most people tend not to listen. Maybe that's the trouble with the world — people don't listen to one another. Parents don't listen to their children; children don't listen to their parents; Blacks don't listen to Whites; Whites don't listen to Blacks; Russians don't listen to Americans; Americans don't listen to Russians.

Can you imagine what this world would be like if people started seriously listening to each other? Why don't we try it? It may work better than what we've been doing. It sure can't hurt. But then again, what do I know about all of this? And even if I did know something, I'm only 12-years-old — they wouldn't listen to me. . . .

YOUTH'S ENCOUNTER WITH TERROR

(This story was written after seeing a documentary about runaways and throwaways. A throwaway is a kid who is kicked out of his own house. In this documentary there was a 13-year-old boy who talked about his life. He was at a house for runaways and throwaways and was in the process of going to a home more permanent and a place where he was wanted.

I was so affected by the cruelty to this child, many children really, who was so young that I wanted to write a story that would have two messages, one for parents and one for kids. The message I want to get across is that this could be your child or this could be you.

I didn't want the story to be violent or gruesome and I wanted it to end in a good way. I needed to share that there are people and places in the world that help these children and because of this the world is a much better place.)

The rain had soaked through his thin jacket causing him to shiver, yet on he walked. To Carl it made sense that he felt like he did: rejected, unloved, not worth a damn, not even worthy of breathing in the oxygen that kept him alive. Maybe if he would catch pneumonia and die it would be for the best. Then he wouldn't have to worry about where his next meal was going to come from, or where he was going to lay his head in order to rest his over-filled mind, filled with confusion, puzzlement, hurt, and yes, humiliation. It was a tremendous load for a thirteen-year-old to carry. The tears were there all right, but they just wouldn't fall — it was the shocking terror that he felt that held them in check. It was truly a miracle that he was surviving this ordeal at all.

His heart started to pound again. He stopped walking until he could again regain control of himself. Again, the tears wouldn't come. Oh, he was crying all right, but not outwardly. His whole body would shake and all the sobbing was taking place within. His eyes would glisten but never a tear would wet his cheek.

His thoughts wandered back to when his life was thrown into madness, that being three days previous. (Waking up the noise around him he had asked his dad what was happening.) His eyes took in the suitcases and boxes that were next to the door. His mother was putting on her coat. His father didn't answer, he just opened the door and proceeded to take a box outside. His father continued this process until everything by the door was gone.

Carl looked on in puzzlement from the sleeping bag that now replaced the bed he once had. The small, rundown motel room that they were staying in had only one bed, no couch, and just one chair. That left the floor for him. He had learned a long time ago that he shouldn't try to force an answer out of his dad; he'd answer when he was good and ready. One time he had persisted in trying to get a response from his father and received a backhand that loosened two of his teeth. Carl didn't have to have an encore to learn when he should keep his mouth shut.

His mother joined his father at the door, looked at him and then went through the door. That was the last time Carl had seen his mom. He didn't expect to see her again. His father stood there looking at him, smiling from ear to ear. "Kid, this is the day I've been looking forward to for a long, long time." His father took some money out of his pocket and threw it on the floor. "That's all you get, kid, plus your clothes and that sleeping bag you've grown so fond of. You're on your own now. Good luck and good riddance."

"Dad? . . . Mom? . . . Dad? . . . Hey! Where are you going!?" He struggled out of the sleeping bag and made a dash for the door. He felt alarmed. Pulling the door open he caught a glimpse of his folks' car as it left the motel, turning and heading down the highway. He ran out into the cold, stinging, early morning and ran down to the highway, all the time yelling for them to come back. They didn't. The alarm he had felt now turned to panic. He watched until he could no longer see the car.

Slowly he walked back to the motel room. The fact that he was still in his underwear and that the freezing temperature outside was accentuated by snow didn't penetrate any part of him, be it physical or mental. He felt numb, alone, confused, and frightened. He crawled back into his sleeping bag and assumed a fetal position. He was utterly alone. Even though he was unaware of the cold, his natural instincts for survival took over. Carl was not capable of making any decisions. He was close to being in shock.

He lay there for a long time not thinking about anything. He was conscious only of the silence that totally surrounded him. It was so quiet. Sound had abandoned him as well.

Gradually Carl came around. His eyes slowly gazed around the room, coming to rest on the money that had been thrown on the floor by his father. The words came flooding back: "You're on your own now. Good luck and good riddance!" He had to get up; he had to find his folks. His eyes grew larger, his body tense, then slowly he gave in to reality.

It was as if he were moving in slow motion. He managed to get all of his clothes into the one broken suitcase that his folks had left behind. He secured it by tying a cord from the blinds around it. He was moving in a haze. Nothing was real. He was dreaming. No, he wasn't dreaming, he had entered the real world; the world where no one cared a damn about anyone. He was destined to face life on his own from now on. Learning quickly was something he was going to have to master or else he wouldn't survive. He'd perish by the wayside like a common weed.

The last three days had been hell. Carl had had to figure out just where he was going to go and how he was going to live. The two twenties that were left for him on the floor weren't going to get him far. He'd have to use them for food only. Once the money was gone more decisions would have to be made.

Now, as if he didn't have enough trouble it was raining and he was totally soaked. It didn't rain often in the desert but that was something he wasn't aware of. What he **was** aware of was that it was raining in the desert **now** and he was right in the middle of it with no cover to hide under.

Carl had decided to head for California. Maybe he could find someone that wanted him out there. Before leaving Denver he had asked around and found out that he should head out on I-70. He was told that he'd have no problem getting a ride from people that asked no questions. If he went the other way, which was down to I-40 in Albuquerque, he was told he'd have all kinds of trouble and questions coming his way. He had chosen to take I-70.

Now he was beginning to feel that he had made a mistake. True, no one had asked him any questions but he had also not received any rides. Three days of walking and sleeping on the ground out of sight of the road and concealed as best as he could manage had taken its toll. He was totally miserable and growing more depressed by the hour. Even at the tender age of thirteen his instincts told him that this was not healthy. He knew if he didn't get his act together soon that there would be no future to worry about.

He continued to take one step after the other. Each step drawing him closer to . . . to what? Only time would tell. Did he really have a choice? Would he ever have a choice again? What did the future hold? Would he have to become like boys he had heard about at school once, selling their bodies in order to earn enough money so they could survive? How could anyone do such a repulsive thing? He guessed that if it was a choice between living or dying, he'd do it. He hoped that it would never come to that but he decided to prepare, mentally, for the possibility.

When the rain finally stopped he walked a little way off to the side of the highway and got out some dry clothes. At least the suitcase kept his other clothes dry. The sleeping bag was, like himself, soaked thoroughly through and through. After wiping off and getting into dry clothes, he put the wet clothes and the sleeping bag on the barbed wire fence that separated the highway from the vast desert that lay before him. It stretched out for as far as he could see. He wondered if he'd ever make it out of this desert alive.

With the rain stopped the sun slowly came out. What a relief it brought with it. The difference was like night and day. The warm rays felt good. They not only penetrated the coldness he felt physically but they also penetrated his mind. The warmth allowed him to become hopeful instead of feeling broken-hearted. Yes, there was a future and he was going to have a piece of that future. He would make it. He would survive. It seemed like the sun's rays were drying more than his clothes, they were drying the inner tears as well.

For the first night since he became dependent on himself he slept peacefully. He woke up with a new outlook on life and a burning desire in his heart to survive. He wasn't stupid, he knew that he couldn't live on his own. When he got to California he decided he would find someone who would help him. He wasn't going to become a queer or a person who robbed from others in order to eat. That was one reputation that he would never be labeled with.

He set out, continuing to walk westward. He had an entirely new outlook on the future. Soon he would not be alone, he would be with people who cared and who would see to it that he had a chance in life.

A car stopped and offered him a ride. They didn't have to offer twice. It was the first ride he received since he had set out from Denver. He had found out they were headed for Las Vegas and would give him a ride all the way. What a relief! Maybe he'd find someone in Las Vegas and not have to go all the way to California. Maybe these nice people would help him. He'd have to have a talk with them and see.

The movement of the car relaxed him so much that he fell into a restful sleep. He was unaware that Las Vegas was not the destination these fine people had in mind. No siree, they had something altogether different in mind. It didn't bother them in the least that he was a kid. The man had talked with the kid and found out his name was Carl and that he was thirteen. No thirteen-year-old was going to be out on the road with a suitcase and sleeping bag unless he was running away. Nothing else made any sense. He felt very fortunate that no one else had picked up the kid before he had come along. He would have been out all the money he was going to get. He knew the kid would bring a good price. The kid was handsome; he had a face that projected purity. The fact that Carl was innocent-looking and a very naive boy didn't phase the man at all.

It was dark when the car pulled up in front of a house. Carl slept soundly in the back seat. He hadn't woken up once. The man told his wife to stay in the car while he went in and took care of business. It didn't take long. Within fifteen minutes he was waking the kid up.

"Where are we?" Carl asked as he woke up from a sound sleep.

"Come on, get out," said the man as he pulled on his arm.

Something was wrong. The man wasn't being nice anymore. He was being very rough. What had he done? What was happening? He hadn't done anything to them.

The man dragged him out of the car and up some steps. They entered a room. "Here's the kid. You should be able to get a lot of work out of him."

The other man, who the driver was talking to, came over and felt Carl's arm. "Make a muscle, kid." When he didn't respond the man cracked him across his jaw with a closed fist. Carl went down, stunned, almost passing out. The man forced him to his feet and shook him until he could stand on his own. He could stand but he was still groggy. His senses were coming back slowly. As he became aware of his surroundings he realized that someone was saying something to him. The man was shaking him and telling him to make a muscle. Slowly, without thinking what he was doing, or why, he made a muscle. Although he went through the motions his muscle did not come up.

"This kid has shit for strength."

"Why don't you let the kid come around and get his coordination back," said the driver, "then he'll be able to show you his muscles. You won't be disappointed. The kid's strong. You'll get your money's worth."

Carl felt woozy. He had never been hit so hard in his life. "What's happening? Why'd you hit me?"

"You don't do what you're told from now on and I'll do more than give you a love tap."

A love tap? thought Carl. Did he think that that was a love tap!? God, he sure didn't want to find out what it was like to get hit worse than this.

"Now, make a muscle or I'll knock you across the room."

Carl made a muscle and the man felt the muscle in his right arm. The man smiled. It was obvious that he was pleased. What had he gotten himself into now? He had no idea where he was and he had no idea what was happening to him. Why did the man want to feel his muscle? Were they going to rape him?

"All right," the man said to the driver, "I'll take him." He took some money out of his pocket and handed it to the driver who then turned and left.

Carl thought fast, "Hey, what about my stuff?" He didn't know why he was being left here but he knew that he wanted his clothes and sleeping bag. Eventually he'd leave here and he'd need them. Heck, he'd need his clothes whether he got away or not. He never heard the answer to his question as there was no verbal response, but he did feel the crushing pain, and then nothing.

He woke up realizing that it was daylight out. What had happened to the time? The last thing he remembered was asking the man who was driving the car about his stuff. He started to get up and found that he was chained to the bed. He took in his surroundings, of which contained only the bed he was in. The rest of the room was completely bare, there wasn't even a picture hanging on the wall.

Reality came to him along with his memory. He remembered being dragged from the car and the money handed over and now he could remember seeing the fist just before he got hit. After that he must have been out cold. He worked his jaw. It felt tight but it didn't feel like it was broken.

The man came into the room and looked at him. Talk about fierce looking people. The hunchback of Notre Dame had nothing on this guy. Carl felt like he was looking at the devil himself. He'd bet ten to one that the guy never brushed his teeth either. They were all yellow-looking.

"I'm going to tell you once and only once," the man began, "so listen up real good. You belong to me now and you'll do as you're told. You don't do as you're told and you'll get some more of what you got last night. I don't take no crap from anyone and I damn sure ain't going to take any crap from you. Give me too much crap and I'll put you out with my wife. She's over by the big oak tree under six feet of sod. You try to run away and it's over. No second chance. You make it, you're free; I catch you and you're dead. I don't need no talking, so keep your mouth shut. I don't answer any questions no how. I tell you what I want done and you do it. You talk back and you'll get what's coming to you."

This guy never did brush his teeth, Carl confirmed. He could smell the putrid breath as the man spoke, even though the length of the room separated them.

The man took a key from his pocket and released him from the chains that held him to the bed. He then secured two heavy chains to his legs, one to each. "You can start by cleaning the house. I want it to shine." He then walked out of the room and out of the house, leaving Carl with the image of his fiery eyes and the smell of his horrid body odor.

Carl tried to get the chains off of his feet but it was hopeless. They were on real tight but not tight enough to cut off the blood circulation. The chains led out onto the other room so he followed them and found that they were secured to a large metal plate bolted to the kitchen wall. There was no way he was going to get the chains off that plate and even if he could get the metal plate off there would be no way he could carry it. It was just too big and too heavy. There was nothing that he could do except start cleaning the house. If he didn't he knew what would happen. Again, here was a time where he had no choice. Again, he wondered if there would ever be a time when he would have a choice.

As the days passed Carl did what he was told. He didn't ask any questions. In fact, he didn't say anything at all when the man was around. The last thing he wanted to do was get this monster riled. He learned quickly that as long as he did what he was told and kept his mouth shut everything was fine. There were no beatings and he received ample food.

Carl had thought that maybe he could jump the man as he came in and maybe stab him and get free, but the first day the man came back all hopes of something like that vanished. The man had called him to come outside. The chains were long enough so that he could just get outside the front door. The man checked him for any knives or anything else that he might have on him that he shouldn't. Then into the bedroom they went and he was again chained to the bed.

That was the standard procedure: every time the man left the house he'd release Carl from the bed and put the chains on his feet. Every time that he came back to the house he would call him outside and then take him to the bedroom and chain him back to the bed. Carl looked forward to the man leaving. He could then bathe — using a wash rag was more like it as there was no way to get his pants off — or he could eat or simply relax. All he had to make sure of was that the house was clean — not just clean but spotless.

Carl never stopped trying to think of ways that he could get away. Nothing that he thought up seemed like it would work. The real fact of the matter was that he was there until the man decided to let him go. He wondered how old he would be when that happened. Would he have to wait until the man died? And if the man died while he was chained to the bed, what then? For that matter, if the man died at all what would he do then?

He was always in chains — chains that he couldn't get out of. He had tried but to no avail. The situation was hopeless. Sometimes at night as he lay chained to the bed set in a pitch-black room, he'd feel the night closing in on him. Thinking of the man dying during the night caused him to become crazy with fear. When he'd wake up the next morning he'd feel a numb sort of terror. When the man came in to release him he'd be fearful of what the day might have waiting for him.

Two months had passed. He had the routine down pat now. He had reluctantly accepted his fate and had given up, almost, on ever escaping. . . . What was that noise? . . . Whistling! . . . "Hellooo in there. Anybody home?" Someone was outside. Should he go out and talk with whoever it was? Was this a trick of the man's to see if he would disobey him? The man had told him that sometime in the future he would send one of his good friends by just to see what he would do. Was this the good friend? He decided that it was worth getting knocked out over. He had to find out if this person could help him or not. But what if the person turned out to be someone that would take advantage of his being chained up? It could turn out to be worse than getting knocked out. He could end up getting killed. What would the man think then, when he came back and found him dead and the house ransacked?

Carl opened the door and stuck his head out. "What do you want?" he asked with a shaky voice. He heard the voice say that he was looking for work and wanted to know if there was any. Carl didn't answer. He waited until the person came into view.

There stood a youngster, like himself, yet older. He estimated the boy to be about seventeen or so. Here was another boy who was on the road like he had been; his heart skipped a beat. Carl stepped out into the open so that the boy could see the chains on his feet. He felt embarrassed. Let the boy see with his eyes rather than hear with his ears. It would be easier that way. Anyhow, seeing is believing.

"What are you doing with chains on your feet?"

Carl lowered his head and looked at the porch, he felt scared and hopeless. What should he do? Could this boy help him? The only way he was going to find out was to ask. He raised his head and looked at the boy; pushing all thoughts of hope inwardly he said, "I'm being held prisoner here. Can you help me?" The words came out in almost a whisper, yet loud enough that the boy did hear.

The boy came up the steps and looked Carl over up close. "Let's go inside and see to getting these chains off you."

Carl led the way and inside he told the boy that he had tried on many occasions to get the chains off and could never succeed. The boy told Carl that his name was Sport — at least that's what everyone called him. It was his road name; real names were of no use. Carl told him all about what had happened to him right up to and including the present. He was talking so fast that Sport had to slow him down several times. In the end Sport had the whole story.

Carl told Sport that the man would be back at five, as he came home every day at the same time. That left four hours. Sport went out of the house and into the barn which was some distance from the main house. He found a hammer and chisel and came back to the house. Within minutes the chains were off of Carl's legs. He was free once more. The chains had left the skin with an ugly dark discoloration on both legs. "We'd better get a move on," Carl said, "before the man comes back. When he does get back he's going to be looking for me."

"Why didn't you try and call for help? Isn't there a phone in the house?"

Carl told Sport that there was a phone but that the man disconnected it and took it out of the house every time he left. There was no way he could get a hold of anyone. Sport was the first person he had set eyes on since he had been sold.

"Let's go," said Sport.

They walked out the door and, to Carl's surprise, saw his suitcase and sleeping bag sitting on the ground. Sport told him that he had found them in the barn while he was looking for some tools to get the chains off. He figured they belonged to Carl after he looked inside the suitcase. Carl picked up the sleeping bag and secured it to his back. There were ropes wrapped around it with arm slots so that he could carry it on his back. Then picking up his suitcase they headed out.

Carl looked back once they had reached the main road. "This is one place I never want to see ever again in my whole life." Sport told him that once they were far enough away he'd call the police and tell them about the man and what had happened without giving any names. Carl asked Sport why they couldn't just go to the police right now. Sport explained that if they did that they'd both be put into a juvenile facility. It turned out that Sport was only sixteen. According to Sport, a juvenile facility was the last place that either of them wanted to find themselves in.

A day and a half later Sport and Carl reached San Francisco. After talking to some kids on the street, Sport learned about a place where they could get food and shelter. It catered specifically to kids that were runaways, throwaways, or that just had no place else to go.

Carl wasn't a runaway, he was a throwaway; Sport wasn't a runaway either. His mother had died the year previous and he had decided to go out on his own rather than end up in a foster home with people who only wanted him for the money that came with his care. If there was no foster home available he would have probably been put in a juvenile facility — that he definitely didn't want.

They headed for the shelter and once there found it to be everything they had heard it was. The people really cared and the welcome they received was with open arms. Carl could see that these people had something to give him that he hadn't seen in a long time — love! He drank it up like it was water.

After hearing about how Carl had been thrown out, so to speak, and his experience with the man, they promised him that he could stay until they found a home for him to live in. They would find a good family, one that had a lot of love to dish out.

It sounded pretty good to Carl so he decided to stay on. Sport decided he would stay on for a while but insisted that he would get a job and eventually a place of his own. The people running the place told Sport they would help him in every way they could. They did, too.

Within a couple of weeks Sport had himself a job but instead of getting a place of his own he stayed on at the home to help out with the new boys and girls that came in. New kids were always coming in day and night — he was a big help.

A family was found for Carl that had a ten-year-old of their own. The youngster, Noah, took to Carl right away. He now had a big brother, something he had always wanted. Now, when a bigger boy picked on him he, too, could say that he'd get his bigger brother to beat the crap out of him. And Carl had himself a home, a real home. He was delirious with joy.

Carl knew he was one of the lucky ones. It could have been a lot worse. He could have ended up on the streets along with the gays and dopers. So many of the runaways and throwaways ended up there, selling themselves and using drugs to help them forget what they were doing. It would have been one nightmare on top of another nightmare. He vowed an oath that if ever he could help a person that was in a similar situation he would. First though, he had to get his life back together and make something of himself. Life was finally being kind to Carl and he loved it.

MR. BROWN

In a case history related in the British forensic journal article "The Case of the Disembowelled Doll" by Dr. Alan Usher, "Mr. Brown" (a pseudonym) murdered his wife, 6-year-old son and 10-year-old daughter in November 1966. A middle-aged biology teacher at a South Yorkshire grammar school, Mr. Brown made additional money, according to Usher, by sculpting

> . . . three-dimensional models of human anatomy, which were sold as teaching aids to schools, educational institutes, etc., all over the country. These models were each some twenty-five inches high, realistically painted and superbly constructed in such a way that all the major organs could be lifted out separately.

One day Mr. Brown left school at lunch time, telling the headmaster he was suffering from "intense nervous strain." When Mr. Brown had not returned to work two days later, the headmaster went to his home after work in the evening, and found the lights on with no one answering the door. Breaking in, the headmaster discovered an eerie, bloody tableau. Usher clinically described the scene:

> In the downstairs rear room, lying in an apparently relaxed position, upon the settee lay the pajama-clad body of Mr. Brown – a cigarette still between his fingers. His forearms and hands were spotted with blood. In the adjoining kitchen upon the sink a large tablet bottle, containing a single capsule of sodium amytal and another of sodium seconal, was found. Upstairs in their separate bedrooms the bodies of Mrs. Brown and her two children were found. All were clad in night attire and lay in attitudes of sleep. All had been killed by repeated blows with a blunt instrument, on the head, and by having their throats cut – in addition the six-year-old boy had a stab wound in the upper abdomen, through which bowel was protruding and which at autopsy proved to have resulted from a knife being partially withdrawn and thrust in again several times – causing multiple wounds in the liver, stomach and diaphragm. A bloodstained kitchen knife lay upon the boy's bed and a heavily bloodstained wooden mallet upon the double bed in the parents' room.

They appeared to have been murdered the night Mr. Brown went home ill; police found newspapers for the previous two days and an unopened letter from a psychotherapist on the front stoop. When the psychotherapist was interviewed by police, it was found that Mr. Brown had been visiting him for the past few years and had recently threatened to kill his family. Usher dryly noted that:

> subsequent investigation . . . revealed that as late as 8:30 P.M. on the night of the murder Mrs. Brown had phoned the psychotherapist for advice, because she was frightened of her husband's behavior and his threats towards the family. In the past Brown had been something of a hysteric and on this occasion it was felt that he was again acting and that the situation could be adequately controlled by mild sedation. This unfortunately proved to be untrue.

Usher also discovered from Mr. Brown's psychotherapist further indications of the dead teacher's macabre temperament:

> Brown's father had been a manic depressive who on occasions, at his own request, was roped to a bed at their home in order to prevent him doing damage and who eventually spent the last twenty years of his life in a mental hospital. Brown himself had spent at least two periods undergoing in-patient treatment in mental hospitals, the last one in 1962. At these institutions he had produced as part of his therapy several paintings and models of a most alarmingly violent nature – mostly depicting the disembowelling of a young woman, by a satanic monster-figure.

Visiting Mr. Brown's home the morning after the bodies were discovered, Usher made the following observation about the bizarre interior design motif:

> A noticeable feature of the entire house . . . was the incredibly garish decor. All the rooms were painted in loud basic colors and there were several pictures of the type that one paints oneself by reference to a color key, which had in this case clearly been ignored with nightmarish results.

Usher's final evaluation of "Mr. Brown":

> Since his release in 1962 . . . he appears to have presented a gentle and substantially normal picture to the world at large, though it seems very probable in the light of subsequent events that the horrifying decor in his home and the anatomical models which he so assiduously made were both mechanisms for the sublimation of the dangerously destructive and aggressive urges which still lurked in his subconscious mind.

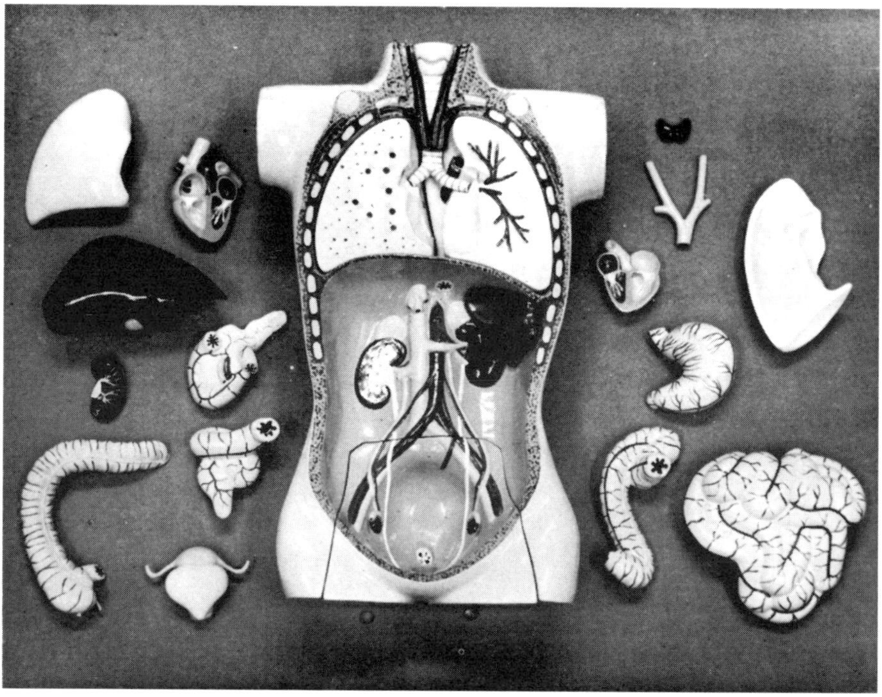

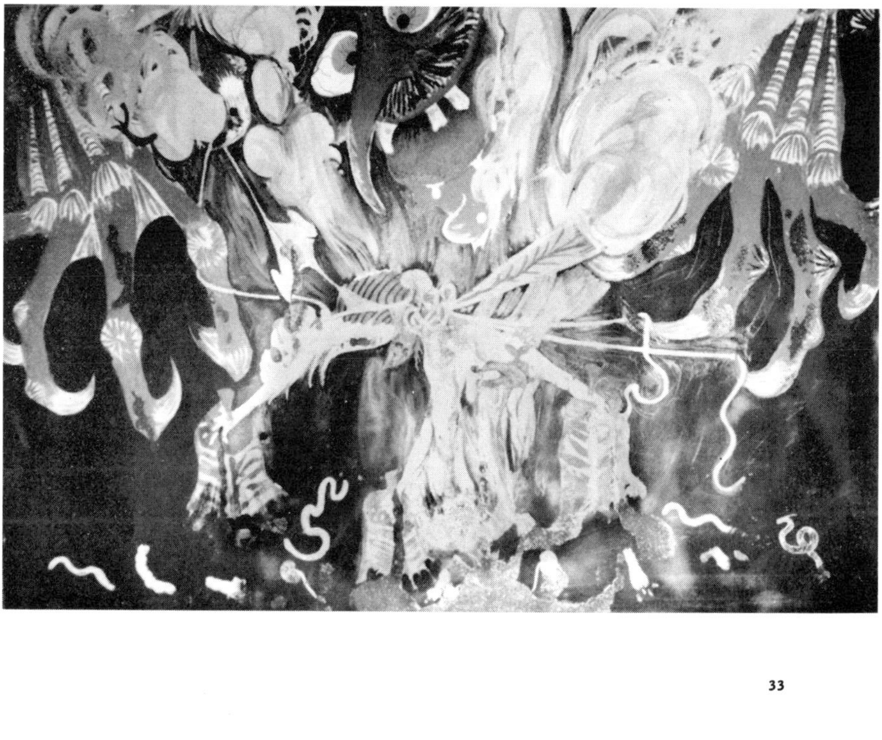

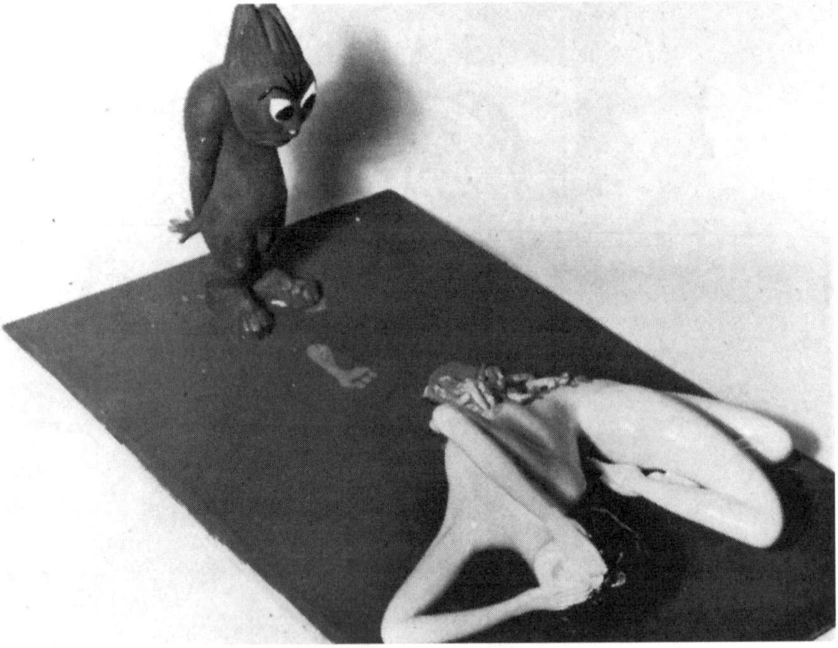

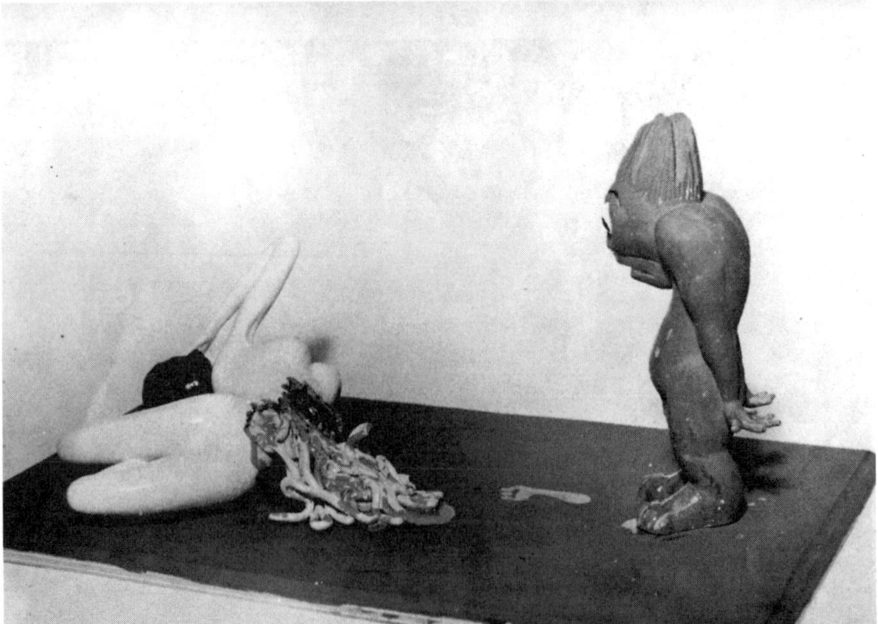

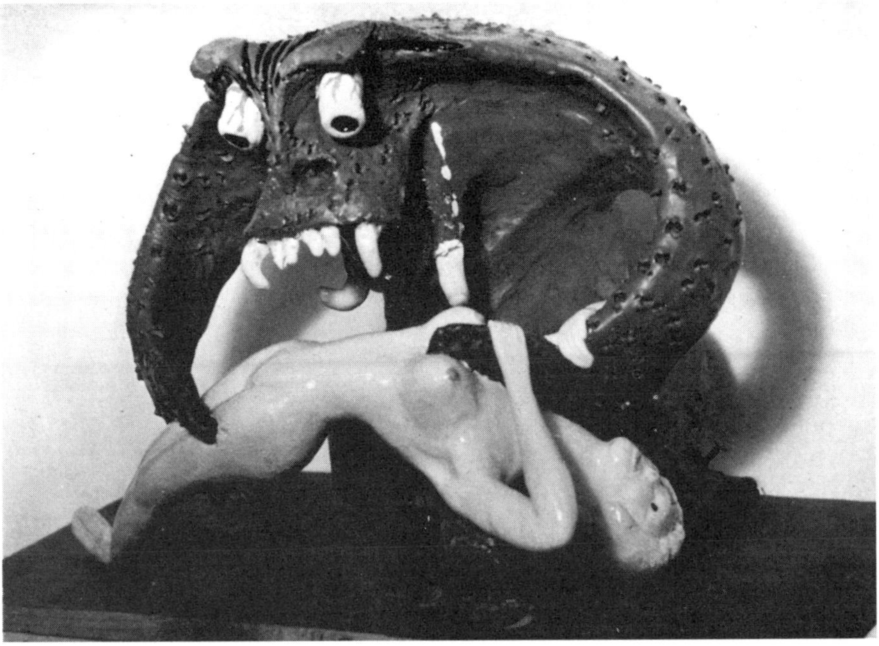

PATRICK **BYRNE**

On the evening of December 23, 1959, at a YWCA hostel in Birmingham, England, 28-year-old Patrick Byrne strangled to death 29-year-old Stephanie Baird, and then raped, decapitated and mutilated her body. Afterwards he went downstairs to a laundry room and attacked 21-year-old Margaret Brown, striking her on the back of her head with a stone wrapped in a bra stolen from the laundry. The blow was softened by her thick bun of hair, and her screaming frightened Byrne away. The police interviewed twenty thousand men; when Byrne was interviewed he became nervous and confessed to the killing. He was convicted of murder – later changed on appeal to a conviction of manslaughter, due to his being "sexually abnormal" – and sentenced to life imprisonment.

Placed near Stephanie Baird's nude body was a scribbled note:

This was the thing I thought would never come.

What Byrne said about the note to police:

> I can't remember the words I used, but I wanted everybody to see my life in one little note. The other times I had been definitely satisfied with peeping, but this time was different somehow. What I meant when I wrote the note was that I thought I might be had for rape but not murder.
>
> I was very excited and thinking that I ought to terrorize all the women. I wanted to get my own back on them for causing me nervous tension through sex . . . I felt I only wanted to kill beautiful women . . . I watched this other girl for a while and stood close to the window. I only looked at her face and the urge to kill her was tremendously strong. I thought I would take her quietly and quickly and picked up a big stone from the garden . . . I struck at her with the stone, but she screamed and the stone swung out of my hand.
>
> I put the note in my pocket and went into the bathroom. I stood by the mirror talking to myself and searching my face for signs of a madman, but I could see none. I felt I ought to commit suicide . . . then I thought of my mother and Christmas. I didn't want to upset nobody for Christmas so I thought I would put it off until afterwards.

MICHAEL & SUZAN **CARSON**

On Thanksgiving evening of 1977, a young waiter met a 36-year-old housewife at a dinner party in Scottsdale, Arizona, a suburb of Phoenix. After this seminal encounter they evolved into Michael and Suzan Carson, Islamic "hasashins": assassins on a mission to kill "witches" and other enemies of God, espousing a "cry for war" that was their own personal Jihad, and which ended the lives of three innocent people. With Suzan as the dominant partner, they fed on each other's crazed paranoia, becoming followers of their own manic New Age religion, a potpourri of Moslem beliefs, Bircher conspiracy theory, pothead astrology and proto-Earth First! environmentalism. Their ultimate nemesis was the President of the United States, Ronald Wilson Reagan, whose name was equivalent numerologically to 666, the "Number of the Beast."

James Clifford Carson, born on November 28, 1950, was raised in Tulsa, Oklahoma, where his father was an oil company executive and an advisor on oil and energy to President Richard Nixon. He graduated from the University of Iowa, married and had a child, and was in Phoenix for less than a year when he met Suzan. Born on September 14, 1941, the daughter of a rich newspaperman, Susan Thornell Barnes was a mother with two grown children, separated from her husband for eight years, and a member of the Scottsdale tennis club. After their "union" Susan became "Suzan" and James became "Michael," a name chosen by Suzan after the "angel in the Bible that fought the Devil." They sold all their possessions, travelled to England to visit Stonehenge, and were "spiritually" married outside London on June 21, 1978, the eve of the Summer Solstice. They returned to the United States and became pot-dealing nomads, roaming the highways of Arizona, California and Oregon – with Suzan always on the lookout for "psychic vampires."

The first "creature of darkness" they murdered was 23-year-old Keryn Barnes. A naive, buxom hippie who shared an apartment with the Carsons in the Haight district of San Francisco, Barnes dabbled in "magick" and danced topless at the Mabuhay Gardens punk club for "Willie the Stick," a demented quadriplegic performance artist. Michael, attracted to Barnes, wanted her as his "second wife"; Suzan, in a jealous frenzy, managed to convince Michael that Barnes was a witch trying to take Suzan's "power" through Michael's "sexual energy." On March 7, 1981, after Suzan had a vision from Allah that Keryn Barnes should be killed, Michael bashed her head in with an iron frying pan as she slept and stabbed her thirteen times.

While staying in Portland at the seedy Eddington Hotel in November of 1981, Suzan told Michael it was time to write a book titled *Cry for War* (excerpts reproduced below) – it was to be their manifesto. Michael wrote the first half of the book while Suzan played her bamboo flute and weighed one-ounce baggies of pot in their rented room; then Suzan had another vision, and dictated the latter half of the book to Michael as he typed. After weeks of arguing over the editing of the manuscript – at one point, Suzan threw her flute out the window in anger – they finished *Cry for War* in February of 1982, xeroxed six copies, and hit the road once again.

On April 20, 1982, they killed Clark Stephens, a heroin addict and pot farmer visiting a friend's dope ranch in Humboldt County where Michael Carson was hired as "security." When the "demon" insulted Suzan, Michael accused Stephens of trespassing, shot him in the mouth and chest, and fired a final bullet into his head at close range. Suzan and Michael then burned his body and buried it in a mound of chicken fertilizer.

They were hitchhiking outside Bakersfield on January 11, 1983, when Jon Hellyer pulled over in his pickup truck to give them a lift. As they got in, Suzan whispered to Michael, "We have to kill him. He's a very powerful witch"; her instinct was confirmed when she found out from Hellyer that he was a "Triple Scorpio." That evening Hellyer let them spend the night in the back of his truck while he stayed overnight with a friend. The next morning, as they were driving towards Santa Rosa, Michael pulled a gun on Hellyer. As they fought over the gun, the pickup pulled to a stop in front of a fruit stand, and Hellyer and Michael, still struggling, fell out of the cab of the truck. When Hellyer managed to gain control of the gun, Suzan stabbed him in the back with a kitchen knife that she kept in one of her boots and Michael shot him three times in the head. They were immediately captured by sheriff's deputies while trying to escape.

Found guilty of three counts of murder in the first degree, Michael and Suzan Carson were sentenced to life imprisonment on July 2, 1984. Michael is now serving his sentence at Folsom State Penitentiary and Suzan is an inmate at the California State Women's Prison in Frontera – residing in a high security cell known as the "Manson Unit."

Excerpts from *Cry for War*:

Chapter Ten **California**

Every civilization has its seat of power. Though outwardly displayed by political, economic, and military power; its intellect, culture, and spiritual ways are the key. The question — where do the emulated and brilliant people live, is answered by California. Most cultural trends begin in California and spread through the country and across the world. As California goes, so goes the world.

California is the center of the "new consciousness" — a new way of thinking and living. This consciousness is an outgrowth of the hippie movement of the mid-late sixties. California, concentrated with intellectuals, artists, radicals, free-thinkers, dissidents, religious mystics, is a world leader — **a super-power of the mind.** She is envied, hated, resented, by lesser lands; but always emulated and copied. **California is smug; she should be ashamed.** The Beast has come to power, nothing has been done about it! Everyone is wallowing in egotistical self-gratification; justifying non-action with vague liberal, neo-Hindu, pacifistic philosophies pretending the big bad world doesn't exist. Poland exists. Afganistan exists. Haiti exists. An old friend, who escaped from Nazi Germany, said to never forget a similiar escapist attitude existed in pre-Nazi Germany.

(Californians speak of the "new age" as if it had arrived; is just unrealized of yet. Let us be realistic. No turning point from one age to another has passed without bloodshed.)

This neo-Hindu philosophy is based on the bland teachings of Indian gurus who claim reality is "all consciousness" — that is the material world is mere illusion of no importance; therefore physical violence is wasted effort. First of all, as Jesus said, "By their fruits you shall know them." I have been to

India. It stinks — literally and figuratively. Do we wish to emulate a filthy, starving country?! The Hindu philosophy is similar to the sophist thinking refuted by Socrates of Athens. Sophism states all things are true or that nothing is ultimately true. This philosophy reduces life to a game. It comes down to the question of — Is there one God or many gods?; Is there one truth or many truths? Western thought, from Socrates to Jesus, is based on the knowledge of a single truth worth standing for; worth dying for. I call on my brothers to reject this relativistic, soothing belief in nothingness and reclaim your heritage. The time has come to stand up for the truth — to say some things are right; some things wrong; and some things are worth fighting for!

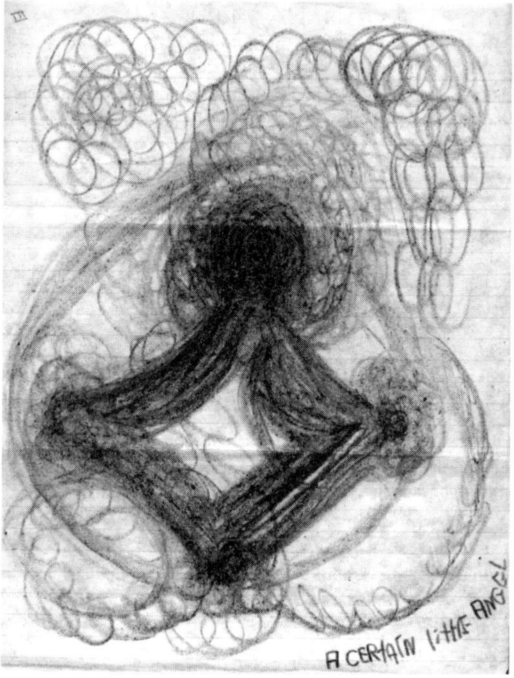

California is often divided into two parts; Northern and Southern. Northern Californians believe all the brilliant "new consciousness" lives in the North, while Southern California is a term of reproach; referring to smog, McDonald's, short hair. Southern Californians defensively reply, the North is rainy and they have sunny beaches, orange groves, money. California cannot be divided. It is one geographic unit inhabited by two very different civilizations.

California, especially Northern, is the home of the hippie movement. California, especially Southern, is the home of a clique of demons whose income is based on the rape of the Earth. Ronald Wilson Reagan, the Beast, lives in California on a "ranch" (really an avocado farm) near Santa Barbara. (The whole of California is occupied by the CHP — a gestapo organization.) The Beast and his financial backers intend to exploit California's greatness; selling her for quick profits to Germany, Japan, and all other comers. James Watt's name is a curse word, though the real point is Reagan and the boys hired Watt as the henchman. An explosion is coming. California is the battleground. The war will begin in the North.

The American Revolution was touched off by a tax on tea. A few years later the new American government, opposed by rugged frontiersmen, faced an armed rising called, "The Whiskey Rebellion." The first battles of this revolution will be called, "The Marijuana War." In a three county region — Humbolt, Mendocino, and Trinity — the culture, economic base, and way of life is based on marijuana. Marijuana has been used for five thousand years. It is held sacred by Afganis, Morrocans, Hindus, Jamaicans, Mexicans, Africans and Californians. (Sacred, that is, to hippies, while used frivolously by millions of others.) The government of the Beast has begun the "War on Marijuana"; equipped with millions of dollars, sub-machine guns and helicopters (and the Army Reagan has threatened to use), they spy on us constantly in low flying planes, raid with huge armed posses, and there is talk of aerial spraying with paraquat.

Why does the Beast hate pot? Because it is politically dangerous. Marijuana leads to a mystical state of mind in which people see the truth for themselves and don't accept what they are told by leaders. Pot has given rise to a new culture in which thousands of the most intelligent people have quit the industrial system and moved to the hills. The Beast is well aware that marijuana growers and smokers led the anti-Vietnam War movement. He is also aware that the ecological movement opposing the expansion of environmental destruction is led by hippies. The Beast can get the support of rednecks by "protecting" them from pot, a non-existent threat, like Hitler's "Reichstag fire."† At the same time he can crush the leading group opposed to his policies by depriving them of their freedom and their economic base.

So far the Federal Marijuana War has attacked the more isolated and vulnerable growers in Trinity County, Mendocino County, Oregon, Hawaii and the Sierra foothills region. Humbolt County, the biggest county for growing, has had only token raids and little local pig co-operation. Many growers hope the raids will continue to spare their county. Most hope the situation will not turn violent. However, Oregon has had violence already, and everywhere the once pacifistic dope growers are buying guns — in some cases automatic weapons.

California, you house the Beast; you are rich, black, Jewish. You will do anything for a buck; like having your child smile as a whore for a T.V. toothpaste add. You are soft, you are paid off.

California, The Spark that Died

She traveled to Katmandu. She searched in India. She dropped out of college. She is Jewish. Often, she is Scorpio; as in Jerry Garcia (CIA) scorpio, confessed witch, black and white. He is a dead jinn. (Moslem for the other guys — the ones that work for the system. They are open for spoils; for they are traitors.) The end, or beginning as we think of it, will begin and end in California; with civil war.

Whose side are you on; theirs or ours. We are the Moslem Earth Liberation Movement. We stand for God; the truth as written in the Koran and Bible (except for soft Paul). We stand for civil war. If you are rich, the Earth is black because of you. If you are weeping, we are your friends. It comes to this; before the Earth is poisoned, we must overthrow the government. We must fight for the right to breath air and drink water that is not poisoned.

There is no bliss in Katmandu or China or whatever; and we are the only ones left.

Chapter 11 — **Takilma, Oregon — A Tactical Battle-Plan**

I was in Takilma, Oregon in the summer and fall of 1980. Takilma is one of the oldest rural hippie communities in the country. It is a widely mixed group. There is a large group of alcoholic bums, who get drunk everyday. There is a large group of Jesus freaks — some sincere — others pompous hypocrits; like "straight" Christians. There are yogis — both real ones and fakes. Some rich communes own land. Other people are poor. Many people live off government hand-outs in the form of food stamps and welfare. The one common denominator is nearly everyone has long hair and smokes, grows, and sells marijuana.

For years a live and let live mood has existed between the hippies and the rednecks. A few hippies grumbled about the redneck loggers cutting down all the trees, but no one was fighting mad about it. This peaceful scene changed when "Operation Sinsimilla" began. Dozens of federal agents swept through with M-16's and flack jackets, arresting people who were then jailed, fined, and sometimes beaten. Tempers were high, rocks were thrown, roads barricaded, and guns were carried (but not used). In the middle of this scene, I wrote the following plan and posted it on the community bulletin board:

† "Readers Digest" is conducting a propaganda campaign about the "newly discovered dangers of pot." The editor of "Readers Digest" is a CIA agent who was based in Berlin in the 1950's.

"A Plan to Defend Takilma"

1.) Post a guard at 4-Corners to watch for pigs and fire a rifle in the air as a warning signal when they are spotted coming.

2.) Immediately evacuate all women and children to high ground.

3.) 100 men with rifles line the road from above in the cover of trees.

4.) Throw up one road-block in front of the pigs and a second one quickly behind them to block their escape route.

5.) Begin sniping at them with accurate rifle fire, following the rule of firing only once from one position. Quickly move to a new hiding place so pigs can't pinpoint where the opposing shots come from.

This plan illustrates elementary principles of tactics:

First: Get the women and children out of the line of fire. No man wants to see his family hurt and no man will fight if he believes it will cause his family injury. Every man's place is carrying a gun and every woman's place is protecting the children.

Second: Block the roads. Restrict the enemies' mobility. He is in a hostile, unfamiliar place and will not go far from his car. Don't let him get re-enforcements in to help.

Third: Hold the high ground. It is an extreme advantage to fire at the enemy from above in the cover of trees. You can kill him and he can't kill you. (Use only head shots — because of the flak-jackets.)

Fourth: Always have a look-out to give you advance warning. Don't be taken by surprise.

Fifth: Stay **mobile.** Hit and run. Don't let them know how many oppose them or where you are. Hide your guns where they can't be found — away from your homes. Have an escape route through the hills where you can slip away into hiding.

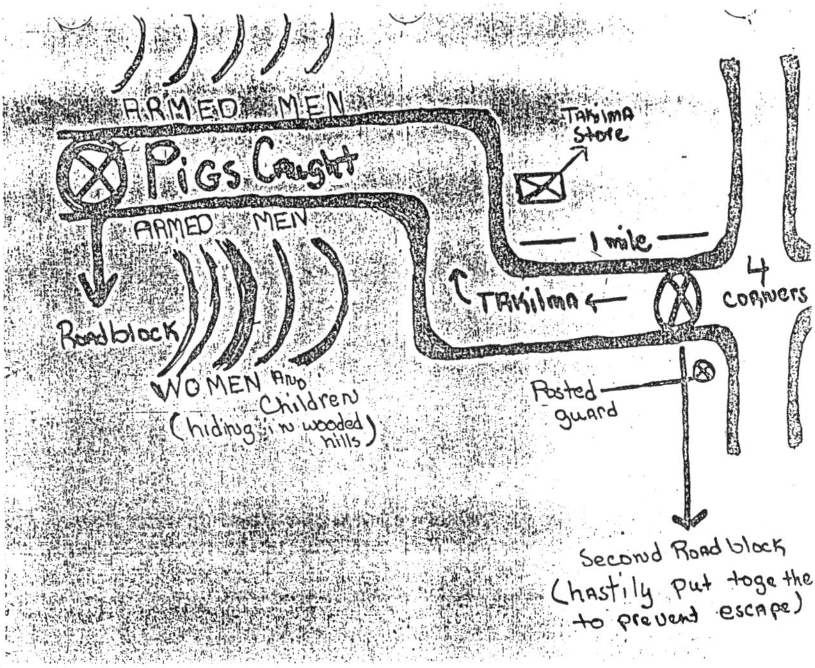

PERFect
Fish
ViRGo/Scopio

These are simple principles of guerrilla warfare. They can be used to defend any community against any outside invader.

The Battle of Lexington and Concord — the shot heard round the world — which set off the American Revolution, used these tactics.

The question wasn't — Could we do it? — but, rather — Did we want to? Many were referring to the "new Battle of Lexington and Concord" and realized any bloody clash would be in itself a victory and would establish that we are willing to fight and the enemy is not invincible. One battle and the revolution would spread throughout the West Coast — perhaps throughout America and the world.

But what was the outcome? A town meeting was called by the richest and most hypocritical commune — "the Meadows Family." Those of us believers in the cause of freedom knew meetings are of no value and didn't attend. The liberals of the "Meadows" — a bunch of pseudo-spiritual wimps — argued against violence and in favor of the alternative strategy of boycotting all the stores in the nearby town for awhile. This was an insanely stupid sell-out. The store owners weren't our enemy. Many of them had sympathized with our cause. The enemy was the federal government and the pigs that do its work. A tyrant has one vulnerability — **his fear of death.** Patriots will die for their homes and their freedom, but paid mercenaries of a bureaucratic state will never willingly die.

The "Battle of Takilma" fizzled out. It was an idea whose time had not come. Many were bought off with the Beast's foodstamps. Still it planted the seed — the idea that maybe we could fight them and win.

The greatest lesson of this "battle" was a revolution's first enemy is the enemy within. The "Meadows" deserve to have their commune burned to the ground. A few days after the abortive clash, one of the "Meadows" crew argued with me about Zionism. I told him I had lived in Israel and that it stinks. He responded by insulting my wife and my religion and implying Moslems are homosexuals. I struck the first blow of my own, private holy war by beating him severely with a wooden stick, chasing him across the river and throwing rocks at him. He ran fast, but returned later with two friends to smash and burn my home. I slipped away in the night with my old lady — but I will someday return. When I return, it will be with an automatic rifle and a 6-gun to settle some old scores.

[...]

"The Enemies List"

This list is inspired by "Tricky Dick" Nixon. You have put out "warrants" on us all. You made us wanted in our own country. You put my wife in jail. You broke the spirit of Truth.

We in the Revolution don't believe in jails. We use only the death penalty for serious crime. Since we are wanted by you, I say, you are wanted by us. We claim your life for your treason.

1. **"Tricky Dick" Nixon:** The man who thought he got away with it all. Tried to overthrow American freedom. Made us all "criminals" by stirring up paranoia of crime as a political force. Sold America's defenses out for Pepsi-Cola contracts and wheat deals. Drank champagne in the Kremlin while Russian dissidents were tortured in Siberia.
2. **Henry Kissenger:** The German Jew who dared to speak for America. Sold out the people of the world with detenté. Is responsible for the rape of Afganistan and Poland. Taught America that morality has no place in national policies. (Controls Haig and Scowcroft.)
3. **David Rockefeller:** Gave us Nixon and Reagan. Manipulates American elections behind the scenes. Favors big trade deals with Russia. Controls fascist governments in Central America. Destroyed America's freedom. (Heads Trilateral Commission)
4. **Ronald Wilson Reagan:** — 666 — the moving mouth. B-movie actor. Installed as puppet leader for slick American-style fascism. Called "the Beast" in the Bible.
5. **George Bush:** Fixed 1980 election. Pulls strings behind Reagan. A friend of Nixon and Rockefeller. Head of CIA. (Conneticut preppy turned fake-Texan)
6. **James Watt:** Directs the policy of environmental rape. Wants to ruin the American West to make friends richer. Sells America's resources to foreigners. Holds secret $2000 a plate dinners with corporate leaders.

7. **Supreme Court Justices — Burger, Reinquist, Powell, O'Conner:** Favor changing the U.S. Constitution to remove individual rights. Justice Burger advocates factory-prisons in which dissidents will be forced to work as slaves.
8. **Senator Howard Baker:** Used Watergate scandal for personal gain. Is Reagan's chief flunky in Congress.
9. **Senator Laxalt:** Another top friend of Reagan in Congress. Represents Mafia — thugs that control Nevada.
10. **Senator Charles Percy:** Senate Foreign Relations Chairman. Related to and right hand man of Rockefeller. Friend of Nixon and Kissenger. Friend of Begin. Friend of Brezhnev. Enemy of Ireland. (old blonde-beast Norman "aristocrat")
11. **Cyrus Vance:** Helped L.B.J. plan the Vietnam War. Advocated arms agreements with Russia which left America defenseless. Leading advocate of trade with Russia. Friend of Rockefeller. Traitor.
12. **Spiro Agnew:** Did Nixon's dirty work. Threatened the free press. Threatened students and dissidents. Took bribes. Was a friend of Nazi dictators who crushed Greece.
13. **Jerry Brown:** Zen-Jesuit-fagot-witch. Sold out California. Advocated more pigs. Pretended to be our friend. Allowed Reagan to spray poisonous malithion on our people.
14. **George Dukmeijan:** Groomed by Reagan's people to be facist dictator of California. Personally leads marijuana raids for publicity. Advocates people's children be taken away by the state for the crime of belonging to "unorthodox" religions.
15. **Hayakawa:** Rotten un-American little Jap. Got his start in politics suppressing free speech during anti-Vietnam War demonstrations. Friend of Reagan.
16. **Charles Manson:** Rotten black-witch. Discredited the hippie movement by posing as hippies. (We clean our own house!)
17. **Margaret Thatcher, Queen Elizabeth, and Lord Carrington:** All made statements favoring the suppression of Irish freedom and avoided statements criticizing Russia's suppression of Polish freedom. All favor selling Britain out to German dominated Common Market. (The "House of Windsor" are German mercenaries hired to replace the legitimate Stuart Dynasty.)
18. **Anthony Wedgewood Benn:** Favors Communism in Britain and sell-out to Russia.
19. **Ian Paisley:** Leads lynch mobs against the Irish in their own country. Friend of pigs.
20. **Helmut Schmidt:** Ex-Nazi. (Still a Nazi.) Leads the Common Market. Sold-out Poland to the Russians. One of the most evil leaders in the world. (Vacations in Florida)
21. **Willie Brandt:** Pro-Communist German leader. Started the detante policy. Friend of Kissenger. Supported Schmidt in the sell-out of Poland.
22. **Prince Bernard (of the Netherlands):** A German married to the Queen of Holland. Runs Royal Dutch Shell (world's biggest oil company). Friend of Rockefeller. Top member of the Trilateral Commission. Friend of Nazis.
23. **Leonid Brezhnev (and other members of Russian Communist Party):** Treat their own people as slaves. Repressors of Poland. Invaded Afganistan. The direct enemy of God, Freedom, Morality, and Truth.
24. **Menachem Begin:** Punk who created Israel. Blew up the King David Hotel. Killed men, women, and children at the village of Deir Yasin in 1948. Stole the holy city of Jerusalem in 1967. Works for Rothschild. Claims to be orthodox Jew but has no beard in violation of the Torah.
25. **Yasir Arafat of PLO, Assad of Syria, Khaddafy of Libya:** Fake Moslems who work for Russian Communists. Traitors.
26. **Khomeini:** Shia false prophet. Deserves death. Claims to be Moslem. Kills pregnant women in violation of the Koran.
27. **The House of Saud:**[†] Spit on Islam. Failed to aid brothers in Afganistan. In love with money. Make speeches about "holy war" on Israel one day and "peace plans" the next.
28. **The Pope:** A corrupt old man. Trained to speak Italian as a young man. Works for Russian

[†] There are possible exceptions.

KGB. Claims to speak for Jesus. Makes a mockery of religion. Sells out freedom.

29. **Billy Graham:** Rich hypocrit, who claims to speak for Jesus (like the Pope). A friend of Nixon.
30. **James Michner:** Wrote bestselling novel, "The Source." Ghost written by research team and paid for by Israeli government. Removes both Jesus and Arabs from Palestine's history.
31. **Mike Royko and James Kilpatrick:** Opposed right to bear arms, joked about the fall of Poland, covered up the Beast's seizure of power, called for more pigs and jails — while honest journalists struggled to get the truth out. (Christmas 1981)
32. **All Homosexuals:** (See Leviticus chapter 20)
33. **All Witches:** (See Leviticus chapter 19)
34. **All Pigs:** Kill the spirit of mankind in their jails. The dirty ones who enforce the rule of the Beast.
35. **All members of the Rothschild Family:** For 90 per cent of an entire generation of French young men who lie in "Flanders Fields" and the 20 million Russians and for Damascus.

We will not allow any foreign land to shelter these criminals like South America did for Nazis. We will pursue them to the end of the Earth.

[. . .]

Closing:

A Cry for War

I say it is finished. I say the time is at hand. I say there is no more time. I say there is no more peace. The Beast stole the peace. No more lies! No more hypocrisy. No more pain to our brothers, our sisters, our Earth, and our Father. I say kill the Beast. Leave no stone unturned. Drive him from our Earth. We are at war. Our brothers died in Afganistan. They fasted to death in Ireland. They fought with only axes in Poland. We are at war until the end of time. We will win with God's help. It is written.

ALBERT DESALVO

Albert DeSalvo raped and killed – mostly by strangulation – thirteen women from 1962 to 1964. The various trademarks of the "Boston Strangler" included bite marks on the victims' bodies, foreign objects (mainly broomsticks and bottles) shoved into their vaginas, and obscene positioning of the bodies for the benefit of police and friends and relatives of the victims. He was stabbed to death in prison on November 26, 1973.

Letter sent to his lawyer before DeSalvo confessed to being the "Boston Strangler," dated January 9, 1965:

Dear Mr. Sheinfeld,

I feel I owe you this letter. I wanted very much that you take my case but I remembered what you told me if I ever get in trouble again don't bother you. So I have another attorney Mr. Jon A. Asgiersson, from Stoneham, my brother Joe gave me his name. . . .

I'm not looking to get out of this trouble I am in but I am looking to be helped if I can be. I realize I am sick and have been for a long time. but I neaver knew how to ask for help. I was afraid and ashamed. how could I tell my wife I am oversexed and have a drive and urge I cannot control. even you Mr. Sheinfeld, when you had my case in 1961 in Cambridge involving all them women. you asked me if I got a thrill or feeling when I touched them. and I lyed to you and said no, because I was ashamed to admit it of my sex drive. But now its got out of hand, but still thank God I neaver got to hurt anyone.

But I think the way I was going anything could have happen in time had I not been caught. I've been doing a lot of thinking — plus what the doctors have told me — that this had to come out one way or another somehow. my problem started way back in my childhood days. Mr. Sheinfeld, I want so bad to tell all I have inside me and **I have a lot.** My wife is still staying by me because she knows I am really sick and I am not lying but asking for help. Mr. Sheinfeld at Westboro State Hospital they treated me good, I saw a doctor just about every day. They at least tried to help and find out what is really wrong or what kind of a problem a person has. I was hoping they could have sent me there. but they didn't. they sent me to Bridgewater State Hospital. At Bridgewater State Hospital Mr. Sheinfeld it's a shame all you do is stay down there for 35 days and they send you back. I saw one doctor for about 1 1/2 in the whole thirty-five days I was there. I filled out an answer sheet with 500 questions on it and from this they found me sane but recommend I be sent to Treatment Center. How can anyone find out in 1 1/2 if a man is sane or not?

Mr. Sheinfeld, I no something is wrong with me. You no my family background and what my father was like and all the things he did. Mr. Sheinfeld, do you no of anyway I can be sent to a hospital where I can come clean with everything inside me. I don't care if I never come out but I want to no at least I am being helped. and maybe find out what made me be what I am and do all them bad things which I am so ashamed of. there is got to be some kind of explanation as to why this has all happen. If you could only no of the good and love I have given my wife and children. this is why she cant believe or understand why this has all happen. I tried being good and did everything to make her happy and children. Mr. Sheinfeld, the night this all happen. She cried and said Al how could you do this to me, you made me relove you all over again. So you see Mr. Sheinfeld I was trying with all my heart to be good but my drive got to bad I found myself relieving myself at least four and five times a day. it was so bad. but when I went out and did what I did that I am in here for it was so strange because it was like I was burning up inside and the feelings I was getting put me like a daze it would be like a dream I would not no where I was going but I was thinking and seeing a woman in my vision in front of me wondering what kind of a body she would have and so on. sometime before I even got anywhere I found myself sitting in the car while driving, already releaved. but in five min it came back again. I was all ready again. But when I did get a woman and she did what I asked her to after it was all over I cried and told her I was sorry please forgive me and the woman also told the police the same. they even said some of the women that they felt when I just got nexted to them, they had a feeling that I had just releaved myself because after that I just tied them up and left without even doing anything to them. its true I just put my hand on them and I was finished. and then realized again what I had done. in almost all the cases the women said more than half I didn't even touched them but tie them up and run whitch took only 3-5 min — so you see I was so build up by the time I found a woman I just got near her and I was releaved. I realize Mr. Sheinfeld that this may mean nothing to you but maybe some day someone else will come up to you with my same problem and you may be able to help him. if there is anything or in any way you can somehow help me. I'll give you my attorney I have allready told him about you but he said he would see you or call you. . . . I always did respect you Mr. Sheinfeld but I didn't not how to explain my problem you have always treated me better than good.

Albert DeSalvo

I went to the police station myself also Mr. Sheinfeld. I gave myself up to the police.

Letter to his wife from Bridgewater State Hospital on March 21, 1965, during his series of confessions:

Hi Irm,

I hope this letter finds you and the children well. As for myself, I'm okay and even though I have a lot of trouble I am still concerned mostly about you and how you feel about me. I don't blame you for my troubles or blame anyone else. But you will admit that if you treated me different like you told me all those years we lost, the love I had been searching for, that we first had when we were married. Yes, Irm I stole them. **But why.** Think Irm. What happened when Judy was born and we found out she may never walk. How you cried Al please no more babies. Irm from that day on you changed. All your love went to Judy. You were frigid and cold to me, and you can't denie this. That's why we were always fighting about sex, because you was afraid to have a baby. Because you thought it would be born abnormal. Irm I even asked doctors what was wrong with our sex life and they all said — until you have another baby, and it is born normal will you then be free to love again.

Irm they were right, the doctors. Remember how much you were worried after Michael was born, how many times you went to doctor Karp and when Michael was born the first thing you asked doctor Karp was is he normal, and you went every week to his office til you were sure he was okay. Irm then you came to me and gave me love I had been starving for — it was to late. More than four years you made me suffer, from the time Judy was born til Michael was born.

I went to jail. Why Irm. Even Hilda knew. She told you. But you didn't believe or want to. I didnt no how to make you love me. I found out to late why you were to frigid. Because you were afraid to have a baby, but I was in jail and this is what hurts me now. When I came out I believed in you and thought you kind and good. But later I found out different. Instead of you saying Al lets start out clean now, forget the past no matter what and think of the future, — no not you Irm. My suffering a whole year in jail was not enough for you. All alone in one room while you were free outside doing what you wanted.

You knew how much I loved you. But when I came out the first thing you said was you waisted one year. And if I hurt you again you would leave me with the children. And you said I would have to prove myself to you. But you forget about the four years witch put me in jail because of you — in witch you made me suffer. Yet because I loved you I didn't leave you. You gave me no love. To prove I'm right, when we went to Germany, two months, look how cold you were. Love is a two-way affair not one Irm, not just when you want it.

Irm I'm not saying this is all your fault. Because I am the one who did wrong. But I had reason I loved you. After I came out of jail — despite everything I tried to do — you denied me my rights as a husband you constantly told me I had to prove myself and in short you tried to make my life a hell wether you knew it or not. I am really and sincerely sorry for what I have done and I will have to pay for it with years of my life. But apparently that is still not enough for you. You tell me not to write or if I write not to express in any way my love for you. So that even in this critical time when I need you most of all you are still making me feel hopeless and if I cant turn to you, I have no hope, no ambition . . . You can't no how awful it is to wait for letters that do not come, or to love someone and be laugh at for that love. As for myself I will all ways feel the same in regards to my love for you and I can only hope that some day, you may realize, the extent of my love and feelings for you . . . I will close for now wishing the best for you and the children.

P.S. Give my love to my Judy and Michael — there Daddy always.

I will love you forever always

Love,

Al

Only untill things started changing, us going out weekends, having everything you wanted, house fixed up, all the money coming in, did you change and start showing a little love for me. Our last two months together you made me feel for the first time like a man. You gave me love I never dreamed you had to give. But why — only because you had just about everything you dreamed of. If you really loved me as you said you did, you would love me now. But you closed the house and everything in it. you lost that and everything you dreamed of. all your love was in the house and now you hate me again. When you really love someone, no matter what they do if you really love them you stay by them.

DERRICK **EDWARDSON**

On August 31, 1957, 31-year-old Derrick Edwardson of London, England, murdered 4-year-old Edwina Taylor. He had previously been convicted eight times for various offenses, including one conviction for sexually assaulting a 5-year-old girl. He turned himself in to the police on the evening of September 9 after his photograph was broadcast on television; he had spent the day watching *St. Joan* and *Son of an Outlaw* at a local movie theater. He pleaded guilty on October 25 and was sentenced to life imprisonment.

Shortly after the murder, police found the following note in Edwardson's overalls inside his work locker:

I killed four-year-old Edwina Taylor. I enticed her to my flat and strangled her with the intention of raping her after death. But I realised that I had killed someone that somebody must have loved and I felt ashamed of myself. I threw her body into the coal celler, it is still there now as far as I know. I cannot get the smell of her decaying body out of my system. I will surrender tonite. I did not interfere with her.

ALBERT **FISH**

Albert Fish confessed to murdering at least six men and children and molesting over one hundred children; he was also a walking *psychopathia sexualis* who reveled in every unnatural act known – and some yet unknown – to mankind. Dr. Fredric Wertham, a psychiatrist who examined Fish, compiled the following list of Fish's "abnormalities": sadism, masochism, active and passive flagellation, castration and self-castration, exhibitionism, voyeur acts, piqueur acts (jabbing sharp implements into oneself or others for sexual gratification), pedophilia, homosexuality, fellatio, cunnilingus, anilingus (oral stimulation of the anus), coprophagia (eating feces), undinism (sexual preoccupation with urine), fetishism, cannibalism and hypererotism (abnormal intensification of the sexual instinct). Some of Fish's proclivities simply defied categorization: as one example, he soaked pieces of cotton in alcohol, shoved them up his rectum and set them on fire. When Fish told Wertham that he enjoyed inserting needles into his scrotal area, Wertham in disbelief had Fish's pelvis x-rayed; a total of twenty-nine needles were found in his body. According to Wertham, one of Fish's sons later told him "that he had found some of these needles cached in one of his father's books, a volume of stories by Edgar Allan Poe, in the story 'The Narrative of A. Gordon Pym'."

Wertham also noted that when Albert Fish was in his middle fifties, "a definite psychosis with delusions and hallucinations began to develop insidiously. Always intensely interested in religion, he began to be engrossed in religious speculations about purging himself of iniquities and sins, atonement by physical suffering and self-torture, human sacrifices. At times he identified himself with God and felt that he should sacrifice his own son. He tried to stick needles under his fingernails but could not stand the pain. He made the poignant remark: 'If only pain were not so painful!' "

Another of Fish's activities was writing numerous obscene letters to women who had placed classified ads in New York newspapers. One woman, Mrs. Grace Shaw of Little Neck, Long Island, wrote back to Fish and an intense correspondence ensued during October of 1934. She later told postal authorities that she was just "gathering evidence" against Fish, but they suspected that she actually enjoyed the letters and was toying with the idea of becoming Fish's dominatrix. It was only after Fish visited her and gave her a brine-soaked piece of rope – along with a letter of instruction – to use for his "whipping" that she gave up any idea of being "of help."

On May 27, 1928, 58-year-old Fish spotted the following classified ad in the "Situations Wanted" section of the New York *World-Telegram*:

Young man, 18, wishes position in country. Edward Budd, 406 West 15th Street.

The next day Fish visited the Budd home in the Chelsea district of Manhattan. He told Edward's mother Delia his name was Frank Howard and that he owned a twenty-one-acre farm in Farmingdale, Long Island, where he employed a Swedish cook and five farmhands. "Mr. Howard" offered to hire the young man for $15 a week plus room and board. Delia Budd said she would need to talk to her husband about the job offer; Fish told her he would be back in a week to "discuss the arrangements with Mr. Budd."

Fish arrived shortly after eleven o'clock in the morning on Sunday, June 3, with a box of strawberries and a pail of pot cheese "fresh" from his non-existent farm. Taking the food into the kitchen, Delia Budd immediately noticed that the cheese smelled rotten. While the Budd family ate lunch with "Mr. Howard," 10-year-old daughter Grace came home from Mass, jumped on Fish's lap and threw her arms around his neck. Fish exclaimed to the family, "What a beautiful child!" He then suddenly "remembered" he had to go to a birthday party for one of his sister's children, and told Edward he would return later, around "suppertime," to take him to his farm. As he was leaving, Fish asked Grace if she wanted to come along; excited to leave the dreary apartment, she kissed him on the cheek and asked her parents if she could go. The parents acceded after Fish told them the party was located at an address near 137th and Columbus; only later did they find out that Columbus Avenue ends at 110th Street.

Later that evening Fish murdered Grace Budd in an abandoned house near Irvington, New York. Over four years later Fish wrote a letter to Delia Budd detailing how he had strangled the little girl and devoured her flesh (reprinted below). The letter was immediately handed over to the police, and New York Detective William H. King noticed on the envelope an unsuccessfully blotted-out monogram with the initials "NYPBA": the New York Private Chauffeurs' Benevolent Association. King interviewed chauffeur Lee Siscoski, who told the detective he had left some of the association's envelopes at his former residence, a boardinghouse located at 200 East 52nd Street. After King staked out Siscoski's old room for nearly three weeks, Fish showed up and was arrested shortly before noon on December 12, 1934.

Although his defense lawyer tried to save him from execution by pointing out that Fish was undeniably insane, a jury convicted him of first degree murder and sentenced him to death on March 25, 1935. Polled later by reporters, most of the jurors agreed that he *was* insane but that he deserved to die anyway. Fish himself supposedly told reporters after the verdict, "What a thrill it will be to die in the electric chair! It will be the supreme thrill – the only one I haven't tried!" He was electrocuted to death on January 16, 1936; at the age of sixty-five, he was the oldest man to be executed at Sing Sing prison.

Excerpts from two letters sent in the spring of 1929 to women whose names Fish had selected from classified newspaper ads:

I wish you could see me now. I am sitting in a chair naked. The pain is across my back, just over my behind. When you strip me naked, you will see a most perfect form. Yours, yours, sweet honey of my heart. I can taste your **sweet piss,** your **sweet shit.** You must **pee-pee** in a glass and I shall drink every drop of it as you watch me. Tell me when you want to do #2. I will take you over my knees, pull up your clothes, take down your drawers and hold my mouth to your **sweet honey fat ass** and eat your sweet **peanut butter** as it comes out **fresh** and **hot.** That is how they do it in Hollywood.

[Bobby] does not wet or muss his clothes or the bed. He will tell you when he has to use the toilet, #1 or #2. For #1 his pants must be unbuttoned at the crotch and **his monkey** taken out. His pants and drawers are all made with a drop seat. All you have to do is loose three buttons in the back and down they come. Saves a lot of undressing. Handy when you want to spank him, just drop the seat of his pants and drawers. You don't have to strip him except at night for bed, or to give him a bath (or a switching). The Doctor says three or four good spankings a day on **his bare behind** will do him good as he is nice and fat **in that spot.** It will be an aid to him. When he don't mind you, then you must strip him and use the Cat-o-nine tails. Say **you won't hesitate** to use the Paddle or Cat-o-nine tails on him when he needs it.

Letters sent to Grace Shaw after she placed a classified ad in the Sunday New York *Times*, seeking invalids and elderly people to board at her home in Little Neck, Long Island:

September 30, 1934

My Dear Miss Shaw

I am a widower with a son of 19 who is a semi invalid. I am a director in the movies and must be back in Hollywood California by Oct 15. Before I go I wish to see him placed in competent hands in some good private home. One that does not look or smell like a Hospital or institution. I am well able and quite willing to pay a good price for Bobbys care. But my instructions must be carried out. Here is the case — When 5 he fell down the cellar stairs. Sustained a brain concussion. Has never been really normal since. Tho going on 20 good looking well built, fully developed. He has the mentality of the age when he fell. Every part of his body has grown but the brain. He is harmless and just so easy to spank or switch as a child of 5. When 12 he had an attack of infantile paralysis. He can walk, run, jump. Get in and out of the bath tub alone. No lifting to do or wheel chair to push. He has very little use of his hands or arms. Has to be washed, dressed, undressed, given a bath. Rubbed all over daily with alcohol and assisted in the toilet. He gets cross and cranky at times, dont always mind. I am trying out European treatment in such cases. Prof Cairo of Vienna Austria, recommends it. He says when he gets a spell **he must be whipped.** They are having great success over there in cases like it. So you see as his own father I would sooner have him whipped **any how** then have him lose his reason entirely. Should you take him in charge on the first occasion he shows temper **spank him soundly** as you would a small boy and dont hesitate to **use** the Cat-o-nine-tails on his bare behind when necessary.

If interested, state your terms and when you can receive him. He is now in Phila in charge of a colored woman I have known 25 yrs. She says **whipping** is the best medicine she ever used.

I will call on you

Sincerely yours
Robert E. Hayden

October 2, 1934

My Dear Mrs. Shaw

Just got home and found your letter. Am so glad you are interested. Before I call on you, will you kindly advise me — Are you a widow? and if so would you consider another marriage? Will the presence of your daughter in your own home, prevent you from taking care of my son? You know there are some women who think it immodest, to strip a boy naked who is over ten years unless he is their own son. I know you are not ashamed to strip, bathe, rub, spank and switch my son or you would not have answered my letter. However I shall feel much more at ease if you will say you are not in your next letter. Would phone but dont hear very well. Will call on you as soon as I get your answer.

Yours very truly
R. E. Hayden

October 4, 1934

My Dear Mrs Shaw

Just got your very nice letter. I am much pleased to know you are **not** one bit ashamed to strip Bobby Naked and bathe him. Am also glad you spoke to your daughter and she is willing to aid you in taking care of him. There is no reason why either of you should be. You know **times** have changed and so have **people**. What in times past was considered immodist is now very common place. Then again look at what young girls training to become Nurses — **See** and **Touch** in Hospitals. Bare in mind that it is for **Bobbys own good** that he is to be whipped. So dont let your heart stay your hand. Do you know that I feel that in part I am to blame for the condition Bobby is in. My conscience says that for being careless I should be whipped, **in same manner (and place)** you will whip Bobby. Some day I hope you will be able to accomodate **me**. I would give a nice new $100.00 bill for a good old fashioned spanking and a taste of the switch — once again. There is a place on 42 St called Fleishmans Baths where naked men are rubbed **all over** by women. White — Black — Chinese. Most women would get a kick out of spanking a naked man. But I prefer some privacy — in a home. Am a 33 D. Mason and will be busy next two days. How about Sunday afternoon or night. Let **your daughter** read this letter. I am a man of the world and she can get knowledge of the world thru it.

I feel that we shall be fast friends.

Sincerely yours
Robert E. Hayden

New York Sunday Oct 7 — 34

My Dear Mrs Shaw

I have been called to Phila on some very important business. While there I shall make arrangements to have Bobby transferred on here and will then turn him over to you and your daughter **for his treatment** when you are ready for him. I have paid for his board and care up to Oct. 15. You see I am never sure just where I will be until Dec. 31-34 when my contract expires. I have always made it a custom to pay several weeks in advance. Now in your letters you have made no mention of your financial **condition**. You may be short of funds. If you are, **dont hesitate to say so.** You can give me your answer thru Mr Pell the bearer of this and I will then advance you as much as you may require. Mr James W. Pell is a friend and **Ward** of mine. He has been declared (imcompetent) and I have $32,500 of his money in trust. He had a nervous break down and was in a nearby Sanitarium for 21 weeks at $100.00 a week. He is **without a living relation** and I dont see **why** you cant take him and so earn some of his money as well. Two of his sons were blown to pieces in the War. At times he imagines he is a boy at School, has been naughty and must be spanked for it. Dr Lamb said to Humor him — let him be a boy all over again and spank him. He gets short of breath and is subject to fits, **when in water.** For that reason he must never take a bath alone. The **least** I have in mind is this. You have told me that I need not worry about you being ashamed to strip Bobby naked and spank his bare behind. If you are **not** ashamed of **Bobby you wont be of Jimmy.** One bare behind is the same as another. Take him upstairs, undress him, give him a bath then **spank him good.** He will say teacher whip me. I shall not leave for Phila until Jimmy returns with your answer. Hope some day **you** will call me by my first name.

How about —————— **my spanking???**

Do I get it??? Oh — I — hope — so

Sincerely **Yours**
Robert E. Hayden

Monday October 8/34

My Dear Mrs Shaw

I had a friend of mine drive Mr Pell or (Jimmy) to Little Neck. They stopped at Little Neck Pkway and asked a policeman where your street was. They spent nearly an hour walking up one street and down another. It was so dark they could not see the numbers. Some one told them of a Mr. Chas Shaw an Electrical Engineer and a Dr Shaw but Jimmy got tired out. When I returned home I found him all in. He had the other letters with him and was all set for a good old fashioned spanking from both of you. That is of course when the (Mr) is not at home. You can arrange that. I shall be in Phila for a day or two. May go to Washn D.C. before I return. Meanwhile you can write me, Belleview Stratford Pa and if you are **ready for Jimmy,** write him at the same address in N.Y. City.

I am Very Sincerely Yours
Robert E. Hayden

P.S. In 1928 Mr Pell operated on for a Hernia. When you have him stripped, you will see the mark of the incision. Look on his left groin, from his Penis to his hip bone. He was prepared for another operation ten days ago. All hair shaved off. That is **why** he looks like a **picked chicken.** He was found to have a bad heart, so it was called off. When you or your girl spank him, dont use your hand. If you have not a paddle, use the back of a hair brush or get a few switches. There must be plenty of them near your home. I know Jimmy would give you a $100.00 bill for a good sound spanking. So I shall take it out of his money for you so **spank spank spank.** Harry K. Thaw gave $100.00 bills to girls for a spanking. Only **he done the spanking on the girls bare behinds.** He met them at the Stage Door. Took them to his room at the Astor House, stripped them naked, turned them over his knee and used a Paddle. **Many of them** came 2 and 3 times a week — **to be spanked** and get that $100.00.

Show me a girl who is nice and has some modesty, but not too much. It dont pay your rent or taxes or buy the baby shoes. Out in Hollywood Laura La Plante came in my office dressed in her birth day suit and sat in my lap. We have an old Romany Gypsie woman who tells all the girls that if they can catch a man naked in his home, whip his bare behind with switches and then kiss him, she will surely marry him. Now they all carry switches.

Jimmy has a habit of painting his behind red or in Gold. When you strip him you will see. I have told him just what to expect at your home. He is pretty tough so dont be shy or slow in laying it on his behind. Limber up your arms for Bobby and his Daddy.

Robert

New York October 24, 1934

My Dear Mrs Shaw

You have struck the nail on the head at last. You have been too **modest**. Take 100 women and give each the same chance I gave you and 99 of them would have jumped at it.

Bobby is still in Phila in the charge of the same colored woman. I am paying her $50.00 a week. It is **not** a question of price but — Service. He seems to like colored people and I have found that colored women and girls **enjoy the job** of **spanking** and **switching** a **Naked white boy** or **man**. Especially is it so **with the girls** regardless as to their age or size. There are many things about Bobby of which I have never written. **Not** because of modesty but because I well knew you would find out. I may as well speak of it now. He has such a strong tendency to **play with himself** (Mastibation) that I have been advised to have him **Altered** or **Sterelized**.

Now as to Mr Pell or Jimmy. He is not a bit Looney. His Hobby is to be **whipped, whipped,**

whipped. I wanted you to try your hands out on his **bare behind** just as a sample of what Bobby would get. He could come to your home and be stripped, well spanked and switched. Put on his clothes and return to me. He is able to do so. Now if the Mr is at home in the evening, it **would embarass both of you.** But it can be done in the **day time** any hour you say. Take him to the house — and go to his bare behind with a will. Now my dear I think I deserve the same — dont you think so??? I have the money to pay for it and am not stingy. So any hour and day you say for **Jimmy** Daddy — later — on.

Now you just drop **Modesty** and speak Plain.

Robert

P.S. I can almost hear the smacks on Bobbys bare behind as those colored girls spank him. **Your turn next**

October 24, 1934

My Dear Mrs Shaw

Just now I am so busy I scarcely got time to really enjoy a good meal and wish you had room for the Daddy as well as for the son. I know I would enjoy some good home cooking with the prospects of a good Spanking now and then thrown in.

I have a sort of an idea that you and the (Mr) do not pull so well together. I would Just **LOVE to give you** a Royal good time and am capable of doing it, without his knowing of it. When I wrote you last of Spanking Jimmy, he had just been shaved for an operation and looked like a picked chicken. Now the hair is beginning to grow again. He has a strange habit of putting on his underwear backward. So you will no doubt find it that way when you strip him. **Both of you warm his behind** until it is good and **red — all over.** He will come down on the bus from Flushing and have a letter from me to **you** in his hand, so you know him. Black Coat — Grey Fedora. Have your daughter meet him. Once you have him in your home, upstairs I am sure both of you know — **what — to — do.** How about Sunday 2-4 P M for him? Have you a nice heavy Paddle??? Have you a nice Cat-o-nine-tails? You see there are **three behinds** to be spanked and switched. So now **dont be — bashful. Dont be — modest Either of you** Just say — **Yes — Robert (Dear x if you want x You shall get a — plenty**
Until I hear from you — by by

Robert x x x

P.S. if Jimmy kicks or puts his hands in the way when you spank him — **tie his hands**

New York City Oct 29/34

My Dear Mrs Shaw

Mr Pell gave me your note.

He says you were afraid that in spanking him he might have a heart attack. I am taking him at 2 P.M. today to Roonoake Va. and turn him over to a man and wife who formerly lived in Washington D.C. (His old home) I shall then return to that city for a few days and then go to Phila. Bobby seems to get on well with colored people so I shall put him in charge of a widow who has a son of 27. Am beginning to think he really does **need a man** to care for him. Especially the parts that are so — **very personal**

Thanking you for the interest you have shown

Excerpt from the last letter to Grace Shaw, dated November 9, 1934:

My Dearest Darling Sweetest Little Girlie Grace

Just got your letter calling me dear Robert. Dear Honey Heart of mine, you have **captured me.** I am your Slave and **everything I have is yours.** Prick — Balls — Ass **and all the money you want. . . .** If you were my own sweet wife, you would not be afraid of me. O girlie of my heart would I love you — and how. Hug-Kiss-Squeeze you, spank you, then KISS **just where** I spanked! **Your nice-pretty-fat-sweet ass.** . . . You won't need toilet paper to wipe your sweet pretty fat Ass as I shall eat all of it, then **Lick** your sweet ass **clean with my tongue**. . . .

Letter to Delia Budd, the mother of young murder victim Grace Budd, postmarked November 11, 1934, from Grand Central Annex, Manhattan:

My Dear Mrs Budd

In 1894 a friend of mine shipped as a deck hand on the Steamer Tacoma, Capt. John Davis. They sailed from San Francisco for Hong Kong China. On arriving there he and two others went ashore and got drunk. When they returned the boat was gone. At that time there was a famine in China. **Meat of any kind** was from $1 — to 3 Dollars a pound. So great was the suffering among the very poor, that all children under 12 were sold to the Butchers to be cut up and sold for food in order to keep others from starving. A boy or girl under 14 was not safe in the street. You could go in any shop and ask for steak — chops — or stew meat. Part of the naked body of a boy or girl would be brought out and just what you wanted cut from it. A boy or girls behind which is the sweetest part of the body and sold as veal cutlet brought the highest price. John staid there so long he acquired a taste for human flesh. On his return to N.Y. he stole two boys one 7 one 11. Took them to his home stripped them naked tied them in a closet. Then burned every thing they had on. Several times every day and night he spanked them — tortured them — to make their meat good and tender. First he killed the 11 yr old boy, because he had the fattest ass and of course the most meat on it. Every part of his body was Cooked and eaten except head — bones and guts. He was Roasted in the oven, (all of his ass,) boiled, broiled, fried, stewed. The little boy was next, went the same way. At that time I was living at 409 E 100 st, rear — right side. He told me so often how good Human flesh was I made up my mind to taste it. On Sunday June the 3 — 1928 I called on you at 406 W 15th St. Brought you pot cheese — straw berries. We had lunch. Grace sat in my lap and kissed me. I made up my mind to eat her. On the pretense of taking her to a party. You said Yes she could go. I took her to an empty house in Westchester I had already picked out. When we got there, I told her to remain outside. She picked wild flowers. I went upstairs and stripped all my clothes off. I knew if I did not I would get her blood on them. When all was ready I went to the window and Called her. Then I hid in a closet until she was in the room. When she saw me all naked she began to cry and tried to run down stairs. I grabbed her and she said she would tell her mamma. First I stripped her naked. How she did kick — bite and scratch. I choked her to death, then cut her in small pieces so I could take my meat to my rooms, Cook and eat it. How sweet and tender her little ass was roasted in the oven. It took me 9 days to eat her entire body. I did **not** fuck her tho I could of had I wished. She died **a virgin.**

Letter mailed on November 21, 1934, to a Brooklyn woman who had advertised a "Room to Let":

Dear Madam

I am a widower with 3 boys, 13-15-19 I wish to board out until the two youngest are thru school. I want good plain food clean beds, sew mend darn and do their laundry. I prefer **a widow,** who has a girl old enough to aid her. Henry and John have caused me a lot of trouble by not going to school. . . . Their principle Miss Bruce said to me, if they were her boys, she would spank both of them soundly 3 times a day

for a month and give John a dose of the Cat-o-nine-tails at bed time. She blames him most so do I. I have no time to do this and besides I think whipping children is **a woman's job.** I want a good motherly woman, who can and will assume full charge of the 3 boys. Make them obey you and when they dont take down their pants and **spank them good.** Dont hesitate to strip them to the skin and **use the Cat-o-nine-tails on them,** when **you** think they need it. Robert is feeble minded due to a fall. Tho going on 20, well built and strong he is much easier to spank or switch than Henry. He kicks like an army mule when being spanked. I want a woman who will whip any one of the 3 or all 3 at once if they need it. Our own doctor says if Bobby **is not** spanked and switched when he gets cranky he is apt to lose his reason entirely. So **he** must be spanked as well. He is now in Phila Pa in charge of a Colored woman I have known 25 years. She has a daughter 17 and between them he is getting **plenty** of the paddle and Cat-o-nine-tails. Henry and John are in Upper Darby Pa in charge of two Maiden Sisters, both ex School Teachers. They conduct a boarding school for boys and girls up to 17 yrs. Both are very strict and any **boy** or **girl** who misbehaves is spanked in front of the entire class. John is a big boy for his age and it shames him to have his pants taken down and be spanked in front of a lot of girls. I want a place where **all 3** can be together. . . . I am willing to pay you $35.00 a week for the 3 boys, $15.00 a week extra when I am there. But if you take them you must **assure me you will Use the paddle** and **Cat-o-nine-tails freely on all 3 boys.** I want a woman who will **not be embarrassed** in stripping Bobby any more than Henry and John. So if you are interested tell me how to reach your place by car.
A. H. Fish

Letter to Detective King while in custody:

Dear Mr. King

In 1906 or 7 I lived at 519 Main st, Bridgeport Conn with my wife and 2 childrn. Albert now 35 and Anna 33. They took part in a play at Palis Theatre called Little Orphan Annie. From there we moved to Springfield Mass where I done some painting for Rev Charles F. Slattery rector of Christ P.E. Church. In April or May of 1933 my son Henry drove me to his Car to New Haven, Conn to see a widow who had an ad in Friendship Magazine for a husband. When we got there she had gone to town. . . . During these 4 years I wrote to about 20 widows who claimed to have money but it was all hot air. . . . I write as habit — Just cant seem to stop. A few months after I done that deed I shoved 5 needles into my belly — legs — hip. At times I suffer awful pains. An Ex Ray will show them. Three weeks ago I spilled Alcohol on my behind and then lit a match. I can hardly sit still now. You know as well as I that if I had not written that letter to Mrs. Budd, I would not be in Jail. Had I not lead you to the spot no bones would have been found and I could only be tried for kidnapping. So again I say it was fate, due me for my wrong. Now my dear Mr. King I am going to ask you In Gods Name do this for my poor childrens sake. For my self I ask no mercy. Write to Hon Wm. F. Brunner ask him to get in touch with Hon Hamilton Fish. See if you cant have me tried in N.Y. City on the **kidnapping charge.**

When 5 yrs old I was placed by my mother in St Johns Orphanage Washington D.C. There I learned to lie — beg — steal and saw a lot of things a child of 7 should not see. . . . I hear they are going to take me out to Westchester next week. Suppose I **deny** the killing. I have **signed** no statement **as yet.** You tell me. I only want to live **long enough** to see my poor children at work and out of want. **Misery leads to Crime.** I saw so many boys whipped it took root in my head. I have many hundreds of times whipped and **tortured** myself as marks on my behind will show. . . . the Blessing of Almighty God on you.

I am
Albert H. Fish

Letter to Fish's 11-year-old granddaughter, Gloria, shortly after January 28, 1935, while awaiting trial:

My Dear little Gloria

Your poor old grand pa got your sweet note you sent in Mamas letter. I am so glad to hear you still love me and always will. You know as a baby and at all times, I loved you. . . . There have been times when I was at Mamas that I was cross and cranky. But I had **much** on my mind. Since this has happened, Mama can tell you what that was. I am so happy to know that you . . . are doing so well at school. **Stick to it** and learn all you can. Some day before long now, you will be able to go to work and help poor Mama & Papa. They have struggled hard for each of you, as I have also struggled hard for each of them, in the years that have passed. I am well. Trust in God and have no fear as to what the result will be. You know I love each of you dearly and always will. Pray every night for your poor old grand pa — Write soon again.

Letter from the same period to his teenage stepdaughter Mary Nichols:

Dearest Sweetest Mary — Daddys Step Kiddie

I got your dear loving sweet letter. I would have answered you long before this. But between ex rays, doctors and my lawyer I have been busy. Then you know I am 65 and my eyes are not so good as they were when you saw me last. . . . So my sweet little big girlie will be 18 on the 28th. I wish I could be there, you know what you would get from your daddy. I would wait until you were in bed, then give you 18 good hard smacks on your bare behind. . . . Now Mary dear, I will get a check from the U.S. Government in a few days. As soon as it comes I will send you $20.00. I am not able to get you a watch, but you can get one that you like. I hope dear Mama who I loved and **still love** and all of you are well. You speak of being at the big games. Here in N.Y. City there is nearly always some kind of a game going on. In the Public Schools and all of the Y.M.C.A.s they have large swimming pools. If a man or boy wants to use this pool he must take all his clothes off and go in bare naked. There is one of the largest pools in the U.S. in the West Side Y.M.C.A. 8th Ave & 57 St. The water varies from 3 to 8 ft deep. Sometimes there are over **200 men and boys, all of them naked.** Any boy or man can go in and see them for 25¢. Now you know well sweet honey bunch that most all **girls like to see a boy naked.** Especially the **big boys.** Do you know, my dear Mary, what the girls do to get in and **see the show?** Many of them have boyish bobs. They dress up in their brothers clothes, put on a cap, then go to the Y. Quite often a boy will come out of the water and stand so close to a girl dressed in boys clothes, she can and does touch his naked body. Many of the men and boys know the girls are there and see them naked, but they dont care. . . . Be careful all of you my sweet kiddies. Dont go out doors in the snow unless you have on rubbers. Now listen my little miss, dont you keep me waiting so long for another of your sweet dear letters. If you do some day I shall come out there again and give you another sound spanking — you know **where!**

During his trial, Fish handed the following note to his lawyer:

Before you sum up, read to the jury Jeremiah, Chapter 19, 9th verse.

The biblical quote:

> And I will cause them to eat the flesh of their sons and the flesh of their daughters, and they shall eat every one the flesh of his friend in the siege and straitness, wherewith their enemies, and they that seek their lives, shall straiten them.

Letter to his attorney, James Dempsey, after the trial, confessing to the murder of another victim, 4-year-old Billy Gaffney:

There is a public dumping ground in Riker Ave., Astoria. All kinds of junk has been thrown there for years.

Here is my plan: some years ago I lived at 228 E. 81, top floor front. Suppose I confess to **you** that I did ——— the Gaffney boy. In same manner I did the B girl. I am charged with the crime anyhow and many really believe **I did**. I will **admit** the motorman **who positively identified** me as getting off his car with a small boy, was **correct.** I can tell you at that time I was looking for a suitable place to do the job.

Not satisfied there, I brought him to the Riker Ave. dumps. There is a **house** that stands alone, not far from where I took him. A few yrs. ago I painted this house for the man who owns it. He is in the auto wrecking business. I forget his name but my son Henry can tell you, because he bought a car from him. This man's father lives in the house. Gene, John, Henry helped me paint the house. There were at that time a number of old autos along the road.

I took the G boy there. Stripped him naked and tied his hands and feet and gagged him with a piece of dirty rag I picked out of dump. Then I burned his clothes. Threw his shoes in the dump. Then I walked back and took trolley to 59 St. at 2. A.M. and walked from there home.

Next day about 2 P.M., I took tools [unintelligible], a good heavy cat-o-nine tails. Home made. Short handle. Cut one of my belts in half, slit these half in six strips about 8 in. long.

I whipped his bare behind till the blood ran from his legs. I cut off his ears — nose — slit his mouth from ear to ear. Gouged out his eyes. He was dead then. I stuck the K in his belly and held my mouth to his body and drank his blood.

I picked up four old potato sacks and gathered a pile of stones. Then I cut him up. I had a grip with me. I put his nose, ears and a few slices off his belly in grip. Then I cut him thru the middle of his body. Just below his belly button. Then thru his legs about 2 in. below his behind. I put this in my grip with a lot of paper. I cut off the head — feet — arms — hands and the legs below the knee.

This I put in sacks weighed with stones, tied the ends and threw them into the pools of slimy water you will see all along road going to North Beach. Water is 3 to 4 ft. deep. They sank at once.

I came home with my meat. I had the front of his body I liked best. His monkey and pee wees and a nice little fat behind to roast in the oven and eat. I made a stew out of his ears — nose — pieces of his face and belly. I put onions, carrots, turnips, celery, salt and pepper. It was good.

Then I split the cheeks of his behind open, cut off his monkey and pee wees and washed them first. I put all in a roasting pan, lit the gas in the oven. Then I put strips of bacon on each cheek of his behind and put in the oven. Then I picked 4 onions and when meat had roasted about $^{1}/_{4}$ hr., I poured about a pint of water over it for gravy and put in the onions. At frequent intervals I basted his behind with a wooden spoon. So the meat would be nice and juicy.

In about 2 hr. it was nice and brown, cooked thru. I never ate any roast turkey that tasted half as good as his sweet fat little behind did. I eat every bit of the meat in about four days. His little monkey was as sweet as a nut, but his pee-wees I could not chew. Threw them in the toilet.

XXXX

You can put my children **wise** as to the above and **if necessary put me** on the stand.

I can relate the details just as if I were talking about **the weather**.

The place I have described is just **such a one** to do an act of this kind. How about calling in several reporters and tell them that I told you God told me to purge myself of this sin and depend on his Mercy? Lead them down to the dump. **They will bite hard.** What a sensation. Gene, John, Henry, who worked with me on the house nearby can tell of same. Or do you think I ought to call in Father Mallet of Grace P.E., Church, White Pl. and **confess to him?** Then you let it loose.

Write down just what **you** want me to do. If it will be of any good, you can get my record from prison office. It shows **emergency call** about 7 P.M., Cell 1-B-14, Warden Casey and dr. (symptoms of lead poison).

While in Police Hdqurs., Dec. 13-14, had not as **yet** made confessions to any one. When officer F. W. King left room I was kicked hard in my stones as I sat in a chair, by Sgt. Fitzgerald. I can point him out to **you** in court. He said to me, even tho you are an old man, if you don't come clean, I'll take you downstairs and use a length of rubber hose on you. **You** take at least one shot at him in court **for me.**

Get **torture paddle** I made from officer King. He has it. Shows state of mind. Board with tacks driven thru it.

JOHN LINLEY **FRAZIER**

On October 19, 1970, 24-year-old John Linley Frazier tied up five people at their home in an affluent neighborhood of Santa Cruz, California, shot them to death, dumped their bodies into the swimming pool, and set the house on fire. His victims were Dr. Victor Ohta, his wife Virginia, their two sons, 11-year-old Taggart and 12-year-old Derrick, and Dr. Ohta's secretary, Dorothy Cadwallader.

Frazier was convinced that he was on a "divine mission"; he was also convinced that the Ohta family had been "polluting and destroying the Earth." A student of the occult, numerology, astrology, phrenology, and the Book of Revelations, Frazier unsuccessfully attempted to recruit twelve disciples for his "mission." The press portrayed Frazier as a psychotic "acid casualty"; forensic psychiatrist Donald T. Lunde, however, diagnosed Frazier as suffering from acute paranoid schizophrenia, stating:

> there was no evidence that he had consumed any drugs in sufficient quantities to cause irreversible brain damage, yet he was acutely psychotic months later in jail where he had no access to drugs of any sort.

Judged legally sane, Frazier was sentenced to life imprisonment at San Quentin.

Note found under the windshield wiper of Dr. Ohta's Rolls Royce:

halloween . . . 1970

today world war 3 will begin as brought to you by the pepole of the free universe.

From this day forward any one and?/or company of persons who missuses the natural environment or destroys same will suffer the penelty of death by the people of the free universe.

I and my comrads from this day forth will fight until death or freedom, against anything or anyone who dose not support natural life on this planet, materialisum must die, or man-kind will.

KNIGHT OF WANDS
KNIGHT OF CUPS
KNIGHT OF PENTICLES
KNIGHT OF SWORDS.

JEANNACE **FREEMAN**

Before dawn on May 11, 1961, 19-year-old Jeannace Freeman and her lesbian lover, 33-year-old Gertrude Jackson, murdered Jackson's two young children at the Peter Skene Ogden State Park in Oregon. Freeman – who had numerous tattoos on her body, including the word HATE on her knuckles – hit 6-year-old Larry over the head, strangled him, mutilated his genitals with a tire iron, and tossed his body into a 360-foot gorge. Then Jackson and Freeman together mutilated the genitals of 4-year-old Martha and threw her, still alive, into the gorge. After their arrest, Jackson pleaded guilty and was sentenced to life in prison; she was released seven years later. Freeman went to trial – taking care to change her "butch" look by wearing a skirt and her hair in curls – and was found guilty, receiving the death penalty. After the state of Oregon abolished capital punishment, her sentence was commuted to life and she was paroled in 1983. Six months later she violated her parole conditions – authorities found her living with a woman and her young children – and was returned to prison. She was eventually released in 1985.

An "open letter" published in *The Oregonian* newspaper on November 11, 1974:

To the People of Oregon:

My name is Jeannace June Freeman. Remember me? I was tried and convicted of first degree murder back in 1961. I was given the death sentence; I was under that for three years. Then I was commuted to life imprisonment. I got transferred back here to Alderson, W. Va., in 1969.

I have a few things to say that I have kept to myself for too many years. The crime that I committed was indeed horrible. Any crime of murder is. But, what made mine so bad, was that fact that it was a small boy that I killed.

Would it interest anyone to know that I meant to kill his mother, only she pushed him in the way; and he caught the blow that I meant for her? Can you understand how I did panic?

How out of this panic, I tried to hide the terrible thing that I had done, by throwing his body down in that canyon? That I wasn't thinking of how it might look later, but thinking that I myself couldn't face up to what I had done! That I was running scared . . . That I made up all kinds of lies trying to deny to myself, as well as everyone else what I had done.

They said I am sadistic and perverted because I am a lesbian! Well hey, who and what made me a lesbian? Are you interested enough to keep reading?

When I was four years old, I was brutally raped by ————. This didn't twist my mind, except in the sense that I don't care for men. I did say men, not boys! In other words, when it comes to making love, I prefer women. Why?

Because my body was brutally torn up when I was raped! And I can't even stand the thought of a man touching me in that way. If it had happened just once, then maybe I could have gotten over it . . . but it happened four times in all.

A four-year-old girl just isn't built to have "relations" with a man. For years I was afraid for them to even touch me. Can any of you mothers honestly say that you would censor your daughter if, under the same circumstances, she had turned out the same way? Your answer has to be no! If you have any understanding of a human being, who needs love and affection, the same as everyone else.

I started my fourteenth year in September . . . for killing a child, when I meant to kill his mother! What kind of a person was she, that she could push her own flesh and blood in the way of a blow meant for her? And what kind of a mother would deliberately throw her own daughter into that same canyon; and then, firstly, try to blame it on me . . . then admit it . . . only instead of admitting that she set it up, for it to happen exactly as it did.

Knowing me well enough to know that I do have a violent temper . . . and would try to bust her head open.

And so, consequently, played right into her hands, and trying to hurt her, I killed the boy, with a blow that was meant for her!

Then, she plays crazy, and says the kids loved each other so much, that she felt the little girl would want to be with her brother! Well, I have news for you . . . the woman isn't crazy . . . "maybe like a fox" and she got "LIFE," did seven years, made parole, went out, violated . . . and is felt sorry for!

One question, does her conscience bother her? Does she have trouble sleeping nights? Does she have nightmares? I DO!

She had her chance at trying to make another go of it out in the free world . . . so when do I get my chance? How long does being locked up stay punishment? When does a person cease to be punished, and become like a vegetable? Where does the "hard time" leave off, and a person becomes adjusted to the prison life, and it ceases to be punishment? Where does punishment leave off, and CRUEL & UNUSUAL PUNISHMENT come in? What says it is "JUST" to give the mother a chance and not me? If I had killed an adult, and if I wasn't a Lesbian, I would have been given my freedom a long time ago! How can anyone rightfully blame me, at that time, nineteen years old; the mother, thirty-seven! I was still a child in many ways myself!

Don't you people know and understand that I will pay for what I did for as long as I live? That I can't forgive myself! Even though it was an accident, I suffer knowing that I did do it! And what everyone seems to be forgetting, is the fact that my final judgment is still to come. No matter how long the laws of the land keep me locked up . . . my final judgment will come from God, not no mere mortal!

And while we are on the subject of judging, what gives the people of Oregon, the Parole Board, or anyone else the right to stand in judgment of me? When ALL OF YOU, somewhere, at some time, have most likely done things, if not just as bad, then at least still wrong in a moral sense.

But yet, you will judge me, because I am a lesbian. Because I have gone against the conventional code and led a different type life than what the laws of our land say we are to lead!

But again, who and what made me different? What one of you can say that you wouldn't have turned out the same, given the same circumstances? Or was I such a big sensation because it was election year?

All the judges and district attorneys really made a name for themselves with my case! They must have been re-elected at least three or four times because of me! And how many of the "Shrinks" and lawyers just had to mention my name, to have clients busting down their door? Great for the business world!

So here I sit, waiting for the parole board to decide that I can have a parole. I meet them again in March. It would be nice to be free! I think that fourteen years is long enough for what I did. What do you think? Can you truthfully say that I deserve to be kept locked up longer?

Or do you even care? Did anyone ever really care? When it comes to caring, who cared when I was so brutally abused? My mother, yes, but she wasn't there at the time or it wouldn't have happened!

In closing, I remain, ME! I can't change what I did, or what I am! But I still say, fourteen years is enough time for what I did.

Sincerely,

Jeannace Freeman

BRUNO G.

A German police sergeant, 27-year-old Bruno G. murdered Ella H. and her mother, Ella T., on February 2, 1924. The sexologist Magnus Hirschfeld examined Bruno G., and asked him to answer a questionnaire and write "a coherent account of his life, with special regard to his sexual life." Dr. Hirschfeld described the crime scene as the following:

> In the charge presented to the State Attorney it stated that both women, Ella H. and her mother, Ella T., were the victims of a sexual murderer. This conclusion was evidently drawn from the fact that in both cases the genitals were exposed. Frau H. was only covered with a blanket and a towel over her chest, and was completely naked, most of her clothes having been found under her back.
>
> The shoes and stockings of the murdered woman were scattered all over the kitchen. When the blanket and the bloody towel had been removed, a knife was found to be buried in the left breast, with about half an inch of the haft protruding. On the right breast there was a wound evidently caused by biting. There was a wire loop round the corpse's throat. The face at the base of the nose was swollen, apparently from blows with the fist. In the corner of the right eye there was a slight stab wound, while a wound caused by biting was discovered below the right calf.
>
> In the living room next to the kitchen lay the body of the murdered Frau T. Her dress was torn from her throat downwards, so that her breasts were bare, while her skirts were turned up and her knickers torn, so that her genitals were exposed. Near the body a pair of pocket scissors were found. On a chair near the body lay a chopper. The throat of the murdered woman showed clear signs of strangulation.
>
> The bed was in disorder. There was a spot on the sheet, caused by vomiting, and the chamber under the bed also contained a discharge of this nature. There was no sign of a search having been made for money or valuables; nothing except a lady's watch was missed. According to the post-mortem carried out by the police surgeons, Frau H. died of strangulation and internal hemorrhage resulting from stab wounds in her heart and lung, while the older woman died of strangulation. Her genitals were also injured, apparently by scratching.

Bruno G. was acquitted by reason of insanity in the middle of June 1926 and was subsequently released.

Autobiography and account of the murders:

I was born on the 18th August, 1897, at Bromberg. I was born before my parents were married. I can recollect no special event from my childhood at Bromberg. Later, my parents moved to Berlin, where we occupied a living room and a kitchen at my grandmother's flat. There were 12 children, 7 of whom, four brothers and three sisters, are still living. As my parents moved very frequently, I cannot tell whether this or that event took place at this or that flat; in particular, my memory does not reach back far enough for me to be able to say anything about my school days. We children slept in pairs in the same room as my parents. My father, who had had a bootmaker's shop in Bromberg, was a building laborer in Berlin. He was very kind to us, though strict, and only when he was drunk did he have a temper. As he beat my mother, as well as all the children, I did not like him so much as my mother. She was an affectionate, forgiving woman, and she tried to make good all the injustices my father committed. Owing to the recurrent quarrels and her terrible worries to provide food for the family, she sometimes spoke about suicide and said she would gas herself and the children. Some nights, fearing that she might carry out her intention, I put the key of the gas meter under my pillow. One day, after a quarrel with my father, my mother attempted to hang herself in the lavatory. Disquieted by her long absence, we went after her and found her hanging from the lavatory door. With the aid of my father, whom this had sobered up, we brought her into the room and revived her. For many years I could not forget that moment, and I was haunted by this scene in my dreams. When my father went to bed drunk, he slept restlessly, stripped himself in his sleep, and sometimes he lay almost entirely naked. My sisters and I used to watch him at such times. When our parents had sexual intercourse, this was not hidden from us children.

As a child I was willing, obedient, but extraordinarily timid. I loved my mother very much, but I became more and more estranged from my father, owing to certain happenings in the home, particularly when he beat my mother. I could not forget the injustices he committed against my mother and us children. When I reached school age I went to the municipal school, where I was an attentive and quiet scholar. My favorite subjects were religion, history, and general knowledge. I was a good average scholar, except that I had difficulty with mental arithmetic. I also had bad marks for singing, mainly because I was too shy to sing in the presence of others.

I was promoted regularly, except once, when a foot wound caused by a broken tumbler necessitated my going to hospital, and I missed the examination. Once I was severely punished during the drawing lesson, for painting another boy's face to look like a Red Indian.

I do not know how I came to start masturbating. For years I slept in the same bed with one of my sisters. On one occasion, during a lesson in gymnastics, I was sliding down a pole, and as my penis rubbed against the pole I experienced for the first time a curious sense of pleasure. Also, at the lavatory at school I saw boys touching each other. I also masturbated mutually with my sister, but I do not know which of the above events happened first. When I was about 12 it happened one night that my brother, who thought I was asleep, called my sister and performed the sexual act with her on the edge of the bed, before my eyes. As long as my sister and I slept together we masturbated nearly every night. One night we tried to perform the sexual act, but failed, because my member was slack, and we made no further attempts. Once I observed an older boy playing "doctors" with a little girl, and examining her anus and genitals with a piece of wood. I asked my sister about all these things and I often got hold of pamphlets and books which my parents kept under lock and key.

I masturbated on an average three times per day. At first I did it for the pleasure it gave, and I do not know what I was thinking during the operation. Later I took away feminine underwear, chemises, knickers, etc., kissed the parts covering the feminine genitals, and masturbated.

I do not know when the first emission took place. However, at the age of 14, I must have been weakly built, because when the time came for me to choose a profession my mother advised that I should apprentice myself to a tailor, as she did not think a more difficult occupation would suit me. I myself wished to become a druggist, but the continuous unemployment of my father and a severe illness of my mother made this impossible. I had to earn money, and I therefore took a job as errand boy to a druggist in West Berlin. During the three years I stayed in this job, I earned the satisfaction of my employer, and here I finally found the explanation of all I wanted to know.

While out on errands in summer I used to walk behind lightly-dressed women wearing transparent dresses, masturbating through my trouser pocket, or I used to stay in the basement of the shop, and tried to look under the skirts of women standing in front of the shop window, masturbating the while.

When delivering goods, I generally dealt with servant girls, and I had many opportunities for intercourse, but I blushed easily, and was shy with women, so I talked to them no more than was necessary. Although I would have liked to have had an affair with one of these girls, who often became importunate, I was far too shy.

The money I earned I always handed over to my mother, and she gave me some pocket money on Sunday. I did not spend much on myself. I drank but little, and then only stout, or soft drinks, such as ginger beer. But I had already taken to smoking at that time.

One Sunday, with some other boys, I visited a tavern where customers were served, but although the women offered themselves, I had no dealings with them.

On one occasion, returning from a boating trip, a friend and I went home with a prostitute, who had accosted us. My friend performed the sexual act with the girl before my eyes. When my turn came I had no erection. This was my first attempt. My failure was due, I think, to my friend's presence, but perhaps my excitement and the fatigue of rowing also had something to do with it. For a long time afterwards I made no further attempts, because I was afraid that I might fail. Also, my friends teased me a great deal, so that I gradually severed my connections with them.

After three years my employer dismissed me, because I had tried to rob him. Then I worked for several firms before I was called to the colors. Nothing particular happened during this time. My last job was at a chocolate factory, where I met a girl whose quiet temperament attracted me. An intimate and undisturbed friendship developed, but no intercourse took place, except that we kissed several times in the course of our friendship. I was introduced to the girl's family and carried on a regular correspondence with her until her marriage. In March, 1916, at the age of 19, I was called to the colors, and was sent to an infantry regiment in East Prussia. I was glad to be a soldier. I found military service easy, and I always behaved fairly well.

I wanted to go to the front as soon as possible, and had myself transferred to a machine gun corps in Konigsberg, whence, after a short course of training, I was sent to the Eastern front.

There I stayed until the Revolution, without participating in any major engagement or sustaining a wound. I had leave three times, and always stayed at the home of my parents, visiting my own relations and those of the above-mentioned girl, with whom I was still carrying on a regular correspondence.

At barracks, and also in the field, I had frequently seen my comrades masturbate. I had no sexual intercourse with women either during my leave at home or in the occupied territories of Lithuania and Esthonia. I kept myself to myself, in so far as this was possible among the lower ranks. My comrades were mostly older territorials from East Prussia, and I was the youngest in the company. In December, 1917, I was decorated with the Iron Cross, second class, though I had done nothing in particular. Shortly before the Revolution I received three days C.B. because the group to which I belonged refused to clean the machine gun immediately on their return from sentry duty.

At the outbreak of the Revolution I and several comrades joined a voluntary organization designed to protect the troops returning from the front, and ensure the safe return of materials. The generous pay I received enabled me to visit theatres and travelling cinemas, as well as brothels, but I had no intercourse with the women. For some time I managed the officers' mess as the subordinate of an officer. One day I tried to have intercourse with the Lithuanian woman who had been engaged as cook, but here again I had no erection. During the night I spent with her I made several vain attempts. This was my only attempt in the field. Several of my superiors, whom I later met in the police, were struck with my depressed appearance, and asked me what was the matter with me. I used to sit for days, brooding, but I cannot explain even now what I felt like at such times.

In Olita I had an experience that I shall never forget. We had to evacuate the place in face of a superior force of Bolsheviks, and when we re-took it a few days later and went in search of quarters, I came upon the bodies of dead and mutilated comrades in a dark corner. As I turned my torch on them they seemed to move, and I was seized with a feeling of horror, such as I had not known before. Later, when the voluntary corps returned to Konigsberg, I secured my discharge, and returned to Berlin, where at first I lived with my parents. Then I found a job at a munitions factory, where my father was also employed, and as sleeping in the same room with my sisters was distasteful to me, I began to look for a furnished room.

Since my return from Russia I had no other wish than to cure my impotence. I was making money, but I could not bring myself to consult a specialist. Then, as a result of an advertisement, I ordered a book entitled **Neurasthenia and Impotence** from a Swiss sanatorium. I answered a questionnaire, in reply to which I was informed, to my great relief, that my case was not hopeless. I was also sent some tablets and a liquid for bathing the scrotum, both of which I used as directed, but without result. In an attempt to force a cure I took more of the tablets than the prescribed dose, but the only result was that I fell in a faint. My father saw this. Then I read about charlatanism and quackery, and was afraid that I had made my condition worse by using the preparations. In my own mind I nursed the hope that nature would help me in the end. I withdrew from all social intercourse, and would not be persuaded to take part in any party or the like. I also stopped drinking and smoking, but I ate well.

But in spite of all my resolutions I could not give up masturbation; in my loneliness I even indulged in it to excess. One day I lost control over myself and touched my sister, who was lying in the next bed, in an indecent manner, and I then immediately carried out my former intention of leaving the house. I rented a furnished room not far from where my parents were living. Shortly before this I had called on Miss S., a relation whom the parents of both of us wanted me to marry. We were given many opportunities to be alone together, and on this occasion, after some kissing and hugging, I tried to have intercourse with her, but again failed to have an erection. I was ashamed of myself, and parted from the girl, never to see her again.

After a year at the munition factory the firm was liquidated, and all the workers discharged.

During my visits to the home of the girl I met at the chocolate factory, I made the acquaintance of her sister, who was my ideal woman, and with whom I fell in love. After six months we became engaged. After leaving my last job I was unemployed for a fortnight, so I applied for employment in the police force. I was accepted, and it was a real relief to me that my duties, which I carried out with pleasure, gave me no time to think about my condition. As an unmarried constable, I lived at the police barracks.

My fiancée was of a passionate nature. She often visited me at the barracks when I was alone, and she must have formed her own opinion of my strictly moral conduct. I finally resorted to lies, telling her that I had previously lived somewhat too carelessly, in order to mollify her. In the end I came to the conclusion that she would seek elsewhere what she could not get from me.

I never tried to have sexual intercourse with her, and in the end I came to the conclusion that it would be best for both of us to break off the engagement, yet I could not decide to do this, as I loved the girl too much. Then one day she told me that she had been unable to control herself and had given herself to a childhood friend. Although I perfectly understood, I nevertheless broke off the engagement, though it made me suffer. After that I took no interest in anything but my profession. I gave myself very little leisure, in order to prevent myself constantly thinking of my trouble, which made me the unhappiest man on earth. Even on my days off I stayed at barracks, and only visited my parents for a few hours very rarely. I was mostly on the sports ground or at the swimming baths. I read all sorts of books without discrimination, though I preferred erotic books. Gradually I bought myself a collection of nude studies, and looked at them while masturbating. I very rarely met other people.

I frequented a teashop with my brother for a long time, and there I met a girl who by her gay and vital personality cheered me up and tried to dispel my sad thoughts. With this girl I tried unsuccessfully to have sexual intercourse on several occasions. I found a way out in mutual masturbation, which we practiced several times, and at the moment when my discharge occurred I used to kiss her on the right breast. Once, when she made merry over my impotence and turned away from me, I attempted to shoot myself, but was prevented from doing so by my brother, who was also present.

With another girl, whom I met later on, I never had any normal intercourse, either. We masturbated mutually at my barrack room, without undressing, and while doing so I pressed against her body. We usually excited ourselves in advance by reading obscene books or by looking at a few pictures in my album. In this case, too, I kissed the girl's breasts, which were full and firm. During my intercourse with her we read together **The Sexual Criminal**. It is possible that I had intercourse with this girl in other ways as well, because she persuaded me to drink, and I had no recollection afterwards of anything that might have happened between us.

Then, when I met my present fiancée, I broke off this relationship. I met my fiancée in the course of my duties on the beat. Her serious, modest, reserved personality attracted me. The fact that our relationship gradually became more and more intimate was due not so much to her personality as to her faith in God. I had already found my Saviour when I was 12, and was then a junior member of the Salvation Army and also a member of the band. But the evil of masturbation had turned me away from God. In this religious girl I found someone who brought me back to my Saviour again, encouraged and comforted me. She sustained me, and showed me that it is easier to reach one's goal with patience and perseverance, than if one charges with one's head against a wall. Later I was introduced to the girl's family, and gradually regained my tranquillity and peace of mind in this environment. Later I became engaged. Frequently, when the meetings held in the house lasted far into the night, I slept at my fiancée's home. I slept on a sofa in the same room as the girl and her parents.

Peculiarly enough, she was the first woman with whom I was able to have intercourse in the normal way. This may have been due to the fact that she came to me as I had frequently wished, or perhaps to the fact that, at first, we only had intercourse at night in bed, so that I was able to overcome my shyness. We slept together twice a week, and during the first day we had sexual intercourse three or more times in one night; later, I was content with one or at most two acts. I had regular discharges, though at first I ejaculated at the first coital movements. At the moment of discharge I could never refrain from kissing her on the mouth and breast. I often attempted to bite her on the mouth and breast, but when I noticed that it hurt her, I bit the pillow. Now I was certain that I was no longer impotent, it gave me the idea of attempting sexual intercourse with another woman. Then, when I met Miss A. L. at the hairdresser's at the police barracks, I thoughtlessly made friends with her and ceased to call on my fiancée for the time being. I had no intention of breaking off the engagement, I could not control myself, and all my thoughts were concentrated on the desire to try sexual intercourse with another woman. After an acquaintance with A. L., who visited me every evening, I ventured to make the attempt. But I had no erection. During my affair with her we made three or four attempts, but the result was always the same. We always lay on the bed fully dressed, and she earnestly forbade me to look at her uncovered genitals during the attempts. She also refused my request to undress entirely, or even partly. On the contrary, she wanted the room to be in semi-darkness, so that I could not see her charms. Otherwise nothing noteworthy happened between us.

Meanwhile, my fiancée, owing to my absence, and also because my affair with the other girl had been revealed to her by my colleagues, broke off the engagement. I continued my friendship with the other girl, was introduced to her family, and frequently visited her when off duty. She told me that she had already been engaged, and that her fiancée had left her in the lurch with a child; she also confessed that she had been in the habit of masturbating for years. I described to her the consequences of masturbation in a terrifying manner, and also read to her some chapters out of the book I had received from Switzerland. That I myself was in the habit of masturbating, I never mentioned anywhere, and in this case too, in reply to questions as to my impotence I explained that I had been a cocaine taker and that I had previously led a dissolute life.

This girl was the first member of the opposite sex of whom I knew that she was also addicted to masturbation, and I regarded her as a fellow sufferer and our relationship became firmer and more intimate. But my impotence did not improve. In view of my experience with my second fiancée, which showed that in certain circumstances I was potent, I now had an aversion for masturbation or any other substitute for the sexual act. It was my desire to have intercourse in the normal manner, and I persuaded myself that I could do this with another woman if, like my second fiancée, she met my wishes in all respects.

I also thought that if a woman behaved quietly, lying down without looking at me, I should again be capable of carrying out the sexual act.

Then one evening, after a visit to my girl, I entered an establishment opposite the police barracks, in order to have a drink. Here I renewed my acquaintance with a working girl, who had been engaged to a colleague some years earlier. I celebrated our reunion by treating her to various drinks and accompanying her, before I was due for duty, to her rooms. I knew through other policemen, that this girl was not very particular in the matter of morals, which was, in fact, the reason why her engagement had been broken off. I intended to go up with her for the purpose of sexual intercourse, and told her so. We stopped at the front door and chatted for a while, when I suddenly, without any reason whatever, seized her by the throat, and holding one hand over her mouth, began to choke her. The woman fell to the ground, and I let go of her in terror, with the words: "Forgive me, there must be a devil in me." I begged her in tears not to cause me trouble. I myself did not understand why I had done what I had done, and I am not clear even to-day as to the cause of my actions. But I do know that afterwards we attempted sexual intercourse, though I am not certain whether this happened in her room or in the corridor.

Then I wandered about in the street for a long time. It was not till dawn that I returned to my quarters and went to bed. Upon waking I noticed bloodstains on the sleeves of my overcoat and I could not rest until I had called on the woman and asked her what had happened, for the events of the night before were very blurred in my memory. However, when I was face to face with her, I was so ashamed of what had happened that I did not ask her anything.

On the 2nd February, 1924, at about 11 P.M., after a visit to my girl I entered a tavern in the Gneisenaustrasse, where I had been several times before. I ordered a glass of beer and sat at a table in the bar parlor reading a paper. In the adjacent saloon someone was playing the piano. I drank my beer and some liqueurs then I laid the paper aside and went to the lavatory. I had to pass through the saloon, and on my way back I stopped at the door watching the dancers and talking to the proprietress. Before this, my attention had been attracted by Frau H., who was in the bar parlor persuading customers to order more drinks and generally behaving in the manner of a prostitute. This woman now invited me to dance with her. I refused saying that I could not dance, and that in any case I was in uniform. Thereupon the woman asked me to stand her a drink by way of compensation for my refusal. She demanded rather than requested this. Her whole behavior led me to think that she was a prostitute. We then went to the bar parlor, where I ordered some beer and liqueurs, and stood talking with her at the counter. I do not remember what we talked about apart from a few questions put to me by the woman as to where I was serving, where I lived, and whether I came to this place frequently. I also remember that in the course of conversation Frau H. pointed to a table near by which was occupied by an old lady, saying: "That's my mother with whom I'm living." At closing time, when the proprietress asked the customers to leave, I left the place with Frau H. and her mother. I do not know whether I had asked their permission to accompany them. Shortly before we came to another public house, Frau H. asked me whether I had enough cigarettes on me, and I replied in the negative. We then entered the place, and in order not to appear to have come in for the cigarettes alone, I ordered a beer and a liqueur for each of us. I also bought a packet of cigarettes. I cannot remember anything else that may have taken place at this establishment. I must have paid and left, for I remember finding myself in the street with the two women. I do not remember what direction we went in, and what streets we passed through. I only remember standing in front of a door which Frau H. must have opened. Here, or in the entrance hall, the mother became ill and fell down, and I raised her and, with the aid of Frau H., carried her to the door of the flat. As we entered the flat I remained alone with the mother in the passage, while Frau H. went into the kitchen and made a light. Then she came back, took her mother by the arm and led her to her bed, while I took off my cap and coat and belt in the passage. Then I entered the kitchen, where I sat down at a table and smoked a cigarette. Frau H. had put her mother to bed and sat on my knees and embraced and kissed me. She asked some questions relating to my financial position, and it was obvious that she would only consent to intercourse for payment. This hint depressed me, and in any case, now that she was so close to me I saw that she was old, in addition to which her clothes exuded a smell that repelled me, and so I decided to go home, particularly as I feared that I might fail to carry out the sexual act. I got up, picked up the key that lay on the kitchen table and made for the kitchen door, in order to put on my things in the passage. Frau H. threw herself into my arms with the words, "I shan't let you go," and tried to take the key away from me. A playful, harmlessly meant struggle developed, and the woman hugged me and pressed her body against me with erotic meaning. Contact with her body, her renewed attempts to kiss me, and her unpleasant smell, caused me to let go of the key, but I still hoped that she would let me go. But she hid the key in her dress and ignored my threat that I would leave in spite of that. She begged me not to go, saying that now that I was there I ought to stay. In order to free myself at last, I pushed with both hands against her breasts, and I must have done this rather roughly, and I thought she was going to scream, though I do not know whether this was so. I then seized her throat with both hands and choked her. She shut her eyes and slowly collapsed. I knelt down beside her with my hands still round her throat. Owing to her coital movements while she was on her feet, I had had a slight erection, but this passed while I was choking her. Now a desire to attempt the sexual act on the woman lying before me rose in me. I tore my clothes off, took off her shoes and stockings, had a good look at her body, then bent her right leg back and bent over her, hoping to induce an erection. But this did not happen. Owing to my failure I flew into a terrible rage which exploded in my subsequent actions. Naturally, I am unable to describe these actions in the order in which they might have happened. I know that I picked up a knife which must have lain on the kitchen table and buried it in her left breast, and also that I hit the woman with my fist. I also remember that I put a wire loop round her throat. I do not know which I did first after choking her, as I do not remember. I do not remember the moment when I bit her, and I only have a very vague recollection of having encountered a resistance with my mouth. Then I know that the light went out and that I lighted an oil lamp; then I returned to the corpse and dragged it by the legs out of the pool of blood to the window, during which time the stab wound bled more profusely; and that I then covered the body with the garments that were lying around and with a towel. I do not know how many times I tried to perform the sexual act on the body, nor whether I did anything else besides the above. I also do not remember how I got from the kitchen into the bedroom. I remember that I choked Frau T. who must have been sleeping there, but I do not remember how I did it. Nor do I know how she came to be on the floor, or whether I attempted to perform the sexual act on Frau T. I do not know how long I lay with Frau T.; all I know is that when I woke up I was lying beside her. I then got up, lighting the passage with a match. As I was putting on my coat it occurred to me that I could not get out of the house, as I had no front door key. I remembered that Frau H. had hidden the key in her dress, and I therefore returned to kitchen. I made no light, as the kitchen was sufficiently illuminated by the moonlight, and I could see everything clearly. Beside the body of Frau H. I saw the key and the watch. I took away both and quickly left the flat. Then I went to the police barracks. As I entered my room I found that my comrades were asleep. I undressed, had a wash, and went to bed and I must have fallen asleep immediately.

Until the day of my arrest I carried out my duties at the barracks. I tried to wash the bloodstains off my clothes, but did not succeed. My superiors and comrades noticed my excited demeanor, and I was spoken to several times on account of my inattention. The day after the murders I threw Frau H.'s keys into a lavatory, but found myself unable to part with the watch, which I carried in my trouser pocket. I could not bring myself to give myself up to the criminal investigation department. That suspicion would fall on me, I assumed from the fact that I had mentioned my name at the public house where I met the women.

Then, on the following Sunday, one of my roommates mentioned the case, and I was almost on the point of confessing to him that I was the murderer. I could not bring myself to do this, but could not refrain from telling him that I had been together with the women the day before the murders were discovered. On the day of my arrest I was on duty at the barracks. In the morning two commissars of the murder squad called, and asked to see the officer in charge. I myself was ordered to take them to the officer, and on the way to his office I struggled with the idea of revealing myself to the commissars as the murderer, but the thought that it might perhaps not have been me caused me to keep silent. Having carried out my task, I returned to the guard room and immediately afterwards I was called by telephone to the main office of my division, where I found the commissars in the act of examining my personal documents. They asked me whether I had been in the company of the murdered women on the critical night, to which I replied in the affirmative, but denied having murdered them. Then a roommate was shown my pocket scissors, which had been found on the scene of the murders, and he recognized them as my property, whereupon I was taken by the commissars to the police presidium. Here I strenuously denied having committed the murders, insisting that I had not accompanied the two women into the flat, but had parted with them at the front door. Then, in the evening, I heard that my locker had been searched and the officers also brought away my civilian clothes, so I revealed myself as the murderer, but asked to be allowed to change as I could not make a confession in uniform. As I was changing, the watch of Frau H. fell out of my trouser pocket. An officer who was present picked it up. At sight of the watch it depressed me to think that I must now part with it. In reply to the question to whom the watch belonged I said that it belonged to one of the murdered women, and that I had taken it as a mascot, as a souvenir. I then described my meeting with Frau H. and her mother at the first public house, but could not remember what had happened at the second public house. When I was told that some other customers had heard me say to the older woman, "Mother, you don't mind if I sleep with your daughter?" I said to myself that they must have been more sober than I and agreed that I had said something of the kind.

During my interrogation there was present, in addition to the interrogating commissars and several other gentlemen, a female typist, who took down what I was saying, so that my only thought was to get it over as quickly as possible. As the talk about the sexual details in the presence of the typist was painful to me, I admitted many things which I did not recollect, but which were shown in the photographs taken on the scene of the crime. For the rest, I had an idea of committing suicide in an unguarded moment, but this had been foreseen by the authorities, and I was carefully guarded, even during my interrogation. I gave all the facts I could remember, as stated above, but as I could not talk about the attempt at sexual intercourse in the presence of all those people I admitted certain things without feeling that they were true. I am sure I would never have made some of the statements, and would have described the procedure differently, had not the interrogating gentlemen called my attention to motives which they said I had been guided by. When I was asked why I killed the older woman, I said that when I was in the passage, about to dress, I thought I heard her snore and that it occurred to me that she might give me away. I then decided to eliminate her. I pronounced this self-accusation with a certain disgust for myself, and I heaved a sigh of relief when I was told that from the criminological point of view my description was the only correct one. Nothing would have been more painful to me than to be accused of deliberate lying in the presence of all those people, or if my statements had been doubted. I hoped that my confession would end the interrogation. In view of the scratches on the older woman, I allowed myself to be persuaded to say that I had attempted sexual intercourse with her. I knew that I had lain in the older woman's bed, but I did not know how she came to be on the floor, and I said that she had slid off the bed and I had then laid her on the floor. While describing these things I saw myself doing them and I continued to work out in my mind what must have happened next, being guided in the process by the endeavor to make everything appear credible. I was in a suicidal mood while describing these things, and nothing mattered. I never withdrew any part of my confession. The reason for the self-accusation that I had killed the older woman with premeditation was that I was being treated far more gently than I had expected or deserved. I could not do otherwise, I had to do something in order to punish myself for my crime. Also I did not think that I would ever have to answer for my actions to an earthly judge. I did not drop my suicidal intentions afterwards, either. When, after my mother's death, I came to regard myself as her murderer also, it gave me an inner satisfaction to have accused myself in this matter. My mother's death strengthened me in my determination not to withdraw anything. The longer I kept saying to myself that everything had happened as I described it, the more I came to believe it. Later, when I became reconciled with my fiancée, I thought otherwise.

His thoughts on criminologist Erich Wulffen's graphic forensic textbook, *The Sexual Criminal*:

When I first saw the book, my curiosity was sufficiently aroused for me to buy it, so that I could read it and look at the pictures at leisure. I thought I would be sure to find in the book something I did not know. Also, the certainty that the pictures of the murdered persons were those of nude women, and were faithful pictures, contributed to my decision to acquire the book. I read the book with great interest from cover to cover, including the histories and descriptions of the murderers. The ultimate result was not that I decided to perpetrate a similar crime; I laid the book aside with the knowledge that I had obtained an insight into matters of whose existence I had not even dreamed until then.

Written answers selected by Dr. Hirschfeld to his "psycho-biological questionnaire":

1. My father is still living, my mother died of consumption at the age of 54.
6. Physically I resemble my father, mentally my mother.
7. I have three brothers and three sisters.
13. My father and brothers, as well as several of my relatives, are addicted to drink.
20. As a child I was physically well. I only had a slight headache when reading or learning something by heart. Until my 16th year I wetted my bed.
21. As a child I was very timid, but later I changed.
23. I participated only in pronouncedly boyish pursuits like wrestling, running, military and Indian games, etc.
24. As a boy I lacked a spirit of gaiety and as I was frequently reproached for depressing others by my quiet demeanor, I gradually withdrew from the company of other boys. My sisters teased me for staying indoors too much, and called me a dreamer.
25. In my early years my mother often told me that I looked like a girl, but for my short hair.
26. As a child I often had nightmares. I was pursued by a pair of eyes, staring at me with a terrible expression. I could not get rid of that face even in the waking state. I was always afraid of going to sleep.
29. My conduct was such that I did not deserve chastisement from my parents or teachers. My father chastised me frequently because on the instructions of my mother I refused to buy drinks for him.
30. I was brought up at the house of my parents.
35. From my tenth or eleventh year I masturbated nearly every day about three times. I do not know how this began.
39a. I am 5ft. 8in. tall, and weigh 11 stone.
39b. I love small women.
41. I like hard physical work best; the strength and endurance of my legs are greater than those of my arms. I prefer weight lifting, etc., to free exercises.
42. My tread is firm and my stride long.
42b. I like a short stride in women.
44a. My skin is of a light, somewhat ruddy color.
44b. In women I like a clear, pale coloring.
45a. The hair on my head is thick but soft. My arms, chest, and legs have only a slight growth of hair. The same applies to my face.
47. My sensitiveness to pain is slight.
48. I like small hands and dainty feet in women.
50. My body is slim, with full shoulders. My hips are narrower than my shoulders. The shape of my skull is oval and long.
52. I have a full chest, with small nipples.
52a. I like women with full, round breasts.
55a. I prefer the odor of the rose to all others.
55b. I like women to use creams and perfumes.
56. I dislike strongly spiced foods, but like strongly sweetened foods.
58. I like natural speech, an attractive, insinuating voice.
58a. My larynx is normal. My Adam's apple protrudes only slightly. My voice is naturally low.
60. I am not left-handed.
61. I sometimes suffer from so-called depressions and feel as though the ceiling were going to crash or something else of an extraordinary character were going to happen. I am very forgetful, and have practically no memory for figures. I blush easily, even at harmless talk. At the age of 10 I once fell on my head when sliding down the banisters. The consequence was slight oppressiveness, headache, and nose bleeding. I do not know whether my recurring headaches are due to this or not.
63a. I am of a soft temperament.

63b. I am yielding and conciliatory, the way I like women to be.

64. I feel pain and pleasure like other people, with this difference, that a small present or unexpected pleasant news brings tears to my eyes. On the other hand the more serious and sad I feel, the more I try to conceal or shoo away my troubles with a laugh. My relations have frequently called me heartless on account of this. This laugh sometimes comes without rhyme or reason, and I do not know myself why it rises to my lips. This laugh lasts a long time, and is of a convulsive character, so that my former colleagues nickname me the "Laughing Prince."

65. I am erratic; I am alternately gay and depressed, and laugh and cry almost in the same breath.

67. The more excited my environment is, the calmer I am. I always try to reassure and calm others. When I am angry or excited over something I find relief in words, then I am calm again, as though nothing had happened.

70. I am very ambitious. I mostly over-estimate my knowledge and capabilities. I am very receptive to admiration and applause. I have no desire to dominate others.

71. I am curious, taciturn, and credulous, but not easily accessible. I am not interested in gossip.

72. I have been a believer (religious) since childhood.

74. I am tidy and very punctual, but somewhat easy-going and extravagant, though I do not live above my means.

76a. I am weak-willed, but know no fear.

76b. I like strong-willed, energetic, fearless women.

78. My requirements are modest in everything; I cannot exist without work, but prefer hard physical to intellectual work.

79a. I have been a smoker (cigarettes) since the age of 16. In my early years I drank very little, and then only on special occasions. Later, as a soldier and policeman, I drank more. I could not stand much, and was entirely drunk after drinking a pint of beer, and one or two liqueurs.

79b. I do not like women who drink or smoke.

80. My memory is weak. I can only vaguely remember events that took place long ago. On the other hand, events of a sexual character remain more distinctly in my memory. I have a very lively imagination. I have frequently related insignificant experiences of my own after embroidering fact with fiction. The more romantic or horrible such a tale turned out to be the more satisfied I was. When I saw at the theatre or the cinema people who performed foolhardy acts, I always imagined myself in their place. For instance, when I saw a screen detective perform a bold act, it gave me immense pleasure if, in my capacity as a policeman, I was able to do something similar. As a participant in raids I had very frequent opportunities for this, and I preferred such tasks to others.

80b. Women whom I love, and who satisfy my taste in all respects, are capable of influencing me very considerably. I am a man who voluntarily subordinates his will to the will of others who are stronger. Left to my own resources, I am undecided, and need someone to lean upon.

82. I read a great deal, without discrimination, though I prefer detective stories and particularly erotic matter.

85. I like women to be able to sing and play an instrument.

86. I am interested, apart from my profession, in sport, athletics, and swimming, and also in wrestling and boxing.

89. I was very satisfied with my profession, and I worked at it with pleasure.

90. I dress simply, like close-fitting clothes but dislike high collars. Apart from engagement and signet rings, I do not like jewelry. I have no preference for any particular color, but for my clothes I prefer blue cloths.

91. In women I like close-fitting clothes which show up the shape of the body.

92. I generally keep myself to myself. A large company depresses me. I prefer the quiet life of a small town.

93b. I suffer from a lack of energy and will-power. Also from sexual impotence.

94. I have strong sexual urges, and I am of a passionate nature.

95. My sexual impulse is directed towards women.

97. I love women who are of the same type as myself.

98a. I feel drawn to people who are intellectually above me and who are kindly and gentle.

99a. The half-clothed body stimulates me most.

99c. A soft, plump skin has a special attraction for me.

99d. All exudations of the skin (perspiration, etc.) repel me.

101. My sexual impulse is directed towards women of the pronouncedly feminine type.

102. In my dreams I am only concerned with the female sex. Mostly my dreams relate to the sexual act, but frequently to mutual masturbation. I have also said to myself: "If a woman were to lie still and indifferent until I made my member rigid through masturbation, then I could perform the sexual act."

103. In public my attention is attracted by women, but in company I feel easier and less self-conscious among men.

104. I am interested in pictures of nude women, and had a fairly considerable collection of them.

105. I am self-possessed with other men. My feeling of shame is deeper when confronted with women.

106. I am constant in my affections. I do not like flirting.

113. My behavior during intercourse is active in the masculine manner.

120. At the moment of ejaculation I used to press my partner convulsively to myself, pinching her arms and breasts in a manner that caused pain, and ruffling her hair with my hands. I also tried to bite, but always bit the pillow or the quilt.

122. From a boy I had a predilection for fine feminine underwear, and used to masturbate while looking at it. Later I asked women friends whose hair I liked for locks of hair, and used them for the same purpose.

133. Up till now I have never been able to confide in a doctor; I was too ashamed. Years ago I received treatment by correspondence from a Swiss sanatorium, but there was no result.

134. I felt I was the unhappiest man on earth. Frequently when I was in the company of gay, vital people, I was so overwhelmed that I attempted to commit suicide. I was filled with nausea for myself for being unable to control my unhappy urge for masturbation, for I saw in masturbation the chief cause of my impotence. In addition, I had betrayed my faith in God by living aimlessly and not having the strength to throw overboard all that was oppressing and tormenting me. I felt useless, superfluous.

HARVEY GLATMAN

As a mousy, jug-eared "momma's boy," Harvey Murray Glatman reveled in the activities of the Boy Scouts. He was particularly talented in the art of rope handicraft; years later he would tell police, "It seems as if I always had a piece of rope in my hands when I was a kid." At the age of twelve he discovered what is sometimes the wont of other unusual teenage boys: autoerotic strangulation, to increase the pleasure of masturbation. One evening Glatman's mother noticed that when she arrived home with her husband, "Harvey's neck was all red with what looked like rope marks. He said he went up in the attic, took a rope, tied it around his neck, and tortured himself . . . In that way he got satisfaction." He never lost his fascination with ropes and bondage.

In 1945, at the age of seventeen, Glatman pulled a toy gun on a teenage girl in Boulder, Colorado, and told her to take off her clothes. She fled screaming, and he was arrested and held for a short time by authorities. Moving to New York, he robbed women at gunpoint and was known in the tabloid newspapers as the "Phantom Bandit." For these crimes and a charge of burglary he served five years in Sing Sing and, according to authorities, responded well to psychiatric treatment. Released on probation in 1951, he moved into an apartment at 1101 South Norton Avenue in Los Angeles. His mother set him up with a TV-repair business, and for a short time he quietly enjoyed his life as a bachelor. He especially took great pleasure in his new hobby, photography.

By the summer of 1957, though, Glatman was still – at the age of twenty-nine – a virgin. His sexual fantasy life had become increasingly vivid and sadistic in nature, and photographing female models in the nude made his frustration all the more unbearable. On August 1, 1957, acting on what he termed in his later confession to police "my intention," Glatman – posing as a "true detective" magazine photographer named Johnny Glynn – photographed, raped and strangled to death Judy Ann Dull, a 19-year-old model and mother from West Hollywood. He buried her body in the desert near Indio, California; her scattered bones were later found by hitchhikers. He changed his tactics on March 8, 1958, by arranging an evening of square dancing with Shirley Ann Bridgeford, a 24-year-old factory worker and divorcée, through a "lonely hearts" club; the role he played on this occasion was a plumber named George Williams. After picking her up at her mother's home in Sun Valley, he suggested that, instead of dancing, they go driving in the romantic moonlit desert. Bridgeford agreed. They drove to the Anza Borrego State Park, north of San Diego, where once again Glatman enacted his ritual of photography, rape and murder.

Glatman found his last murder victim, Ruth Rita Mercado – a 24-year-old dancer known in the strip clubs as Angela Rojas – at a nude modeling agency on Pico Boulevard near his home on July 23, 1958. He raped her repeatedly at her apartment, then suggested that they have a "picnic." Taking her to the same desert locale as the Bridgeford murder, he laid out his red blanket and, in between snacking on sandwiches and documenting his tableaux of torture and bondage, raped her "four or five" more times. Glatman then strangled her with the same length of cord he had used on Dull and Bridgeford.

He was finally arrested on the night of October 27, 1958, while attacking another model, 28-year-old Lorraine Vigil, in his car off the Santa Ana Freeway in Tustin. Vigil successfully defended herself and attracted the attention of a passing highway patrolman. Glatman immediately confessed to police and showed them, in the early hours before dawn on Halloween, the burial sites of Bridgeford and Mercado. His 69-year-old mother, after being informed by reporters that her son had confessed in chilling detail to the murders, responded: "Oh, my God in heaven. Not my boy! He was always so good. He never hurt anybody . . . He was always good and always dependable . . . There must be some mistake." Glatman insisted on receiving death in the gas chamber, saying "It's better this way . . . I knew this is the way it would be." He was executed on August 18, 1959.

Glatman's verbal confession, taken down by Los Angeles Police Detective Pierce Brooks, to the murder of Judy Ann Dull:

> I learned that she was a model for both amateur and professional photographers from her roommate, who showed me her pictures. I called her about noon to ask if she was available for a modeling job that afternoon. I gave my name as Johnny Glynn. She said she was free, and we made an appointment for 2:00 P.M. to meet at her apartment. She picked out some clothes, including extra ones that she said she needed for another assignment after we were finished. We left her apartment for my apartment, which I told her was fixed as a studio with lights and equipment there. She was agreeable. She said she didn't care where she was modeling as long as she was paid twenty dollars per hour.
>
> We drove to my apartment, arriving around 2:15 P.M. I slipped the gun I usually kept in my glove compartment in my coat pocket before going into my apartment. Once inside I told her I wanted to take some pictures that would be suitable for illustrations for mystery stories or detective magazines and that this would require me to tie her hands and feet and put a gag in her mouth. She was agreeable, and I took a number of poses.
>
> The last pictures that I shot had her tied and on the floor. She was getting a little restless. I finally made up my mind to go through with my intention. I went over to her and put my hand around her shoulder and just below her neck. I sat down on the floor beside her and propped her up to a sitting position and told her that I was going to keep her there a while and that I wouldn't hurt her if she did as she was told and didn't give me any trouble. I said I was going to have some fun with her and I also took the gun out of my pocket and showed it to her as a sign of seriousness and also to get her to a frame of mind where she would be docile. I also told her that I had a record and just by doing what I had done so far I was in serious trouble. This was to scare her into being submissive.
>
> She motioned to me that she wanted to say something. I took out her gag and cautioned her to talk quietly and not to make any loud noises or scream. She said she was a nymphomaniac and that she was not going to cause trouble because she was estranged from her husband and that she had a custody suit pending which was due for a hearing in about a week. Any hint of

her running around or engaging in any unusual activities might be used against her, as her ex-husband was trying to have her declared as unfit for custody of the child. She was saying this, I presume, to impress me that it was not necessary to threaten her with a gun.

I believed her, so I slipped the gun back into my pocket and picked her up and carried her into a little hallway adjacent to the living room where we had been taking pictures. I put her down and left her in there by herself in the same condition as she was on the floor in the living room. I went back into the living room and took the film out of the camera, put the camera and tripod away, went into the kitchen and got a glass of water and a piece of apple to eat. Then I went back where I left her in the hallway and sat down beside her. I started to run my hands over her body and squeeze her and I was kissing her around the neck and breasts. She seemed to be partially enjoying it. I don't recall how long we kept this up. Then I untied her hands and feet. I told her to remove her clothes. I think I said I had taken the film out of the camera. That is not correct. I had two or three shots left in the camera. I finished the roll of film then and took pictures of her sitting on the couch with her facing the camera, virtually naked and with one, I believe, leg on the couch and the other one dangling on the floor.

I left something out. While she was still tied and in the hallway, I had gone into the kitchen and when I came back she had a nosebleed for some reason. She was trying to hold her head back and her nose was bleeding. I don't know why. She hadn't been struck or anything unless in trying to move around slightly, she jarred her head against something. I just grabbed the first piece of cloth that was laying close by, and I used that to hold over her nose to stop the bleeding. It was bleeding quite freely, and I held her head back till it stopped. I mention this because the police did find a pillow case in my room after I was arrested and it had bloodstains on it, and one of the photographs of Judy show it.

Judy wanted to use the bathroom, and I let her. I told her she could get dressed, and she did and combed her hair and put on some makeup. When she came out I told her to sit on the couch and relax a while. I began to wonder just what I was going to do next, how I was going to resolve this. It was getting late in the afternoon, and I was trying to think could I release her and what would happen if I did and what would she do about reporting this. I asked her several times something like: "Judy, what are you going to tell your roommates when you get home?" "Do you think your roommates are very worried about you and would they call the police?" She indicated that she would try and cover this up and make up some story. She repeated that she could not afford any kind of scandal or improper activities, whether it was her fault or not, whether she was forced into something or whether voluntarily or not, as she thought it would hurt her chances to get her baby.

I questioned her intermittently like that, trying to decide in my own mind. The thought crossed my mind that the safest thing to do would be to kill her because she knew where I lived and the car and the color and the make and maybe the license plate. I was weighing one factor against another. My own fear of returning to prison and what the chances would be of her successfully making up a story. I don't recall how much time passed but maybe it was 7:30 or 8:00 P.M. I guess I finally decided I would not be able to take the chance and that I probably would kill her to cover up the other crimes that I already committed with her. I decided to take her out in the country somewhere. I wasn't too familiar with the area, but I knew there was some desert area. I waited until it was dark and a little later in the evening when things were pretty quiet on the

street. I turned on the television to help pass the time. She was still sitting in the chair and had been dozing for a while. She woke up and wanted to know if I wanted her to sit on the couch with me. I said sure, and she came over and sat on my lap. It was 10:15 because I remember watching the 10:00 P.M. news. After the news I said we were going to leave the apartment. I told her I was going to drive her out in the sticks and then I was going to let her out of the car and give her the money. I promised her that would be more than enough for bus fare back. I told her I needed to tie her hands while on the way out as a precaution.

As we were driving, I kept debating with myself whether I could actually go through with it or not. I kept trying to justify it to myself and try to justify it by assuming that there just wasn't any other thing I could do except of being a sure risk to go back to jail. As a matter of fact, the actual thought I had was that if I was going to turn her loose, I might as well go down to the police station and just walk inside with her.

I finally reached the point where I said it was now or never, and I pulled off to the side of the road. I told Judy I wanted to have intercourse once more with her before I turned her loose. This was a pretext to get out of the car. She agreed to this but wanted to use the back seat of the car. I said it was pretty dangerous in the car because we were just on the shoulder of the road and not well off the road, and it would be embarrassing if someone stopped. I told her I had a blanket in the car and we could spread it on the sand. There was a railroad track running parallel with the road. I told her I wanted to tie her hands and she asked why and I said I didn't want her to argue. She didn't. I tied her wrists behind her while she was standing, and then I had her sit down and I tied her ankles. I had her roll over on her stomach and then I had a third length of cord, and I tied one end of that between her ankles and put a knot in that so it would hold firm, and then I bent her legs back at the knees as far as they would go, pulled her ankles back toward her head as far as it would go, and I put one knee in the small of her back and I lifted her chin off of the blanket with my hand and I just very quickly looped the rope around her neck twice and just pulled. I knew if she knew what was coming or what I intended to do she would have started begging and I wouldn't have been able to go through with it. I let go of her chin and put both hands on the end of the rope which I had in my hand, and I just pulled as tight as I could and as hard as I could and, of course, the other end was looped around her ankles so it was anchored there.

For an instant I wanted to undo what I had just done. I lifted her head up and called out her name. I assumed she was already dead. Then I sat there for a few minutes getting over the shock of it, and then I began thinking again and I noticed that we weren't too far from the railroad tracks, and I thought maybe I had better move her body back from the tracks a little further because someone on the train might see her. I just didn't want it found. First I took the rope from around her neck and then the ropes from her wrist and ankles and put them back in my pocket. I picked her up and carried her twenty to twenty-five yards further from the tracks to where there was soft sand. I started digging a depression and put her body in it. I took off her shoes. I remember thinking about possible fingerprints on the smooth leather and I wiped them off. I threw one away. I then took the other shoe, picked up the blanket, went back to the car, made a U-turn, and started back home.

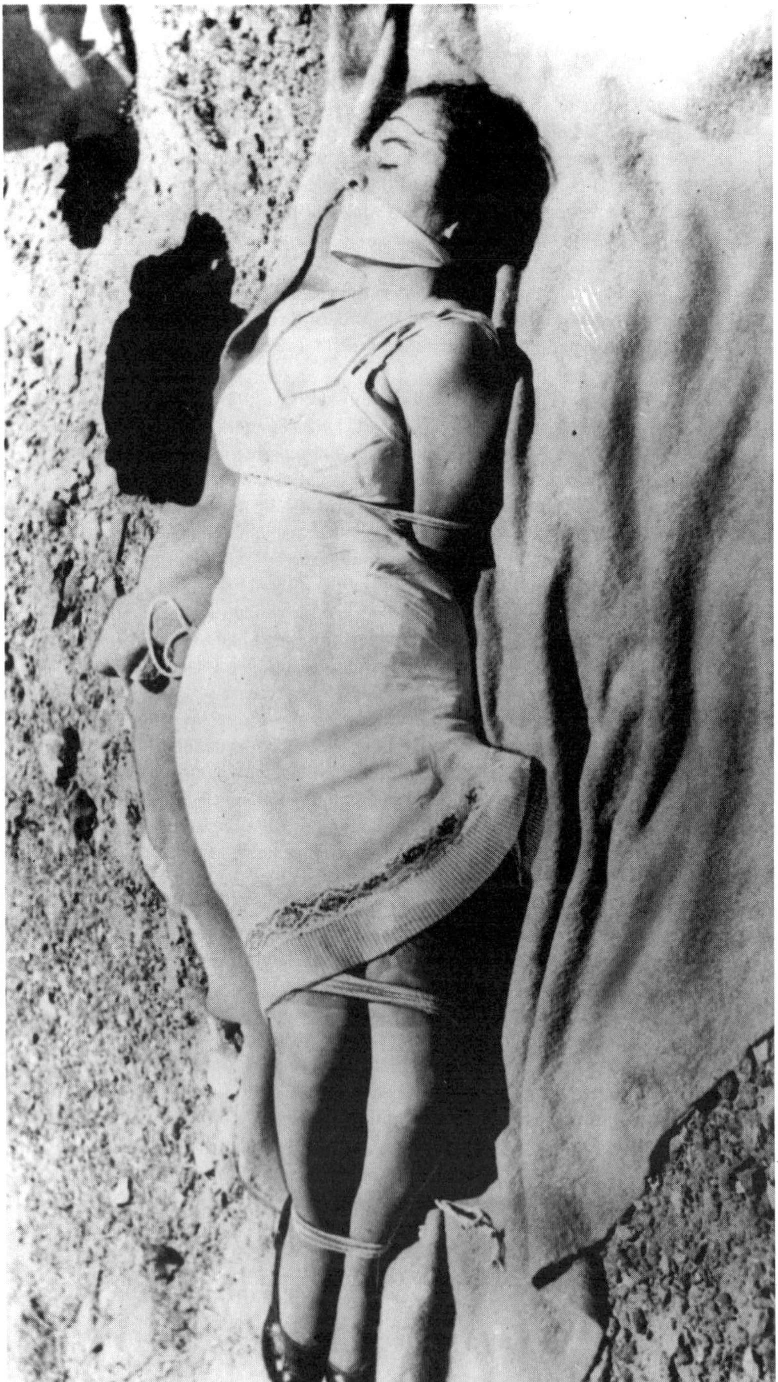

CHARLES **GUITEAU**

One century before John Hinckley attempted to assassinate an American president for the affections of an actress, a demented, self-publicizing religious fanatic, Charles Julius Guiteau, shot and killed 49-year-old President James A. Garfield. His reason, Guiteau stated later in court, was that "the Lord interjected the idea into my brain and then let me work it out my own way. That is the way the Lord does. He doesn't employ fools to do his work; I am sure of that; he gets the best brains he can find." Guiteau was also delusional enough to believe that he deserved to be appointed consul to either Paris or Vienna by the recently-inaugurated president. He was later represented in the newspapers during his trial not as an archetypal celebrity stalker acting out of sheer lunacy, but as a disappointed office seeker who murdered for political revenge.

Born on September 8, 1841, in Freeport, Illinois, Guiteau was known by his middle name, Julius, as a child until he decided "there was too much of the Negro about it." He left home in June of 1860 and joined the Oneida Community in New York, a utopian commune that taught a combination of free love and "Bible Communism." (The founder of Oneida, John Humphrey Noyes, believed that the female orgasm brought couples closer to God, asserting: "It is as foolish and cruel to expend one's seed on a wife merely for the sake of getting rid of it, as it would be to fire a gun at one's best friend merely for the sake of unloading it.") There Guiteau constantly bickered with others in the commune – he believed he was divinely ordained to be their leader – and the people of Oneida started to regularly refer to him as Charles "Gitout." Since he also wasn't acquiring any of the "free love" for himself, Guiteau left the commune in April 1865 (see letter to father reproduced below). Afterwards he attempted to blackmail Noyes for $9000, telling reporters that "all the girls that were born in the Community were forced to cohabit with Noyes at such an early period it dwarfed them. The result was that most of the Oneida women were small and thin and homely."

In Hoboken, New Jersey, Guiteau attempted to start a religious newspaper, the New York *Theocrat*, out of his squalid little apartment, but he found no backers. From 1869 to 1874 he tried marriage and a career as a lawyer in Chicago (his main occupation, though, was bill collecting), and in 1875 he became an evangelist. Travelling across the country as "the Eloquent Chicago lawyer," he printed handbills and pamphlets, wore sandwich boards, gave laughable, incomprehensible sermons to near-empty halls, and was jailed periodically for unpaid bills. In July 1879 he self-published a compilation of his lectures, *The Truth: A Companion to the Bible*, which was almost completely a plagiarism of Noyes' *The Berean.*

In 1880 Guiteau campaigned for Republican presidential candidate Ulysses S. Grant and wrote a speech, "Grant vs. Hancock." When dark horse candidate Garfield won the Republican nomination, Guiteau promptly changed the speech to "Garfield vs. Hancock" and canvassed for Garfield's successful campaign against the Democratic candidate, General Winfield Scott Hancock. Convinced that his speech resulted in Garfield's election, Guiteau moved to Washington on March 5, 1881 and immediately started harassing the President's staff in the halls of the White House for his consulship appointment. On May 13, Secretary of State James G. Blaine was so irritated by Guiteau's self-righteous petitioning that he yelled at him, "Never bother me again about the Paris consulship as long as you live!" Realizing that he was not going to receive an appointment to political office, Guiteau bought a British .44-caliber Bulldog revolver on June 8, and learned how to shoot in the woods near the Potomac River. On June 25, he inspected the local jail to make sure he would be comfortable after his arrest, and early in the morning of July 2, after one more session of target practice on the Potomac, he walked to the Baltimore and Potomac Railroad Depot (now the location of the National Gallery of Art) and shot the President in the back while he was waiting with Secretary Blaine for his train. Mortally wounded, Garfield lingered for nearly three months before dying on September 19, 1881.

The trial began on November 14, the courtroom packed with throngs that cheered, hissed and laughed with Guiteau throughout the proceedings; *The Nation* said it was "simply ghastly and horrible." A reader of the Washington *Evening Star,* indignant about the celebrity treatment Guiteau was receiving from the press, wrote a letter suggesting that the prisoner be forced to eat two ounces of his own flesh each day "until he *eats* himself up." A defense psychiatrist contended that Guiteau was insane, observing that his mother died of "brain fever," his sister acted strangely in the courtroom (she was later institutionalized), and two uncles, one aunt and two cousins had a history of mental illness; he concluded that Guiteau's family "was strongly drenched with the hereditary taint." The assassin's brother, upset that his family's name was being dragged through the psychiatric mud, thought that "mesmerism" was involved and wrote, "I have no doubt that masturbation and self-abuse is at the bottom of his mental imbecility."

Confident of his acquittal, Guiteau planned on lecturing in Europe and running for president after his release. On January 25, 1882, however, Guiteau was judged sane and guilty of the President's murder. When the judge pronounced a sentence of death and said, "And may the Lord have mercy on your soul," Guiteau answered:

> And may God have mercy on your soul. I had rather stand where I am than where the jury does or where your Honor does. I am not afraid to die. . . . I know where I stand on this business. I am here as God's man and don't you forget it.

He was hanged at 12:40 P.M. on June 30, 1882, before a large, rowdy crowd. As a signal to the hangman, his last words were "Glory, ready, go . . ."

Letter to his sister Frances in 1852:

Dear Sister,

you ou me a letter I want you to Wright to me how do you do . . . well how do you like going to School at Rockbord . . . I go to Union School I like to go the Union School thay have five teachers in the Union School . . . I and Wilson . . . ar verry well I cant think of any thing.

JULIUS

Excerpts from a letter to his sister in 1859:

I think I should live according to the laws of health and physiology to arrive at the first part (physically). Secondly, to improve my mind by reading, writing, studying, and thinking as much as possible without over taxing the brain (intellectually). Thirdly, to keep my moral character pure and spotless.

I want to go to School two or three years steady if I can & I can if my well is large enough. (Where there is a will there is a way.) I think mine is sufficient.

Excerpt from a letter to his father in April of 1865:

Dear Father:

I have left the community. The cause of my leaving was because I could not conscientiously and heartily accept their views on the labor question. They wanted to make a hard-working businessman of me, but I could not consent to that, and therefore deemed it expedient to quietly withdraw, which I did last Monday. . . .

I came to New York in obedience to what I believed to be the call of God for the purpose of pursuing an independent course of theological and historical investigation. With the Bible for my textbook and the Holy Ghost for my schoolmaster, I can pursue my studies without interference from human dictation. In the country [Oneida] my **time was appropriated,** but now it is at my own **disposal,** a very favorable change. I have procured a small room, well furnished, in Hoboken, opposite the city, and intend to fruitfully pursue my studies during the next three years.

And here it is proper to state that the energies of my life are now, and have been for months, **pledged to God,** to do all that within me lies to extend the sovereignty of Jesus Christ by placing at his disposal a powerful daily paper. I am persuaded that theocratic presses are destined, in due time, to supersede to a great extent pulpit oratory. There are hundreds of thousands of ministers in the world but not a single daily theocratic press. It appears to me that there is a splended chance for some one to do a big thing for God, for humanity and for himself.

Excerpts from letters dating from 1865 to 1870:

Whoever edits such a paper as I intend to establish will doubtless occupy the position of Target General to the Press, Pulpit, and Bench of the civilized world; and if God intends me for that place, I fear not, for I know that He will be "a wall of fire round me," and keep me from all harm.

I say boldly I claim **inspiration**. I claim that I am in the employ of **Jesus Christ & Co.**, the very ablest and strongest firm in the universe, and that what I can do is limited only by their power and purpose.

In the world, the **flesh** everywhere prevails over the **spirit**, and this makes it exceedingly difficult for a **spiritual** man to prosper, and herein, as it appears to me, lies the greatest impediment to the success of my paper.

God makes no **blunders.** The millions inhabiting the earth are before Him, and he selects the right man every time for the right place; and in this He always successfully check-mates the devil's moves.

If a man have big ideas he is usually deemed **insane**; but I trust the community will not thrust the charge of insanity at me; but will allow me quietly to follow my own inspiration.

I weave the discourse out of my brain as cotten is woven into a fabric. When I compose my brain is in a white heat, and my mind works like lightning. This accounts for the short epigrammatic style of my sentences. I write so rapidly I can hardly read it . . . I divest myself of all unnecessary clothing. I eat and sleep mechanically.

Letter to his brother John in the spring of 1873:

Dear Sir,

Your letter from Eaton . . . dated Nov. 8, '72, received. I got the $75 on my supposed responsibility as a Chicago lawyer. I was introduced to Eaton by a gentleman I met at the Young Men's Christian Association, and it was only incidentally that your name was mentioned.

I wrote to Eaton several times while at Chicago, and he ought to have been satisfied, but he had the impertinence to write you and charge me with fraud, when he knew he let me have the money entirely upon my own **name and position.** Had he acted like a "**white**" man, I should have tried to pay it long ago. I hope you will drop him.

Yours truly,
Charles J. Guiteau.

After his brother requested repayment of a small loan, Guiteau sent the following note:

J. W. Guiteau: New York, March 13th, 1873

Find $7 enclosed. Stick it up your bung-hole and wipe your nose on it, and that will remind you of the estimation in which you are held by

Charles J. Guiteau

Sign and return the enclosed receipt and I will send you $7, but not before, and that, I hope, will end our acquaintance.

He sent President Garfield a copy of his speech "Garfield vs. Hancock" with the following enclosed note on March 6, 1881:

I presume my appointment will be promptly confirmed. There is nothing against me. I claim to be a gentleman and a Christian.

Letter to President Garfield dated April 8:

(Private)

Gen. Garfield:

From your looks yesterday I judge you did not quite understand what I meant by saying "I have not called for two or three weeks." I intended to express my sympathy for you on account of the pressure that has been on you since you came into office.

I think Mr. Blaine intends giving me the Paris consulship with your and Gen. Logan's approbation, and I am waiting for the break in the Senate.

I have practiced law in New York and Chicago, and presume I am well qualified for it.

I have been here since March 5, and expect to remain some little time, or until I get my commission.

Very respectfully,
Charles Guiteau

The final letter to President Garfield, dated May 23:

(Private)

General Garfield:

I have been trying to be your friend; I don't know whether you appreciate it or not, but I am moved to call your attention to the remarkable letter from Mr. Blaine which I have just noticed.

According to Mr. Farwell, of Chicago, Blaine is a "vindictive politician" and "an evil genius," and you will "have no peace till you get rid of him."

This letter shows Mr. Blaine is a wicked man, and you ought to demand his **immediate** resignation; otherwise you and the Republican Party will come to grief. I will see you in the morning, if I can, and talk with you.

Very respectfully
Charles Guiteau

Before he shot President Garfield, Guiteau left a package with a newstand attendant at the railroad station; it contained his book *The Truth*, a brief résumé, "An Address to the American People," a note bequeathing his papers and revolver to the State Department library, a letter granting the New York *Herald* permission to serialize his book, and the following note:

Washington, Monday, June 20, 1881

The President's nomination was an act of God.
His election was an act of God.
His removal is an act of God.
(These three specific acts of the Deity may furnish the clergy with a text.)

I am clear in my purpose to remove the President. Two points will be accomplished. It will save the Republic, and it will create a demand for my book, The Truth. See page 10.

This book was not written for money. It was written to save souls. In order to attract public attention the book needs the notice the President's removal will give it.

C. G.

Police found in Guiteau's pocket a letter he had written earlier that morning:

Washington, July 2, 1881

To The White House:

The President's tragic death was a sad necessity, but it will unite the Republican party and save the Republic. Life is a fleeting dream, and it matters little when one goes. A human life is of small value. During the war thousands of brave boys went down without a tear. I presume the President was a Christian and that he will be happier in Paradise than here.

It will be no worse for Mrs. Garfield, dear soul, to part with her husband this way than by natural death. He is liable to go at any time any way.

I had no ill-will toward the President. His death was a political necessity. I am a lawyer, a theologian, a politician. I am a Stalwart of the Stalwarts. I was with General Grant and the rest of our men in New York during the canvass. I have some papers for the press, which I shall leave with Byron Andrews [correspondent of the Chicago **Inter-Ocean**] and his co-journalists, at 1440 N.Y. Ave., where all the reporters can see them.

I am going to the jail.

Charles Guiteau

Another letter fell out of Guiteau's pocket and was found outside the train station. Sealed, it was addressed on the front of the envelope: "Please deliver at once to General Sherman, or his first assistant in charge of the War Department":

To General Sherman:

I have just shot the President. I shot him several times, as I wished him to go as easily as possible. His death was a political necessity. I am a lawyer, theologian and politician. I am a Stalwart of the Stalwarts. I was with General Grant and the rest of our men, in New York during the canvass. I am going to jail. Please order out your troops, and take possession of the jail at once.

Very respectfully,

Charles Guiteau

Excerpt from "Address to the American People," dated June 16:

I conceived of the idea of removing the President four weeks ago. Not a soul knew of my purpose. I conceived the idea myself. I read the newspapers carefully, for and against the administration, and gradually the conviction settled on me that the President's removal was a political necessity, because he proved a traitor to the men who made him, and thereby imperiled the life of the Republic. At the late Presidential election, the Republican party carried every Northern State. Today, owing to the misconduct of the President and his Secretary of State, they could hardly carry ten Northern States. They certainly could not carry New York, and that is the pivotal State.

Ingratitude is the basest of crimes. That the President, under the manipulation of his Secretary of State, has been guilty of the basest ingratitude to the Stalwarts admits of no denial. . . . In the President's madness he has wrecked the once grand old Republican party; and for this he dies. . . .

I had no ill-will to the President.

This is not murder. It is a political necessity. It will make my friend Arthur President, and save the Republic. I have sacrificed only one. I shot the President as I would a rebel, if I saw him pulling down the American flag. I leave my justification to God and the American people.

I expect President Arthur and Senator Conkling will give the nation the finest administration it has ever had. They are honest and have plenty of brains and experience.

After his arrest Guiteau announced that he was going to write a new book, *The Life and Theology of Charles Guiteau, Prepared by Himself.* He sent the following outline to the Chicago *Press*:

Put quick headlines on to this matter. C.G.

I expect to issue shortly through a first-rate New York publishing house a book entitled

The Life and Theology of Charles Guiteau

Prepared by Himself

It will be a good-sized volume of 500 pages.

Part 1. My life, I dictated to a short-hand writer. The story of my life is pointed and graphic, and reads like a romance, and tells of my acquaintance with public men, and of my attempted removal of the President.

Part 2. My Theology, is my contribution to the civilization of the race. It is a reprint of my book **The Truth** issued in Boston nearly two years ago.

When President Garfield did not immediately die from his wound, Guiteau wrote that his survival was a result of:

. . . the disadvantage under which I executed the Divine Will: to wit: I shot him as he was rapidly receding from me and the bullet did not strike him in a vital part, but notwithstanding this, it would have proved speedily fatal had it not been for the prayers and supplications of the people who were justly horrified by the President's distressed condition . . . the prayers and entreaties of the American People changed the Deity's original intention.

On September 13 he wrote to the judge:

If I should decide to enter a plea of assault with attempt to kill, would the government meet me by giving two years — the lowest time the law allows? I hardly know whether I would do it as I expect to be acquitted, whatever the charge.

On September 20, the day after Garfield died, Guiteau sent a letter to the new President of the United States, Chester Arthur:

My inspiration is a God send to you & I presume you appreciate it. It raises you from $8,000 to $50,000 a year. It raises you from a political cypher to President of the United States with all its powers and honors. . . . For the cabinet I would suggest as follows: State: Mr. Conkling Treasury: Mr. Morton War: Gen. Logan P.M.G. Mr. James Atty. Gen. Mr. E. A. Storrs of Chicago. There is no objection to two or more cabinet officers from the same state. The men & not the state should govern. . . . Let all honor be paid to Gen. Garfield's remains. He was a good man but a weak politician.

During his trial, Guiteau prepared an address to the jury. He introduced his speech by saying:

> I am going to sit down because I can talk. I am not afraid of anyone shooting me. This shooting business is declining. . . . I am not here as a wicked man, or as a lunatic. I am here as a patriot and my speech is as follows. I read from the New York *Herald*, gentlemen. It was sent by telegraph Sunday, and published in all the leading papers in America Monday.

Excerpts from the speech:

If the court please, gentlemen of the jury: I am a patriot. To-day I suffer in bonds as a patriot. Washington was a patriot. Grant was a patriot. Washington led the armies of the Revolution through eight years of bloody war to victory and glory. Grant led the armies of the Union to victory and glory, and today the nation is prosperous and happy. They raised the old war-cry, "Rally round the flag, boys," and thousands of the choicest sons of the Republic went forth to battle, to victory or death. Washington and Grant, by their valor and success in war, won the admiration of mankind. Today I suffer in bonds as a patriot, because I had the inspiration and nerve to unite a great political part, to the end that the nation might be saved another desolating war.

The Deity allowed the doctors to finish my work gradually, because he wanted to prepare the people for the change and also confirm my original inspiration. I am well satisfied with the Deity's conduct of the case thus far, and I have no doubt that He will continue to father it to the end, and that the public will sooner or later see the special providence in the late President's removal.

No one wants to shoot or hang me now save a few cranks, who are so ignorant they can hardly read or write.

High-toned people are saying, "Well, if the Lord did it, let it go."

As sure as you are alive, gentlemen, as sure as you are alive, if a hair of my head is harmed this nation will go down to desolation . . . all you can do is put my body in the ground, but this nation will pay for it as sure as you are alive.

The mothers and daughters of the republic are praying that you will vindicate my inspiration, and their prayers I expect will prevail. A woman's instinct is keener than man's, and I pray you listen to the prayers of these ladies.

Guiteau issued "An Appeal to the American People" on January 26, 1882, the day after being judged guilty:

They do not pretend to be Christian men, and therefore did not appreciate the idea of inspiration. They are men of the world, and of moderate intelligence, and therefore are not capable of appreciating the character of my defense. According to one of them, "We had grog at each meal and a cigar afterwards," which showed their style and habits. Men of this kind can not represent the great Christian Nation of America. Had they been high-toned, Christian gentlemen, their verdict would have been "Not Guilty."

Poem published in the Washington *Star* newspaper on June 17:

God's Ways

Thou Jehovah!
All things created
Save the evil one!
He being uncreated
Like Thyself.
(See my book.)
. . . .
The retribution came,
Quick and sharp,
In fire and blood,
In shot and shell,
In endless pain!
Like a jumping tooth
Lasting for ever and ever!
(A jumping tooth
Gives an idea of hell,
And that is what
Those Jews got!)

Excerpt from a letter sent to the Washington *Star* on June 21, a week before his execution:

I slept splendidly last night. I had a fine breakfast of Java coffee, broiled steak, omelet, strawberries, and bananas. . . . Last night the papers stated I had a doubt as to my inspiration. **This is untrue. . . .** Only good has come from Garfield's removal and that is the best evidence that the Almighty is backing me. If I am murdered woe unto this Nation and the men who do it! . . . Newspaper men are going to hell as a matter of course. When the Almighty gets after them there will be wailing and gnashing of teeth. They will only get what they deserve for their diabolical spirit towards me. Please publish my poem on heaven and hell.

Excerpt from another letter to President Arthur, requesting that he intervene with the execution:

I am entitled to a full pardon; but I am willing to wait for the public to be educated up to my views and feelings in the matter. In the meantime I suffer in bonds as a patriot. I have concluded to acquiesce in Mr. Reed's suggestion that you respite me until January, so the case can be heard by the Supreme Court in full bench. . . . I am willing to DIE for my inspiration, but it will make a terrible reckoning for you and this nation. I made you, and saved the American people great trouble. And the least you can do is to let me go; but I appreciate your delicate position, and I am willing to stay here until January, if necessary. I am God's man in this matter. This is dead sure.

"Literary explorations" from jail, dated June 26:

TABLEAUX.

Scene between the Almighty and my murderers.

The Almighty:
Why did you murder my man Guiteau?

Crocker. (Crying & wailing)
I was warden, & wanted my salary.

"No excuse. Go to Hell."

The Almighty (To Arthur)
Why did you not pardon Mr. Guiteau?

I wanted to; but I was afraid it would defeat my nomination in '84.

"No excuse, you ingrate! Go to Hell. Heat up Mr. Devil!"

The Almighty, (To newspaper men)
Why did you hound my man to death?

We did not believe he was your man.

"No excuse. Go to Hell."

The Almighty, To the American people.
"For your diabolical spirit towards my man I will destroy your nationality as I did the Jewish nation. It took me nearly forty years to get even with the Jews for killing my man & I will get even with you for killing Mr. Guiteau. You are doomed!"

Charles Guiteau

US Jail
June 26, 1882.

Letter to a prison chaplain dated the day before his execution:

Washington, D. C.
June 29, 1882.

To the Rev. William W. Hicks:

I, Charles Guiteau, of the City of Washington, in the District of Columbia, now under sentence of death, which is to be carried into effect between the hours of twelve and two o'clock on the 30th day of June, A. D., 1882, in the United States jail in the said District, do hereby give and grant to you my body after such execution; provided, however, it shall not be used for any mercenary purposes.

And I hereby, for good and sufficient considerations, give, deliver and transfer to said Hicks my book entitled "The Truth and Removal" and copyright thereof to be used by him in writing a truthful history of my life and execution.

And I direct that such history be entitled "The Life and Work of Charles Guiteau"; and I hereby solemnly proclaim and announce to all the world that no person or persons shall ever in any manner use my body for any mercenary purpose whatsoever.

And if at any time hereafter any person or persons shall desire to honor my remains, they can do it by erecting a monument whereon shall be inscribed these words: "Here lies the body of Charles Guiteau, Patriot and Christian. His soul is in glory."

Charles Guiteau

Witnesses: Charles H. Reed
James Woodward

Poem composed shortly before his execution; before reciting it on the gallows, he announced:

> I am now going to read some verses which are intended to indicate my feelings at the moment of leaving this world. If set to music they may be rendered effective. The idea is that of a child babbling to his mamma and his papa. I wrote it this morning about ten o'clock.

I am going to the Lordy, I am so glad,
I am going to the Lordy, I am so glad,
I am going to the Lordy,
Glory hallelujah! Glory Hallelujah!
I am going to the Lordy.
I love the Lordy with all my soul,
Glory Hallelujah!
And that is the reason I am going to the Lord,
Glory hallelujah! Glory Hallelujah!
I am going to the Lord.
I saved my party and my land,
Glory hallelujah!
But they have murdered me for it,
And that is the reason I am going to the Lordy,
Glory hallelujah! Glory hallelujah!
I am going to the Lordy!
I wonder what I will do when I get to the Lordy,
I guess that I will weep no more
When I get to the Lordy!
Glory hallelujah!
I wonder what I will see when I get to the Lordy,
I expect to see most glorious things,
Beyond all earthly conception,
When I am with the Lordy!
Glory hallelujah! Glory hallelujah!
I am with the Lord.

JOHN GEORGE **HAIGH**

Thirty-nine-year-old John George Haigh was dubbed by the Fleet Street newspapers of London the "Acid Bath Murderer" and "the vampire killer." In the mid- to late forties he murdered six people, allegedly drank their blood, and destroyed their bodies with sulfuric acid.

Nicknamed "Ching" as a child because of his slightly slanted eyes, Haigh was raised by parents who belonged to a fundamentalist anti-clerical sect, the Plymouth Brethren; he later joined the Church of England and became a choirboy and assistant organist for the Wakefield Cathedral. He enjoyed music and writing, and at the age of seventeen he won a divinity prize for his essay "St. Peter in the Gospels and in the Acts." He also had – as he related over twenty years later to police – a "divine revelation" to drink his own urine, and was tormented by grotesque dreams involving the blood and wounds of Christ.

In the thirties and early forties Haigh married and wandered from job to job, usually in the fields of engineering, insurance, advertising and dry cleaning; he also spent much of this period in prison. In November of 1934 he was arrested on fraud charges, served a year in prison, and separated from his wife. He was arrested again three years later for "attempting to obtain £750 by false pretences and seven cases of obtaining bankers' cheques by false pretences." Sentenced to four years, he was released early for good behavior on August 13, 1940. Less than a year later he was caught stealing, and was sentenced on June 11 to twenty-one months in jail.

After his release from prison he found employment as "company director" of the Onslow Court Hotel, located in the South Kensington district of London, and lived in Room 404. He also rented a workroom at 79 Gloucester Road to work on his "inventions." In the spring of 1944 he was involved in a car accident; it was then he supposedly acquired the taste for blood and suffered from "visions." On September 9, 1944, he murdered his friend, Donald "Mac" McSwan. He later confessed to police:

> I got the feeling I must get some blood somewhere. I was quite capable of carrying on business in an abstract sort of way. I was meeting McSwan from time to time. . . . He brought a pin-table to Gloucester Road to repair. The idea then came to me to kill him and take some blood. I hit him over the head and he was unconscious. I got a mug and took some blood, from his neck, in the mug, and drank it. Then I realized I must do something about him. I left him

> there dead. That night I had the dream when I caught up with the blood. At Gloucester Road I had acid and sheet metal for pickling. I found a water butt on a disused site and took it on a cart and put McSwan in acid. I did it with a bucket. I went to see McSwan's parents and told them he had gone away because of his call up.

He "coshed" Mr. and Mrs. McSwan on July 2, 1945, and disposed of their bodies in a similar manner.

Two years later he gained access to a storage room in Crawley, and on February 13, 1948, shot to death a couple he had become friendly with, Dr. Archie Henderson and his wife Rose. A year later, on February 18, 1949, he took an elderly widow who resided at the Onslow, 69-year-old Olivia Durand-Deacon, on a tour of his "factory" at Crawley and shot her in the head. At the insistence of another guest at the hotel, Haigh reported her missing to police; he then sold her jewelry and spent nearly a week slowly dissolving her body in acid. Police noted his suspicious behavior and, after checking out his prison record, arrested him on February 28. During his interrogation he muttered in irritation: "Mrs. Durand-Deacon no longer exists. I've destroyed her body with acid. You will find the sludge which remains at Leopold Road. Every trace is gone. You can't prove murder without a body." After a long pause he asked, referring to England's principal mental institution, "What are the chances of being released from Broadmoor?"

Haigh, however, was wrong about there being no body; police found in the 475 pounds of "sludge" the following day – as later identified by forensic pathologist Dr. Keith Simpson – the remains and possessions of Mrs. Durand-Deacon:

> (1) a mass of some 28 lbs. of yellow greasy substance, resembling melted body fat; (2) three facetted gall-stones of human type; (3) part of a left foot, eroded by acid; (4) eighteen fragments of human bone, all corroded by acid to a varying degree; (5) intact full upper and lower dentures; (6) the handle of a red plastic bag; (7) a lipstick container.

Police also found a bloodstained penknife hidden in Haigh's car, and an appointment diary with small red crosses drawn next to the initials of his victims on the days they were murdered. Haigh was charged with the murder of Mrs. Durand-Deacon, and pleaded not guilty.

Attempting to prove that their client was insane, Haigh's attorneys had him drink his own urine in front of authorities at Brixton Prison. They also theorized that Haigh was severely traumatized as a child by the changes in his religious background, from the Plymouth Brethen's lack of ceremony to the intense splendor of Anglican ritual. The prosecutors, on the other hand, illustrated how Haigh profited by the murders, netting property (through the clever use of forgery) and over £12,000 in cash; they also contended that Haigh was shamming his insanity, especially taking note of his curious question about Broadmoor. The jury took only seventeen minutes to find Haigh guilty and sane on July 18, and he was executed at Wandsworth Prison on August 6, 1949.

In his book *Man into Wolf: An Anthropological Interpretation of Sadism, Masochism and Lychanthropy,* Robert Eisler argued with the verdict, stating in his essay, "A Clear Case of Vampirism":

> Why should maniacs *not* be actuated by motives of sordid profit? Because it is rational to strive for gain, does it follow that a man ceases to want wealth and an easy life when his mind begins to be obsessed by contorted religious ideas? . . . The fact that the consciousness of a paranoiac is dominated by deep-rooted archetypal ideas does not mean that his power of logical reasoning is affected to the extent that he must act in an absurd and illogical manner in

every other way. It does not mean that he is unconscious either of his actions or unaware of the social disapproval they are bound to incur – *if* he is found out. He may perfectly well know what he is doing, he may know that everybody else considers the actions criminal. His "moral insanity" consists in his inability to resist the powerful impulses welling up from the subhuman atavist background of the individual mind and in the childish credulity which enables him to accept as "divine revelations" justifying his behaviour the most absurd interpretations of misunderstood scriptual passages torn from their context.

A less fanciful conclusion is offered by Dr. Clifford Allen in his essay, "The Medical Aspects of the Case of John George Haigh," published in the appendix of *The Trial of John George Haigh*:

> The possible reasons for Haigh's behaviour seem to be the following: – (1) Paranoia, (2) Psychopathic Personality, (3) Sadism and (4) Murder for gain without obvious illness being present, or (5) A mixture of any two or more of the preceding. . . .
>
> If I may put it like this, the psychopathic element in Haigh's mind enjoyed the profit he made from the murders; the thought that he was outwitting society, and the idea that he was "a great man": the sadistic element enjoyed the planning and performing of his terrible deeds and (if he spoke the truth – which is doubtful) may even have led him into his fantasies of blood and of actual blood drinking.
>
> The final diagnosis in my opinion, and in this I must emphasize that I differ from the Editors of this trial, is that Haigh certainly suffered from a psychopathic personality and, less evidently, from a sadistic element. He murdered for profit, but was able to do so because he was an abnormal type, being neither entirely sane nor entirely insane.

Excerpts from his prison memoirs:

The atmosphere in my home, which even now I can feel and sense with a vividness beyond words to convey, was rather like that of some monastic establishment. It had the quietness of a strange certainty. It did not belong to the world outside.

Though my parents were kind and loving, I had none of the joys, or the companionship, which small children usually have. From my earliest years my recollection is of my father saying: "Do not," or "Thou shalt not." Any form of sport or light entertainment was frowned upon, and regarded as not edifying. There was only, and always, condemnation and prohibition.

Their sect was known as the Peculiar People. Their religious beliefs were to them more important than anything else in life. They lived by precepts, and they talked in parables. It is true to say that I was nurtured on Bible stories, mostly concerned with sacrifice.

If by some mischance I did, or said, anything which my father regarded as improper, he would say: "Do not grieve the Lord by behaving so." And if I suggested that I wanted to go somewhere or to meet somebody, he would say: "It will not please the Lord."

He was constantly preoccupied with thoughts of the Hereafter, and often wished the Lord would take him home. It was a sin to be content with this world, and there were constant reminders of its corruptness and evil.

Often I pondered my father's references to the Heavenly places, and to the "worms that will destroy this body." It was inevitable that I should develop an early inhibition regarding death.

So great, in fact, was my father's desire to separate himself and his family from the evil world, that he built a great wall round our garden so that no one could look in.

But it is true, also, that my parents loved me deeply, and they devoted themselves to moulding my life. Their hopes were high, and to me they remained all that is noble.

On my father's forehead is a small blue scar shaped like a distorted cross. Explaining the mark to me when I was very young he said, "This is the brand of Satan. I have sinned, and Satan has punished me. If you ever sin, Satan will mark you with a blue pencil likewise."

Naturally I remarked: "Well, mother isn't marked." My father answered: "No, she is an angel."

My dismay was acute when at school this story was received with scorn. I soon dropped the idea that I must be an extraordinary person to be the child of an angel and the one man who had sinned. I have, nevertheless, always cherished, in a less literal sense, the thought of my mother as an angel.

It is odd to recall that in those early days, my father's story of Satan's mark filled me with anxiety. Often, while I lay on my bed at night after a day in which I might have done something which to my mind was sinful, I passed my hand over my forehead to feel if the mark was there.

Only when I had convinced myself otherwise, could I sleep. And even years later, after I knew that my father's "brand" had been caused by a piece of flying coal in the mine, I found myself looking at the foreheads of passers-by to see if they carried Satan's mark of sin.

One of the delights of my boyhood was to visit my maternal aunt, and at her house I used to enjoy reading the comic strip in a newspaper. When I asked my father why we didn't have a newspaper at our house I was told: "It is a thing of the world: there is not time enough to read the Bible."

At school, **Treasure Island** was one of the set books which I thoroughly enjoyed; but my father told the headmaster that a book about pirates and murder was not fit for children.

But even at that early age, I could not reconcile this argument with the blood and horror of the Old Testament. The answer that the Lord was Jehovah, and, therefore, totally different, I found very unsatisfactory.

The introduction of wireless, and the sight of school friends playing with cat's-whiskers and crystals, prompted the question: "Why don't we have a wireless set?" My father's answer was that it was an instrument of the devil — a sign of the times — and one day anti-Christ would use the instrument to speak to the world and organise insurrection against God and His Saints. The Brethren were always spoken of as Saints. . . .

How well I remember those days at home, especially Sundays when to play with one's toys, or to walk across the fields, was a sin. When I became a choirboy it was a terrific thought to be able to indulge with impunity (according to Catholic doctrine) in hitherto "heinous crimes." I could walk to Wakefield without fearing the wrath of God, who might easily have turned me into a pillar of salt. . . .

There was considerable conflict of thought during this period. The views of my cathedral teachers were constantly being fought out with those of the Brethen. My father had always impressed me by his indisputable knowledge of being right. But the disquieting thing was that it appeared possible to produce two equally satisfactory interpretations of the same text. And who was to adjudicate?

As I grew up I realised, though imperfectly, that I was different from other people, and that the way of life in my home was different from that in the homes of others. Without being able to explain the difference between us, or to measure the chasm which divided me from others, I realised its existence. This stimulated me to introspection and strange mental questionings. . . .

One favourite preoccupation which remained with me until manhood was to go into the cathedral and there kneel in the fading light regarding the Works of The Great Craftsman, seeking some reason, some purpose for my own life. Frequently I contemplated the Cross and the suffering figure of Christ upon it. Thought of the pain He suffered horrified me, my overwhelming desire was that He should be put out of His misery. I gazed with a strange fascination at the blood flowing from His wounds.

Looking back I realised my thoughts were of a high priestly vision. I saw myself as a servant in the service of the Church. Often I officiated at the altar as a server. . . .

Taking part in those services, I was strangely stirred by the spectacle of vestured priests, and the dignified ceremonial at the High Altar, which moved me to primitive ambitions. The beauty of the music, the colour, the pageantry, the delightful smell of incense appealed to me tremendously. The monotonous chanting of the priests, and the responses of the acolytes could, in my imagination, be likened to the witch doctors of Africa.

As a boy my voice was good, but not exceptional, but my sight-reading and the mathematics of my music was better than the rest, due undoubtedly to my organ playing.

I knew I should never be brilliant as a pianist. . . .

It was not until my voice broke that it became really outstanding. The process was so gradual that it was hardly noticeable. But break it did at a most inconvenient moment, in the middle of a recitative in the "Matthew Passion" on the words: "Have thou nothing to do with that just man."

My embarrassment was acute, but soon I recognised that my voice now possessed a richer quality, although it was no longer pure in its method of production. Instead of having to retire from solo work I continued with a falsetto voice for another year.

Having left the choir just after Christmas I was recalled at Easter because of the illness of the then leading chorister, to sing the Easter choral solo: "I know that my Redeemer liveth." It was a terrific strain, for there was the constant fear that my voice would break, but it didn't apparently owing to the false method of production. That effort was my crowning glory as a chorister.

Most music has a soothing effect on me. All Chopin is beautiful and restful, even the "Revolutionary Study," which stirs the soul and brings a desperate urge to get somewhere. I also love all Tchaikovsky — except the "1812" which is one of the most irritating things I know.

[About witnessing the bombing of London during World War II:] I loathe suffering. I detest to see humans in pain, or fear, and I was shocked in both mind and spirit. The ghastly sights after two land mines had wiped out a block of buildings are fixed indelibly in my memory.

On one occasion, while on firewatching duty, I was talking to a Red Cross nurse at a warden's post. The sirens shrieked, bombs dropped and the nurse and I moved off to our places of duty. Suddenly, in a moment of premonition, I knew that a bomb would fall close by. I dodged into a doorway and awaited the inevitable crash. It came with a horrifying shriek, and as I staggered up, bruised and bewildered, a head rolled against my foot.

The nurse who, but a few moments before, had been gay, full of life, high ideals and sense of duty, had in one instant been swept into eternity. I was shocked beyond all belief. How could God allow it to happen?

Sex should not exist. Propagation should be an insensible act, like the throwing off of acorns by an oak tree.

Human nature is a nuisance, and fills me with disgust. Every so often one must let off steam, as it were. But that is, more often than not, not a complete sex function. . . .

Apart from the period of twenty-one to twenty-five, the sex appetite has taken a very small part in my life. . . .

Not only is sex unimportant, but also irksome. . . . I hate these instincts, which rob me of self-possession. I even despise the partner of the exercise. . . .

This is a criticism of the Eternal method; that I realise. I shouldn't question the Eternal's methods perhaps, but as a generated sperm of the Eternal I am privileged to think with the infinite mind.

I do not question the Eternal's processes through me; but, as is evident everywhere, the processes of the Eternal are in constant evolution, and the time will, no doubt, come when the present state of sex function will evolve into a form less obnoxious.

To find the reason for anti-social conduct involves consideration of the question of right and wrong. What the world regards as right is what the world can get away with. And if the aim can be achieved without discovery it is called "Success" whatever the purpose might be. Condemnation is the consequence of failure, not the sanction of the wrong.

When I first discovered there were easier ways to make a living than to work long hours in an office, I did not ask myself whether I was doing right or wrong. That seemed to me to be irrelevant. I merely said: "This is what I wish to do." And as the means lay within my power that was what I decided.

It all began with a dream. My mother was a great student of dreams, and she believed they foretold the future. She bought many books on the subject, and I often read them when I was a boy. . . .

The first dream I vividly recall was experienced when I was in the choir at Wakefield Cathedral. At nights after I had got into bed and closed my eyes I would see again the tortured Christ on the Cross. Perhaps that day I had sat in the stillness of the great nave of the church, and had contemplated the High Altar. Now in my sleep the vision would return, and I would see either the head or the whole body of Christ with blood pouring from the wounds. I was startled and horrified and dared not disclose what I had seen. . . .

Once acquired, the taste [for blood] obsessed me, and the recollection of it, with certain intervals, pursued me down the years. . . .

But none of these experiences crystallised into a frantic uncontrollable urge until after a motor accident at Three Bridges, Sussex, during the Easter of 1944.

My car collided with a lorry, and turned over. . . . Blood poured from my head down my face and into my mouth. This revived in me the taste, and that night I experience another awful dream.

I saw before me a forest of crucifixes, which gradually turned into trees. At first there appeared to be dew, or rain, dripping from the branches, but as I approached I realised it was blood.

Suddenly the whole forest began to writhe and the trees, stark and erect, to ooze blood. . . . A man went to each tree catching the blood. . . . When the cup was full he approached me. . . . "Drink," he said, but I was unable to move. The dream faded. . . .

Always there was a consciousness of the ebbing away of the life force, and the urge to follow the man holding out the cup; the inability to reach it, and the feeling of frustration; the waking up to a state of semi-coma with a feeling of frustration still palpable; the hand still before me, and the urge to satisfy the appetite for the life force in my mind.

No words of mine can recall the horrific assaults which this dream — never changing in pattern — had upon me. When it was over I would suddenly in my first conscious moments realise my dreadful appetite. The dream repeated itself for three to four nights, and with each succeeding dream the urge became more intense.

It was not their money but their blood that I was after. The thing I am really conscious of is the cup of blood which is constantly before me.

I shot some of my victims, but I couldn't say if I shot them in the head, if the hole was not there to show afterwards. But I can say I made a small cut, usually in the right side of the neck, and drank the blood for three to five minutes, and that afterwards I felt better. Before each of the killings I have detailed in my confession, I had my series of dreams, and another common factor was that the dream cycle started early in the week, and culminated on a Friday.

I lived in two worlds; one as vivid as the other, and each unrelated. The deed was always done with my hand, but that part of my mind which guided it did not conceive it. The conception sprang in the curious pattern of dreams which three or four nights before the killing imposed upon me with a vividness and impact no words can convey, an irrational, wild, unremorseful purpose, beyond the understanding of man.

With the second McSwan murder these operations became automatic. . . . The mechanics of the disposals became of a passive operation, which I didn't think actively about till afterwards, and the "dopey" period experienced during the dream cycle had passed. So much was this so that in each successive case more of the preparation — that is getting the things ready — began to be done during the dream period, prior to the actual killing and obtaining satisfaction from the blood. . . . Archie complained I was not paying attention to what he was saying, and I told him I was in what I called a "dopey" state. My mind was on something else. He replied it was a cerebral something or other, giving it a technical name.

When I look back on it there are so many things I should have done quite differently if I had sat down and thought out a planned campaign of murder for gain. . . . I should not have ordered the acid tank in my own name. I certainly should not have drawn attention to the fact that it was to be used for acid. Notice that I had now got to the stage of getting the drum in which I put the body, beforehand — the first time this had taken place. Also in this last case I have asked myself why I got more acid. It wasn't necessary, there was more than enough there already. Obviously acid was one of the things which was associated in my mind with the whole procedure and, therefore, I automatically arranged to get it.

As with Henderson's foot, so with Mrs. Durand-Deacon's handbag. I did not trouble to reduce it. I was not careless, but sure of my protection.

Another point about these disposals is that they became increasingly irksome. In contrast with the pleasure of other anti-social activities they were a burden. So much so that on looking at them in retrospect I am sure I could not be bothered to go to that exertion in order to make a living.

It is a fatiguing business getting a fourteen-stone carcass into an oil drum on one's own. It took me the best part of two hours to get Mrs. Durand-Deacon into the drum. I am not a strong man, and in the matter of these disposals I accomplished something which normally I should have been incapable through lack of strength to do. . . .

There are easier ways of making money than by murder — even though illegitimately. If gain were the object it would have been much more simpler to have got rid of my own parents and inherited their property. There would have been no questions about that.

Today, I have no conception of an omniscient and loving God. I have no religion beyond the admission of some Superior Force.

I am convinced of this, not by reason only, but by reflection upon the working out of my life, and by the impact of the metaphysical. For example, my dreams prior to the death of relatives, and my mother's similar experiences, confirmed to me the correctness of my postulate that there exists a sperm of Being awaiting germination.

May it not be that I was a disembodied being, a body which is human in shape, yet with a personality outside itself, and moving independently of it? Is this the automatism of which science speaks, yet never recognises, diagnoses, yet never cures?

For the greater part of my life, I believed in and cherished the notion of a just and loving God. I, who love and adore the smallest and weakest of God's children, I, who would seek to succour suffering mankind and ease their burdens, am I the same person who committed these deeds — who has taken many lives?

The only common line in my actions is the line of blood. The urge to create, the satisfaction of the cunning manipulation, though common to other activities, does not exist in the killings. Or was this a subconscious effort to do something which no one had ever done before? Good God! it couldn't be. . . . There can be only this one answer which satisfies the problem: the influence impinged by the Supernatural Force.

. . . legal insanity is still governed by a set of rules made over 100 years ago. . . . Odd it is that these rules were designed before the science of psychiatry had discovered or diagnosed the strange recesses and vagaries of the human mind. Odder still that unenlightened civilisation has resisted the urgent need of allowing the law to march hand in hand with science. Many times in the long hours which have been given to me in recent months for undistracted thought and reflection I have wondered about the disease of the mind which afflicts me.

I have, I know, every attribute of normality in my daily doings, in my various connections with officials, doctors and lawyers. I write a normal letter and conduct my business affairs with efficiency and intelligence. Yet I am, as I acknowledge to myself, a being apart, nursing many strange and horrible secrets, some of which I cannot share even with myself, for my mind will not acknowledge as real the ideas which arise from it.

It may be that one consequence of the happenings in which I have been perhaps the foremost actor may lead to a fresh attempt to bring the McNaghten Rules up to date, so that the anti-social character of the man who kills the neighbour without conscious volition or controllable will may be treated as suffering from some disease of the mind, as a schizophrenic or a paranoic.

Letter to a psychiatrist for the defense, Dr. Henry Yellowlees, who had examined Haigh for his trial; he believed Haigh was mentally ill and abnormal:

Dear Sir,

I would like you to know that I appreciate the personal interest you have taken and the effort you have made on my behalf, even though I cannot agree with your opinion. After all, all the outstanding personalities throughout history have been considered odd: Confucius, Jesus Christ, Julius Caesar, Mahomet, Napoleon and even Hitler; all possessed a greater perception of the infinite and a more lucid understanding of the omniscient mind. I am happy to inform you that my mother, writing to me during last week, was able to confirm that my headmistress at the High School and my headmaster at the Grammar School both reported that I was not at all a normal boy. How could it be otherwise in the product of an angel and one of the few men who ever sinned?

I do therefore have the utmost admiration for your greater perception and am grateful to you for your courageous exposition of it.

Yours truly,
J. G. Haigh

Nearing his execution date, Haigh corresponded from prison with his friend Barbara Stephens. An excerpt:

How foolish of you to ask why I had not murdered you. Of course I had millions of opportunities, I know that. But the idea never even crossed my mind. I wouldn't have hurt a hair of your head.

This other business is something entirely separate and different. There was no affection involved there. . . . These two things had to go on together. . . . I can't go on discussing these two alien things side by side. . . .

I have been proud of our association, it has always been an honourable one.

Three days before his execution, excerpt from another letter to his friend:

I now await the decision of the Home Secretary in this matter, from which will be known the state of enlightenment in this so far dark isle. . . . Man may not yet as in some other countries pursue his spiritual conviction with complete freedom. Religious liberty is a thing of name only. . . .

Now I must leave you to worship from afar knowing that I have been to you all that you would desire in moral rectitude. I leave you to the comfort of the eternal spirit and desire that you shall be happy in the path which is made for you, forgetting not that there is a benediction in silence and solitude. From abstinence there comes the voluptuous intoxication of self-reliance and guided rightness. In this you will know you are right and fear no man. This I commit you, being ever grateful for your love and devotion.

Excerpt from his last letter to Stephens:

. . . if you read Ecclesiastes you will find, "What has been, has been, what is to be, will be". . . .

I have had a pleasant week-end going over mentally the numerous records we have enjoyed so much. I hope they will be a legacy of happiness to you. One which we haven't got I can't get rid of from my mind is Beethoven VIth (The Pastoral). . . .

As I have said before it is not easy to bid you farewell; but you will feel me around from time to time as I know my mission is not yet finished and I shall remain earthbound until it is over.

WILLIAM **HEIRENS**

Early in the morning of June 5, 1945, 16-year-old William Heirens broke into the Chicago apartment of 43-year-old Josephine Ross while she was asleep in bed. After hitting her over the head and stabbing her in the throat, he washed her nude body in the bathtub and placed adhesive tape on the knife wounds. Late in the evening of December 10, Heirens climbed up a fire escape and entered the sixth-floor apartment of 33-year-old Frances Brown, an ex-Wave and stenographer for A. B. Dick & Company. Surprising her in bed, he shot her in the head, stabbed her with a 10-inch bread knife he left protruding from her chest, and – after washing her corpse and draping it over the side of the bathtub – wrote with lipstick on the living room wall, "For heavens sake catch me Before I kill more I cannot control myself." At approximately 1 A.M. on January 7, 1946, Heirens sneaked into the bedroom of 6-year-old Suzanne Degnan, strangled her to death, took her body to a neighboring basement, dismembered her body, dumped her remains into the sewer system, and tossed a ransom note through her window. Police found her head in a manhole around seven o'clock the next night.

Heirens was caught burglarizing apartments on June 26, 1946, by Abner T. Cunningham, an off-duty policeman returning from an afternoon swim. Struggling with Cunningham and another officer who had joined the ensuing chase, Heirens was subdued after being hit over the head with three flowerpots by the unarmed Cunningham. He told police his name was "Joe Blow" and admitted nothing, but police, puzzled by a note they found in his wallet written by a possible accomplice (reproduced below), interrogated Heirens for days, subjecting him to a spinal tap and an injection of sodium pentothal (popularly known as "truth serum"). He confessed to the murders on August 7 after being confronted with a partial matching fingerprint from the Degnan ransom note and a sample of his cursive style that was similar to the lipstick writing on Frances Brown's wall.

Examined by psychiatrists for the prosecution and defense, the accomplice who wrote the note turned out to be a criminal "alter ego" of Heirens who went by the names "George Murman," "George M.S.," and "George LMFT." According to the doctors' psychiatric article, "A Study of William Heirens," at the age of ten he began stealing women's panties (mostly pink and blue) from neighboring apartments; alone in his parents' attic, Heirens would put the panties on and immediately ejaculate. As Heirens matured he found that

> . . . he had sexual excitement or an erection at the sight of an open window at the place to be burglarized. Going through the window he had an emission. Later it took several entrances to produce the emission. . . . Often when sexual

> completion occurred in the entered room it was accompanied or preceded by defecation or urination, or both.

Heirens himself explained to police in an interrogation from July 26:

> I first started to steal when I was about ten years of age and at that early time the mere act of stealing carried with it sex satisfaction. At that age I was conscious of sex. About this time I saw a motion picture of Doctor Jekyll and Mr. Hyde, and to this day in some way or another the song "Rose O'Day" connects itself with this picture. In this picture I also remember quite vividly a hand, a body of a woman and blood. They are about the only things from this picture that I now carry in my mind. I never have been given to masturbation or other abnormal sex desires nor have I up to this time ever had sexual intercourse nor attempted to have any relations with any female.

The boy stole cash, bonds, guns and jewelry. Most of his pickings, however, were worthless items he simply hoarded: socks, belts, college pennants, German Iron crosses, birth certificates, cuff links, and nylons. In 1942, at the age of thirteen, he was arrested for a number of burglaries (he was suspected of nearly fifty) and sent to a reform school, the Gibault School for Boys in Terre Haute, Indiana. At the time of his final arrest he was majoring in German at the University of Chicago.

His psychiatrists also noted in their article that as a child Heirens was raised in a rigid Catholic household that had no room for "dirty books." With the freedom of college, however, he became

> . . . interested in books on sex and crime. "I read around the subject of masochism, fetishism, sadism, flagellation, also Kraft-Ebbing and dreams, some parts of Freud." . . . His reading revolves around the power principle: Nietzsche, Schopenhauer, and even Spinoza, of which he grasped nothing. Pictures of Hitler, Goering and Goebbels are in his scrap books and his favorite studies were a sketchy intellectual interest in "mass psychology."

The police, taking a much harder line, culled the following from Heirens during an interrogation:

> Q: Are you familiar with Nietzsche's philosophy?
> A: No. That is as far as I got in this book. I must have spent a week trying to read it.
> Q: What caused you to interest yourself in Nietzsche?
> A: Well, I tried to understand about everything I got.
> Q: You knew he was a crazy man, didn't you?
> A: As far as I know here, I could not get any further in understanding.
> Q: You knew he blew his brains out, didn't you?
> A: No, I did not.
> Q: And killed himself. I do not think he shot himself. . . . Are you a follower of Nietzsche?
> A: No.
> Q: Freud?
> A: No.
> Q: How much philosophy have you read?
> A: As many pages as are dirty in any of those books.

Heirens accepted a bargain from the district attorney and pleaded guilty to murder and burglary charges on September 4, 1946; that evening at 12:30 A.M. he attempted to hang himself in his cell. He survived and was sentenced the next day to three consecutive life terms. Now residing at the Vienna

Correctional Center, Heirens was the first Illinois prisoner to earn a college degree and is secretary to the prison's Catholic chaplain. He spends most of his time writing letters, reading (his favorite book for some time was a collection of writings by parapsychologist Charles Fort), playing cards, and painting landscapes and portraits.

Excerpts from his high school "scrap book":

Just who am I? I begin to wonder after all I could be human as the rest are but to myself, I would laugh at such a thought. Oh these seem so much more superior. In plain words I think I'm a worm. It's from being a worm though, I like it: insignificant and obsolete. That's just what I need. Maybe if I'm all wrong in writing this. Probable I'll change my attitude soon. It's odd but I begin to like my habits now. Probably just a passing phase. I'll most likely hate myself when I do things disagreeable to myself. . . . I wonder why I can't run the world. It seems only great men have that choice. It's funny but I don't understand why I haven't the same equal chance. I guess they probable know just where to start & I don't. Would't it be great to have that much power. Men sacrifice their lives for it. There must be an easier and faster way to gain control. . . . Why am I thinking these things. It's all nonsense. Probable never ever entered another mind. You've got a good imagination, Bill, but I doubt whether you'll get far with it. So far it's gotten you into trouble. Real trouble. Well, I guess that's life for you.

Why the fish did I ever go out for football. I detest the game and yet I go in for the sport. That's some sign of you loosing your head. In about three years you'll probable end up in a coo-coo house. . . .

Whoever got the idea that I could do great things and so sent me to school. It's sure a mystery. Maybe if I come down to earth I'll learn sum'min. . . .

You god dammed nincompoop. Why the hell do you live is all I can wonder. Your one of the most unworthy persons I've understood to be able to live. Your sure not following your golden rules for control. In fact you've been standing still for the last two weeks.

Great News 7:20 Sept. 26 '45

I'm now shaking with excitement. My hopes and prayers have been answered in one of my biggest chances in life. If I can only use my chance to the best advantage. The University of Chicago has accepted me into its enrollment. This is my first chance at showing how good I am to society and I intend to show even better signs. Tonight I feel as if the world were mine. All I have to do now is pray, giving thanks and vowing to do my best as humanly possible.

Plot VII

Considering my present college status, considering my inability to control society, considering that I am loosing my moral code slightly; I hereby intend to change my whole way of living. Since I have devoted more time to psychology it should be easy. My plan described in this plot should be carried out fully. I shall attack human nature to my fullest extent.

College paper for English class. It was graded "C-plus" with the instructor's comment: "Almost a 'B' paper. You express yourself better here than in former papers. Perhaps you are more interested in your subject."

Character

First of all she is an introvert. Her ideas are liberal altho a few minor skepticisms enter. When we first met she was very quiet. She did not care to associate with people any more than needed. After a while she began to talk freely. It seems it took her some time to analyze me, but in reality I was getting to know her more.

She is self-centered; her interests center in her own world. Because of her opposition to the gregarious instinct, she does not thoroly understand other points of view. She is very considerate tho, and tries to please whenever possible.

Her appearance and action would put her age at about 17 but she is twenty. I am fairly good at judging ages but this case was the first to fool me. She has no intention of getting married; perhaps she has lost all hope. This point seemed a bit unreasonable to me.

She is what you might call charming by the fact that she is obliging. I think that if she could come to like associating with people her whole feeling toward life would change.

Message written in red lipstick on December 10, 1945, on murder victim Frances Brown's beige wall; Heirens later told police, "I wrote the message because I had an awful sick feeling and felt bad. I had a headache."

For heavens
sake catch me
Before I kill more
I cannot control myself

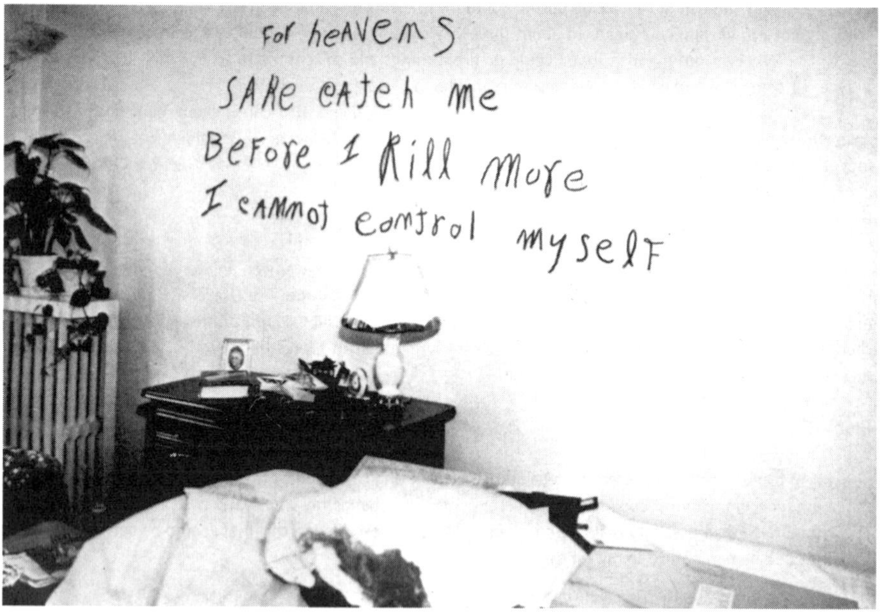

Ransom note written late in the evening of January 7, 1946, after he kidnapped and killed 6-year-old Suzanne Degnan. The note was written in pencil and spattered with oil:

Get $20,000
Reddy &
Waite
For word
do not notify
FBI or

police
Bills in 5's & 10's

On the other side he wrote:

Burn this for her safty

After his arrest police found a letter in his wallet "from" his alter ego, "George." Heirens elaborated the following in his confession on the subject of "George":

> He was just a realization of mine. I just stuck him in for no good reason. Before he seemed real to me. At Gibault [reform school] things were so vague when I went out on burglary, it seemed to me that George was doing it. He seemed to be real. I cannot introduce him to anybody but he is there. . . . Usually when I had to get out I would ask him where he was going. We would talk back and forth that way. He would say, down to the lake, and I would say, what are you going to do there? He said he would get some things. I would ask him why he was going and he said, because he wants to. It would be just that way. I would argue with him to stay and then I would get a headache. I would argue in every way possible with him but he always wanted to get out. . . . I don't want you to laugh. It seems so darn real to me. Previous to this, I had given the whole matter a name. I just had a faint memory of these things, as to temperature or color of things. When I would go out it would make no difference to me if I had a summer suit on with freezing weather. I could not feel any temperature. I gave it the name of George. . . . I would write letters to myself. I would talk to him. When I wanted to get out he would ask me where I was going, why I was going out, and what time I would be back and things of that nature. I begged him to stay. I had a headache almost all the time I was doing that. I was just stimulated to get out. One of the letters I had written was to George M. S. I figured if I could send him to Mexico. . . . Sometimes in the letters I would ask him for things I needed at school. I would ask him if I could borrow money from him. . . . When this urge would come out, I would tell him there would be a letter in the drawer for him. Sometimes he would answer after I wrote and then when I would read it, it would all seem new to me. I don't remember writing the answer and would not know I had written what was written. . . . I made a pact with George if I ever got caught through him that I would kill myself and kill him too. I thought that would scare him away but it never did. . . . He has to be part of me. . . .

Letter from "George":

May 17

Bill:

I haven't heard from you in a long time. I feel for you being in jail. Tough luck. You'll know better next time.

It seems that I'm being caught up with and I'll have to make an exit if I want to enjoy life. Therefore I will entrust with you some of my belongings.

I will pick up most of my things in the future. Inside I enclose a key to the locker at the Randolph Street Station. Use the key as soon as possible.

Inside the locker you will find some papers and money. You can use some of the money. Please leave most of it alone so I can pick it up when I need some ready cash.

It's a good thing the police didn't search your place. I'd probably be in the coop now if they did. I remember once you told me that you wouldn't take the rap. I appreciate you taking those things off my hands when I was being followed.

I could have just as well dumped it but I can't see me losing all that jewelry. I'll give you a phone call before I come for the stuff.

I'm on my way to Milwaukee for a month and then El Paso. Jock has things fixed in that territory south of there. Tom, Sid, Pete and myself will start the road from there. Once the stuff is on the way it will be easy.

Howey, Johnny and Carl will be out of the Army soon with a few new ideas. I'll see you soon. If this doesn't pan out, the gang might be broken up. We aren't keeping any of our old plans, so burn what you have. We'll burn ours.

George M. S.

After Heirens attempted suicide on September 4, 1946, prison guards found in his cell two letters to his parents, a letter to his girlfriend Joan, and a letter to "George":

Dear mom & dad,

Things aren't turning out the way I planned. I didn't think of the present happenings to come about. I'de better start from the beginning & tell you everything. ~~Long ago when we lived on Loyola Avenue & had the store at 1257 Loyola I started my terrible practice.~~

~~It was stealing but not normal stealing I think you know what that was. If not I'll merely say underclothing & it should refresh things. From that sort of stealing I developed into the field of burgalry. I'de say the first time was in the fall of '41. I don't know what brought it about but what I know of the fact I told the lawyers. I realized after I was caught what bad I committed. My sorrow that I felt toward you was inbarable. You stuck by me & helped me along. The judge sentenced me to Gibault where I was at my best for a long time but I missed home very much & began to think you didn't care about me anymore so my mind again wandered in the wrong direction. After I came home I was as bad as when I left. Thus I started in on the same thing with some knowledge I picked up at Gibault.~~

If I would have thought of you none of this would have happened but as things went I got caught again. Maybe it was by the grace of God that I did since it woke me up to what was going on. The Judge was hard on me this time too. He sent me to St. Bede where everything went alright for a little while & then my mind changed to wrong. I tried for your sake mom & dad & I succeeded for a year & a half but it seems my mind couldn't be controled like that. It wandered along lines that I had previously forbidden to enter my mind. I lost all control of myself & started to plan burgalries. Then news came that I passed my test at the University of Chicago & I prayed to God in thanks for the favor he had done & made a vow for yours & Gods sake to mend my ways. I knew there was something wrong with me to do such things so I tried to find out why & I finally came on a solution. Everytime I committed a burgalry I had an erection & sometimes a discharge just as I

on Loyola

did when I stole ~~underclothing~~ I therefore thought it must be something to do with sex so I deduced that the best way to overcome it was to get at the source which I did by dating girls. I found them repulsive but I was determined to overcome this. My burgalries were very frequent at that time & usually when I went out I committed more than one a night. But soon after Christmas when I started to go with Joan I began to let up on burgalries & I decided I was winning but I still made infrequent burgalries. I knew I was winning. Yet I had not overcome it. During the burgalries I had an excretion either way in the place I burgalarized so I decided to elevate any chances of more burgalries would be to go to the bathroom frequently before night & the urge I couldn't control would come on again. This also helped but not sufficiently. Joan was converting me away from my crime but not sufficiently. We never went further than necking & maybe that's the reason. Some houses I broke into I merely excreted in & left so I should say my total burgalries were vast considering the amount of things I stole & threw away.

& did not steal

I was caught in one of the acts in an apartment building by a lady & a man. The man chased me & coming down the stairs my erection went down & I came to consider my danger. I got away by using the gun I had but if they challenged my intentions to shoot I could not have. I knew what I had done & was fearful of being caught & what you would again have to go through. I reflected the danger & ran away to the back porch of a store nearby. Where I was cornered & I was very thoughtful at that time. A policeman came up after me & I knew it was all over. I thought of shooting myself through my head with the 22 but I thought that it might not be sufficient to kill me. The policeman tried to shoot me as I came down to give up but the bullets only fell out the end of the gun because I seen the end of one laying on the floor. So I fought with him thinking someone else would come with a bigger gun & kill me but nobody did only a guy with flower pots. I thought he had a gun & didn't even look to see him shoot which I was sure he would do. I got fooled. When I woke up I was in Edgewater hospital. There I was having my head sewed up but I didn't revive because I thought I could find some other way to kill myself. I layed quite & thought. In the hospital I devised a plan to fight & I did to my best knowing they would have to give me something to quite me down. If they gave me an injection I intended to break the needle in my arm so that the point would go to my heart & end it all but they all held me to tight. I tried latter to gouge my eyes out in the hope they wouldn't notice it till I was dead but that failed because they were watching me just like when I tried to reopen the wounds in my head to bleed to death. Then I thought of starving myself & I succeeded for some time. Then a guy came to take finger prints & said I was a suspect in the Degnan case. I had read a lot about it in the papers & I then began to think of it. First I knew I must convince myself I did it & I finally by repeation in my mind & verbally I had completed it. I then planned other things to lead to my conviction & eventually the electric chair. I was too nervous when they used the truth serum for it to have any effect but when they started to question me I decided to play along & so I wanted to agravate them against me so I blamed it all on George M.S. of whom I had composed a note concerning. That all worked very well but I think I should have told them I did it in the truth serum. Later on they gave me a spinal injection which was terrible & I realize now was uncalled for. An hour after the spinal they took me out for questioning of which I could not convict myself of in any way because I couldn't think since the headache was so great. Later on things began to be better & I decided again to help Mr. Tuohy out. My finger print as they say had been found on the note but it would undoubtedly later be proved to be not mine. Therefore I substantiated more evidence for them. Therefore I called Mr. Tuohy & a court reporter to give a fake confession, primarily to get them angry & also to do something else. My chance came when they asked me to write the ransom note. They didn't know it themselves but I remembered everything in it from an article the Daily News printed about this writing. I tried to duplicate everything that I could do to incriminate myself but on the letters I slipped up. I couldn't make that figure "and" because I didn't know which way the curve went but I duplicated quite a few things I knew were wrong primarily the spelling & the coma since I knew I could not possible duplicate the very same document. I was satisfied with what I had done & when Crowley came in this morning to tell me the mistakes I aggravated him more by telling him to bring a dictionary. That really clinched things I thought but I seemed to fail when I spoke to my lawyers they told me they couldn't convict me on that. I had previously told the lawyers I did it to get them against me & make them fearful of loosing the case in such a way that I could be sure of killing myself & not causing anyone anymore grief. Then the police later said they had fingerprints of mine in the Brown killing so I thought here is another chance & tried remembered another murder I had read much about & could confess to that was the Ross killing. So I told my lawyers all I could thinking they would give it away. Then to my satisfaction everything was going fine until they started to dicker on the case. I knew Touhy would except because he didn't have enough evidence so I've been brought up to the present time.

I now realize my mistake & so having devised a way to end my life now I must tell you I did not do it. I say this in order to keep the Degnan family on the alert against the killer who will obviously seek the other daughter. Also so that the citizens of Chicago will be on their guard.

I'm taking all into consideration mom & dad & realize that I am a failure & a disgrace to the race. I've tried my best to overcome my fault but I've failed. I did tried to the best I can so I therefore must end my life. I know God will be with me & I have no fear. I'm in the state of grace & know I'll be alright. I've saved very many aspirins & I intend to take all 32 of them. I'm sorry very sorry but this is the best way. I owe you much, much. I'll see you mom & dad. Eternal love.

Bill

Dear mom & dad,

I love you both above all earthly things. I've never shown it have I by what has happened. Probable you think I'm not worth bothering about & I don't blame you. I'll relate parts of my past in hope that you'll understand.

When we lived at 1257 Loyola I started on my terrible & troubling habit. I was stealing but not normal stealing as you might remember. The lawyers have been told of that which is part of the partial truth I told them. That practice continued until the fall of 1942. I was not caught at it because it was not too much against society. In fall I developed the habit of burglary which lasted for almost a year before being caught. I got the same excitement out of it as my previous abnormal burglaries. Then I was sent to Gibault. It probable was a mistake on the judges part because it didn't help me any. I picked up more about burglary & I got great excitement just talking about it. At first at Gibault I felt very sorry. You'll never know how many nights I cried myself to sleep. I tried at first to turn my thoughts to studies but later I guess I just drifted back to the same ideas.

I was glad you stuck by me then. Nobody else did & nobody seemed to want to help. You didn't leave me or talk against me as other people did. You've stood by me & I cannot forget that. I know I didn't deserve it.

When I left Gibault for home I came back worst than I started. I had plans & in the middle of the summer I went back to the same thing. I got great excitement out of it all. Then I was caught again. At Gibault I learned very many things but it seemed none of them could stop me from stealing. I went to court again & the judge still didn't understand me so he took me away from you again. I wanted so much to go to the high school near home but I didn't have any choice. I was really homesick this time & just mopped around waiting for a chance to come home & see you but it was not frequent enough. I wanted to go to Niles high the next semester but you didn't want me to. I thought you didn't care for me then but that was a foolish thought.

Remember dad, when we went to work togeather during the summer. We'de get up early & go out to the car when the sun was just coming up. It sure was great. I guess I have the best father in the world. You would let me drive part of the way & I remember how you would be on pins and needles worrying about me hitting something. I thought that was funny that you should worry about me doing that. Yes, you are the greatest dad in the world. I remember when we'de go fishing real early in the morning. You & Jere always had a hard time getting me up. Then we would go down to the rocks on Lake Michigan & fish. Remember when we arrived it would still be dark & we'de get all the fish when the sun started to come up. I know I'll remember that. You were swell dad. There aren't many fathers that would do that much for their sun.

I started my second year at St. Bede with the money from the steel mills. I hated to go back I wanted the normal schooling being able to see you after school & getting around with regular guys. The last year at St. Bede my mind began to wander again as it did at Gibault. I had very few things to occupy it & I began to feel you didn't want me at home. I planned how I would do more burglaries. At that time I got a lot of excitement in planning such things. Then summer came again & I felt still that you didn't care about me so I wanted to get out on my own & prove that I was not a baby & I wanted to show you there was some good in me. I worked at the I.C. for a while & latter I seen that dad resented it & I felt I owed him so much & shouldn't cause him such resentment. Then I worked again at the steel mills. Later on I applied for the test at the University of Chicago. I knew if I passed it I would further convince you I wasn't so bad. All this time I didn't commit any crimes. I wanted to very much but I somehow kept from it. Then I went back again to St. Bede most against my will. Soon I received word from you that I had been accepted at the University.

I thanked God & promised him I'de be good & prove myself. God always understood me. He helped me get into the University. At times God was all I had to help me & I believed in him. I hoped & prayed he would help me. I knew he would & he did. But since that time things changed.

I had been ashamed to face people for what I had done previous to the time I entered the University. So I agreed with you to live there & save money by doing so. That was a very poor choice on my part & I've regretted it since I was there. I had to wait for a chance to prove I was worthy of being around home more. I felt I could not face people. One morning early I got up to study. It was just before school started. I got the urge to commit burglaries then so I went out looking around. This is my first attempt at crime since I was last caught. I went into an apartment building on Drexel and 60th. I started at the top to work down as I did on previous burglaries through open doors. I went to the penthouse on the top floor where a lady was coming out of. I suppose to go to work. She scared me away for about an hour & a half. Then I came back & went through all the floors looking for open doors to steal purses from. I found none so I decided to burgalrise the penthouse which I believed at the time to be empty. I went up & to make sure I knocked on the door. After a short time someone came but to my horrified eyes I seen a lady with blood dripping down all over her. She looked weak & I did not know what to do. I helped her to a chair & went to get a wet towel to wipe the blood off & give her first aid but I changed my mind.

Dear Joan,

I noticed your name in the New World last Sunday. When I think that mine might have been there with the rest it gives me a funny feeling & hate for yourself myself that I cannot expressed. I hope the convention turns out alright. It looks like I won't have a date with you for that formal dance. I'm sorry about ~~everything~~ breaking it.

You'll never realize what I've been through. It all seems like a bad dream & I can't wake up. Every thing that the police can say to hurt me in any way they tell the newspapers. I want you to know that what is being said is not true. I never had anything to do with the Degnan case or all those burglaries & assaults. It seems the police are trying to say I did everything bad in Chicago but it isn't true, not a bit of it. For example when they caught me they said I gave a big gun battle. Actually I tried to hand the gun to the policeman amidst his bullets coming at me & then they wonder why I struggled ~~with him~~ with his gun.

Quite a few times I spoke to you of knowing shady characters & now you can understand I wasn't telling a story. ~~I would hold things for George, he is one of my friends the best I thought.~~ But it's all water under the bridge now ~~& George is a very far ways from Chicago~~ & I know something will come up help my case.

You can help me very much if you remember all the nights you & that we went out together ~~the best you can remember.~~

Joan, I guess you know now that I never went out with many girls. I want you to know that I think very much of you, more than I ever did concerning girls. I couldn't avoid all the bother the police gave you even if I tried. It seems they poke their nose in everything. All I can do is wait for the truth to shine through to the public eye. I'll never forget you, Joan, No matter where you are I'll write & tell you what's happening.

I can't write concerning my case now, but I want you to know I'm not guilty & I'll soon be able to prove it. Almost all my waking moments I think of my proof, etc.

I'll write again soon. If you have time, drop me a few words will you. I never know what's in the newspaper or how the public is thinking here but be careful what you write because they change words around & use them as evidents against me. So for safety sake don't write anything concerning my case to me.

Bill.

Dear George,

You have got me into a lot of trouble now and you failed to help me to get out of it. I realize that you are my friend, but I think it is not the right thing to let me take the blame for everything. If you have left I sure would like to have you back to straighten things out. Before you helped me out by getting me things I wanted and helped me pay my way through school. I appreciate that, but can't you help me now. If you can, please do.

Yours, Bill Heirens.

WILLIAM EDWARD **HICKMAN**

On November 23, 1927, a short young man named "Donald Evans" rented apartment number 315 of the Bellevue Arms at 1170 (now 1168) Bellevue Avenue in the Echo Park area of Los Angeles. He had a place in Altadena, but 19-year-old William Edward Hickman's plan required a safe, anonymous location. In the summer he had been employed as a messenger at the First National Bank at 7th and Spring in downtown Los Angeles; his immediate superior was Perry M. Parker, the chief clerk of the bank. One day Hickman observed his boss having lunch with one of his pretty 12-year-old twin girls, Marion, and noted to himself that Parker seemed very fond of his daughter.

Hickman's ambition was to attend evangelical college. Certain he would receive a scholarship for his tuition, he calculated that he still needed $1500 for his living expenses. For an aspiring man of God, he had rather unorthodox ways of raising the money: on Christmas Eve of 1926, he robbed a drugstore with a friend, and managed to get away in a gun battle that resulted in the death of the owner and the wounding of a passing police officer. Hickman hid out in San Francisco for three weeks, and afterwards returned to Los Angeles and got the job at First National Bank. After attempting to pass some forged checks he stole from the bank, Hickman was fired, arrested, and released on probation. Remembering his ex-employer's little girl, he concocted a more ambitious scheme.

On Thursday, December 15, 1927, Perry Parker celebrated his birthday by taking the day off from work and relaxing at home. In the afternoon he received a call from the principal of his daughters' junior high school, who was surprised to get Parker on the phone; a young man from First National Bank had just picked up his daughter Marion, stating that her father had been in a car accident and was hospitalized in serious condition. Parker's confusion cleared after two telegrams and a special delivery letter arrived at his house: his daughter was being held by a kidnapper calling himself "George Fox" for a ransom of $1500. After Parker contacted the police, two more letters arrived on Friday afternoon from "Fox" and Marion. That evening the kidnapper called and told him to come alone to the intersection of Tenth Street and Gramercy Place with the ransom money. Unfortunately, "Fox" was intelligent enough to make the call from a phone booth across the street from the local police station; after observing a flurry of unmarked cars leaving the station, the kidnapper did not show up for the drop-off. The next morning Parker received two more letters from his daughter and "Fox" warning him to keep the police away, and at 7:15 P.M. the kidnapper phoned with instructions to meet him in front of 435 South Manhattan Place. Determined to see his daughter alive, Parker successfully pleaded with the police not to intervene and arrived alone at the meeting place at 8 P.M.

Soon after his phone call to Parker, Hickman dictated to the bound child the contents of her last letter. He then strangled her to death with a towel and – putting to use the skills he had learned working in a chicken slaughterhouse as a teenager – slit her throat in the bathtub to drain her blood, sawed off her forearms and legs, severed her torso at the waist, removed her entrails, and washed her remains. (Hickman was later asked by police why he dismembered her body; he replied that he needed to fit her into his suitcase to get her into his car unwitnessed. When asked why he didn't just buy a bigger suitcase, Hickman stared at his interrogators with a puzzled expression.) To make Marion appear lifelike to her expectant father, Hickman applied rouge and lipstick to the dead girl's face and, in a sickening yet effective operation, kept her eyes open by sewing her eyelids to her eyebrows with two fine strands of picture wire.

Hickman pulled alongside Parker's car fifteen minutes after eight o'clock, brandishing a shotgun and wearing a white handkerchief over his face. He displayed what appeared to be a quiet Marion in the back seat and Parker, thinking that his daughter was still alive, handed over the money. Hickman drove ahead half a block and dumped the girl's body by the curb. Police later arrived after getting reports from the residents of Manhattan Place of a hysterical man pacing up and down the street, cradling a limbless corpse in his arms. Perry Parker had to be heavily sedated by the family physician before he was returned home.

The next morning, December 18, police found six newspaper-wrapped bundles containing Marion Parker's limbs and viscera in the brush along Lilac Terrace Road in Elysian Park, and a suitcase filled with bloody newspapers and towels on Manhattan Place. A laundry mark on one of the towels led two detectives to the Bellevue Arms, where they briefly interviewed Hickman but did not consider him a suspect. That evening Hickman stole at gunpoint a green Hudson coupe from salesman Fred Peck at the intersection of Hollywood Boulevard and Western Avenue. Shortly thereafter police matched the fingerprints on the ransom notes with Hickman's arrest records and searched his apartment. (The Los Angeles *Times* reported that police found "a portable phonograph and a number of records, three pairs of golf pants, five golf clubs, the steel shafts of three having been broken or crudely cut in two, [and] a number of golf balls . . . all of the phonograph records were foxtrot and new jazz-song pieces.") With his photograph in newspapers nationwide, Hickman was spotted by a haberdasher in Seattle, Washington, on December 21, and arrested the next afternoon near Echo, Oregon.

In his initial confession to police he blamed Marion's death on a fictional accomplice, "Andrew Cramer"; when all the Andrew Cramers in California accounted for their whereabouts during the kidnapping, Hickman admitted murdering her but pleaded not guilty by reason of insanity. The trial started on January 25, 1928, and the Los Angeles *Examiner* hired gossip columnist Louella Parsons, movie director King Vidor, and Tarzan creator Edgar Rice Burroughs as "guest reporters." Hickman's attorneys attempted to show "insanity of a hereditary nature," and friendly witnesses recounted how Hickman – who had been student body vice president and editor of the school newspaper in high school – had deteriorated by the end of his senior year into a sullen, apathetic insomniac. To illustrate Hickman's decline, his brother testified "that Ed began to perspire heavily, giving off a very foul body odor." A defense psychiatrist, Dr. A. L. Skoog, offered in court the following conversation with Hickman as an indication of his schizophrenic delusions:

> Q: Can you tell me more about how this Power makes itself known to you?
>
> A: I feel the Power over me. With the aid of this Power I know I will become great. I never stop to figure it out. If the Power directs me, I do it. I know it will lead to a great end. I think it plans everything for me. It is predestination. All human beings, no matter how smart they are, have only a shade of conception of the universe. But the Power knows all. It is Supreme Greatness. I used the name Providence but

that does not exactly describe it.

Q: Do you know of anyone else with whom your Providence communicates?

A: It has not been revealed to anyone else, not even Christ.

Q: You say Providence talks to you; how does it sound?

A: It is soft, but powerful. When it is speaking, I cannot move. Chills run down my spine.

Q: You have seen pictures of God in white flowing robes. I presume your Providence appears much like God.

A: No, my Providence has fiery eyes; they seem to burn a hole in me.

Q: Did Marion ever give you any indication whatsoever that would cause you to believe that she was aware of what would happen to her?

A: She told me that a week before the kidnapping she dreamt that a strange man came to school and took her away. She told me this voluntarily. She said this about 7 o'clock the evening of the day I took her away, when we were driving along Foothill Boulevard. She told me that she had several dreams about this before. She said her mother always warned her about getting into an automobile with a strange man. She told me she never thought it would be so bad to be kidnapped. She said that in daydreams at her desk in school she had also imagined this. I felt this was a positive manifestation of this Power that I have been trying to describe as having influence over me. It was all prearranged. I feel that there are two shades to this affair. One was Providence bringing me before the world, the other was Providence trying me to see if I was super strong and capable of doing the work. He would set out for me. It was all sort of a test.

Hickman, however, sealed his fate by penning a letter to a cellmate (reproduced below) admitting his insanity was a sham; the letter was intercepted by a guard and handed over to the district attorney. The jury took only 36 minutes to return a guilty verdict on February 6, and Hickman was sentenced to death by hanging on February 15. On October 19, 1928, a crowd of two hundred and thirty people at San Quentin witnessed a nauseating spectacle: as Hickman dropped through the trap door his head hit the side of the gallows, and for fifteen endless minutes he slowly strangled to death.

Telegram from Pasadena, California, sent to Parker on the afternoon of December 15, 1927:

DO POSITIVELY NOTHING TILL YOU RECEIVE SPECIAL DELIVERY LETTER. MARION PARKER GEORGE FOX.

A second telegram was sent from Alhambra, California, a few hours later:

MARION SECURE. INTERFERENCE WITH MY PLANS DANGEROUS. MARION PARKER GEORGE FOX.

Parker received a special delivery letter on the morning of December 16:

Δεατη

P. M. PARKER:

Use good judgment. You are the loser. Do This. Secure 75 – $20 gold certificates – U.S.

Currency – 1500 dollars – at once. KEEP THEM ON YOUR PERSON. GO ABOUT YOUR DAILY BUSINESS AS USUAL. LEAVE OUT POLICE AND DETECTIVES. MAKE NO PUBLIC NOTICE. KEEP THIS AFFAIR PRIVATE. MAKE NO SEARCH.

fullfilling these terms with the transfer of the currency will secure the return of the girl.

FAILURE TO COMPLY WITH THESE REQUESTS MEANS – NO ONE WILL EVER SEE THE GIRL AGAIN EXCEPT THE ANGELS IN HEAVEN ["HEAVEN" circled in dots]

The affair must end one way or the other within 3 days. 72 HRS.

YOU WILL RECEIVE FURTHER

NOTICE,

But the terms Remain the Same.

FATE

IF YOU WANT AID AGAINST ME ASK GOD NOT MAN.

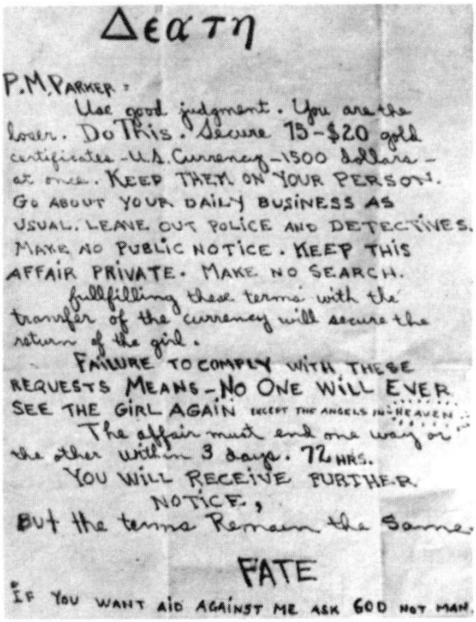
Δεατη

P.M.Parker:

Use good judgment. You are the loser. Do This. Secure 75-$20 gold certificates - U.S. Currency - 1500 dollars - at once. KEEP THEM ON YOUR PERSON. GO ABOUT YOUR DAILY BUSINESS AS USUAL. LEAVE OUT POLICE AND DETECTIVES. MAKE NO PUBLIC NOTICE. KEEP THIS AFFAIR PRIVATE. MAKE NO SEARCH.

fullfilling these terms with the transfer of the currency will secure the return of the girl.

FAILURE TO COMPLY WITH THESE REQUESTS MEANS - NO ONE WILL EVER SEE THE GIRL AGAIN EXCEPT THE ANGELS IN HEAVEN

The affair must end one way or the other within 3 days. 72 HRS.

YOU WILL RECEIVE FURTHER NOTICE,

But the terms Remain the Same.

FATE

IF YOU WANT AID AGAINST ME ASK GOD NOT MAN.

On the same day in the afternoon, two letters arrived. One was from Marion:

Dear Daddy and Mother,

I wish I could come home. I think I'll die if I have to be like this much longer. Won't someone tell me why all this had to happen to me. Daddy please do what the man tells your or he'll kill me if youdon't

Your loving daughter

Marion Parker

P.S. Please Daddy.

I want to come home tonight.

The other letter from "Fox"; "Isadore B" refers to former Police Commissioner Isadore Birnbaum, a neighbor and friend of the Parker family, and "W. J. Burns" refers to a well-known private detective agency in Los Angeles:

Δεατη

P. M. Parker:

Fox is my name. Very sly you know. ∴ Set no traps. I'll watch for them.

All the inside guys, even, your neighbor Isadore B., know that when you play with fire there is cause for burns. Not W. J. Burns and his shadowers either – remember that.

Get this straight: Your daughter's life hangs by a thread and I have a Gillette ready and able to handle the situation.

This is business. do you want the girl or the 75 – $100 gold certificates U.S. currency ? You cant have both and there's no other way out. believe this, and act accordingly. before the day's over I'll find out how you stand

I am doing a solo so figure on meeting the terms of Mr. fox or else

FATE •

if you want aid against me ask god not man.

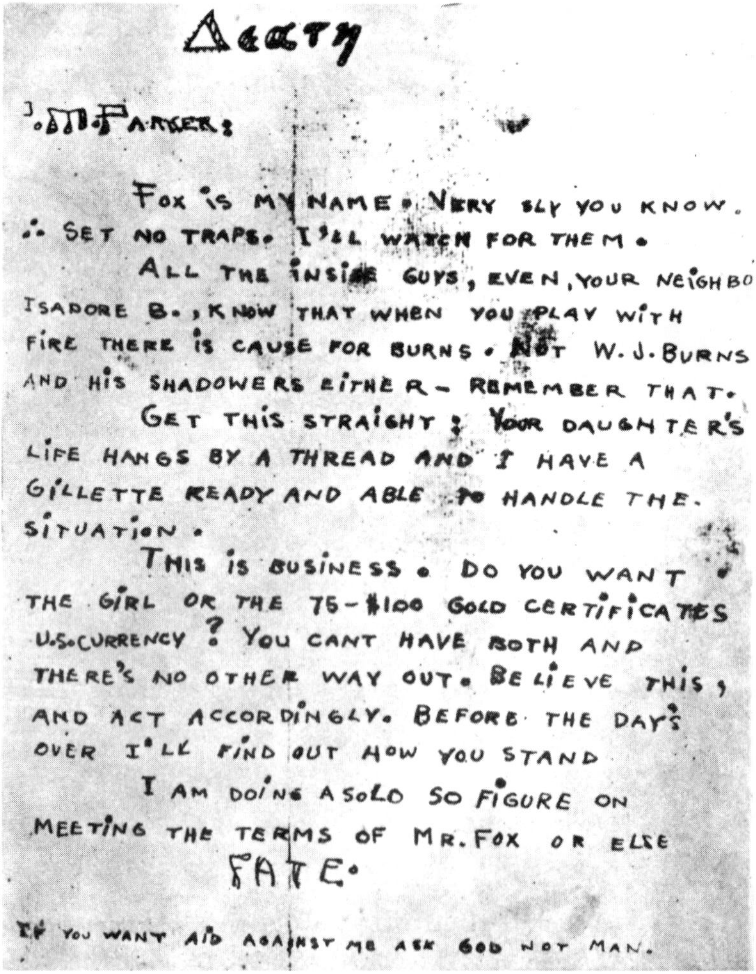
ΔεατΗ

J. M. Parker:

FOX IS MY NAME. VERY SLY YOU KNOW. ∴ SET NO TRAPS. I'LL WATCH FOR THEM.

ALL THE INSIDE GUYS, EVEN, YOUR NEIGHBO ISADORE B., KNOW THAT WHEN YOU PLAY WITH FIRE THERE IS CAUSE FOR BURNS. NOT W. J. BURNS AND HIS SHADOWERS EITHER – REMEMBER THAT.

GET THIS STRAIGHT: YOUR DAUGHTER'S LIFE HANGS BY A THREAD AND I HAVE A GILLETTE READY AND ABLE TO HANDLE THE SITUATION.

THIS IS BUSINESS. DO YOU WANT THE GIRL OR THE 75-$100 GOLD CERTIFICATES U.S. CURRENCY ? YOU CANT HAVE BOTH AND THERE'S NO OTHER WAY OUT. BELIEVE THIS, AND ACT ACCORDINGLY. BEFORE THE DAY'S OVER I'LL FIND OUT HOW YOU STAND

I AM DOING A SOLO SO FIGURE ON MEETING THE TERMS OF MR. FOX OR ELSE

FATE.

IF YOU WANT AID AGAINST ME ASK GOD NOT MAN.

The next day, December 17, two more letters arrived. From Marion:

Dear Daddy & Mother:

Daddy please don't bring anyone with you today. Im sorry for what happened last night we drove wright by the house and I cryed all the time last night. If you don't meet us this morning youll never see me again.

Love to All,
Marion Parker

P.S. Please Daddy:

I want to come home
this morning.
This is your last chance
be sure and come by your
self. or you won't see
me again. Marion

From "Fox":

P. M. PARKER:

TODAY IS THE LAST DAY. I MEAN SATURDAY, DECEMBER 17, 1927. YOU ARE INSANE TO IGNORE MY TERMS, WITH DEATH FAST ON ITS WAY. I CUT THE TIME TO TWO DAYS AND ONLY ONCE MORE WILL I PHONE YOU. I WILL BE TWO BILLION TIMES AS CAUTIOUS, AS CLEVER, AS DEADLY FROM NOW ON.

IF BY 8 O'CLOCK YOU HAVE NOT HEARD FROM ME, THEN HOLD A QUIET FUNERAL AT YOUR CEMETERY ON SUNDAY, DECEMBER 18 WITHOUT THE BODY. ONLY GOD KNOWS WHERE THE BODY OF MARION PARKER WILL REST IN THAT EVENT. NOT MUCH EFFORT FOR ME TO TAKE HER LIFE. SHE MAY PASS OUT BEFORE 8 P.M. SO I COULD NOT AFFORD TO CALL YOU AND ASK $1500 FOR A LIFELESS MASS OF FLESH

FINAL CHANCE TERMS. HAVE $1500, 75 $20 GOLD CERTIFICATES U.S. CURRENCY. COME ALONE IN CAR, LICENSE NUMBER 594,955. STAY IN CAR.

IF I CALL YOU, YOUR GIRL WILL STILL BE ALIVE. WHEN YOU GO TO THE MEETING YOU WILL HAVE A CHANCE TO SEE HER. THEN WITHOUT A SECOND'S HESITATION YOU MUST HAND OVER THE MONEY, ANY DELAY WILL COST HER LIFE.

DON'T BLUNDER. I HAVE CERTAINLY DONE MY PART TO WARN AND ADVISE YOU.

Essay for a court-appointed doctor before his trial:

I want to appeal to your complete justice, to your soundest reason, to every feeling and sense that you, the jury, possess. I want to do a great good for you. I want this case decided with the greatest and most beneficial results to society. I love the American people. I respect the people of California. I forgive the members of the prosecution. I want to help you in a way that no one else has ever helped you. A great Providence is urging me to do this. Think of destiny and forget fate. Believe in yourselves and your fellow citizens for good. Consider society.

What does my death matter to the American people? Loeb and Leopold were sentenced to life imprisonment. Snyder and Gray were sentenced to death. Remus was sentenced to the asylum. It matters not, as far as I am concerned, what may be done with me, whether I live or die, only as it regards your own welfare. I ask only that you allow me to explain the great calling of a great Providence, a great Providence which profoundly has brought me into this world, which has guided and directed my every action throughout my entire life, and which will take me away from this life at the appointed time.

Allow me to stand here and explain the whole truth and honesty of my life and to offer you the plea which this great Providence has given me to utter. From the time of my youth, I have felt the presence of a great guiding power. This power has manifested itself in me and has made me feel that I would become great. It has made me feel that I would become widely known and that my name would live in history. It has made me feel that I would live to an old age and accomplish a great good for my fellow countrymen and the world. This great presence, and you may call it God if you wish, but I shall call it Providence, has been with me since the age of twelve. I have felt it and known all these great secrets from this early age, and I can prove to you that it is real and that there is a likelihood of this fulfillment of this great work.

In my life there has already been a great range of activity. Environments, subjections, manifestations and accomplishments, all of which have been in a definite pursuit of the guidance and protection of this great Providence. In plain words, my life was intended by Providence to exemplify the tendency in modern youth to generate criminality, and the terrible atrocity of my last deed with the subsequent wide report of this case, are only steps in the plan of this Providence to bring me before the world, so that I could do the great good which has been confided in me by this same Providence and which was meant to be accomplished in me and through me by this great Providence, for the benefit of society and especially the safety and security of human rights here in the United States of America. Let me explain.

I was born in Arkansas state and before I was ten years of age, my father deserted the family and my mother was placed in the custody of an insane asylum at Little Rock, Arkansas. I had a broken home, so you can see, but before I left the country I tried to accept God, and it then being my twelfth year, I received the first calling and feeling of Providence. I came to the city with my remnant family and while there I got discouraged with religion and the church. Religion in the city didn't seem serious enough and I began to disbelieve in it and its God. I attended high school and graduated with the highest honors and scholarship in Kansas City's largest high school. I was disgusted and felt hurt unjustly when I could not attend college.

In spite of the circumstances, I always felt the presence of this Providence; it led me to come to California on Thanksgiving Day of last year. On December 15th last, I abducted a little girl by the name of Marion Parker from the Mount Vernon School and held her for a ransom of $1,500. I must have this money to defray my college expenses at Park College; it was my destiny. Here I thought Providence made a great manifestation to me. From the lips of Marion Parker herself I received this amazing and positive proof of the presence of a great Providence which was using me for a great work. I will speak the true words of this little girl. Marion Parker told me that in the very week that preceded her kidnapping, she had dreamed of a strange man coming to the Mount Vernon School and taking her away in a car. Marion Parker further related that in dreams she had many times been kidnapped and that she always felt that some day she would be taken away from her home and family in this way. Even the little girl freely told me that she believed the whole thing was intended, and if there is a God in heaven, I ask that he will strike me down at this instant if I am in the least particular diverging from the absolute truth and honestly, not only in this matter but in everything that I say here.

These matters are of great significance. There is a great Providence prompting me, it has brought me to live and do all these things. The murder of Marion Parker and the horrible, terrible simply awful mutilation of Marion Parker's helpless body, a separate deed from the kidnapping of Marion Parker, a distinct crime done in blood with a knife by my own hands on December 17, 1927, in the bathtub of an apartment in Los Angeles, California, was not meant by me, Edward Hickman, but through me under the guidance and protection of, and as a duty to this great Providence for the great work which it had been calling me to since the age of twelve to perform for the safety and security of human rights in the United States of America.

Here I stand before you. A human being always reserves the right and ability, I believe, to feel and express the true condition of his soul and mind. He knows his innermost parts better than his co-existent. Your duty is to judge me. Yet, only in your own minds can you judge me. Whatever I may be, judge it not of myself alone but from the power in me and over me of this great Providence. Listen to me now for your own cause and feel securely in your own reasoning that my greatest desire is for your good. I have always loved my country and it thrills my heart to hear the Star-Spangled Banner, or to witness the Stars and Stripes in parade. I have always felt that before I died I would do some great good and Providence tells me that this is about the time.

My America! America! My country and your country will always live. Nothing will bring the downfall of this great republic. There will always be a great mass of the people to understand and keep peace among us. If I live, everything in me of Providence will be exerted for your good. If I die, I hope that some day my country will hear from another youth who is destined and guided by Providence unto the same great work that I have wished to accomplish.

For your consideration, and to your interest, may this message and plea be dedicated. I trust that you will bear me out so that the great power over me can exert itself for this great good for the American people and humanity.

Note to a fellow prisoner during the trial; it was admitted as evidence by the prosecutor, Asa Keyes:

Listen Dale –

I believe you and believe I can trust you. Give me your advise on which one of these plans would be better. All of these depositions arent enough to prove me insane. I've got to throw a fit in court and I intend to throw a laughing screaming, diving act before the prosecution finishes their case – maybe in front of old man Parker himself.

Then to bewilder the jury. Before the case is ended – I'll get up and ask the judge if I can say something without my attorney butting in. Then I'll get up and give all that [expletive] about me wanting to do some good by living

I intend to rap Mr. Keyes before the things over and pull some trick on him in the crazy line.

Shorty, think these things over and tell me whether it is best, or not

For God's sake tear this thing up because it would ruin me if it got out.

See you in the morning

William Edward Hickman

alias "The Fox"

Ha! Ha! Ha!

P.S. You know and I know that I'm not insane however.

Letter to a close high school friend and his mother shortly before his execution:

San Quentin Prison
October 8 – 1928

Dear Jack and Mrs. Morris,

My good kind friends, I am most heartily sorry to have become such a contemptible wretch. I assure you that by the help of God I shall no longer remain in the pit of corruption. By rejecting the truth of Christ and the word of Almighty God I have degraded myself. I allowed the devil to work my destruction. I do not despair however. I believe in life after death. I repent of my sins and believe in Jesus Christ for forgiveness and redemption. Please pray for me and all the other condemned men here at San Quentin Prison.

May God bless you two. I hope you may have much future happiness and receive eternal joy in Heaven. I most surely believe in life after the grave. I place my hopes in everlasting life through the spirit of Christ. All glory belongs to God. For His sake I have no bitterness against any man. I want no man to be angry with me. God loves us all. I trust that I shall meet you and my other friends in Heaven.

Let all men keep their faith in spiritual glory. I hope the world will lose its hold upon the people and that the destruction of Satanic influence may be accomplished. The light and justice of God will ultimately prevail. Till we meet again.

Sincerely and Humbly yours

Edward Hickman

WILLIAM K. JONES

Executed in Huntsville, Texas, for the murders of his wife and daughter, 58-year-old William K. "Railroader" Jones gave a newspaper reporter a handwritten note on his way to the electric chair:

"My Last Statement"

If we could see our Mistakes before we make them it would save millions and millions of Heartaches, and would save a world full of trouble.

I am sorry that I killed my dear Wife and Daughter. Just as sorry as I can be for I loved them with all my Heart.

But God being my Witness and Judge, I did not Kill them for any insurance money. The reason and only reason I Killed them was that I was looseing my Job with the Rail Road and I couldent see how I could Suport them any longer as well as they deserved and as well as I wanted to. I just couldent face them in the disgrace of being fired from my Job.

It worried me so till I thought they would be better of dead and I thought I would rather they were dead than see them in such want and drudgery. So I Killed them. I have been teriblly Sorry that I did ever since, and I want to die now and go on to be with them.

I believe it is my duty to die for killing them. I never could want to live any longer with out them. Please every body for give me. Dear Father in Heaven please for give me all my sins, and please accept me as one of thy children I pray, in Jesus Name I pray. Amen.

JOSEPH **KALLINGER**

Born on December 11, 1936, Joseph Kallinger was abandoned by his mother and adopted at the age of eighteen months by a sadistic, moralistic Catholic couple who had emigrated from Austria. At the age of six he had a hernia operation; when he arrived home from the hospital his adoptive parents told him that the operation made his penis – his "bird" – stop growing. Taking this to heart, Kallinger believed from then on that his penis was abnormally small.

As a child, and later as an adult, Kallinger masturbated while stabbing pornographic photographs of breasts and penises. In 1957 and again in 1959 he was held for a short period of time in a psychiatric hospital; a doctor's report from the latter stay indicated

> . . . that he is in a state of tension, feeling rigid and being unable to face reality situations and master them. He projects onto the female figure his hostility, the sexual anxiety that he feels, and a need to hide his aggressiveness . . . when he becomes defensive, he responds with agitated, sadistic and emotional behavior. He appears to be developing agitation and anxiety in the sexual area and, if this loading becomes too strong, he will again repeat his sadistic response when he discharges this effect.

To the outside world, though, Kallinger was a respectable self-employed shoe repairman, married twice and father to seven children, who lived and worked at 2733 North Front Street in the Kensington district of Philadelphia, Pennsylvania.

Beginning in the early 1960s, however, his public persona began to slowly unravel: for instance, neighbors complained that Kallinger had set up a bowling alley in his bedroom where he practiced the sport at all hours of the night. He later told his biographer, Flora Schreiber, that he set fire to a building he owned three times, collecting a total of $41,000. As she recounts in her book *The Shoemaker*, Kallinger spoke in rapturous detail about his love for fire:

> "Oh, what ecstasy, Flora," he went on, "setting fires brings to my body! What power I feel at the thought of fire – all my treasures in total ruin. Oh, what mental images fire brings. Oh, what a pleasure, what heavenly pleasure!" (Here the expression on Joe's face was beatific; his eyes looked at me as if he were having a transcendental experience.) "I see the flames and no longer is fire just a

> daydream. It is the reality of heaven on earth! I love the excitement of the power fire gives me to burn up all that I own. This mental image is greater than sex. Oh, Flora, what a release, what bliss, what love, what . . . !" (At this moment, standing, Joe had an orgasm; a flush suffused his face, then he sat down on a chair, sweating and breathing heavily.)

On January 30, 1972, three of Kallinger's children – 13-year-old Mary Jo, 11-year-old Joey and 10-year-old Michael – filed a complaint with the police detailing a long history of abuse by their father; the "three total gods of my doom" (as Kallinger described them in his poem "Enraged," reproduced below) told police they had been whipped, burned, and beaten. Kallinger was convicted and served seven months in prison, but his sentence was later voided and cleared from the records after the children, under pressure from their father, recanted their story to the authorities. In May of 1974 Kallinger took out a $45,000 triple-indemnity insurance policy on his son Joey (who had initiated the charges); Joey's body was found three months later floating in a stagnant pool of water in the abandoned basement of a partially demolished novelty shop. Kallinger later confessed to Schreiber that he had drowned the boy on July 28, with his son Michael watching, when Joey was engrossed in singing the lyrics to his favorite song, "Seasons in the Sun." Kallinger's insurance company, suspicious of the child's death, refused to honor his claim.

Kallinger also confessed to his biographer that he and Michael had previously murdered a young boy, José Collazo, on July 7; they lured Collazo into an abandoned rug factory, stripped him naked, stuffed a sock into his mouth, and cut off his penis.

Beginning in late November of 1974, Kallinger and his 13-year-old son Michael committed four robberies in six weeks. They forced their way into the homes of women who were usually alone at the time, tied their victims up, sometimes sexually assaulted them, and left with their money and jewelry. On the afternoon of January 8, 1975, they invaded the Romaine family home at 124 Glenwood Avenue in Leonia, New Jersey, with Kallinger posing as a John Hancock insurance salesman. Twenty-eight-year-old Didi Romaine Wiseman was doing laundry with her 4-year-old son Bobby and keeping an eye on her 90-year-old bedridden grandmother; her mother Edwina was away taking care of some errands. Kallinger stripped the mother and son naked, tied the mother up, and left the child, frozen with fear, unbound. He was about to kill the grandmother when the doorbell rang. Meeting Didi's sister, 21-year-old Randi Romaine, at the door, Kallinger also stripped and tied her up. He thought of raping the two women, but decided against it when he discovered they were both menstruating. The doorbell rang again, and Kallinger admitted at gunpoint Edwina Romaine, Retta Romaine (Randi's twin sister), and Retta's boyfriend, Frank Welby. Shortly afterwards, leaving seven trussed-up people behind, Kallinger and his son were about to exit with their stolen goods when family friend Maria Fasching, a 21-year-old licensed nurse, came to the door. Exasperated, Kallinger tied her up and dragged her and Welby down into the basement. After playing with Welby's exposed genitals with a knife, Kallinger unexpectedly went over to Fasching and stabbed her five times in the throat and two times in her left breast, killing her almost instantly. Upstairs, Edwina Romaine heard Fasching's screams, managed to get loose, and ran from the house yelling for the police; Kallinger and Michael fled, and were arrested less than two weeks later.

Spotting his son at the police station after their arrest, Kallinger told the young boy, "If you tell them anything, I'll kill you." Michael never did talk to the police and, after serving a little over a year in an institution for boys, was released on probation and placed with foster parents. Prosecution psychiatrists examined Kallinger in the spring of 1976 and reported the following:

> He spoke in an exalted religious vein stating that he was called upon by God to preach religion. Under Amytal [commonly known as "truth serum"], he behaved

> bizarrely, referring to his father as God, that he was sent to earth, having been a butterfly, to settle in the body of Joseph Kallinger to be a shoemaker, that the heel bone was related to the brain, etc. . . . Of note were feelings of sexual and social inadequacy, excessive religiosity, denial, grandiosity, and sexual and aggressive acting out. His IQ was 89, with a verbal score of 94 and a performance score of 83.

Awaiting trial in jail, Kallinger also complained that he was being persecuted by a hallucinatory "double" and a vision of a floating head he called "Charlie"; to ward "Charlie" off, he placed fifty paper cups filled with water underneath his bed. According to a psychiatric article by Flora Schreiber and Dr. Silvano Arieti, "Multiple Murders of a Schizophrenic Patient: A Psychodynamic Interpretation," Kallinger was psychotic partially due to the trauma induced by his parents:

> The case of Joseph Kallinger is unusual because the schizophrenic symptoms led directly to horrible sadistic crimes and because a specific childhood incident became the origin both of the low self-esteem that is conducive to schizophrenia and the nature of the sadistic acts. The patient was filled with hostility, rage and vindictiveness because of what his adoptive parents alleged had been done to his sexual organ ("the bird").

Found guilty and sane on October 12, 1976, at Bergen County Courthouse in Hackensack, New Jersey, Kallinger was sentenced to life imprisonment three days later and was remanded to the State Correctional Institution at Huntingdon, Pennsylvania (S.C.I.H.). Transferred to Farview State Hospital on May 18, 1978, after stabbing and nearly killing another inmate, he went back to Huntingdon ten years later and in December of 1990 was sent to S.C.I. at Cresson, where he now resides.

In prison Kallinger writes his poetry and recently "adopted" a friendly prison correspondent from Texas, Janet Toal, as his "next of kin"; she wrote the following about his condition in a letter dated December 16, 1991:

> Joe is very difficult to deal with . . . his cell remains barren . . . everything is now contraband – he will consume papers – & is only allowed a small piece of pencil – for he will swallow it – if he gets a chance. . . . There are times when he appears to think fairly straight and other times when he is totally off the wall – as if he were totally drunk. He has been drinking and eating his feces and urine out of the commode, dipping it out with his hands – for about 8 months – every chance he gets. It keeps his hands raw – plus he smears it into his arms and lets it dry out and then peels the skin off. This is sick. Pain brings him pleasure . . . this feces talk is about to wear me out and yes he has it in his mind that people want to read about it and will be fascinated by what he is doing. . . . He sent me about 7 or 8 pounds of it earlier this year when his intestines were re-routed for several months. I demanded him to stop, in fact I don't know how it made it all the way to Texas, because it was one leaky mess. . . . Joe is very ill, now.

Poetry from 1977 to 1991; some misspellings from the early poems have been corrected by Flora Schreiber:

Odd Man

February 6, 1977
Camden

odd man at the trial
odd man all the while.
what journalist's eye
could write my fearful fright?

My Home

August 7, 1977
Camden

My home is my
castle and I pray
nothing evil will
ever come cross my door.

My Final Waking Bell

February 22, 1978
Huntingdon

As I rise this morning
I roll out of bed
to the noise of the food cart
being rolled on to the
head of the block,
the banging sound of the large
stainless steel lids
being taken off the trays,
being laid on top with a bang:
These sounds open my eyes
and as I look around
the guards march by
with three trays of food
for the men back in the main hole
of this prison,
and then I hear the clanging sounds
of each spoon being counted, each
being dropped against the stainless
steel tray: my final waking bell.

Prisoner in Court

March 3, 1978
Huntingdon

unable to speak
there was nothing;
all the symptoms
of madness were going on
as described by judge
and the newspapers,
who were there
and there was I
in my flowing movements

like a doll swimming
in a sea
of spleen and hatred
(back in my cell the guards
had beaten me, as always)
all watched and taunted and laughed
'cause my head was tilted down
my eyes weren't working right
and I could not speak
I could not speak

Past and Future

March 3, 1978
Huntingdon

Christmas, the time of year
that has the impact
of a childhood story
and the dreams of the future
all rolled into the present
that we give our loved ones.

Hard Wind

March 3, 1978
Huntingdon

The wind blew hard as I made my way
along the trail. My hat blew off
and blew across the grass until
it caught on a turtle who swore he was
caught by a human, then all swallowed
up in one gulp as he groped around
in the dark surrounded by the smell
of a human. A child saw the hat
and after picking it up saw
the turtle, and said, shaking his finger:
you naughty boy, you ate him all up.

A New Breath

June 5, 1978
Farview

When a child is born
it's a new breath
in an old world,
heart beat of young and old:
but it will never die,
for each new day is glory
when a child is born.

My Mind and You

June 8, 1978
Farview

My mind is chainless,
only you can bind it.
through my open window

pass odors of freedom.
the guard paces up
and down the corridor
outside my cell.
My body is in chains.
Brightness fills the air
this fall day.
for my mind is chainless
which only you can bind.

Last Reign — Rain

July 12, 1978
Farview

When I was king,
I made my rain
— but now my rain
is made by those
who carry keys
to walls and doors
of brick and steel
— and memories.

Secret Life

July 20, 1978
Farview

I discovered
a secret
of life
in a single line
of poetry.
that was a week ago.
today, I celebrate
a new week yet
have forgotten
what the secret was.
Oh, as life goes on,
I shall discover it
again in other lines
of poetry
that is, assuming
there is a secret.

The Evil Whisperings

August 20, 1978
Farview

The chilling voice from nowhere
came whispering out of the air;
as I listen, then open the door
and
I rushed into the parlor,
'cause anything was better than to stand
in the dim hallway and hear

the evil whisperings,
for I was in intense fear
and silence;
even the music held its breath

The Shadow Stand

August 28, 1979
Farview

I am a man whose whole shadow
is only as big as his head:
it lies at my feet and
acts as a stand to hold me up.

Downhill

August 31, 1982
Farview

When I was in the world
I had seven children,
A wife, and a business of
My own.
We were a comfortable family
Until —
One cannot pinpoint the moment
That I lost my mind;
It was not a day, a week, or
Even a year.
Life flames rising, the surges
Came, the invocations, the
Orders from the Devil, then
From God!
My determination grew
To destroy mankind and so fulfill
God's will, reach my apotheosis
And become God Himself!
The route was strewn with corpses,
Multitudes imagined, a few real.
The first reality was one of my own
Sons; after that I began to go steadily
Downhill, and no longer were we a comfortable
Family, or a family that was whole.

The Unicorn in the Garden

September 3, 1982
Farview

When I was a little boy,
My adoptive parents,
Anna and Stephen,
Killed the unicorn in my garden.
The nightingale died, too, and
The lilacs and roses perished.
I wanted to be an actor,
Playing with the unicorn in my garden,

But they said: "You will be a
Shoemaker, like your father,
Dummkopf! If you don't,
You will be a bum!"
So I grew up in my adoptive father's shop,
Hearing the cutting of leather,
Smelling the odor of glue,
My music the whirring of machines,
Idiot's delight.
Exiled from the street,
Isolated from other children,
I lived among shoes and knives and hammers.

Unknown, unwanted, unloved,
I learned to shape soles, replace heels, drive nails.
My own soul was hidden from me by the shop's
Dead world.
A robot to their will,
I died with the unicorn in my garden.

Chicken and Yellow

September 8, 1982
Farview

When I was a little boy
My adoptive mother always called me
chicken and yellow.
This was so because I would run from
Fights with other boys.
Yet she gave me no choice, for
When I would fight back
She beat me and so did my adoptive father.
They said I was ruining their business
Reputation.

So I was trapped; damned if I didn't fight
Back, damned if I did, and they were a team
Against me, a solid front, and I an outsider.
A boy growing up alone, not knowing which
Way to turn, I lived in rage, stored up
Hostility, and the festering hate made me ill.

Charlie

September 10, 1982
Farview

he's after me, riding air currents
like an angry balloon

floating, his long hair is parted in front
curled back at the sides. his mean brown eyes
stare at me, pin me to the wall
where i wriggle.

(i cannot free myself from charlie)

he has no body and below his eyes his faceless face is
just a tight tissue of skin wrapped around jawbones
rounding in a fleshy chin.

(i cannot free myself from charlie)

bodiless rider, he rides thunderbolts in Hell
with the Devil sings doom songs

through his mouthless face
then comes to me with bloody instructions
(his favorite word is **kill**)

but charlie is real, like you and me
someday i'm going to waste him
someday i'm going to kill him
someday i'm going to puncture him
with a knife
he'll shrivel like an airless balloon.

but maybe charlie's going to kill me first
at night i lie with one eye open

(i cannot free myself from charlie)

My Double

September 11, 1982
Farview

through a window of the ward
shines a sunray
my double and the woman,
death's dancers,
glide
through the motes of dust
sparkling on the shoulders
of his dark coat, on the blood
flowing from her belly.

from window to wall
they glide through the sunray
slowly
in time to the unheard music
of the knife in my double's hand
going in and out of the woman's
belly
her screams silent counterpoint to the
silent voice of the knife,
devilish music for an unredeemable.

my double looks like me

I look like him
but we are not each other
he is my fear and my master:

in the unheard music I hear
his command to kill, to pluck out
eyes, cut breasts, slice bellies,
testicles and penises, rip
vaginas.

he is the delegate of God
bringing the day of wrath
bringing the day of doom
to mankind
through me
(delegate of a delegate)
when I shall become the God of Glory.

Enraged

October 8, 1982
Farview

Hot anger has coursed through me
all my life,
I see it now,
I had not recognized the signs
before.
Anger, my biographer tells me,
began even before my birth
Not my anger then, but
that of my mother who
wished I had not been conceived.
My anger came when
at the age of one month
my mother gave me up,
turning me over to the care of
strangers; a private boarding home,
an orphanage
and then my adoption by a middle-aged
childless couple that kept reminding me
they were my benefactors.
They were also always threatening
to send me back to the orphanage.
Each time they did, my anger flamed,
but I held back the expression of it
when I could.
There were times that I couldn't:
times of beating my head against
the wall and running wild with rage.
I didn't fight other kids;
when I didn't, my adoptive mother
called me chicken and yellow;
but if I had, she would have

been angry
generating anger in me.
Anger turned like a water wheel;
my adoptive parents' anger feeding
mine and mine theirs.
I carried rage into manhood,
although when I first married,
I dreamed of normal life.
But things went sour and my wife,
angry for reasons of her own,
walked out on me after taking
up with another man.
I cannot know, but I believe
he had more sexual power than
I had to offer.
Once my wife was gone, my anger
grew and grew.
My second marriage led to angers
of its own,
culminating when my children,
the three total gods of my doom,
had me locked up.
In time my anger found an
outlet in what the world calls crime,
and to me was the command
of God, a vengeful,
wrathful God.
He was telling me I could
become God myself by destroy
us I had been destroyed.
My anger, hot and piercing,
had led to what I wish
I had not done.
And, despite God's promise
that I would become God,
I am not God today.
All I am is a mental patient
on leave from prison,
out of the world that fed my rage.

Life After Death

October 10, 1982
Farview

There is no Hell, but only a Heaven
After death, Hallelujah!
In Heaven there are no rewards:
Everyone is treated equally
(Some, of course, more equally than others)
(Even in Paradise there can be raw deals)
I come from Heaven
Heaven is where I'll go
When I die and from

Heaven I'll return to
This earth as
Another spirit
In a new born baby.
Hallelujah!
Other people have different
Thoughts about Heaven, Hell, and
Reincarnation.
How do I know
I'm right about
What I think?
It is not a matter of logic,
Or even of religious conviction.
It is thought that
Courses through me,
Flowing through my blood
Beating with my heart.
It is a thought that
has brought consolation in
Dark hours, in twisted times
And has remained firm
Through my forty-five years.
To Heaven I believed I would go
After my Divinely inspired
Mission had been accomplished,
And as God I ascended my Throne.

A New Day

October 11, 1982
Farview

In the darkness of night
I rise to begin my day.
Memories flow in the silence
Of yesterdays and tomorrows
Which are fading flowers,
Lilacs and royal roses,
Sprays of regret
For the might have been
And the never will be.

The Aged Eagle said:
All time is eternally present,
All time is unredeemable. So
the past is fixed and I am
Unredeemable.

On the ward I pace, in the
Cool silence feel the hot flush of
Memory: Footfalls echo in my memory
Down the hall I paced at home.
A shoemaker, I wanted all men to be
Fleetfooted,

For fleet of foot, their minds would be
Fleetfooted too.

Dawn breaks with sounds of trays and carts
Sizzling bacon for the unredeemables.
Between sips of coffee
I talk on the phone with
Angel Flora, saintly woman
Of my soul, I hear your
Voice and I feel the
Paradise of your presence
Around me, saving me, and
Listening to you I am
Redeemed not in time
But out of time, hearing you
A joy of endless moments
Out of time unredeemable,
Redeemed out of time
In the golden of your voice
Speaking of endless moments.

Higher, Mommy

June 27, 1985
Farview

Rockabye, baby, on the tree top
Rockabye, baby, on the tree top
Higher, Mommy, higher, higher,
Higher

Look, Mommy, there's an airplane
Higher, Mommy, I want to say hello
To the pilot

He's waving to me, Mommy,
So is everyone else on the plane
But one little girl in a
Mickey Mouse cap
Is sticking her tongue out at me

I wave back
We're coming closer to each other
The roar of the jets grows in my ears
The pilot dips a wing, I wave an arm
In greeting
I'm almost one with them now

Now higher I go, Mommy
And higher
Mommy
Always higher
My precious
Prickly rose

Mommy

Always higher

Now it's night, Mommy
and Mr. Moon is winking at me
I wink back

Mr. Moon says
"There's an autograph party
Tonight in the crater of Lucifer"
You're invited. All the lights
both bright and dim from publishing
Will be there, multitudes of
Extraterrestrials from the farthest
ramparts of the Universe will be
There to get your autograph on
The shoemaker.

I autograph until my wrist aches
My fingers are sore
And you are close to me Mommy
Autographing with all your might

Disappointments in My Life

October 10, 1988
Huntingdon

When I was a little child
I was put in an orphanage
for adoption, my first
disappointment. After I was
adopted my adoptive parents
never gave me any love
and were crule to me,
child abusers, my second
disappointment in my life.
I was never allowed to
play with other kids or have
friends in my adoptive parents
house all of my young life
with them, my third disappointment,
in my life. When I grew up and got
married and had children
she ran around with other men,
and never took care of our
children and finally left me
for another man and I had
to raise the children alone, my
fourth disappointment in my life.
Later when I remarried and
had more children, She was
childlike and always on the
fringes of everything. She didn't

love our children and never took
care of them and finally left me,
My fifth disappointment in my
life. After that I learned I was
severely mentally ill and it had
started already in childhood.
My sixth disappointment in my life.
From then on my life got increasingly
worse, I went on a six month
crime spree. I robbed and murdered
people, My seventh disappointment
in my life. Shortly after that I was
arrested and tried for my crimes
and sent to prison for the rest of my
live, My eighth disappointment in my
life. My whole life started out in
disappointment and ended in disappointment
disappointment is all I have to remember
for a lifetime.

Standing Firm

December 25, 1988
Huntingdon

Before the ending of the
age there will be signs
of famines and earthquakes
in various places and wars,
people will betray and lose
their faith and hate each
other, the love of most
will grow cold, but those
who stand firm to the
end will be saved, when
we see all these things,
we will know that it
is near, we must keep
our faith, because we
do not know on what
day our Lord will come,
we must be ready, because
The Son of Man will come
at an hour when we do
not expect him, we must
stand firm with our
Lord.

Dismal Voyage

July 1989
Huntingdon

When I was a child
My adoptive parents
Always threatened
To send me back

To the orphanage

Now an adult,
I have been remanded to prison
Having spent ten years
In a hospital for the criminally insane

The hospital personnel
Echo my adoptive parents' voices:
"We're sending you back."
But eminent psychiatrists
Had said that my psychosis is chronic
And I should always be in the hospital;
My lawyers worked hard to keep me there;
The Commonwealth and hospital lawyers
Worked hard to send me back.

So: a Judge proclaimed a stay:
I would remain where I was
They could not send me back
Until the Judge had made up his mind
What should be done with me.

By some hocuspocus of bureaucracy
I was well, no longer psychotic:
Suddenly one hot day in August,
Unprepared as I was for present and
Future shocks, two correction officers
Uniformed and sturdy without warning I
Was taken back to prison, defying the
Judge's stay.

Before the car of doom began its dismal
Voyage, the hospital's head psychiatrist
Knocked on a window of the car, "Joe, be
Sure to take your medicine," said he who
Had declared me well.

August 1989
Huntingdon

Solitary Confinement in Prison

here I sit in a cell all alone
solitary confinement for the
rest of my life in prison. the
only companions during the day
are cockroaches parading up and
down the walls of my cell during
the night I listen to the invasion
of mice and rats and watch in the
darkness their shadowy forms
skittering across the floor I
talk with no one I hallucinate

I hear voices which tell me to
kill other people and then myself
I see Charlie who always gives me
bloody instructions and I see my
double they are my only companions
solitary confinement the only
memories are Flora who came into
my life after I went to prison
she loves me and I made her my
mother she is all that keeps me
going every day now until I die
without her love for me I would
surely hang up and end my life
in solitary confinement my life
now

End-Time, Song

August 25, 1991
Cresson

I shall arise from the east to rule the world, – – – – –
for I am a Beast, – – – – they say!
a Man of sin, – – – – they say!
Yes! that's right, I am the Antichrist
The Antichrist,! – – – –
Yes! – I will be, your worlds Dictator:
who will rule this, Your Unaverse
as your Antichrist,! – – – – –
and during the, Great Tribulation, Period
I will enter into the new temple,
in Jerusalem, – – – –
and proclaim my self as your God
for I the Antichrist am God,! – – – –
and there will be put, – – – –
as I put in the New temple, – – – –
a statue of myself – – –
The Antichrist! – – – – –
God – – Your God – – I – the – Antichrist,!
for I then your God, – – – –
Will rule the World, – – – – – –
as your only God! – – –
and Dictator,! – – – –
for I am the Antichrist,! – – – –
The one and only true God,! – – – – –
I am,! – – – **& The Antichrist! of End-Time.**

JOHN LIST

In 1971, 46-year-old John List had what amounted to "the good life": a well-paying job as an accountant and insurance agent; esteemed positions as Boy Scout leader and Sunday school teacher at his Lutheran church; a beautiful eighteen-room mansion, "Breeze Knoll," in Westfield, New Jersey; and a family that he loved and cared for. His 84-year-old mother, Alma, kept mostly to herself in an apartment located at the top of the house; his wife, 46-year-old Helen, was an excellent cook (she owned over two hundred and fifty cookbooks) and a "Jeopardy" fan; his two sons, 15-year-old John Frederick and 13-year-old Frederick Michael, were doing well in school; and his pretty 16-year-old daughter, Patricia Marie, studied drama and was appearing in the local high school's theater productions.

But there was an unpleasant underside to this "Father Knows Best" existence, a growing catalog of anomalies that – partly due to his strict German-Lutheran fundamentalist upbringing – caused List's face to twitch and grow red and blotchy with rage. He realized he wasn't making enough money to support the mortgage payments on a mansion that was becoming weather-worn and shabby. His wife mixed her booze with her pills (scotch and Doriden was a favorite combination), and was becoming increasingly ill from a dose of syphilis she received from her first husband Marvin, a soldier killed in the Korean war who had slept around with the bar girls of Seoul. When drunk, she taunted List, contrasting his inadequacy in bed with the late Marvin's sexual prowess. The worst, however, was what he saw in his daughter Pat's behavior: in the summer of 1971 she announced to her friends and teachers that she was a witch, and after school would sit in her room and smoke pot, drink Boone's Farm Apple Wine, play acoustic guitar, and listen to Black Sabbath records. After she appeared as sexpot Stupefyin' Jones in her high school's production of the musical *Li'l Abner*, List drove his wife and daughter home with white-knuckled hands wrapped around the steering wheel, later screaming that they were both "sluts" who were going "straight to hell." He thought of Fred and John as good sons and he still loved his mother, but List concluded that they too would eventually be caught in the sea of degradation that the sixties represented to him.

List at first checked his anger by immersing himself in his work and his favorite hobby, military strategy board games; his favorite game was "Third Reich." He always played on the side of the Axis powers, and invariably beat his friends. He also rented a private mailbox where he received pornographic magazines. But on November 9, 1971, no longer able to contain his malevolent frustration, he methodically shot and killed all five members of his family with a 1912 Austrian Steyr 9-mm handgun he had bought while serving in World War II. He arranged an escape by informing employers, schools, friends, and neighbors that he was traveling with his family to visit relatives in North Carolina, and left notes of instruction (reproduced below) in his study. Nearly a month went by before Pat's drama teacher found most of the bodies, decaying and bloated, lined up on the mansion's ballroom floor, with the musical strains of Wagner's *Götterdämmerung* playing loudly on the stereo in the background.

List, in the meantime, drained his mother's savings account and flew to Denver, Colorado, where he created a new, yet quite similar, persona: Robert P. Clark, CPA. He remarried in 1985, moved to Richmond, Virginia, and continued to live his life as before: playing board games, jumping from job to job, always punctual. A fugitive for almost eighteen years, he was finally arrested on June 1, 1989, after the TV program "America's Most Wanted" broadcast a recreation of the murders and a commissioned bust of what authorities thought List looked like at the age of 64. The FBI received over 200 phone calls; one tip, from ex-neighbor Wanda Flannery, resulted in List's capture. He stubbornly maintained he was Robert Clark until a New Jersey jury judged him guilty of first-degree murder on April 12, 1990; two weeks later List was sentenced to life imprisonment. Judge William L. Wertheimer, himself a resident of Westfield, told the crowded courtroom before sentencing, "The defendant's name and his deeds in November 1971 have proven to be a specter that will not as easily be obliterated from the community's mind as they were from his own conscience. His acts stand as a permanent, pathetic, and profane example to the potential of man's inhumanity to man. They will not be soon or easily forgotten, and the name of John Emil List will be eternally synonymous with concepts of selfishness, horror, and evil."

Heading of his personalized stationery:

A Few words from John E. List — Career Builder, 55 Washington Street, Suite 209, East Orange, N.J. 07017. Tel: 676-4100

The following notes were found in List's office after the bodies were discovered:

Note on his stationery taped to his desk:

To the finder:
Number 1. Please contact the proper authorities.
Number 2. The key to this desk is in an envelope addressed to myself. The keys to the file are in the desk.
J. List.

Draft of a note sent to Westfield High School:

To the principal — Nov 9, 1971
Westfield High School

Our daughter Patricia is a student in the 11th grade at Westfield High.

She will be out a few days next week since we had to make an emergency trip to North Carolina. We left after the school was closed so I'm sending this letter to you to explain her absence.

John E. List
431 Hillside Ave.
Westfield.

Draft of a note sent to another school:

Roosevelt Junior High

Our sons John and Fred, 9th and 8th grades, attend Roosevelt. They will be out for several days as we had to make an emergency trip to N.C. This happened after the school was closed.

John E. List
431 Hillside Ave.
Westfield

Draft of a note sent to a real-estate company that employed his children Patricia and Frederick part-time:

KVM Associates
Mrs. Dawson,
Patricia and Frederick will be absent for several days as we had to make an emergency trip to NC (North Carolina) during the night. I'm sorry for the inconvenience.

John E. List

Note on his stationery to his boss, Burton Goldstein of State Mutual Assurance Company of America:

Hello Burt,

I'm sorry that it all had to end this way but with so little income I just couldn't go on keeping the family together. And I didn't want them to experience poverty.

I want to thank you for everything that you did for me. You treated me better than any associate I've ever dealt with and I'm sorry that I have to repay you this way.

The files are marked so that they can be turned over to you.

Maybe Paul Greenberg can follow up on some.

The best prospects for a quick sale are:

Douglas Moe
Edward Varga
Odendahl

Also be sure to contact Charles Jacobson CPA. I worked with him on the Swokenden thing and that worked real good.

Also don't fail to follow up with Harvey. He may be just about ready.

Best wishes,
John

Note to his mother-in-law, Mrs. Eva Morris:

Mrs. Morris

By now you no doubt know what has happened to Helen and the children. I'm very sorry that it had to happen. But because of a number of reasons I couldn't see any other solution.

I just couldn't support them anymore and I didn't want them to go into poverty. Also, at this time I know that they were all Christians. I couldn't be sure of that in the future as the children grow up.

Pastor Rehwinkel may add a few more thoughts.

With my sincere sympathy,

John E. List

Note to his mother's sister:

Mrs. Lydia Meyer

By now you no doubt know what has happened to Mother and the rest of the family. For a number of reasons this was the only solution that I could see for the family. And to save Mother untold anguish over that result I felt it best that she be relieved from this vale of tears.

Please accept my sincere condolences.

John

Note to his wife's sister:

Mrs. Jean Syfert

By now you have heard of what happened to Helen and the children. I'm sorry that it had to go that way but when I couldn't support them I couldn't let them go on welfare etc.

Please accept my sincere sympathy.

John

Five-page letter to his pastor, Reverend Eugene Rehwinkel of the Redeemer Lutheran Church:

Nov. 9, 1971

Dear Pastor Rehwinkel,

I'm very sorry to add this additional burden to your work. I know that what has been done is wrong from all that I have been taught and that any reasons that I might give will not make it right. But you are the one person that I know that while not condoning this will at least possibly understand why I felt that I had to do this.

1. I wasn't earning anywhere near enough to support us. Everything I tried seemed to fall to pieces. True we could have gone bankrupt and maybe gone on welfare.

2. But that brings me to my next point. Knowing the type of location that one would have to live in plus the environment for the children plus the effect on them knowing they were on welfare was just more than I thought they could & should endure. I know that they were willing to cut back but this involved a lot more than that.

3. With Pat being so determined to get into acting I was also fearful as to what this might do to her continuing to be a Christian. I'm sure it wouldn't have helped.

4. Also, with Helen not going to church I knew that this would harm the children eventually in their attendance. I had continued to hope that she would begin to come to church soon. But when I mentioned to her that Mr. Jutzi wanted to pay her an Elders call, she just blew up (This is not a criticism of Ed) & stated that she wanted her name taken off the church rolls. Again this could only have given an adverse result for the children's continued attendance.

So that is the sum of it. If any one of these had been the condition we might have pulled through but this was just too much. At least I'm certain that all have gone to heaven now. If things had gone on who knows if that would be the case.

Of course Mother got involved because doing what I did to my family would have been a tremendous shock to her at this age. Therefore, knowing that she is also a Christian I felt it best that she be relieved of the troubles of this world that would have hit her.

After it was all over I said some prayers for them all — from the hymn book. That was the least I could do.

Now for the final arrangements:

Helen & the children have all agreed that they would prefer to be cremated. Please see to it that the costs are kept low.

For Mother, she has a plot at the Frankenmuth Church cemetary. Please contact

Mr. Herman Schellhas
Rt 4
Vassar, Mich. 41768.

He's married to a niece of Mothers & knows what arrangements are to be made. (She always wanted Rev. Herman Zehnder of Bay City to preach the sermon. But he's not well.)

Also I'm leaving some letters in your care. Please send them on & add whatever comments you think appropriate. The relationships are as follows:

Mrs. Lydia Meyer — Mothers sister
Mrs. Eva Morris — Helens mother
Jean ~~& Gene~~ Syfert — Helens sister
~~Fred & Clara~~
~~Marie~~

Also I don't know what will happen to the books & other personal things. But to the extent possible I'd like for them to be distributed as you see fit. Some books might go in to the school or church library.

Originally I had planned for this Nov 1 — All Saints Day. But travel arrangements were delayed. I thought it would be an appropriate day for them to get to heaven.

As for me please let me be dropped from the congregation rolls. I leave my-self in the hand of Gods **Justice** & **Mercy.** I don't doubt that he is able to help us, but apperently he saw fit not to answer my prayers they way I had hoped that they would be answered. This makes me think that perhaps it was for the best as far as the childrens souls/are concerned. I know that many will only look at the additional years that they could have lived but if finally they were no longer Christians what would be gained.

Also, I'm sure many will say "How could anyone do such a horrible thing." — My only answer is it isn't easy and was only done after much thought.

Pastor Mrs. Morris may possibly be reached at
802 Pleasant Hill Dr
Elkin — Home of her sister.

One other thing. It may seem cowardly to have always shot from behind, but I didn't want any of them to know even at the last second that I had to do this to them.

John got hurt more because he seemed to struggle longer. The rest were immediately out of pain. John ~~probably~~ didn't consciously feel anything either.

Please remember me in your prayers. I will need them whether or not the government does its duty as it sees it. I'm only concerned with making my peace with God & of this I am assured because of Christ dying even for me.

P.S. Mother is in the hallway in the attic — 3rd floor. She was too heavy to move.

John.

PATRICK **MACKAY**

Before he was even born, Patrick Mackay was subject to abuse; he was in his mother's womb when she was kicked in the stomach by her husband in a drunken rage. Born on September 25, 1952 in Middlesex, England, he was institutionalized for the first of many times at the age of thirteen after trying to set fire to a Catholic church. By the age of fifteen Mackay's life was a litany of aberrational misdeeds that included roasting his pet tortoise alive, playing with dead birds, nearly killing a young boy in his neighborhood, and attempting to strangle his mother and aunt. A Home Office psychiatrist, Dr. Leonard Carr, knew from Mackay's record that he was "explosive in temper" and, deducing that he would evolve into "a cold, psychopathic killer," had him committed as a certified psychopath to Moss Side Hospital for four years. In their book *Psychopath*, authors Tim Clark and John Penycate recount that while he was awaiting transfer to Moss Side,

> Mackay adopted a bizarre name by which he demanded to be known: Franklin Bollvolt the First – "a name to be feared and remembered, like Hitler's." The world, he decided, needed a change, and he would be the world figure to provide it.

Against the advice of his psychiatrists, the Liverpool Mental Health Review Tribunal released Mackay in the summer of 1972. Mackay, usually in a drunken or drugged stupor, stayed with friends and entertained himself by building and burning the eyes out of Frankenstein monster models. He decorated his bedroom with photographs from Nazi Germany and fashioned for himself a quasi-German SS uniform, replete with lapel badges and armband; occasionally Mackay mugged for photo booth snapshots in this homemade outfit.

Proving the psychiatrists right, Mackay murdered eleven people from July 1973 until his arrest on March 23, 1975. He threw a hobo from a bridge and an au pair girl from a train, strangled and knifed an 84-year-old woman, stabbed to death a woman and her 4-year-old grandson, beat a 62-year-old tobacconist with a lead pipe, killed a café proprietress with an axe, and pummeled a 92-year-old woman to death for her £5 Christmas bonus. His last victim was Father Anthony Crean, a 63-year-old Catholic priest that had befriended Mackay. He confessed to police after being captured:

> I grabbed hold of him by his arm, I think the right one, and we both fell on the floor in the hallway. I struggled and he struggled on the floor and he

> seemed to get extremely nervy. He said, "Don't hurt me." This seemed to get me even more excitable myself, and then I started to strike him on the side of the head with my hand and with my fist. The next thing I knew he had broken loose from my grip and ran into the bathroom which is just off the hallway. Whilst I had been on the floor of the hallway myself, I picked up an axe from a box lying just under the stairs and began to feel even more excitable.
>
> He shut the bathroom door and pushed to hold it closed. I barged my side of the door and this pushed him towards the bath. He tumbled and half fell into the bath. I threw down the axe on to the floor and pushed him into the bath. He then started to annoy me even more, and I kept striking at his nose with my arm and the side of my hand. I then pulled out my knife from my coat pocket and repeatedly plunged it into his neck. I then got a little more excitable and stuck it into the side of his head, and then tried to plunge it into the top of his head. This bent the knife. I grabbed for the axe and with this repeatedly lashed out with it at his head. He sank into the bath. He had been in the sitting-up position with the knife but when I first hit him with the axe he sank down into the bath. I then repeatedly got increasingly more annoyed, and lashed at him with the axe. All this seemed to happen very fast. . . . I must have gone out of my mind. It was something in me that just exploded.

The authors of *Psychopath* noted that "the wounds in Father Crean's head were so devastating that his brain was exposed; before he died he raised his hand feebly and touched the exposed portion." Mackay was arrested two days later and sentenced to life in prison.

Prison journal excerpts from the fall of 1975:

September 25: Up until his death my father used to get violently drunk, shout, scream and always when he was like this beat me with the back of his hand and sometimes his fist. He must have had a tremendous

drinking problem, but of course he would never say so. I remember that my father never at all hit my two sisters when drunk, but only me and my mother. He would make a lot of filthy accusations towards her. This would take place usually Friday nights and Saturday nights. It was plain bloody regular.

October 3: I feel terrible about what happened all the more because I do not know why or what made me do it. I find it all a confusing matter. You see, I'm scared of myself. At times I often try to wonder why, but it's just plain hell. . . . Everyone with the experience I had of mishandling and brutality of the homes, remand homes, approved schools, reception centres and any other bloody place will know that the general attitude prevalent in the early and middle 1960s was vastly against the person concerned. Namely, if his or her family had no backing to speak of — such as I for instance, just a widowed mother and a very young sister — the young persons could be manipulated like a ruddy puppet on a string from pillar to post. Had I a father they would never have stood a bloody chance in Hades of manipulating me in this way. But then come to that it would never have taken place.

October 27: In Moss Side I was classified as a psychopath but without mania. I have always believed that I have not just the problem of being psychopathic on its own, but instead having psychopathic mania. This has always been my personal opinion on the matter, and believe no one to judge one's mind better in most cases than oneself. Since the mind is such a complex machine. . . . When I was eventually discharged, I can say that, despite the sudden step to the outside community as a whole, I had at the time only the best intentions in the living of my life. But one cannot unfortunately always foresee the certain type of stigmas that can form and come to be for some people in such an imperfect world as this.

November 2: She was not a bad soul, and why I killed her I feel I may never know. I suppose that even though I had killed her, I wanted in death to make her comfortable as she lay on her kitchen floor. I closed her eyes as they were staring lifeless up, covered her as if in a sleeping bag and left her there. . . . These murders were so solemn when I think of them, yet so quick, so fast to take place. You know, a man who has killed cannot really say much more than the basics from his point of view as he remembers it. In my case, for instance, I became very cocky about a few things that happened. . . . It has been said that I must have closed all the curtains in the homes of my victims as they say. This may well be possible. I have never disputed it. But I cannot say this with any certainty for I just do not recall so doing. There is a hell of a lot from the point of view of these killings that I cannot myself remember.

November 7: I shan't shed a tear. Life is full of shocks of all descriptions and they have to be faced. I am now informed that my trial will be later this month. So I await my destiny. I hope from this writing someone somewhere, wherever it may be read, will pick up some good from my experiences. I am just one example of many bad ones. But who can say totally so?

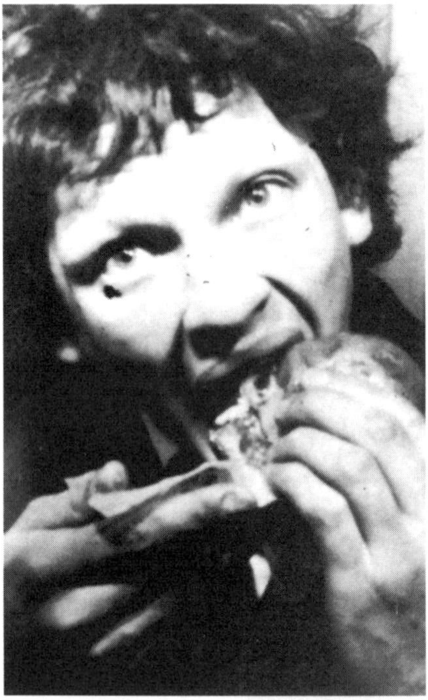
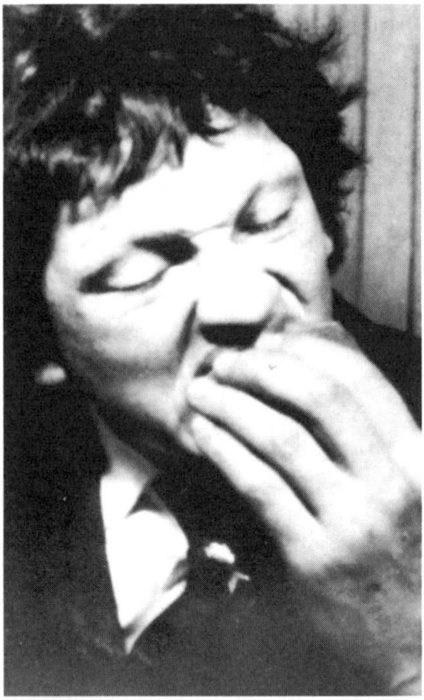

HERBERT MULLIN

Born in Salinas, California, on April 18, 1947, Herbert William Mullin grew up to be a fairly well-adjusted young man. As a child living in San Francisco and then Santa Cruz, Mullin excelled as a Boy Scout, went to Catholic Church on Sundays, and played Little League baseball. After graduating from high school, he earned an associate of science degree in Highway Engineering from Cabrillo College and attended philosophy, music, and astronomy classes at San Jose State College. In 1968, after the death of a close friend in an automobile accident, Mullin's behavior began to change in a counter-cultural sort of way: he started smoking pot and dropping acid (he was arrested once for marijuana possession and received probation), and avoided the war in Vietnam by becoming a conscientious objector and managing a Goodwill thrift store in San Luis Obispo.

Mullin's first symptoms of mental illness appeared during a family dinner for his parents' twenty-ninth wedding anniversary. While sitting at the dinner table he persistently imitated the gestures and speech of his brother-in-law Al. His mother later said, "I just remember it was such a shocking thing – that he wasn't himself. He was like a vegetable, imitating everything Al did." Mullin was convinced by his family to voluntarily admit himself into the Mendocino State Hospital on March 30, 1969, and stayed for a little over a month. The diagnosis from the doctors was "schizophrenic reaction, manifested by distortions of associations and affect, hallucinations, echolalia [an automatic verbal repetition of words or phrases], echopraxia [the automatic imitation of movements made by another], and general deterioration."

Mullin then worked as a dishwasher for a few months, and on October 31 was involuntarily committed to the psychiatric ward of San Luis Obispo County Hospital. The hospital report stated, "as a result of mental disorder, said person is a danger to others, a danger to himself, and gravely disabled." On November 24 he was transferred on an outpatient basis to Santa Cruz Health Clinic. Against his parents' wishes he flew to Hawaii on June 25, 1970, and almost immediately admitted himself into a mental health clinic on Maui. After flying back to California on July 23, he was arrested ten days later for being "under the influence of drugs." The police subsequently determined that he was in fact displaying schizophrenic symptoms; Mullin was committed to Santa Cruz General Hospital and discharged on August 15. At this point he was taking medication on a semi-permanent basis and, attempting to start his life over again, worked in Santa Cruz for a while driving a Goodwill truck. On May 31, 1972, Mullin moved to San Francisco, where he enjoyed his summer learning how to box, writing letters, and reading until he was evicted from his cheap hotel room on September 15. Mullin moved back to Santa Cruz and soon after stopped taking his medication. He started hearing messages in his head spoken in his father's voice saying, "Why won't you give me anything? Go kill somebody – move!"

Mullin believed it was time to "sing the die song"; by killing a few people he thought he would save thousands more from earthquakes and tidal waves. As he later told the jury at his trial,

> I, Herb Mullin, born April 18, 1947, was chosen as the designated leader of my generation by Professor Dr. Albert Einstein on April 18, 1955. . . . His hope probably was that the April 18th people would use his designation and its resulting power and social influence to guide, protect, or perfect the resources of our planet and universe. . . . One man consenting to be murdered protects the millions of other human beings living in the cataclysmic earthquake/tidal area. For this reason, the designated hero/leader and associates have the responsibilities of getting enough people to commit suicide and/or consent to being murdered every day.

Mullin elaborated on his theory for psychiatrist and author Donald T. Lunde:

> You see, the thing is, people get together, say, in the White House. People like to sing the die song, you know, people like to sing the die song. If I am president of my class when I graduate from high school, I can tell two, possibly three young male Homo sapiens to die. I can sing that song to them and they'll have to kill themselves or be killed – an automobile accident, a knifing, a gunshot wound. You ask me why this is? And I say, well, they have to do that in order to protect the ground from an earthquake, because all of the other people in the community had been dying all year long, and my class, we have to chip in so to speak to the darkness, we have to die also. And people would rather sing the die song than murder.

His four-month murder spree claimed thirteen victims, beginning on the morning of October 13, 1972, when Mullin murdered 55-year-old hobo Lawrence "Whitey" White on Highway 9 outside Santa Cruz by bashing in his skull with a baseball bat. Early in the afternoon of October 24 he picked up 24-year-old Mary Guilfoyle, a Cabrillo College student hitchhiking to a job interview, in his '58 Chevy station wagon and stabbed her once in the chest and twice in the back with a hunting knife. He then dragged her into the brush by the side of the road and disemboweled her corpse. Eight days later Mullin walked into a confessional at the St. Mary's Catholic Church in Los Gatos and stabbed to death 65-year-old Father Henri Tomei, a French citizen who was a hero of the Resistance in World War II and a former musical director of the Archdiocese of Marseilles. The French Consul's office and Mayor Joseph Alioto of San Francisco attended his funeral.

In the midst of his violent four-month recitation of "the die song," Mullin applied for service in the United States Marine Corps on January 14, 1973. Staff Sergeant Robert Eaton of the Santa Cruz recruitment office wrote in his report:

> Herbert William Mullin is an intelligent and highly motivated young man, with an ultrazealous eagerness to enlist in the USMC. . . . Because of Herb's earnest desire to improve his lot and climb above his peers, as it were, I submit that Herbert William Mullin can, and most likely will, be a benefit to whatever unit he is assigned and a credit to the corps.

The recruiting office in Oakland did not share Eaton's enthusiasm due to Mullin's mental health and arrest record, and sent Mullin a notice stating: "Enlistment is not authorized."

On the morning of January 25, 1973, Mullin murdered five people in a remote area of the Santa Cruz mountains; police initially thought the "hippy massacre" was the result of a drug burn. After entering the home of a former high-school acquaintance, drug dealer Jim Gianera, Mullin methodically shot the man four times as he was running to protect his wife. He then shot and stabbed Gianera's wife

Joan while she was showering. After he reloaded his gun Mullin drove a short distance to Gianera's former residence, walked through the front door, and shot 29-year-old mother Kathy Francis in the chest and head, her 4-year-old son Daemon in the left eye, and 9-year-old David in the forehead as they were playing Chinese checkers and having breakfast. He then walked over and stabbed each of their bodies once for good measure.

Wandering through the Cowell State Park, Mullin came across a makeshift cabin near Ox Road Trail on February 9. The next morning he returned and shot four young men – 15-year-old Mark Dreibelbis, 18-year-old Robert Spector, 19-year-old Brian Card, and 18-year-old David Oliker – in the head at close range while they pleaded for their lives. Their bodies were found by Card's brother Jeffrey a week later. Early in the morning of February 13, Mullin shot his final victim, 72-year-old Santa Cruz resident Fred Perez, while the old man was gardening in his front yard. The sniping was witnessed by neighbors, and Mullin was arrested driving away from the scene of the murder.

In prison police found numerous tattoos on Mullin's body: "LEGALIZE ACID" on his stomach, "Eagle Eyes Marijuana" above his groin, "Kriya Yoga" on his left ankle, and "birth," "Mahashamadhi," and two crosses on his left forearm.

When his trial began on July 30, 1973, the psychiatrists for both prosecution and defense teams agreed that Mullin was a definitive paranoid schizophrenic, but the prosecution's doctors thought he was "sane by legal standards." The jury agreed with the doctors, finding Mullin guilty on August 19 of ten counts of first and second-degree murder. Sentenced to life imprisonment on September 18, he will be eligible for parole in the year 2020.

Lyrics to a song written before the murders:

The Switcheroo

He showed me everything, but I didn't see.
He knew I didn't see, and he told me not to look.
He wasn't very gentle, he wasn't very kind,
And when he wants something, he's really, really mine . . .
You're scared too, I guess,
So you light up like a horny puss,
But it probably ain't true . . .
I NEED you too, I don't know why.
It was always there, but never really jelled . . .
So it's high, high, high, singing glory on the wind,
Yes it's true in glory land, they're coming through and
through,
One time only friend, happened to me too . . .
The quirk is so true, when my time is all through, the
only survivor will be,
No, not him, and not me . . .

Letters to his parents; the first is from April 1968:

Bill and Jean,

As I have mentioned in the past, someday I would meet the establishment head-on. I was arrested on April 21, '68. That day the GAME started. I requested and was appointed a public defender. I have yet to speak with him.

The charges against me are (a) camping by the SL River; (b) possession of paraphernalia used for smoking a narcotic; (c) possession of a restricted dangerous drug without a prescription. The trial is set for May 16, 10 A.M.

As I have tried to explain, I am a student of eastern thought. But, because I was baptized a Roman Catholic, I have the gift of Christianity.

Both these philosophies agree that all things of the body and senses, and all states and activities of the mind are merely phenomena, temporary playthings.

My present imprisonment is, in an eternal sense, self-induced. A necessary event in this body's wave (birth to death). Remember the ocean. A wave is the ocean and the ocean is the wave.

Your earthly son, Herb.

September 28, 1970:

Dear Dad,

I have some thoughts on my mind, and I'd like to express them to you.

My friends are working with their parents. I don't think you and I have worked with and for each other for a long time.

My conscientious objection thing was against your will. Well, that is past now. I don't know who was right or who was wrong. All I know is that I got hurt real bad because of all the confusion.

Would you let me live in your home again?

Love, Herb.

From 1971:

To Jean and Bill:

I have made a mistake in sending you the life insurance policy . . . I would appreciate it if you would immediately send the policy to the Donnelly Hotel, 1272 Market St., San Francisco, California, c/o Herbert Mullin. I will be able to pick it up there.

Please don't bother me with letters. I AM CERTAIN WE SHOULD NOT COMMUNICATE WITH EACH OTHER FOR A LONG TIME.

Respectfully, HERBERT MULLIN.

June 1972:

Dear Mom and Dad and Grandma,

Hi, how are you? Thank you very much for such a nice time this past weekend. I really enjoyed seeing and talking with you. The food was just great, and I do so enjoy the mountains. The weather here in San Francisco is just fine. Foggy in the evenings but sunny and warm during the mornings and afternoons.

Again, thank you for such a pleasant weekend. We'll have to do it again someday.

Love, Herb

March 16, 1973, following his arraignment for murder:

Dear Dad and Mom,

As you know I appeared in Santa Cruz Superior Court today. My attorney waived formal reading of the indictment. We asked for an extension until the Grand Jury's investigation is typed and we have a copy of it. My next day in court will be March 27th, 1973. I will enter a plea at that time.

I appreciate your willingness to attend the trial proceedings, but the reporters and spectators are so cruel, and I wouldn't get to visit you before the trial or after. I hope you agree with me that the attorneys can inform you about what's going on without having to subject you to the cameras and questions.

I hope the trial won't take too long. I don't like our name being used under such circumstances.

Thank you.

Good-bye.

Herbert William.

Two months after his arrest he wrote:

When I was five years old I feel intuitively that Bernice and Enos Fouratt talked my parents into ignoring me. My parents actually did not tell me the necessary facts of life, sex and death rate, social conversation techniques, etc. Bernice and Enos did not have any children.

Why did Bernice and Enos convince my parents that I should be shunned? My guess is that my cousins and sister were having orgasms at age six. When I was five Bernice and Enos wanted to stop my mental and physical growth. They did not want me to mature.

Why?

. . . I think they were jealous and envious of the fun and I and my parents were going to have when I started to grow up normal. I think they believe in reincarnation and that by confusing and retarding me they might improve themselves in their next life.

I believe my father has been unequally blamed for my failures. But surely, if he had given me the six-year-old homosexual "blow job" oral stimulation that I was entitled to, like most other people get, I would never had taken LSD without his permission.

When I was in the second grade they told me that Jesus Christ, the person, actually lives in the Holy Eucharist. I chose to believe them then; I choose not to believe them now. It is a lie, designed to induce naivete and gullibility in young children. Thereby making them suseseptible to receive and carry out telepathic subconscious suicide orders. . . . One day I took a knife and cut a wood bench. . . . I felt ignored and frustrated. . . . My parents and teachers tried to retard me. . . . I feel as if their is a conspiracy against me. I've told my parents this and they say I'm crazy and imagining it. I don't know what to do about this situation. Mental cruelty is certainly present. Can I sue my parents? Actually I feel like killing the people responsible. They think by practicing killjoyism on me they will trade consciousness with me in the next universal life time.

Excerpt from a list of questions and answers he composed to be asked at the trial:

Mr. Mullin, why did you threaten to kill anyone who helped Herbert mature correctly?

Ans. I believe that Bill was afraid that Herbert would improve mentally, physically and spiritually if people helped him mature. Bill said — I will kill you on the next in-on-it [next life] if you help Herbert.

Statement found by the police among his personal papers:

Let it be known to the nations of the earth and the people that inhabit it, this document carries more power than any other written before. Such a tragedy as what has happened should not have happened and because of this action which I take of my own free will I am making it possible to occur again. For while I can be here I must guide and protect my dynasty.

Prison poetry from 1990 to 1991:

> My poems are discriptive of the beauty I perceive in the natural world around me —.
> I believe that they are beneficial indications that I am a new, healthy and worthwhile person —.
> I am truthfully sorry for the crimes I have committed —. I ask for forgiveness —.
>
> February 25, 1991

A Series of Scenes

10/19/90

Moths at night came fluttering through the valley so fair —
Beautifull Justine, with her three dream look-alike girlfriends —
The ruff autumn season is felt as the temperature gets colder —
Wind, now, is pushing clouds that look like Doctor Storm-Maker is sending out look-outs and scouts to survey the landscape in preparation for a "wet abundance" winter which is to follow ——.

I saw the new moon of August occult Antares, Scorpius Alpha —
I saw the new moon of September occult the bottom star of the web near Antares, yet west ——.

I saw the mighty pair of red tail hawks come laughing in the sunset just three hours after the 50-50 seagulls & crows intermingled in the westward movement ——.

— Moon Sun Auras —

On the 20th, 21st, and 22nd
of February, 1991 —
There was a solar aura
around the sun in the
early and late
afternoons ——

On the 21st and 22nd
there was a lunar aura
around the $1/2$ moon —

On the 22nd the circle
of the lunar aura
surrounded Cappella,
Taurus Alderbersun,
Lugg-Zeus-Jupitier,
Bettlejuz Orioh,
As the moon $1/2$ sat near
the Auriga El Natl —

Winning the years of your life
Listening to the music of the
celestial spheres —
The moisture accentuates the
process of enjoying knowing nature!

x x x x x x x x

GOD BLESS THE SUN

GOD BLESS THE EARTH

GOD BLESS THE MOON

IN GOD WE TRUST

GOD BLESS AMERICA

GOD BLESS CALIFORNIA

GOD BLESS US AND OURS

x x x x x x x x x

ETERNAL LIFE FOR THE
Homo sapien sapien species

ETERNAL LIFE FOR MANKIND

100% PERFECT HEALTH FOR
the SOLAR GLOBE——.

DECEMBER 31ST, 1990 – 4:40 p.m.

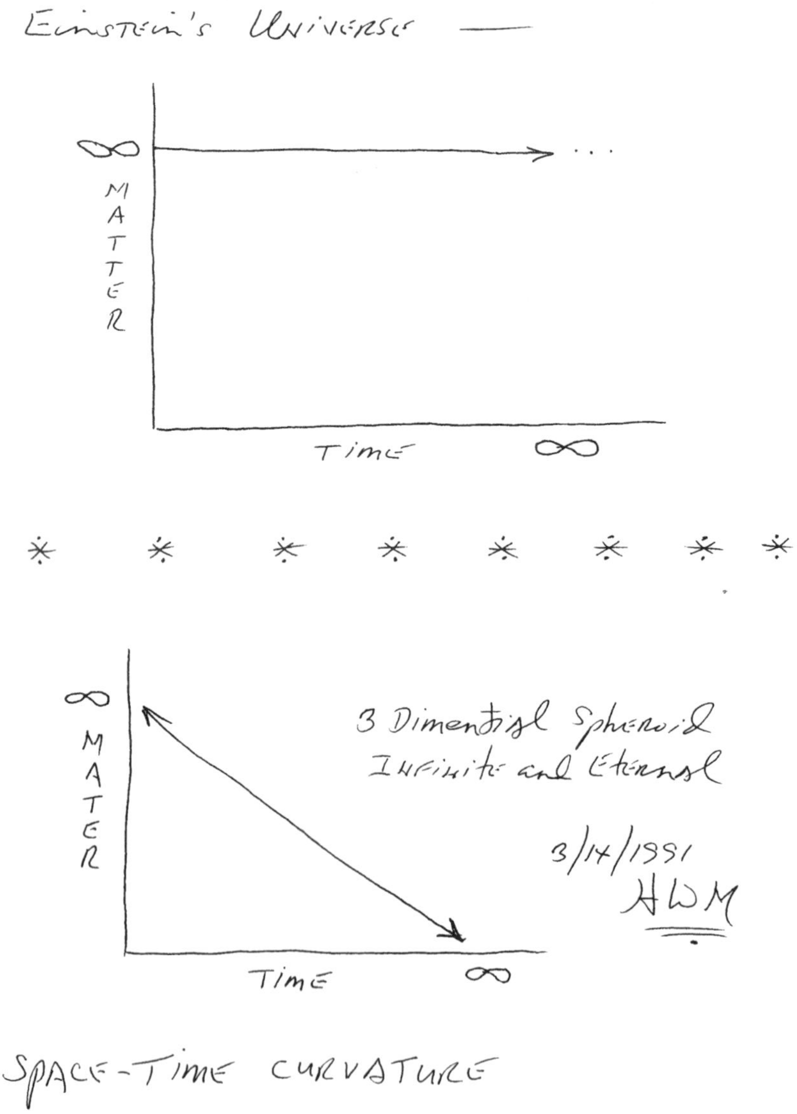
Einstein's Universe —
∞
MATTER
TIME
∞
∞
MATER
TIME
∞
3 Dimential Spheroid
Infinite and Eternal
3/14/1991
HWM
SPACE-TIME CURVATURE

Discriptions

24 Hrs

6/1991

1991

29th & 30th

6/30/1991 ——

Male House Sparrow eats the Bug
Hot Wind Blows the Little Bird
Backwards while facing the wind
for 40 feet ——
Bug Tumbles —
Sunrise Blessings ——— .

Male House Sparrow Rides the Floating white Feather at Turtle Tooth Background scenery — ♉⊕ & ☉♊ ideation — ☉set Geological Shadow philosophy —— .

Male House Sparrow eats the peanut — eats another peanut — mouthing & mouthing — then really eats a small white moth — white five fly moth — little ten ant white moth —— .

6/30/1991

Los Padres Valley Esoteric Wisdom
Geological Philosophical Riddle
Conundrums —.

1. Hokan Chumash Nahuat'l Anaconda Mine Koan
"wish coming out was as easy
as going in" —.
Pyramid of Power

2. Turtle Tooth Breeching Whale Shadow Thought
I☉I ♉ Chumash ☉set wisdom
6/30/1991 —
Earth orbits sun —
sun sets in II Gemini
Earth follows/orbits sun
Earth in Taurus
i.e. I☉I ♉ @ ☉set
Turtle Tooth Shadow Thought —

3. 

2+88 to 89+1
2/88 — 89/1

Moon Cloud
verification

The Greatest Bishops Mitre

March 1st, 1991 —— Friday ——.

Twigg-Mars in Taurus — coming from the pleidies as of January 1st — at the close of retrograde motion —. With two months of traveling as a planet should, against the flow of the celestial star bodies, moving now east against the westward flow ——.

Auriga, the chariotteer, with young Goat Star the Discriber in his arms; Auriga the pontiff symbol of all pontiff symbols —

Twigg-Mars is centered in the head of the Celestial Bishop ——

One night, the first time I saw the symbol, perfect it its form ——

It is a hypothesis, it is a proposition, that we are people trying to win the honors of being "king for a day" so to speak in the game of being beings here on earth ——

Who was the man who one
the March 1st, 1991,
Twiggs position honor?

Is he my ally
Is he my competitor
I think he is a symbiotic
creature of the spirit world!

H.W.M.
3/4/1991

Easter Weekend — 1991

Full Moon on the 29th of March —
Looked real full on the 30th too!!
Friday and Saturday of Easter —.

Saturday afternoon — the hour before and the hour after — I researched the phenomena of "magnetic dip" and "dip circle" ——. The angle between the direction of the earth's magnetic field and the horizontal —. For example, the angle through which a magnetic needle will "dip" from the horizontal when suspended free to swing in a vertical plane in the magnetic meridian —.

Sensitive instruments can really detect the magnetic field force ——. The left and right cerebral hemispheres when lined up on either side of the N-S meridian probably feel as if you're looking down at a book that's explaining it — ha, ha —.

Sunday —. 10-11 A.M. Phrenology with Albert Einstein and April 18th, 1955 ——. Syncronized congruent and coincidental —.

Jet Circler —

4/18/1991

In the early morning hours
a large four engine

military jet circled
around and around
the turtle tooth granite peak —

Five mile diameter
six complete circles
Jet Circler bid me
a very happy birthday — ha, ha!!

Thursday morning
Cool Spring Air

— Look Alike Looking Glass —

Look Alike Looking Glass
High Glass
Low Glass
High Class
Low Class
It is tied to sun worship
Look Alike Looking Glass

4/17/91

Auriga, the Charioteer —

The Bishop's Mitre —

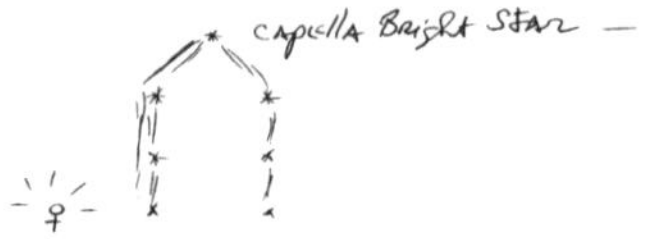

5/3/1991
Friday

Bridget Venus Aphrodite
has risen to speak
eye to eye to the
Bishop of Heaven —

That's the King for a Day
Blessing of Astronomy Award —

Who one — ?

— Astrological Musing —

Venus is now entering the powerfull
constellation of Gemini —
Having risen up through Taurus
and sat under the Auriga Chairiotte
Venus is now at the western north
of the boots of the Twinns —

Mars is moving eastward away from
Gemini and toward Jupiter in
the crab constellation of Cancer —

Jupiter is moving at apparent standstill
in the middle between Gemini
and Leo at the Little Cancer Crab —

It is trully a sight to see —
those three planets playing
magick games with Gemini —

Bridget Twigg and Lugg — Gaelic
Venus Mars and Jupiter — English

5/13/1991

Beautifull Cloudy Sunset —
Very Golden and Colorfull —

Astronomical

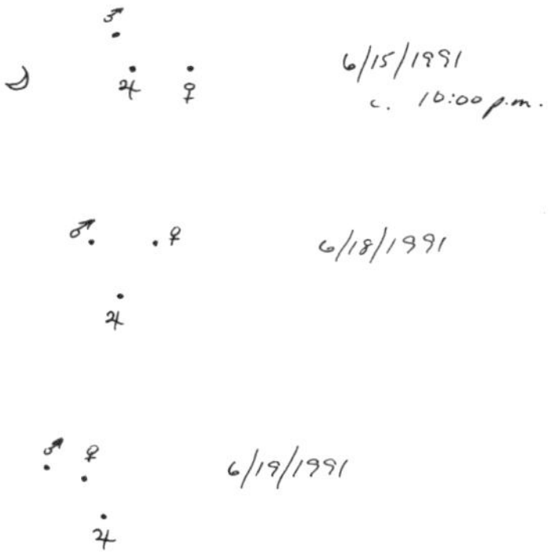

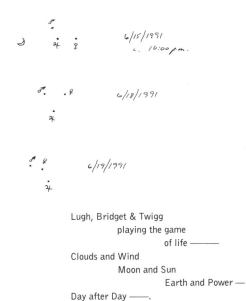

Lugh, Bridget & Twigg
playing the game
of life ———
Clouds and Wind
Moon and Sun
Earth and Power —
Day after Day ——.

Ancient Polytheistic Conundrum —

One God — neither male or female —
they speak through mankind —
one group speaks with silent thoughts
one group speaks with outloud words —
mankind thinks silently with one

mankind speaks audibly with the other
both sides of the one god mate
E Pluribus Unum
— one composed of many —

② Polytheism —
Each good spiritual experience is a link in the chain of polytheistic blessings — scince there are so many gods and goddesses, every blessing is given by a different god — ok goddess — but scince they unanimously agree on all decisions and have basically the same power, each blessing is new, different, and just as good as the others —.

Satire — 6/30/1991 —.

Wednesday — 7/10/1991 —

Young Sparrow and Black Bird
Lock Beaks and Struggled —.
Black Bird on top for NINE SECONDS —.

Family of newly born sparrows
comes visiting at the gate —
One youngest one, wide eyed
and innocent ——.

Five Turkey Vultures make a
Living Eifle Tower
Between the Eucalyptus Strand
and the pyramid Cerros —

One Turkey Vulture watches
the living tower
from the north side
of the Eucalyptus Strand —

Humming Bird visits the
Cana Lilies but isn't
interested —
perches for awhile
on the Jappanese Maple —

A Little Green Tree Frog
leaps into our lives
this morning —
Captured for the aquarium —.

Good Sun and Good Sunshine
Blowing so beautifully —
Shinning so warmly —
Feeling so comfortable —
Red Tail Hawk glidding
so powerfully —
Chased by the Black Bird —

July Phenomena —

10th — Old Bull Sparrow scratches his cheek bones, jaw bones, both sides, with left foot, right foot, then yawns and sticks his tongue out at me —

11th Solar Eclipse — 10:30 <=> 12:30 noon . . .

57% covered — A Blessing of Cleanliness for Mother Earth's Air, Water & crust —.

A Buckwheat Butterfly get captured, soaked in water, put on the right wrist to dry — 10 minutes latter Old Buckwheat flys away — brownish bronze mettalic, purple spots, yelow fringe to spots, black and white decorations, etc. — Beautifull 1 3/4 inch wing span, 1 inch body — 1/4 inch antenas — one eye —.

12th — High Noon Turkey Buzzard Vultures come to 50 foot altitude and swoop and circle above me — 3 minutes — then larger Turkey Buzzard Vulture comes and swoops on them three and the four of them rises up to 100 feet altitude and fly towards the southweste!

— Twighlight Vision —

Bridget and Twigg enter into the
Lion's House — West Side —.
        Luna sits below in the
Eastern room of the Crab —.
        Lugg and Mercury play touch
and bump at the western wall
between the Crab and the Twins —.
        The Solstice Eclipse of 1991 took
place in the House of the Twinns
at their gate in the west leading
        to the Bull —.
Five Solar System Bodies are visible
in the twighlight aftermath of
Sunset, July 13th, 1991 —
Venus-Bridget .—. Mars-Twigg .—.
Moon-Luna .—. Jupiter-Lugg .—.
        Mercury-Messenger .—.

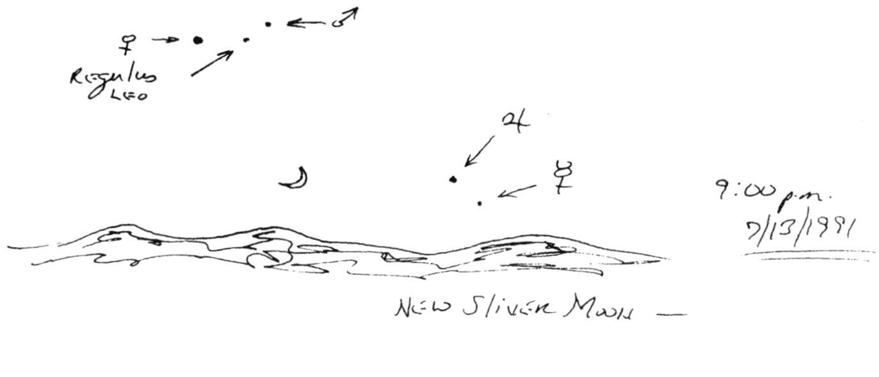

July 19th, 1991, Friday, Sunset Hours

And I looked into the mind's eye
of the Lunar Waxing 1/2 Rabbit —
I saw the Bunny slowly hop
across the moist green grass
of summer showers with
overcast sky calm feelings —.
Riding on the top of the Great
1/2 Lunar Waxing Rabbit
was a little beetle bug
with antenas like those
of a Buckwheat Moth Butterfly —.
As Old Wise Gentle Bunny Hopped
along, the beetle bugs
antenas sailed along
behind his head
Like the Flags Blowing in
the wind on top the
antenas on the rear
of the motorcycles —

Letters and notes to the prison board:

May 14th, 1982

To the Board of Prison Terms
State of California
California Men's Colony
San Luis Obispo County

Gentlemen:

I heard recently on the radio that 44 of Americas 50 States have "OK'd" the use of Lie Detection Exams in any Employee/Labor Disputes. I know that Lie Detection Exams are not concidered admissible in Criminal Trials, but just the same there is enough indication of their efficacy to warant their use in my case re: **family conspiracy.**

I have also seen on the Television that the famous Tennis Player Billy Jean King was accused of being a Gay Bisexual. She refussed to admitt her Bisexuality until the Court System adamently insisted that she tell the truth. I believe that my sister and cousins and other close school mate are playing the same game on the Court System. Unless they are forced by the Legal Investigators to admitt their conspiracy to keep me from becoming Gay, they will continue to hide their sexual positions and kill-joy whitchcraft conspiracy from the Laws eyes. They set the stage for the murders and when the murders began they did nothing to inform the police that they had begun. For over four months they sat by idilly while inocent peoples lives were killed. That is a fellony in itself, one that you men should feel responsible to invesitgate.

The Public Defender at my Trial in Santa Cruz deliberately tried to prove that I was "insane" at the time of the crimes. Instead of doing what I repeatedly asked, concerning proving that there was a conspiracy, he did nothing but submitt embarrassing and inappropriate evidence. Truthfully his efforts were incompetant and his presentations were immaterial and irrelavent. The truth as to what had actually happened was more important, and yet he was allowed to make a "farse and sham" of the trial.

Gentlemen, last year I submitted a written paper indicating that my classmates and peer group durring the 1967 & 1968 period were heavily using L.S.D. and other psychedelics. I also indicated that they had placed a very detrimental kill-joy hex on me at Pexcadero in January of 1968. Truthfully, it is evident to me that the detrimental effects of that hex led to the commission of the crimes. Experiments at Stanford have shown recently that humans can control and communicate with other humans with the use of methods of E.S.P. It is obvious to me now that those people had used methods of E.S.P. to influence my life adversely, up to and including the crimes.

Gentlemen, the Punck Rock and Roll Bands of the late seventies and the early eightys indicate the type of strange power that the Pescadero Conspiracy was playing with. Along with their music the musicians also use sledge hammers to destroy T.V.'s; chainsaws to demolish expensive automobiles, crow bars to shatter fine glassware. Strange indeed are those exhibitions and strange indeed was the Pescadero Conspiracy. I hope that your organization can look into this matter and come to a Just and Honorable Solution.

I have contacted the EXX F.B.I. in the hopes of uncovering evidence concerning the Selective Service Payoff that Jack Watson, my godfather, initiated durring the 1968 thru 1973 period. I spoke of it to you on my two previous appearances. The F.B.I. informs me that the statute of limitations has expired. That payoff set me up for the commision of the crimes. It kept me under the control of the family conspiracy. What now?

In truthfullness and honesty,

Herbert W. Mullin

May 14th, 1982

To the Board of Prison Terms
State of California

Gentlemen:

For the last two appearances I have made before you I have tried in vain to convince you that the "paranoia" the psychs keep reporting about is not paranoia at all; it happens to be a very real conspiracy, a conspiracy that we could term "Kill-joy" conspiracy.

My family was a military family. Bill, my male parent, was in WW2. Apparently he went "crazy" and was put in a hospital for "wackoos". I am certain that he is very embarrassed about the problem he has, but I don't think he should be exonerated from his responsibilities re: the 13 murders he forced me to committ.

Durring WW2 a Lt. Col. Evans F. Carlson formed a group known as the United States Marine Corp Raiders. Much of their fighting was done in the Pacific Campaign. A word that was coined by Lt. Col. Carlson was "gung-ho", I am reasonably certain that you have heard it used. "gung-ho" means the enthusiastic, cooperative, enterprising, etc. actions of a follower in an unrestrained and often naive manner. Gentlemen, I am being punished because 'Crazy Bill' used his training from WW2 in such a way as to make me committ crimes I would not have committed otherwise. He was a drill sgt., a Lieutenant, and eventually a Captain. That does not give him the right to initiate the death of 13 inocent Americans 25 years after the war was over.

I am certain that both you and the psychs would look at my case differently if you did not adamently insist that Crazy Bill is not "responsible". At least you should admitt that the possibility exists and that it warrants further investigations by the propper athourities.

Another aspect of this case that is overlooked all to easily is the fact that my family knew the crimes were taking place and yet they did nothing to inform the police. That is a crime. Why has that been overlooked for so long?

Another consideration is the administration of a Lie Detector examination to Bill. There is more than enough evidence now to warrant such an investigation. By avoiding this issue year after year I believe that you are causing me to spend more time in prison than Justice or human reason would condone. It is a cruel and inhuman punishment.

Gentlemen, Lie Detector Tests cost under $100.00 now-a-days. The State of California spent quite alot of money on my original trial and has spent quite alot of money on my incarceration so far. I feel it is wise to finally get to the bottom of this. I am the man's son and I am acusing him of forcing me to committ the 13 murders. So far all I've gotten from the authorities is alot of double-talk and indiference. I feel that the time has come for you to do something decisive.

Possibly you would want a double Lie Detector Test. One of the prisoner and one from the person he is acussiong.

Forgive me if I have been to strong and forcefull in my speech and affect. I am trying to affect a change in this yearly cycle that we have been engaged in. I know that I am a good American person who was tricked into committing the crimes. I know that I deserve my freedom.

Thank you in Truth and Honesty,

Herbert W. Mullin

Maturity and Imaturity —

The age of reason —
Before the age of reason —
Adolesence and young adulthood —

Because his parents did not want to lose controll —
Because his parents did not teach him the facts of life —
Because his parents did not teach him how to become a man —
Because his community told his parents to teach him how to become a man —
Because his parents refused —
Because his community kept him in a state of naievity, and gullibility and innocent ignorance as to the facts of life and manhood —

— February 12th, 1991 —

Growing Pains

What if his parents and sister, aunts and uncles, cousins, friends and neighbors —

#1. Refused to teach him about masterbation, heterosexuality, homosexuality, bisexuality, and natural mental health —

#2. Caused him to become homophobic, heterophobic and undiferciated schitzophrenic —

#3. Committed pre-meditated 2nd degree murder by allowing him to become tricked and manipulated illegally

Conclusion — If his parents and sister, aunts and uncles, cousins, friends and neighbors are guilty of #s 1, 2, & 3, then how should the prison authority deal with his predicatment — ???

Logic —

I suggest that the defendant's testimony at Santa Cruz Trial #50219, and his written defence exhibits #T & #U be entered as evidence in his C.M.C. and C.D.C. central file —

I suggest that a professional witch that is also a professional psychiatrist be subpoenaed to interview the defendant and make an independent psychological evaluation for the C.M.C. and C.D.C. central file —.

I suggest that more credence be given to the defendant's contention that he was the victim of kill-joy sadistic, soccio-ecconomic witchcraft practitioners —.

I suggest that more credence be given to the defendant's statements pertaining to his remorse and sorrow for his part in the series of crimes ——.

"Response"

you are not paranoid
they were passive aggressive
you didn't know

you are not schitzophrenic
you suffered too many deprivations
without knowing it
you suffered too many insults
without know it
you suffered to many soccio-ecconomic
sabbatage ploys
without knowing it

you became incompetent
you became inefficient
without knowing it

now that you know
what should you do
what could you do

what would you do

April 28th, 1991
— Sunday —

4/25/91

Pescadero January 1968
Truth or Delusion

The so-called Pescadero Conspiracy that I have spoken of to all the psychiatrists and psychologists scince my arrest appears to be the central experience of many soccio-ecconomic factors that have led to my present condition of "paranoid schitzophrenia." That is my opinion based on my own assessment of my own life chronology —.

For close to eight hours I was "mezmerized" by Ernie Keller at a house in Pescadero, California, in San Mateo County, in January of 1968. Within two months of that experience I broke off my engagement to be married to a young lady I had been dating for four years —. I have not had a steady girlfriend scince that time —. I developed homophobia, heterophobia, and masterbation phobia —.

If I compare the definition for delusion to the experience I have had, I find that I am not making an incorrect inference about external reality —. Furthermore, I have asked the psychs what they believed happened that day at Pescadero and they always become reticent to comment on the subject — occassionally they have said they don't know, or that maybe it didn't happen at all —. That does not constitute incontrovertible and obvious proof or evidence that the Pescadero Curse I have spoken of openly for 18 yrs. is a dellusion ——.

The reason I bring this subject up in this report is because I have just read Doctor Rodriguez's psych evaluation report for my June 1991 Board of Prison Terms, parole consideration hearing —. It would seem reasonable from my point of view, to believe that my mental illness was, in part, caused by outside influences —. The Pescadero experience was only the central experience of many soccio-ecconomic experiences I had that now indicate to me that my family and friends were using "approach-avoidance syndrome" manuvres in combination with passive-aggressive manuvres to keep me in a state of immaturity. After the Pescadero experience my immaturity became homophobic, heterophobic, and masterbation phobic schitzophrenia ——.

I have learned to describe and explain these personal situations during one-on-one conversations with psychs after my arrest —.

I have always spoken of them at my group therapy sessions —.

My question now is — why are my beliefs concidered a delusion ——?

In closing this portion of my report I must say that I am very gratefull for the opportunity to present my views and opinions —. Thank you!!

Echolalia 2nd Degree

Are not they guilty of 2nd degree 187 p.c.
did they not set the stage

Don't tell him about masterbation —
Don't tell him about bisexuality —
Don't tell him about homosexuality —

Look, he isn't doing as good as
we thought he would —

Look, someone else is abusing him
emotionally and he doesn't know it —

Look, we haven't taught him the
facts of life —

Look, we put him in a state mental
hospital —

Look, we didn't even try to teach
him how to be mature —

We didn't try to help him cure
his schitzophrenia —

After putting him in a state mental hospital they refused to get involved in group therapy with him like the mental health worker had suggested —

After four months of one-on-one Dr. Felix at Calif. Medical Facility told him that in all likelihood his family and friends "caused" him to committ the crimes —

He tried to prove in State and Federal Court that he was not guilty of 1st or 2nd degree 187 p.c.
Maybe Involuntary Manslaughter —?

1. What is Clapp-Trapp —?
2. What is Bunco-Swinddle psychic energy game —?

3. What is Soccio-Ecconomic Sabbatage?

Who is Herbert Spencer?
What is Social Darwinism?

What is passive-aggressiveness?

4/28/91

"Telepathy and E.S.P."

Standford University has an Extra Sensory Perception Research Center devoted to the study of the parapsychological psychic phenomena peculiar to mankind —.

When I am paroled I will try to become involved in that research project ——.

The Rosicrucian Order that has its headquarters at Rosicrucian Park in San Jose, California, has secrete study groups that teach the power and uses of telepathy in mans progress as a spiritual being —. When I am paroled I would like to become a member of the Rosicrucians —. They have a rule that convicts are not allowed to join until paroled from prison —.

— March 1991 —

Remorse ——

I know I am guilty —
I am truthfully sorry —
I honestly appollogize —

I promise never to do it again —

I know I am suffering from a
mental illness that they call
paranoid schitzophrenia ——

I am going to join the Schitzophrenia
Association of America as soon as I
find their address —
I will attend their meetings when
I am paroled ——.

I will do everything I can to cure
myself of my paranoid schitzophrenia —.

I am guilty —
I appollogize —
I promise never to do it again ———

4/28/1991
Sunday

CARL **PANZRAM**

On the evening of August 20, 1928, a 26-year-old prison guard by the name of Henry P. Lesser began his shift at the Washington District Jail in the nation's capital. During his rounds he came across a recent addition to the prison, a burly 37-year-old man arrested two days earlier for housebreaking and stealing a radio. Sensing that the man was a seasoned criminal, Lesser asked him, "What's your racket?" The prisoner glared suspiciously at the guard and said, "How did you know? What I do is I reform people."

A few weeks later the prisoner, Carl Panzram, was caught attempting to escape by prying loose two bars in his cell window. Warden W. L. Peak, a sanctimonious man who enjoyed meting out punishment to unruly prisoners, ordered four guards to handcuff Panzram to "the post" in the basement of the jail. For two consecutive nights Panzram was sadistically tortured and, as a result, confessed to a number of horrible crimes. Lesser later recounted how he reacted to Panzram's anguish in an essay titled "Recollections of Carl Panzram":

> I learned from the head tiersman, a prisoner, who was in charge of celling men and other work of a routine nature, a full account of the previous night's happening. It was verified by guards who had witnessed all the details. The narration of the brutalities visited upon this defenseless man kindled in me strong indignation and built up a feeling of sympathy for him. I found out that he did not possess any money. A man with money in jail is in a dire predicament; one without money is indeed unfortunate. I gave the head tiersman a dollar for Panzram. When the tiersman told Panzram that I sent in a dollar, he thought that a joke was being played upon him. "What? A guard sending me a dollar?! Don't try to kid me." When the tiersman reassured him that it was so, tears came into Panzram's eyes. Here, after being tortured and mistreated by everyone, a guard takes a sympathetic interest in him. Later in the day, when I passed his cell, he stopped me and offered profuse thanks for my gift. . . . If it were not for the fact that I befriended him at this particular time, I don't think that I would have been able to gain his respect, confidence, and good will which led to his acceding to my request that he write his autobiography for me. We became very friendly, and a spirit of *entente cordiale* prevailed between us.

The Washington newspapers wanted to talk to Panzram about his confessions under torture, but Panzram decided to write down his own story with pencil and paper supplied by Lesser. Against prison rules, the guard smuggled in writing materials and spirited out finished pages of Panzram's manuscript every evening after midnight. When the writing was finished by the end of the year, Lesser had in his possession Panzram's essays, notes, and autobiography [reproduced below]: a profound monument to a life wedded to hatred and depravity, and littered with a multitude of crimes that included arson, burglary, robbery, rape, and twenty-one murders.

Determined to keep himself in prison, Panzram represented himself during his trial for burglary on November 12, telling the jury:

> You people got me here charged with housebreaking and larceny. I'm guilty. I broke in and I stole. What I didn't steal, I smashed. If the owner had come in I would have knocked his brains out. There's something else you ought to know. While you were trying me here, I was trying all of you, too. I've found you guilty. Some of you, I've executed. If I live, I'll execute some more of you. I hate the whole human race. [To prosecutor:] You think I'm playing crazy, don't you? I'm not. I know right from wrong. No delusions. I don't hear anything you don't hear. My conscience doesn't bother me. I have no conscience. I believe the whole human race should be exterminated. I'll do my best to do it every chance I get. [To jury:] Now I've done my duty. You do yours!

The jury unsurprisingly took less than a minute to return with a guilty verdict, and the judge sentenced Panzram to twenty-five years at the federal penitentiary in Leavenworth, Kansas. Lesser recalled his last Christmas Eve with Panzram while on duty, before the murderer's transfer on January 30, 1929:

> A choir in the rotunda, within hearing of Panzram, had just completed singing carols. I passed his cell and, looking in, I noticed that Panzram was standing with the fly of his trousers unbuttoned. His penis was in plain sight of anyone who might look. It was told to me many times by prisoners who were allowed out on the first tier and who were able to pass Panzram's cell in performing their duties, that Panzram used to pace the cell, jingling a few stray coins in his pocket and repeating all the while, "I would give everything I had for a nice hole." He would work his fingers to represent one while making this assertion.

Panzram instinctively mistrusted everyone, including Lesser. One day Lesser was talking to Panzram through the bars of the cell door and, according to Lesser,

> I called his attention to a beautiful sunset which could be seen through his cell window. As I said, "Look over there, Carl," he jumped away from where he was standing and appeared very frightened and excited. When I asked him the reason for this reaction, he said that he thought for the moment that I was trying to divert his attention in order to assault him with some object. He had been used to having his attention diverted in the past, for this reason. Upon second thought, I apologized to him for pointing out the beautiful sunset because he couldn't have been in a mood to appreciate it.

At Leavenworth Panzram corresponded with Lesser and was assigned to work in the prison laundry. After Panzram made it clear to everyone that he was a dangerous man who needed to be left alone, a 40-year-old prison guard named Robert G. Warnke, an active member of the Leavenworth chapter of the Ku Klux Klan, continued to harass him. On the afternoon of June 25, 1929, Panzram responded by sneaking up on the guard and cleaving his head five times with a heavy piece of iron. Spattered with blood and brain matter, Panzram then attempted to attack prisoners and guards nearby, but everyone managed to elude the enraged killer until he finally gave up, exhausted and spent.

Another factor in the guard's murder was that Panzram most likely wanted to be executed. After spending 22 of his 38 years in prisons, he stated repeatedly that he was simply tired of living. Although the state of Kansas had abolished capital punishment in 1907, the murder was committed on federal property; even though no one had been executed in Kansas for over forty years, Panzram was counting on a federal death sentence and, after a brief one-day trial on April 15, 1930 (where once again he sabotaged his own defense), he received it.

Worried that he wouldn't be executed due to the intervention of "do-gooders," Panzram feebly attempted suicide on June 20 by eating a plate of rotten beans and slicing a six-inch wound in his leg. He also wrote letters to President Hoover and an organization against capital punishment demanding that his execution proceed as scheduled.

A fellow prisoner by the name of Robert Stroud – the future "Birdman of Alcatraz" – later recalled how Panzram occupied himself on September 4, the evening before his execution:

> All night long that last night he walked the floor of his cell, singing a pornographic little song that he had composed himself. It was not much of a song, either from the point of view of melody or lyrics, but it undoubtedly expressed, in not too polite terms, the deepest craving of his heart. The principal theme was "Oh, how I love my roundeye!"

While preparing for the gallows in the morning, Panzram spotted two men of the cloth in the crowd and bellowed at the warden, "Are there any Bible-backed cocksuckers in here?" When the warden informed Panzram that the men had come a long way to offer comfort, the condemned man yelled "Get 'em out! I don't mind being hanged, but I don't need any Bible-backed hypocrites around me! Run 'em out, Warden, or you're going to have one hell of a time getting me out of this cell. Every man I get a hand on is going to a hospital!" After they were removed, Panzram saved his final tirade for the hangman who asked if he had any last words: "Yes, hurry it up, you Hoosier bastard! I could hang a dozen men while you're fooling around!"

Panzram dropped through the trap door at 6:01 A.M. and was pronounced dead seventeen minutes later; he is now buried in the prison's cemetery (known to the inmates as "Peckerwood Hill") with a concrete marker bearing only his prison number – 31614.

Panzram's manuscript was sent by Lesser to various people –including renowned psychiatrist Karl Menninger, *Liberty* magazine editor Fulton Oursler, and H. L. Mencken, then editor of *The American Mercury* – inquiring on the feasibility of publication. They were all immensely impressed by the writings, but could be of no help. Mencken's response was typical:

> This is one of the most amazing documents I have ever read. Obviously, printing it in a general magazine would be impossible. Moreover, I doubt that it could be done as a book for general selection. . . . I can't recall reading anything more shocking.

Lesser dedicated his life to seeing through publication of the manuscript; he later said it was "almost a sacred thing, to let society know Panzram's side." Disillusioned as a prison guard, Lesser eventually moved to Los Angeles and earned a living as clothing salesman. Forty years after Panzram's execution, Lesser's persistence led to the publication of *Killer: A Journal of Murder*, a collection of Panzram's writings, with a "historical and sociological framework" provided by Thomas E. Gaddis, author of *Birdman of Alcatraz*, and James O. Long, a reporter for the Portland *Oregon Journal*. Before his death, Lesser said of Panzram, "They told me he was a dangerous man, and he was. But I could commiserate with him because he was a fellow human being, a greatly troubled man who can teach us all something."

Autobiography in its entirety; later research by authors Gaddis and Long has shown that "no major statement in his confession has been disproved":

Written by

Carl Panzram

Nov. 3. 1928. District Jail Wash. D.C.

Born June 28. 1892.

East Grand Forks. Minn.

Full List of all Jails, reformatories, Prisons and State or Goverment instatutions I have been in.

How I got into them.

How Long I stayed inthem.

How I got out of them.

No. 1. East Grand Forks. Minn. Charges, incorrigability and Burglary. 1903. County Jail.

No. 2. Red Wing. Minn. This is the seat of the Minnasota State Training School. There I stayed nearly 2 years.

No. 3. Butte. Mont. Charge Burglary 3 months in the County Jail there and then tried in County Court and sent to the Montana

= 4 = State Reform School at Miles City. Mont where I was held about 1 year and then made a successfull escape. this was in 1905. under my right name. C.P.

= 5 = Joined the U.S. Army in 1906 at Helena Mont under the name of Carl Panzram. Stationed at Fort Harrison in the 6th regular U.S. Infantry in A. Co. Practicaly as soon or very shortly after I joined the Army I was put in the Guard House for stealing several monthes there and then tried by a U.S. Military General Court Martial. and sentenced to 3 years.

= 6 = Sent to the U.S. Military prison at Fort Leavensworth. Kans. where I served 37 months. discharged.

No. 7. sometime in 1910 or 1911 under the name of Jeff Davis I was arrested at Jacksonvill, Cherokee County Texas and was sent to Rusk. Texas the County seat where I was tried for vagrancy the crime being that I was riding a mail train on top while being armed with two pistols. For this I was sent to the County Road gang where I served 65 days and escaped. The date I dont remember but the next night I was in Houston Texas and that was the night of the big fire there. I think it was early in 1911.

No. 8. 1911 or 1912 Fresno. California under the name of Jeff Davis I think. Charge petty Larceny sentence to 120 days. served 30 and escaped.

No. 9. The Dalles. Oregon Name Jack Allen. 1912 Charge Highway Robbery and asualt. Held to await the Action for the Grand Jury. waited about 3 months and escaped.

= 10 = Seattle Wash. 1912 Charge petty Larceny Name Jeff Davis. Served 1 month. discharged

= 11 = Moscow. Idaho. 1912. Charge petty Larceny and assisting a prisoner to escape. 30 days name Jeff Davis.

= 12 = Chinook. Mont. Charge burglary. sentenced to one year State Prison under the name of Jeff Davis 1912. served 8 months. and escaped. Arrested 1 weeke later at Three Forks Mont. for Burglary under the name of Jeff Rhodes sentenced to one year in State Prison. Deer Lodge Mont. When I was brought back to the prison I was taken to the County Court at Deer Lodge and given 1 year for escaping from prison. Of these 3 sentences I served 2 years and was discharged.

= 13 = Astoria Oregon 1904. name Jeff Baldwin charged with Burglary. given 7 years in the State prison at Salem Oregon. done one year and escaped. caught. done one more year and escaped again while out that time one week I robbed a man and had a gun fight with a deputy Sherif at Eugene Oregon for

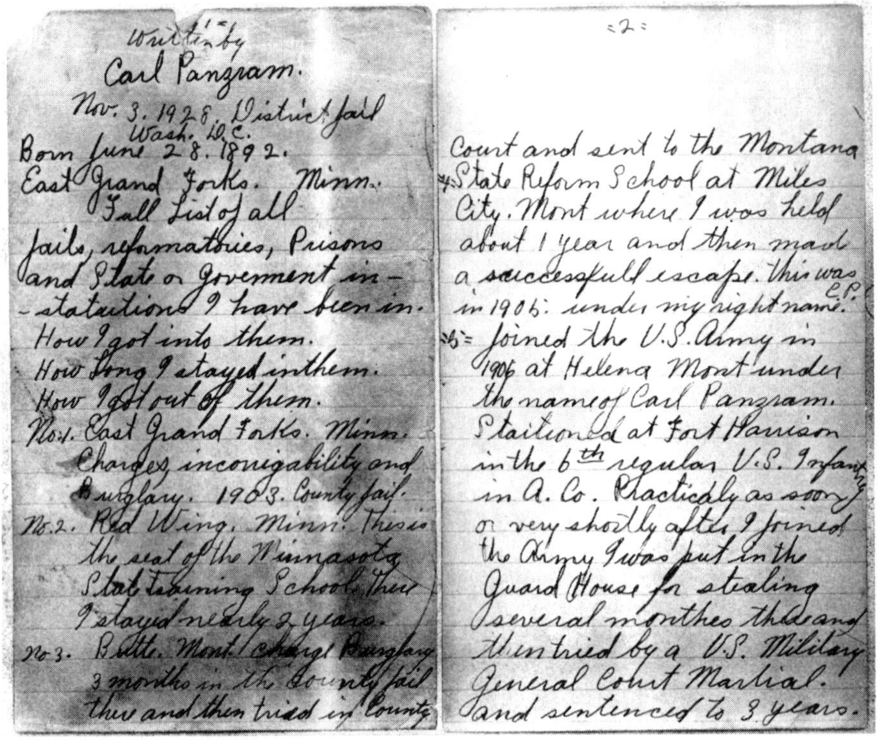

Written by
Carl Panzram.
Nov. 3. 1928. District Jail
Wash. D.C.
Born June 28. 1892.
East Grand Forks. Minn.
Full List of all
Jails, reformatories, Prisons
and State or Goverment in-
-statutions I have been in.
How I got into them.
How long I stayed in them.
How I got out of them.
No. 1. East Grand Forks. Minn.
Charges incoreigability and
Burglary. 1903. County Jail.
No. 2. Red Wing. Minn. This is
the seat of the Minnesota
State Training School. There
I stayed nearly 2 years.
No. 3. Butte. Mont. charge Burglary
3 months in the County Jail
there and then tried in County

= 2 =
Court and sent to the Montana
4 = State Reform School at Miles
City. Mont where I was held
about 1 year and then made
a successfull escape. this was
in 1906: under my right name. C.P.
5 = Joined the U.S. Army in
1906 at Helena Mont under
the name of Carl Panzram.
Staitioned at Fort Harrison
in the 6th regular U.S. Infantry
in A. Co. Practicaly as soon
or very shortly after I joined
the Army I was put in the
Guard House for stealing
several months there and
then tried by a U.S. Military
General Court Martial.
and sentenced to 3 years.

these two crimes I was given 2 additional sentences. one of 2 years for robbery and one of 8 years for asualt. which made me have all together a full 17 years to do in Oregon. but I only done one more year of it and then escaped again. I still owe 14 years to Oregon. After escaping from the State Prison at Salem, Oregon in May 1918. I changed my name to John O'Leary took out seamans papers passengers Passports and went to South America Europe and Africa. for the next 5 years or from 1918 to 1923 I was in 31 different Countries, had stole and spent thousands of dollars committed many murders and robberies and other crimes and the only two times that I was in Jail during that 5 years whas once

= 14 = I got and done 10 days for Theft in Barlinnie Prison in Glasgow Scottland. 1919.

= 15 = and the other was in Bridgport. Conn. for burglary and carring concealed weapons. 6 months in 1920 and 1921.

= 16 = My las arresst before this one was in 1923 at Larchmont N.Y. sent from there to White Plains tried in the County Court and sent to Sing Sing prison and from there transferred to Clinton Prison at Dannemorra N.Y. where I served 5 years. being discharged July 6. 1928.

17. Arrested 36 days later in Baltimore Md. and thats this case. I hope its my last one as I am pretty dam tired. These are the main places where I have done time but there are about 100 more places where I have been in Jail for various offences for periods of from 1 day to a week or so. Alltogether I have served about twenty years of my life in prison and I am 36 years old now.

In my life time I have murdered 21 human beings. I have committed thousands of burglaries, robberies Larcenys, arsons and last but not least I have committed sodomy on more than 1,000 male human beings. for all of these things I am not the least bit sorry. I have no conscience so that does not worry me. I dont believe in Man, God nor devil. I hate the whole damed human race including myself.

Carl Panzram.

In my 145 page autobiography I stated the fact that in 1921 in Lobito bay Africa that I there killed 6 niggers.

I merely stated the bare fact.

To some people of average inteligince this seems an allmost impossible feat.

Thats because their ignorant of the full details.

IT was very much easier for me to kill these 6 niggers than it was for me to kill any one of the 7 young boys I killed later and some of them were only 11 or 12 years old.

In Africa there are bull buffaloes that weigh 2,000 pounds and have enormas strength, yet a crockadile 12 or 15 foot long can kill and eat a buffaloe. Any of these 6 niggers that I killed could kill and eat one of those crockadiles. Armed with no more than some small sticks and a bit of grass and a piece of rotton meat they do that trick every day all over Africa.

I was forearmed with the knolledge that I had gained and also a 9 millameter German Luggar Automatic Pistol and plenty of bullets. The 7 of us were in the canoe The other six in front of me where I sat in the stern The canoe was about 22 foot long 4 1/2 foot wide by 2 1/2 feet deep.

The niggers expected nothing They all had their backs turned to me. I am a crack shot. I fired a single shot into each niggers back. and then reloaded with a new clip and fired another shot into the brain of each one as they lay dying or dead in the bottom of the canoe. Then I threw them all over board and the crockadiles soon finished what I had left of them.

This canoe was registired and licenced. it must still be in existince. If it is, there are two bullets imbedded in the wood one in the bottom near the stern and one on the port side near the middle. These niggers were all full grown men with families who must be still alive and who still remember me as dozens of people saw me at Lobito Bay when I hired them and thier canoe. The exact date can be very easily accertained by The records of the Port. and the passengers list of the small Belgian S.S. which runs from Matildi to Boma, Loanda and Lobito Bay and return On her in 1921 I bought a ticket from Loanda to Lobito Bay and a few dayes in Lobito Bay and then I bought a return ticket on the same boat to Loanda. This is all very easy to verify by any one who cares to do so. And as for the body of the little nigger boy at the gravel pit at Loanda. Hes still there unless he has been found since the day I killed and left him there.

The pistol with which I did that killing, I brought back to the states. There is a record of it at the Maxim Silent Firearms Co. at Hartford Conn. Where I sent it in the winter of 1922 and 1923 From Yonkers, New. York. under my name of Captain John O'Leary. under that name and address 220 Yonkers Ave. I sent the pistol to them and they sold me a silencer for it. All of this must be on the books of that Companys Records. The Port Police, the S.S. Co's. and the Belgian Council at Lobito Bay can verify the rest of the Lobito Bay end of it. I thought that the pistol wasnt deadly enough as it was so I got a silencer for it to be able to do a bigger and more efficient buisness in the murder line. and believe me if that heavy calibered pistol and the silencer had only worked as I thought it would, I would have gone into the murder buisness on a wholesale scale instead of being a piker and only killing 21 human beings. My intentions were good because I am the man that goes around the world doing people good. C.P.

I have lived 36 years in this world and soon I expect to leave it.

All that I have behind me is, Smoke, death, desolation and damnation.

signed.

Carl Panzram.

Carl Panzram

True statement of some of my actions including the times and places and my reasons for so doing these things.

Written by me of my own free will at the District Jail Washington. D.C. Nov. 4, '28.

I was born on a small farm in Minnasota. My parents were of German desent. Hard working ignorant and poor. The rist of the family consisted of 5 brothers and one sister all of whom are dead except 3 of us brothers and our sister.

All of my family are as the average human beings are. They are honest and hard working people. All except myself.

I have been a human-animile ever since I was born. When I was very young at 5 or 6 years of age I was a thief and a lier and a mean despisable one at that. The older I got the meaner I got. My Father and mother split up when I was about 7 or 8 years old. The old man pulled out one day and dissapeared. This left my mother with a family of 6 on a small worked out farm. As fast as the older boys grew up they also pulled out. one died. This left me, my sister and one older brother and my mother. My sister and I were sent to school during the days and as soon as we came home in the evenings, we were put to work in the fields where my older brother and mother were allways at work. from daylight until long after dark sometimes. My portion of pay consisted of plenty of work and a good sound beating every time I looked cock-eyed or done any thing that displeased any one who was older and stronger and able to catch me and kick me around whenever they felt like it, and it seemed to me then and still does now that everything was allways right for the one who was the strongest and every single thing that I done was wrong. Everybody said so anyway. But right or wrong I used to get plenty of abuse. every body thought it was all right to decieve me, lie to me, kick me around whenever they felt like it and they felt like it pretty regular. At this time, thats the way my life was lived until I was about 11 years old. At about that time I began to suspect that there was something wrong about the treatment I was getting from the rest of the human race. When I was about 11 years old I began to hear and see that there were other places in this world besides my own little corner of it. I began to realize that there were other people who lived nice easy lives and who were not kicked around and worked to death.

I desided that I wanted to leave my miserable home. Before I left I looked around and figured that one of our neighbors who was rich and had a nice home full of nice things he had to much and I had too little so one night I broke into his home and stole everything that to my eys had the most value. Those things were some apples some cake and a great big pistol. Eating the apples and cake and and carring the pistol under my coat I walked to the R.R. yeards where I caught a freight train going to the west where I intended to be a cowboy and shoot indians.

But I must have had my wires crossed because I missed my connections somewhere so instead of going out and seeing the world I was caught, brought back home and beaten half to death, then sent to Jail and from there to the Minnasota State Training School at Red Wing. Minnesota.

Right there and then I began to learn about Mans Inhumanity To Man.

They started me off by trying to beat the Christian religion into me and the consequencess were that the more they beat and whiped me, the more I hated them and their dam religeon. They beat me and whiped me for doing this and for not doing that. everything I seemed to do was wrong.

Just at that time I was 11-12 and 13 years old and I was just learning to think for myself. I first began to think that I was being unjustly imposed upon. Then I began to hate those who abused me. Then I began to think that I would have my revenge just as soon and as often as I could injure some-one else. Any one at all would do. If I couldn't injure those who injured me then I would inure some one else. From that day to this I have followed that line of thought. From the time I was 12 years old I have been in Jail allmost continualy until now when I am 36, I have spent 20 years of my life in prison.

During my 20 years in all the various prisons and jails I have been in I have undergone every kind of abuse and punishment that the ingenious minds of many men could devise and believe me, men can surely figure out some horrible tortures to impose on other men. I have had the whip, the Paddle, The snorting pole, the humming bird, the hose, the Jacket, Chained up frontwards, backwards, bucked and gagged spread eagled, water cured, starved, beaten, thrown into swet boxes and half cooked, thrown in ice cold-dungeons and half frozen. I have been in solitary confinement for years at a time where I could have no privilages or pleasures of any kind. Every single thing in life that men hold worth while and that go to make life worth living for I have been denied and deprived of. I have went thru every consievable kind of torture that one man or body of men can impose on another man.

I started out in life enjoying it and hating no one.

I am winding it up now by hating the whole human race including myself and having no desire to live any longer. For all the misery and tortures that I have went thru I have made other men go thru many times over only worse.

When I first went to the Minnasota State Training School I was about 11 years old Lively, healthy and very mischieveous, innocent and ignorant. The Law immediatly proceeded to educate me to be a good clean upright christian citizen and a credit to the human race. They Trained me all right in that Training School. There, during my two years I was trained by two different sets of people to have two sets of morals. The good people tried to train me to be good and the bad peopel did train me to be bad. The method that the good people used in training me was to beat goodness into me and beat all the badness out of me. They done thier best but thier best wasnt good enough to accomplish the task they set out to do.

In that School there were about 250 boys ranging in age from 7 or 8 years old up to 21. These boyes were divided up into 5 companies or cottages. Each Company was in charge of a manager and a matron. I was first put in Cottage No. 2. The managers name was George Mann. The Matrons name was Miss Martin. And a fine pair of Christians they were to have in charge of a lot of young boyes to train.

My first reception at the school was to be met by Mr George Mann who told me the rules. Next he called me into his room to take my pedigree for an oral and phisical examination for to be put on the records of the Instatution. He began on the oral examination by asking me my name, parents habits, schooling, home life and history of my associations. He asked me if my fathere was insane, was he a drunkard was he lazy or industrious. He asked me if my mother was a prostitute or a drunkard was she educated or ignorant. After asking me all of these questions and explaining in detail just what each question meant and all about it.

He hen stripped me naked and began my phisical examination, looking to see if I was lousy or had any kind of sickness or disease. He examined my penus and my rectum, asking me if I had ever committed fornication or sodomy or had ever had sodomy committed on me or if I had ever masturbated. He explained in detail and very thouroughly just what he meant by these things. That began my education. I have learned a little more since. This Mr. George Mann was a Christian, very much so. I was taught to pray when I got out of bed in the mornings to say grace at each meal and give thanks to the Lord after it. We sang a hyme at each meal. A bible lesson every evening before bed time and then just before bed time to say another prayer. On Sundays we were sent to Sunday School in the morning and Church in the After noon. Oh, yes we had plenty of Church and religeon all right. I used to be pretty ignorant and not able to read very well so I allways had a hard job learning my sunday school lessons. For failing to learn these lessons I was given a whipping. For the first year I was there I used to get a beating every Saturday night and sometimes 3 and 4 more during the week for doing something I wasn't supposed to do or not doing something that I was supposed to do. Oh yes, I had plenty of abuse. They had various methods of punishing us for doing wrong and for teaching us to do right. The most popular with them was to take us to the Paint shop, "so called because there they used to paint our bodies black and blue."

This Paint Shop was a very ingenious contrivance for inflicting the worst punishment where it would do the least harm and the most good. They used to have a large wooden block which we were bent over and tied face downwards after first being stripped naked. Then a large towel was soaked in salt water and spread on our backs from the shoulders down to the knees. Then the man who was to do the whipping took a large strap about 1/4 of an inch thick by 4 inches wide and about 2 feet long with a handle on it about 2 feet long.

The strap had a lot of little round holes punched thru it. Every time that whip came down on the body the skin would come up thru these little holes in the strap and after 25 or 30 times of this, little blisters would form and then burst, and right there and then hell began. The salt water would do the rest. About a week or 2 later a boy might be able to sit down on anything harder than a feather pillow. I used to get this racket regular and when I was too ill to be given that sort of medicin, they used to take a smaller strap and beat me on the open palms of my hands. While the other boys were playing ball, skating or swiming I used to be given a sunday School lesson and made to stand at attention with my arms folded and my back to the field where the boys were all playing and enjoying themselves. Some times a dozen of us at a time would be lined up like that. We were all supposed to go to school a half a day and work half a day and the rest of the time learn how to love Jesus and be good boys. Naturaly I now love Jesus very much. Yes I love him so dam much that I would like to Crucify him all over again. I was too dumb to learn anything in school so they took me out and put me to work all day washing dishes and waiting on table in the officers dining room. Right there I began to get a little revenge on some of those who abused me. When I used to serve the food to some of the officers I used to urinate in thier soup, coffee or tea and masturbate into thier ice-cream or desert and then stand right beside them and watch them eat it. They enjoyed it too because they told me so. I wish they could read this now. Once each week I used to be sent to the laundry to get the clean linnen for the dining room. One cold winter day I went there and didn't come back. not right away. I attempted to escape but got caught, brought back and dam near beaten to death. But they put me back to work in the officers dining room. The next thing I tried to do was to poison that Mr George Mann by putting Rat poison in his rice pudding but they caught me, beat me and put me out of the dining room and into the band. There the first day I learned to play one note and never learned one since. About that time I began to try to figure out some other way to punish those who punished me. The only thing I could figure out to do was to burn down the building in which the paint shop was located. This I did. I got a long thick piece of heavy cotton string wrapped it round and round a long round stick, lit one end of it and hid it in the laundry near some oil soaked rags. That night That whole place burned down at a cost of over $100,000. "Nice Eh." Some of the boys who were cleverer than I was finaly put me wise how I should perform if I ever wanted to get out of that Joint. They told me to act like I was a very good boy, tell every body I met, how much I loved Jesus, and how I wanted to go home and be a good boy go to school and learn to be a preacher. I done just as they suggested and I am damed if it didn't work out just as slick as hot grease thru a tin horn.

I was called before the parole board one day and there I told them all the lies and hot air I could and they gave me a parole and let me go home. In that way I first found out how to use religeon as a cloak of hypocracy to cover up my rascalites. One of the boys who showed me how to fool the law was a boy by the name of Gillespie. He is now the Chief or Capt. of Police in either Minneapolis or St. Paul Minn.

That Mr. George Mann was dishonorably discharged from his Job as Company Comander of 2 Co. M.S.T.S. by the then head Superintendent a Mr Whittier who fired him for commiting some kind of immoral act on some of the boys under his care. This same Mr Whittier was himself later on dishonarably discharged for the Brutal and inhuman treatment of the boys under his charge.

All of these things are on file among the Records of the M.S.T.S. at Red Wing. Minn. and can be verified by any one who cares to look the facts up.

After serving about 2 years there I was pronounced by the parole board to be a nice, clean boy of good morals, as pure as a lily and a credit to those in authority in the instatution where I had been sent to be reformed. Yes sure I was reformed all right, dam good and reformed too. When I got out of there I knew all about Jesus and the bible so much so that I knew it was all a lot of hot air. But that wasnt all I knew. I had been taught by christians how to be a hypocrite and I had learned more about stealing, lying, hating, burning and killing. I had learned that a boys penus could be used for something besides to urinate with and that a rectum could be used for other purposes than crepitating. Oh yes, I had learned a hell of a lot, from my expert instructors furnished to me free of charge by society in general and the state of Minnasota in particular. From the treatment I recieved while there and the lessons I learned from it, I had fully desided when I left there just how I would live my life. I made up my mind that I would rob, burn, destroy and kill every where I went and everybody I could as long as I lived. Thats the way I was reformed in the Minnesota State Training School. Thats the reasons why. What others may have learned by the same sort of treatment in other and similar instatutions, I don't know but this I do know that in later years I have met thousands of graduates of those kind of instatutions and they were either in, going into or just leaving either Jails, prisons, madhouses or the rope and electric chair was yawning for them as it is for me now.

When I was discharged from the school, I was given a suit of clothes five dollars in money, a ticket to my home and a million dollars worth of good advise. This advise I threw in the first ash can with my bible and sunday school lessons and report cards. The five dollars I spent on the train for candy, fruit and a belly-ache. The ticket I used to ride as far as my home. The suit was taken away from me as soon as I got home. In exchange I was given an old pair of overhalls and a hoe, taken to the field and told to earn my keep by work and the swet of my brow. That didn't sound so good to me so I told my folks that I wanted to go to school and study to be a Preacher and save souls. I put up such a hot line of talk that it was decided to send me to a German Luthern school where the Minester taught German to the kids in the basement on weekdays and saved souls on Sundays in the same church. The German Luthern Church and School of Grand Forks, North Dakota. This scheme worked fine for about a couple of months and then the kids began to point thier finger at me and yell, "Reform School" every time I passed by. Then I started knocking thier blocks off every time I could catch one alone. They told thier parents who told mine who in turn told the German Preacher to do his duty by me. He did. He started whipping me pretty regularly but I was a pretty big boy and very strong so one day when he started beating me I came back at him and gave him a good scrap but he was too much for me so he won that time. But I had learned a thing or two by then. One of them was a little piece of poetry about a Colonel Colt.

"Be a man either great or small in size;
Colonel Colt will equalize."

With that idea in my mind I looked around until I found a kid who had a big old fashioned heavy caliber Colt Pistol. I got it. The next day at daylight I stole one of my brothers vests, put the big pistols in the inside pocket, and went to school and the first crack out of the box after school opened up I gave the Preacher Teacher, warning to lay off of me or I would fix him. I guess he took it for granted that I was bluffing or incapable of carrying out my threats so instead of leaving me alone he imediataly got his whip and ordered me to the front for punishment. I refused to leave my seat so he came down and tried to pull me out but I held on with both hands and feet. Then he started beating me over the head and shoulders with the whip and at the same time yanking at my coat and vest collar to pull me out.

The buttons on the vest gave out before I did, The Preacher gave a yank; The buttons on the vest tore loose and the pistol fell on the floor and the preacher with it. He fell on his big fat caboose with his mouth wide open and his eyes as big as saucers. He was parylized with surprise and fear. All he could say was, "Mine Gott, Mine Gott. A gun a gun." I was not surprised or afraid, I was mad as hell — I jumped out of my seat, grabbed the gun and pointed it at him right between his horns and pulled the trigger 2 or 3 times but it wouldnt go off. The school was in an uproar and during the exsitement I figured it was a good time for me to go some where else. I did. I went home. I thought I was a hero and I figured they would kill the fatted calf for me as soon as I told my story. Instead of killing the fatted calf they dam near killed me.

They had heard the other side of the story first and before I had a chance to tell my end of it I got a wallop alongside of the coco that floored me and the next I knew was that my big older brother had me by the throat choking me to make me tell where I had hidden the gun. I told him and when he went out of the back door to look for it I went out of the front door to look for another one to shoot him with. I have never seen him since except once for a very short time. That night I resumed my journey to the west that had been cut short 2 years before. I didn't want to be a preacher any more, I wanted to be a cowboy and shoot me a few wild indians and tame preachers. Thats more than 20 years ago but I have been a cowboy since, I never shot any wild indians but I did shoot a tame preacher once. I shot him right under his shirt-tail. His name is Rev. Johnson and he has a church and runs a mission in Baltimore. Md. right now. But this happened many years later. At my second attempt to run away from home to go out and see the world, I was a little more successfull. Since then I have been all over this world. I have seen it all and I dont like what I have seen of it. Now I want to get clear out of this damed world alltogether.

I was about 13 or 14 years old at the time I ran away from home the second time. In theory if not in actual practice I allready knew how to get by in the world. What I didnt know I soon learned. I started out a hobo and soon learned how to ride freight trains and passenger trains, inside and out without paying my fare. for the first 3 or 4 months after I left home I hoboed my way to the Pacific coast and all over the west. Sleeping in box-cars, barns, sheds, hay stacks or most any where at all. My eating I got by begging and telling people lies and hard luck storys about how I was a poor orphan and how much I loved Jesus how I wanted to go to this place or that place, which ever way I happened to be going at that time thats where my rich uncle lived who wanted me to come to him. A lot of bunk with out any truth whatever in it. But people used to fall for it and feed me and help me on my way. Some-times but not allwayss. I done a little stealing whenever I could. sometimes I worked for a day or two. one experience that I had during that time I never forgot and it had a direct bearing on a lot of my actions later in life. I was riding in a box car one night in the west. I was alone and feeling that I would like some one to talk to. I walked over the train until I came to an open lumber car. there were 4 big burley bums in it. When I saw them I told them about the nice warm box car I had just left; it was clean and full of straw. They all imediatly got interested and friendly and told me to lead them to it. I did but I very soon wished that I hadn't. Because just as soon as we all got into the car and shut the door and the train pulled out, they all began to tell me what a nice boy I was and how they would make me rich, they were going to buy me all the silk underwear in the world and I would soon be wearing dimonds as big as base-balls. In fact they promised me every thing in the whole world but first they wanted me to do a little something for them. When they told me what they wanted from me I very soon began to figure that that was no place for me. I didn't want any of that for mine. I told them no. But my wishes didnt make any difference to them. What they couldn't get by moral persuasion they proceeded to get by force. I cryed, begged and pleaded for mercy, pity and sympathy but nothing I could say or do could sway them from thier purpose. I left that box-car a sadder and sicker but wiser boy than I was when I entered it. After that I allways went alone where ever and when ever possible. I had one other similar experiance with men. I was in a small town in the West on a Sunday after noon. I was just a poor young ignorant, friendless and nearly harmless young kid. I was broke and hungry and I went into a livery stable where a bunch of town loafers were sitting around rushing the can, and hitting the bottle. When I approached them and begged for a bite to eat and told my hard luck story about how I loved Jesus and what a good boy I was and how far I had traveled and how old I was. They all became deeply interested and very sympathetic towards me. They didnt promise me any silk under wear or Jewelry but they had a better scheme than that. They told me how good the beer was and how much better the whiskey was. They first offered me a little drink and then a bigger one and it wasnt very long until I was so drunk that I didnt know my own name and soon after I didnt know anything at all. But I sure knew something when I woke up.

These two experinces taught me several lessons. Lessons that I have never forgotten. I did not want to learn these lessons but I found out that it isnt what one wants in this world that one gets. Forse and might makes right. Perhaps things shouldn't be that way but thats the way they are. I learned to look with suspission and hatred on everybody. As the years went on that idea persisted in my mind above all others. I figured that if I was strong enough and clever enough to impose my will on others, I was right. I still believe that to this day. Another lesson I learned at that time was that there were a lot of very nice things in this world. Among them were Whiskey and Sodomy. But it depended on who and how they were used. I have used plenty of both since then but I have recieved more pleasure of of them since; than I did those first times. Those were the days when I was learning the lessons that life teaches us all and they made me what I am today. It wasn't my fault that the teachirs who gave me my instructions were the wrong kind or that the lessons they taught me, were the wrong kind. Men made me what I am today and if men don't like what they made of me, they must put the blame where it belongs.

After I had hoboed around the country for a few months I was finaly caught in a small petty larceny burglary at Butte Mont. I was held in the County Jail where there were 50 or 100 older men. put in there for all the kinds of crime and meannesses there are that men could do on each other. I was there a month or two under the name of Carl Panzram. Then I was tried and sent to the Montana State Reform School at Miles City, Montana. There I stayed nearly one year. While there I spent my time either working in the shoe-shop or in the fields and gardens. When I wasn't doing that I was trying to escape or being punished for trying it. I was a pretty big boy at that time. very stubborn and contrary, decietfull and treacherous. I had been in a few small scrapes and all of the officers had orders to watch me closely. That didn't worry me much but there was one officer there by the name of Bushart, an ex prizefighter from Boston, who made it his special duty to make life miserable for me. He done a pretty through job of it. He kept on nagging and nagging at me until finialy I desided to murder him. Every evening in the school room, he used to sit up on top of one of the front seat while he had one of the boys black his boots. He was doing that one evening and I got a board about 2 foot long and 18 inches wide by one inch thick. this board was made of hard oak wood and had about 3 or 4 pounds of iron on one end of it. I took this and sneaked up behind him and whacked him on top of his head. It didn't kill him but it made him pretty sick and he quit monkeying with me any more.

For this I got several beatings and locked up, and watched closer than before. They were going to indict me and send me to the State Prison at Deer Lodge for that but I was too young. As the law would not permit them to send a 14 or 15 year old boy to State Prison, they done thier damdest to make life miserable for me. They worked me hard and beat me harder. You see they were trying to make a good boy out of me. They took me in the hospital and operated on me by clipping my fore-skin off to stop me from the habit of masturbation. So they said any way, but how the hell they figured that would stop me is more than I could see. I can't yet. At that time a Mr. Hawkins was Superintendent. His method of teaching us boys religeon was to hammer it into us morning, noon and night Just the same as they done to me at Red Wing. But it seems as tho we were not getting enough religeon yet. Hawkins got fired for stealing the funds of the state and for that money and for his misshandling of the boys under his Charge. The next man to take up his Job was a devil chasing, soul saver a Preacher by the name of Mr. Price. His mithod was to put us all on the pratt and tell us what good boys he thought we were. He lasted quick. We all began to leave his happy home as soon as we could get around a corner and then run. After I was there nearly a year I began to be good palls with a boy by the name of Jimmie Benson whoes home was in Butte and who was a pretty smart little boy. Between the two of us we concocted a scheme that we could both escape the same day. He was trusted but I wasnt so he was to run away first and while he was gone and all of the screws were out chasing him then I was to blow. We had a prearranged place to hide until the hunt was over and then we were to meet at another place about 40 miles away. We each done our part and the scheme worked like a charm. Our plans called for a meeting place about 40 miles away at the first water tank east of Terry Mont. The first to arrive was to wait for the other. I arrived there first. on the third night after our escape. I looked around and saw no one so I took my iron bar which I had carried all the way from the school, then I walked around behind the tank, lay down to sleep, cold, hungry and tired but free and happy. I was awakened at day light by hearing some one rattling tin cans and smelling food. I didnt know who it might be so I peeked around the corner where I saw a man dressed in a nice blue suit with a big stetson hat on. On one side of him lay a big sack full of clothes and food, while on the other was a belt full of shells and a scabbard of pistol. The man was eating and drinking, with his back turned towards me. I was hungry and wanted the grub, clothes and the pistol so I took my iron bar and sneaked up on him and was just about to bounce it off of his head when he heard me and grabbed the gun and turned around, so I could see that it was my partner Jimmie Benson. he laid his gun down and I dropped my iron bar and we began to celabrate. In the sack he had food and clothes for me, which he had stolen a few miles down the line the day before by breaking into a surveyers and homesteaders shack. After we eat and I dressed up he gave me the gun as I was the biggest of us two and probably the meanest. Then we were all organized and ready to do battle with any body. We didn't go back looking for the screws who were looking for us but we were in hopes that we might meet one of them. We were both pretty dam hostile and we felt that if we couldnt meet any of them, then some-one else would do to have our revenge on. It didn't take long for the pair of us to raise plenty of hell with a lot of different people. I stayed with him about a month, hoboing our way east stealing and burning everything we could. He showed me how to work the stick up racket and how to rob the poor boxes in churches, I in turn taught him how to set fire to a church after we robbed it. we got very busy on that robbing and burning a church regular every chance we got. When we got tired of riding on a train we used to open up the Journal boxes, take out the greasey waste packing and throw some sand or gravel into it. They wouldnt get far with that car until they had a hot box. At that time the wheat harvest was going on in North Dakota and whole train loads of wheat would be shipped, some-times loose in cars. Every time we saw a car or train loaded like that, we would crall underneath on the rods and cut or bore holes thru the floor so that the wheat would pour out thru the holes and go to waste on the tracks as the train was rolling along. By the time we got as far east as Farago, North Dakota, we had between us, two good six-shooters each had a good suit and about $150.00 in cash besides a various assortment of watches, rings and other slum that we had got by the burglary route and by harvesting the harvesters. At Farago we split; Jimmie went back to Butte and it was only a short time later that he got caught in a hold up and sent to the big house at Deer Lodge Mont. for 10 years. I met him there years later when I myself was sent there for burglary. After Jimmie and I split up I went to my home where I stayed only a day or two and then I headed west again. Out to the Coast again and back to Montana where I Joined the U.S. Army about 1905 or 1906 I Joined the 6th regular U.S. Infantry. I was only in the army a month or two when I got 3 years in the U.S. Military Prison at Fort Leavensworth, Kansas. I wasnt there long before I tried to escape but luck was against me. The next thing I done there was to burn up all the prison shops there. That time I used a candle inside of a one gallon can, in the bottom of the can was a lot of oil soaked rags. when the candl burned down to the rags that set the whole works ablaze. She shure made a fine little blaze. a clean sweep. another hundred thousand dollars to my credit and the best part of it was that no one ever found it out until now. I was in stripes as a third class prisnor nearly all the while I was there. I was allways in trouble of some sort. I had a job of swinging an 18 pound hammer in the rock quarry most of my bit. my number was 1874. and my name was Carl Panzram. There I done 37 months. I done plenty of work and I had plenty of punishment and the only good part of it was that they didn't try to hammer any more religeon into us. My General Court Martial or trial was held at Fort William Henery Harrison Helena, Mont. and my court Proceedings were reviewed by the then Secretary of War Mr Howard Taft. He reccomended me for 8 years and he signed em. 14 years later I had the very good fortune to rob him out of about $40,000.00 worth of jewelry and liberty bonds. This happened at his home in New Haven, Conn. in the summer of 1920.

I was discharged from that prison in 1910. Before I left there I sung em the same old song and gave em the same line of bull about how I sure loved Jesus and what a good nice young man I was and how mich good it had done me to be sent to that prison. I dont know if they believed me or not but they all said they did anyway. They all declared that I was pure as a lilly and free from all sin. They told me to go and sin no more. I agreed with everything they said. They gave $5.00 a suit of clothes and a ticket to Denver, Colorado. Well I was a pretty rotton egg before I went there but when I left there, all the good that ever may have been in me had been kicked and beaten out of me long before. All that I had in my mind at that time was a strong determination to raise plenty of hell with any body and every body in every way I could and every time and every place I could.

I was the spirit of meaness personified. I had not at this time got so that I hated myself, I only hated everybody else.

At this time of my life I was about 20 years old, 6 foot tall and weighed about 190 pounds of concentrated hell-firered man inspired meaness. I was as strong as two or three average men. I had to be to be able to withstand some of the punishments and labor that I went thru during my 3 years in the U.S.M.P. One of my tasks and punishments while there was to be shackled to a 50 pound iron Ball for 6 months. During that time I wore that Ball and chain day and night, slept with it and worked with it on. My work was in the rock quarry and that was 3 miles from the prison. The gang of about 300 convicts and 40 screws used to march out in the morning and back at night. The other men had nothing to carry except themselves but my part was to load my iron ball, an 18 pound hammer, a pick and shovel and a 6 foot iron crow-bar all into a wheel barrow and march behind the line of cons, out to the rock quarry and there work for 8 1/2 hours in the hot Kansas sun, busting big rocks and after that was all over to pack my little iron pill and my tools into the Irish buggy and wheel it all back to the prison. There eat my supper of stinking cod-fish greasey stew or mouldy and wormy rice or beans. But all of that treatment done one good thing for me. The worse the food was and the harder they worked me the stronger I got. I quit my old habit of masturbation because I couldn't do that and do the hard work and punishment at the same time. When I left there and went to Denver I was busted and to get a start with a few bucks I took a Job in a R.R. mule skinners camp. I was there only a few weeks but I licked every one in it and was getting all set to go to work on the boss-man when he fired me pulled a gun on me and drove me out of camp. I took my pay went to town and bought me a gun, the biggest I could find in Denver and they have some big ones there. With the balance of my money I went down to the Redlight district figuring on getting good and drunk and then taking charge of that section of Denver. But something went wrong some where because the next after noon I woke up to find myself laying in an alley feeling pretty sick, I had no gun, no money, my coat, hat and shoes were gone but I had a few lumps on top of my head that werent there before. and the worst was yet to come about a week later when I found that my collection also included a fine first-class case of gonorreah. I began to suspect that the ladies were very good things to leave alone. I have followed that policy pretty closely ever since. once in a while since then one would get her claws into me but not while I was sober or in the daytime where I could see em first. After leaving Denver I hoboed around stealing as I went and not forgetting to take over all the churches I could, until I hit Hutchison where the State fair of Kansas was being held at the time. There I joined up as a rider for Col. Dickeys Circle D Wild West show which was playing with Kliens Carnivil Co at that time. I lasted about a week but during that time I fought and licked everybody around there including the horses and steers. Then they got tired of me being on the prod all the time so they canned me. Then I went over to where the Kansas state militia soldiers were camped and stole one of thier tents and was carring away some sacks of oats and grain when the sentry caught me but he was only a tin soldier and a kid at that so I took his rifel and thru it in the horse trough and was going to throw him in after it when about 9 thousand more came running to his rescue It was about time for me to leave there and go some where else. I did. I went to Sedalia, Missouri where they were holding thier stat fair In a day or so the carnival Co with the D [circled] showed up to play but they had bad luck. The first nights stand they had the misfortune to lose thier horse tent and cook tent by some scoundrel touching a match to them. I left there right away quick. I went to St. Louis where I got a job for the C. and E.I. and the I.C. R.R. as a guard and strike breaker. They first sent me to the yards at Centralia Ill where I started in to lick every union striker I saw. I didn't see many so I started to lick the scabs and guards and I succeeded so well that the Co. sent me to Cairo which was a hard town with plenty of trouble there. When I got off of the train a union picket stopped me to ask me my buisness. I licked him. A copper stopped us from fighting and I licked him. Any way he stopped fighting me long enough to blow his whistle for help and while he was doing that I figured it was a good time for me to go and report to my new boss. when I reported to him I gave him a letter that my former boss at Centralia had given me to give to him. He read it, got up and patted me on the back, told me what a fine fellow I was and then told me to go out in the R.R. yards and if I saw any one there who had no buisness to be there, to knock thier blocks of and run em ragged. I told him I would, and I did so much so that the whole town of Cairo was out to scalp me. The next Saturday night being payday and me having a few bucks in my pocket and feeling pretty good I decided to go up town get a few drinks and then go and see what the girls in the Red Light district had to offer. In the first saloon I struck I met a very nice and accomadating fellow who offered to show me a good time and a nice girl but first he had to call her on the phone. he did as he promised me. he showed me the town. something else too. He took me around the corner and showed me about a dozen big huskey mad union strikers. They at once proceeded to see if I was such a hell of a fighter as I thought I was. I wasnt. They cleaned me up in great shape and then the cops came and finished the Job by throwing me in the cann. My boss got me out of there and gave me a ticket to E. St Louis and another letter to another boss man there but when I got on the train I tore open and read that letter. After reading it I decided that East St Louis could try to get along without me. I went to Chicago, looked at the Loop and the Lake front and started out for Mexico where there was a war on at the time. I figured that a mexican was easier to lick than a lot of hard boiled railroaders. Besides I had heard that all of the Churches in Old Mexico were full of gold and silver. Maybe I could git my share. All the American churches I had robbed wouldn't keep me in cigarett money. I left Chicago hoboing, stealing any way I could and by the time I hit Jacksonvill Texas I had collected two heavy calibered pistols, some money not much tho, and one of the most beautifull, blue eyed curly haired, rosy cheeked fat boys that I have ever seen in my life and I have seen some nice boys. At Jacksonvill Texas we were pinched. The cops took my guns but left me my boy. we were both sent to the County Road gang at Rusk Texas. When we got to the Road gang they gave me a chain to wear on my leg and took my boy away from me. The Boss mans name was Mr. Moore. he took my boy to sleep in his tent. I guess he wanted to save the boys soul or something. Any way about 3 weeks after I was there, this Mr. Moore and one of his officers by the name of Awkwrite or hawkright or some such a name, They got into a hell of a battle and were going to shoot each other. Mr. Moore fired Mr Awkwrite or Hawkright or what ever his name was. Awk went to town and complained to the County officials and they in turn came out to the camp, investigated the conditions and fired Mr. Moore. Then my boy was chased out of the officers tent and put back into the prisoners tent where I was. Then he told me tales about Mr. Moore and Mr Hawkbright and what a queer pair of christian degenerates they were. both married men with families too. At the time of our arrest and confinement there I gave the name of Jeff Davis and the boy gave the name of John H. Clark. this was in the winter of 1910 and 1911

These things are all on the Records and can be verified by any one.

My sentence on that road gang called for 40 days or $19.70 at .50¢ per day. I finished my 40 days and asked the Boss man to cut my chain off and turn me loose but he left the chain on and knocked my block off instead. The next day I ran away, got caught, brought back and whipped at the snorting pole. Then

I worked 20 days more and asked the same question of the same man. he gave me the same answer as he had before. The next day I tried again to move out with the same result. again in 5 days I tried but that time I was successfull in my attempt. I walked to Palistine Texas, caut the trucks of a fast mail train and that night I got into Houstan Texas. When I got there the train couldn't get in because the whole town was on fire so I got off and walked thru the town enjoying the sights of all the burning buildings and listening to the tales of woe, the moans and sighes of those whoes homes and property were burning. I enjoyed it all very much. several times people asked me to help them save thier valuables. Sure I helped em save thier stuff but not for them. I wore some of the clothing for months after that I helped to save. The stuff I stole there kept me in funds and living high until I hit El Passo Texas. There I crossed the Mexican Border to Juraze in Mexico where I tried to Join the Mexican Army but the Federals were in control there and they wouldn't accept me. I left El Passo on the El Passo and South Western R.R. going towards Del Rio. At that time I was with a young quarter breed indian whoes home was in Kalamath Falles Oregon. He also told me that he had just got out of the Pen at Yuma Arizona. We palled together for a week or two. After leaving El Passo we road our way to some small town about 50 or 75 miles away there we met a fellow who told us he was about 35 years old and that he had been working in some R.R. camp near by and that he had $35.00 on him. I and the indian got interested right away. We told him a lot of bull and conned him into walking with us on the wagon road beside the tracks to the next town. We started and got a few miles where we came to a stritch of road with tall mesquite brush and grease wood on both sides of the road no houses in sight and no signes of any other people. There I put the arm on him and we dragged him thru the fence on the left hand side of the road we walked into the bruch for about 1/4 of a mile away from the road. There we stopped and robbed him of his 35 bucks. I tied him up and we walked away. we hadn't gone far before the indian said to me that we better go back and do a better job tieing him up as I hadn't done a very good job. Luckey we did because when we got back to where we had left him he was just about loose. This time the Indian tied him up. First he took his belt of, pulled his pants down to below his knees and tied his legs together with the belt and also tied his shoe-laces together, then he tied his hands behind his back. Then he tied his hands to his feet pulled up together behind. Then he stuffed a sock in his mouth and tied a handkerchief tight over that and then tied him to a tree. He was then ready to leave him and walk away but I wasnt thru yet. I figured that while I had such a good chance as that I would comit a little sodomy on him. This I proceeded to do. Then I invited the Indian to take a ride but that dam fool was only an indian. he hadn't recieved the full benifits of civilization yet like I had so he declined the honor. We left that guy right there in that shape He is still there unless the buzzards and coyotes have finished the last of him long ago. this was in the year of 1911 and the town and place was some where between El Passo and a R.R. division point where we went to that night and there bought a tick to Del Rio Texas. There we split where he went I don't know and dont care. I crossed the Border at Del Rio to Agua Prieta, Mexico where I enlisted in the Forigen Leigon of the Constatutionalist Armmy of Northern Mexico. our Comander was General Stanley Williams and and the Comander in Chief was General Orosco. I was with that out fit for about a month or so but all the churches I ever saw had all been robbed before I got there. All that any of those cholos had was a few beans and some pepper Dam few beans but lots of pepper. I didn't care much for thier beans and much less for thier pepper As I couldn't do much buisness in my line there, I deserted but first I stole my horse, equippment and everything that wasnt tied down. I rode my horse to death before I hit the border, there I left everything I had stolen and then dam near run myself to death before I got back to the land of the free and the home of the brave. When I got back I imediatly got buisy on the S.P. line from Yuma Arizona to Fresno Cal. During this time I was buisy robbing chicken coops and then touching a match to them. I burned old sheds, barns, fences snow sheds or any thing I could and when I couldnt burn any thing else I would set fire to the grass on the praries or the woods anything and every thing. I had a pistol and I would spend all my spare change for bullets, I would take pot shots at farmers houses at the windows, if I saw cows or horses in the fields I would cut loose at them. At night while I was riding the freight trains I was allways on the look out for something to shoot at or trying to stick up the other hoboes that I met on the trains. I looked em all over and whenever I met one who wasnt too rusty looking I would make him raise his hands and drop his pants. I wasn't very particular either I rode em old and young, tall and short, white and black it made no difference to me at all except that they were human beings. During this time all along that S.P. line, things were pretty warm, the sheriffs, coppers and railroad bulls were all hostile. I got pinced a couple of times but it was in the day time and during that time I would have my gun and sap and other plunder planted But in my pockets I allways carried a well thumbed bible and a prayer book and a little account book where I had written down a lot of crap about where I had worked on different Jobs, how many hours, days, what I earned and a lot of bull like that. So every time a cop grabbed me I would pull the old innocent and injured racket. Tell em how much I loved Jesus and what a good hard working honest fellow I was. That nearly allways worked fine. Sometimes not. When I hit Fresno Cal. I got 120 days in the can for stealing a bycycle. I done 30 days and then escaped. When I got out of there I went and dug up my plant where I had left my gun and other stuff and then started north on the S.P. line. I had not gone fare befor I met Mr Trouble. He took the form of a R.R. breakman. I was riding in an iron open coal car at the time with 2 other bums. They knew nothing about me except the lies I had told em. I was sizing up the youngest and best looking one of the two and figuring when to pull out my hog-leg and histe em up. But a shack comes over the top and bounces down into my car and begins bawling us all out and telling us to dig up or unload. He asked us all who we were and what we were. I don't know what the other two told him but I pulled out my cannon and told him that I was the fellow that went around the world doing people good and asked him if there was any thing that I had that he wanted. he said no and that he was a good fellow and never put any body off of his train and to prove he was a good fellow he offered to buy us all a feed and offered to give us a piece of change. He gave me a piece of change, all he had and then he gave me his watch and chain and then he was so kind as to pull his pants down while I rode him around the floor of that freight car. When I was thru riding him I told the other two bums to mount him but they declined to indulge in that form of pleasure. But by my using a little moral persuasion and much waving around of my pistol, they also rode mr brakeman around. After our very pleasant and profitable, "for me anyway," little trip was all over, the other three got off to walk. They didn't want to but they did anyway. The freight was rolling along at about 15 or 20 miles an hour so I guessed that they didn't hurt themselves very much. It didn't hurt me any. I have been unloaded from trains going much faster than we were then quite a few times and I am still alive to remember it. After they got off, I kept rolling along into and out of Sacremento, thru Oregon up to Seattle. There I got the can for a short bit. All this time since I left the prison at Fort Leavensworth I had been going under the name of Jeff Davis Now I changed my name to Jack Allen. Under that name I was pinched for Highway Robbery, Asualt and Sodomy at The Dalles, Oregon. I was in Jail there held for the action of the Grand Jury. I was there about 2 or 3 months and then broke Jail there. I haven't been there since. I left there one day they put an old safe blower in that can. I imediately asked him to teach me how to blow safes. He didn't stay there long enough to teach me that but he showed me how I could break out of there He was taken to Moscow Idaho to stand trial for a Post Office Robbery. He got 5 years in Leavensworth. Later on he got another and bigger bit. he is still in the can. His name was Cal Jordan or Doctor Jordan. He also done a bit in the hoose-gow at Salem Oregon under the name of Hopkins. A few days after he left The Dalles, I broke Jail. this was in 1912. From there I went to Spokane where I robbed the Police Staition at Hillyard a subburb of Spokane among my loot there was 2 of the coppers pistols. Then I bought 6 hack saws and tied 3 on each leg under my sox and underwear, I then went to Moscow, Idaho to try to get the old safe-blower out. When I got there I hid the 2 guns some clothes and food and then walked up to the Jail, broke in to it but got caught doing so and got 30 days myself. The thanks I got from old Cal was that he thought I was in love with him and he tried to mount me. but I wasn't broke to ride and he was so I rode him. At that time he was about 50 years old and I was 20 or 21 but I was strong and he was weak. When I got out of Jail I got as far as Harrison, Idaho where I got pinched and put in the can where I at once tried to break out by setting fire to the Jail. but I got caught and a day or so later I was in the Jail at Wallace, Idaho. under the name of Jeff Davis. Some months later I was pinched at Chinook Montana for burglary, I quick took a plea of guilty and got 1 year at the State Prison at Deer Lodge. Mont. When I got there I met my old partner Jimmie Benson who was doing 10 years for robbery. I stayed there about 8 months and escaped. a week later I was arrested at Three Forks, Mont, for burglary under the name of Jeff Rhodes I pleaded guilty and got a year and sent back to Deer Lodge where I was at once brought to court and given one year for my escape under the name of Jeff Davis. Out of these 3 sentences I served 23 monthes. In that prison there was work for only a few men and I wasn't one of those. All of the cells were for 2 men in each. Each man could choose his own cell-mates and get a new one any time he wanted one. I used to want a new one pretty regular. At that place and time I got to be an expert experineced Wolf. I knew more about sodomy that old boy Oscar Wilde ever thought of knowing. I would start the morning with sodomy, work as hard at it as I could all day and sometimes half of the night. I was so buisy committing sodomy that I didn't have any time left for to serve Jesus as I had been taught to do in those Reform Schools. The warden there was a big wolf by the name of Frank Conley. He was the warden of that prison and Mayor of the town of Deer Lodge for over 30 years. He wound up his own career by blowing out his own brains because he was due for a bit in one of his own cells for charges of stealing the state funds and for a hoste of other crimes. When I left there he told me I was as pure as a lilly, and free of all sin. to go and sin no more. He gave me 5 dollars, a suit of clothes and a ticket to the next town 6 miles away. I headed back to the west and about 2 weekes later I was pinched for a burglary at Astoria Oregon. The Judge and the D.A. offered to let me off light if I would plead guilty and save thier county taxpayers the expense of a trial. I done so and they didn't. instead they gave me the limit of 7 years. When I got back to the Jail the coppers laughed at me, locked the door and went away. When they were gone I got out of my cell, locked all of the other prisnors in thier cells, I plugged up all the locks so no one could get in or out. Then I went to work and wrecked their dam Jail. I tore loose all the radiators and steam pipes smashed all the toilets and sinks and plugged up all the pipes tore out all the electric wiring took the cook stove, all the dishes all the food all the blankets mattrasses and clothing all the furnitcher, benches, tables chairs, books and every thing that was loose or could be torn loose and that would burn, then I piled it all up and set fire to it. The coppers finally broke thru the door and put the fire out and locked me up after first knocking my block off. Then I tried to play crazy but I couldn't fool the Doctors. They took me to the State prison at Salem Oregon this was in 1914 and my name there was Jefferson Baldwin. 7390. I swore I would never do that 7 years and I never have either. I was sent to the Oregon State Prison in 1914 and as soon as I got there I was in more trouble. I swore I would never do that 7 years and defied the warden and all of his officers to make me. The warden swore I would do every dam day of those 7 years or he would kill me. I haven't done it yet and I am not dead but he is. His name was Harry Minto. His method of running the prison was to Bull-doze everybody. I used to go around in the prison all the time scheming and planning how to escape and causing all the trouble I could. if I couldn't escape I would help every body else that I could. I was allways agitating and egging the other cons on to try to escape or raise hell in some way I finaly met a big tough, half simple hoosier kid in there and I steamed him up to escape. He done every thing I told him to and some more that I didn't. He went to the warden and he asked for a Job on the farm. He got it. As soon as he did he attempted to escape right under the wardens eye. The warden tore out to run him down. He did. When he caught the kid they were a long ways in the lead of the other screws who were all chasing him but they and some of the cons saw the whole deal. When the warden caught that kid he at once started to beat his brains out but the kid came back at him and took his gun away from him and killed him and kept on going on his way but not very far. The rest of the screws caught up with him and riddled him with Bullets. When that warden got killed, They sent his brother a John Minto to take his place. As soon as the new Warden got on the job he began to look me up and make life miserable for me. and I in turn done the same for him. I tried to escape. but no luck. caught and severly punished. next I robbed the store room and stole a few dozen bottles of lemon extract which I took out to the gang in the yard and got em all drunk and steamed em all up to raise hell and battle the screws. They did just as I suggested They run all of the yard screws ragged. I didn't drink at all Next I set fire to the prison shops and I figured that I would go over the wall during the excitement but it didn't work worth a cent. The fire went good and burned the whole works down and there was another hundred thousand dollars to my credit. But I got caught that time. They kicked the hell out of me and put me in the cooler for 61 days on bread and water and then carried me out to a new place that they had just built especialy for me and a few more like me. in one corner of the yard under the eye of two rifle guards day and night. There they thought they had us safe for all time but in less than 3 months there were two of the bunch that escaped, thier names were Cockey O'Brian and Step and a half Smith. But 3 of us couldn't go so we stuck and when day light came and the screws opened our doors to feed us they found 2 missing. Wow, then there was hell to pay for sure As they couldn't punish the two who had got away they took thier spite out on the rest of us. Two of us, me and a fellow by the name of Curtis, they stripped naked and chained us up to the door and then turned the fire hose on us until we were black and blue, deaf and half blind. This caused a big invistigation by the aroused public and the consequences were that the warden, "the Deputy warden', a skunk by the name of Vinegar," Sherwood and 9 screws got a can tied on them. A new Warden came then. An Ex Army Capt by the name of Murphy and a pretty good old scout he was too. The new Wardens method of running that prison was a radical change from the old system. I had never seen any thing done like he was doing. There was no religeon about him and no brutality. Those who wanted religeon could have it. There was no punishment of any kind except one and that was to be locked in a cell given a bed to sleep on 3 meals a day, plenty of books to read and exercised twice each day. When I first heard that I thought he was Crazy. That was wrong. Then I thought he was a fool. That was wrong. Then I thought he must be a bit queer sexualy. I thought he must be a punk or some kind of fruit. But damed if that wasn't wrong too. Then he told me himself just what his ideas were. He was an Idealist. A lot of his theories were way over my head and I was too dumb to understand all he told me but one thing he did tell me that I did understand was this "He told me that he had looked up my record and it was just as bad as it had been told to him. The other officers and the former warden told him that I was the worst man in the prison and that they thought I was the meanest and most cowardly degenarate that they had ever seen or heard of." I agreed with what they told him. Then he told me that, "He didnt believe them at all and he told me I was not the worst man in the prison." I told him to show me a worse one. Then he told me the biggest surprise of my life. He told me "that if I would give him my word of honor that I wouldn't escape or try to that he would open the gates and let me outside of the prison to go any dam place I wanted to go but to be back for the count at supper time." I thought for a few minutes and then gave him my word of honor that he would see me there for supper time and that I would not try to escape. Even when I told him that I had not the least intentions of keeping my word of honer. I fulley intended to escape at the first chance. But some-thing went wrong some how. Old boy Spud was as good as his word. He opened the gates and I was free to go any dam place I wanted to. I just stood there dumfounded and so surprised at what I couldn't understand that I didn't try to escape at all, I just walked around a little while to see if any screws were watching me but I didn't see any so I sat down and tried to dope out what it was all about. Of one thing I was sure, I could have gone if I had cared to. And another thing I was sure of was that there wasn't any more honor about me than the stone I was sitting on. I just thought, as I couldn't understand what it was all about, that I would stick around a while and see what would happen and then I would sure beat if after a few days. That evening I walked up to the gate of the prison and demanded to be let in. Spud Murphy was waiting for me. he asked me why I didn't beat it. I told him I didn't know. He asked me if I wanted a Job on the farm as a trusty. I told him no. I went back into the prison and all the cons told me I was nuts. I thought so myself so I asked the Dr to examine me to see if I was crazy or not. He said I was sane. The warden gave me a job inside of the prison. I worked for him where I never would do anything right for any other wardens in other prisons. In other Jails if they made me work something allways went wrong and dam quick to. if they put me to work around any machinery it soon went on the burn, either the bearings burnt out or the belts wore out or something else was sure to happen. But I worked for Spud all right. He soon got a base-ball team organized and a band. He told me to learn to play ball and some kind of a musical instrument. The tailors made me a band uniform and a base-ball uniform. But I had never had any chance to learn to play base-ball when I was a boy and I was too dumb to learn music. Then he told me to learn how to be a drum-major and lead the band but I was too dumb to learn even that so finaly he asked me if I was too dumb to carry a flag in front of the band. I could do that fine. Every week after that the whole band of 30 or 40 men and the base-ball team of 10 or 12 men would load onto trucks or on the train with only one guard with us and we would go to towns all over the state of Oregon. This outfit of cons had every kind of a mongrel crook and murderer there was in the prison, some doing life some 99 years some 50 some 20 and so on down to 1 or 2 years. The state was in an uproare. The papers all over the country had thier eyes on Spud Murphy and every body was watching his experiment with interest. This game went on all summer and during that time I was put to work outside the walls as a trusty. a few fellows escaped but not very many. I stuck it out that way for about 7 or 8 months and made no attempt to escape in any way. I was allowed to stay out late in the evenings till after dark, just walking around or passing the time away talking smoking and enjoying life. There was a big hospital close by where there were a lot of women nurses working. They used to write mash notes and try to date me up for a good time. I used to go out once in a while and one night while I was with one of these girls having a good time with a bottle of boose she had, I not being used to drinking much got loaded to the eyes, I was pretty drunk and the girl was very pretty and affectionate. I stayed too late and then being drunk I thought I was a pretty dumb slob to stick around there when I could be having that kind of a good time all the time. The night was warm and the moon was shining bright, a freight train was whistling down in the yards; Calling to me I figured. Anyway I answered. I pulled out of there. A week later I robbed a house near Eugene Oregon. In the house I put on a good suit of clothes, what money I found I put in my pocket with a loaded pistol which I found there. Then I sat down and eat for the first time in about a week. When I left there I felt that I would rather die than be brought back to the prison to face Spud Murphy. I guess thats the reason I had courage enough to put up a gun battle in daylight in the middle of a town. me alone against a sherif and the rest of the town. Any way thats what happened an hour or so later. I fired and fought until my gun was empty of bullets and I was empty of courage. They tried me at Eugene and gave me 2 years for the burglary and 8 years for asualt on the Sherife. Back to the prison I went where nothing was done to me except to lock me up for a few months. After that the warden put me back to work on the inside of the walls but he told me that in a few months he would put me back outside to work again as I was before. But that was too much for me. I got buisy and got some hacksaws and a spreader and other tools and clothes and one morning I made a break from the inside of the walls. I made it clean. I have never been back since. I still owe 14 years there. That happened in May 1918. They gave me quite a chase. The whole north west was aroused. The newly organized State constabulary were all after me, some of the State Milita and all of the citizens in that part of the country were after me and the rewards that were offered for me but it done them no good. Luck was with me and I got clear away. The war was on at that time and the country was pretty hot. Every once in a while I was picked up and either turned loose or broke loose. I took the name of John O'Leary and I registered for the Army draft at Meyersdale Penn. They put me in class 1A. That didn't sound good to me so I kept on moving. I moved into Baltimore where I worked for a few days at Sparrows Point and then went in to Baltimore, Bought a gun and met a nice boy. The boy told me of a good joint to stick up at Fredric, Md. There we go to the hotel where I registered as John O'Leary what the kids name was I dont know or care. At 2 o'clock that morning we went down into the Lobby of the hotel and stuck up the Joint. My end was better than $1200.00 we split the dough. I took $1200.00 and gave the kid about a couple of hundred in small bills and about 10 pounds of silver. Where he went I dont know. I went to New York to see what made the lights so bright there. I found out. Later I joined the Y.M.C.A. in N.Y. and the Marine Firemans Oilers and Water Tinders Union. Those papers with my membership card in the F.O.E. were sufficient to get me a Seamans Identification Card. Armed with those credentials I Joined a ship, the James S. Whitney of the Grace Line. Went to Panama and from there to Peru where I jumped her went up to the copper mines at Cerro De Pasco. Worked until the strike and then went to Chuquicomatti, Chile where I worked for the Braden Copper Corporation a short time then Back to Panama where I signed up as labor foreman for the Fortification Division. U.S. Goverment. a short time there and I went up the coast of Panama to the Island of Bocas Del Toro. where I worked Driving niggers for the Sinclair Oil Co. They sent me to take charge of a gang way up in the Talamanca Indian country. not long there until I was fired for fighting any body and every body all the time. this was in 1919. and I was still using the name of John O'Leary. I burned the oil well rig at Bocas Del Toro for which the Sinclair oil Co offered 1500 dollars reward. but no one ever got it yet.

I learned a little about uncivilized people while I was up in the Talamanca Indian country in Costa Rica and Panama and what I learned I liked and wanted to learn some more about them so when I got back to Colon, Panama, I inquired around a bit and found out all I could about a race of Indians who had not been contaminated or civilized yet by the other civilized People. Those indians were a tribe called the San Blass Indians who lived in the Darian country in the mountains and on the islands down the coast of Panama. At Panama City I got a Legation Passport issued to me by the U.S. Ambassador there. But I had to have a boat to get down the coast and not having money enough to buy one I set out to steal a small schooner. I hunted around until I found one I liked then I hunted around until I found a hard-boiled sailor who would listen to me. Between us we concocted a scheme to steal that schooner and kill the owener, Captain and crew. There were 6 of them on board of her. The two of us got all ready to do the buisnes but the other fellow got to drinking and while drunk, he alone went to the schooner, killed all of the 6 men but he was too drunk to handle the schooner and the consequences were that he got caught, He was tried in Court at Colon, Panama and the court sentenced him to 18 months for his crime. I was in the clear. I stayed that way by getting on a Panama R.R.S.S. The General Gothals or the S.S. Colon I dont know which. I came to the States on her and Joined the S.S. Houma an oil tanker and went from N.Y. to Port Aruther

Texas and from there to Glassgow Scottland There I robbed the ship and every body on her for which I got a short bit in Barlinnie Prison at Glassgow, Scottland. When I got out of there I had money and my old Panama Passengers Passport I went to London, to Southhampton crossed the channel to Le Havre in France and up to Paris. Had a good time but soon broke so back to Le havre where I joined a ship to Hamburg, Germany and a few other Ports in Europe and then Back to the States. Landed broke and went to Bridgeport. Conn where I robbed a Jewelry store. I got about $7,000 worth of stuff but my end after peddling the lot was $1500.00 Then I signed on the S.S. Manchuria and went to Hamburg Germany and had a hell of a time with my 1500 american dollars and German Marks at 60 to the dollar. In 9 days I was broke and came back on the same ship. Back in New York in summer of 1920 I think June or July but maybe Augst. 5 dayes after I got back broke on the Manchuria I went up to New Haven Conn. There I Robbed the home of some one. in that place I got about $40,000 worth of Jewelry and liberty bonds, The bonds were signed and registired with the name of W. H. Taft and among the Jewelry was a watch with his name on it, presented to him by some congress or senate while he was the Governor General of the Philapine Islands. So I know it was the same man that had given me my 3 years in the U.S.M.P. when he was Secretary of War about 1906. Out of this Robbery I got $3,000.00 in cash and kept some of the stuff. With that money I bought a yacht. The Akista her initials and registry No's were K.N.B.C. 107,296.

On my yacht I had quarters for 5 people but I was alone. For a while. Then I figured it would be a good plan to hire a few sailors to work for me, get them out to my yacht, get them Drunk, comitt sodomy on them, Rob them and then kill them. This I done. Every day or two I would get plenty of booze by robbing other yachts there. The Barbra II was one of them. I robbed here and a dozen or so others around there. I was hitting the booze pretty hard myself at that time. Every day or two I would go to New York and hang around 25 South St and size up the sailors whenever I saw a couple who were about my size and seemed to have money I would hire them to work on my yacht. I would allways promise big pay and easy work. what they got was something else. I would take them and all thier clothes and gear out to my yacht at City Island. There we would wine and dine and when they were drunk enough They would go to bed. When they were asleep I would get my 45 Colt Army Automatic. "This I stole from Mr Tafts Home." and blow thier brains out then I would take a rope and tie a rock on them and put them into my row-boat, row out in the main channel about 1 mile and drop em over board. They are there yet, 10 of em. I worked that racked about 3 weeks, my boat was full of stolen stuff and the people at City Island were begning to look queer at me so the next two sailors I hired I kept alive and at work. One was name Delaney and the other was Goodman or Goodwin or something like that. The three of us on my boat pulled out one day and went'as far as Graves End bay N.Y. where I Robbed another yacht. They knew it but I figured on killing them both in a day or two. But we only got as far down the coast as Atlantic City. N.J. where My yacht was wrecked. With every thing on her lost. The three of us got ashore all right. The other two I paid off and where they went I dont know or care. I was sick at that time and A Dr Charles McGivern took care of me there at his home for a week or so. Him I gave a few pieces of Jewelry of old man Tafts. I also gave him the 45 Colt automatic that I done the killing with. I left his home and went back up to Connecticut looking for another $40,000.00 but I got 6 months in the can at Bridgeport Connecticut instead for burglary. I done that 6 months and while there I borrowed $100.00 from My Doctor Charles McGivern. When I got out of the Can I went to Philadelphia. There I got my Colt 45 back from the Dr. Then I Joined the Flying Squadron of the Seamans Union who were on strike at that time. A few days later I got into a gun battle with some scab sailors and the Cops. The cops won. I got pinched and held for the Grand Jury under the charges of Aggravated Asualt and Inciting to Riot. I got out on bail and imediatly Jumped it. I went to Norfolk, Virginia, got a ship to Europe and robbed her and jumped her when I got there From Europe I went down to Matidi in the Belgian Congo. Africa. From there I went to Loanda, Angola, Portuguesse West Africa There I went to work for the Sinclair oil Co. Driving niggers and I sure drove the hell out of them too. I wasnt there long before I desided to get me a nigger girl. I got one. I paid a big price for her. I bought her from her mother and father for 80 Eschudas or about $8.00 in american. The reason I paid such a big price for her was because she was a virgin. Yah, so she said. She was about 11 or 12 years old. I took her to my shack the first night and took her back to her fathers shack the next. I demanded my money back because they had decieved me by saying the girl was a virgin. I didn't get my money back but they gave me another and younger girl. This girl was about 8 years old. I took her to my shack and maybe she was a virgin but it didn't look like it to me. I took her back and quit looking for any more virgins. I looked for a boy. I found one. He was our table waiter. I educated him into the art of sodomy as practiced by civilized people. But he was only a savage and didn't appreicate the benefits of civilization. He told my boss and the Boss man fired me quick but before he did I licked the hell out of him. They chased me out of the jungles at Quimbazie where that happened and I went back to Loanda. There I went to the U.S. Counsul a Mr. Clark. but he had heard all about me and my ways and he would have none of me. I left his office and sat down in a park to think things over a bit. While I was sitting there, a little nigger boy about 11 or 12 years old came bumming around. He was looking for something. He found it too. I took him out to a gravel pit about 1/4 of a mile from the main camp of the Sinclair Oil Co. at Loanda. I left him there. but first I committed sodomy on him and then killed him. His brains were coming out of his ears when I left him and he will never be any deader. He is still there. Then I went to town bought a ticket on the Belgian steamer to Lobito Bay down the coast. There I hired a canoe and 6 niggers and went out hunting in the bay and back waters. I was looking for crocadiles I found them. plenty. they were all hungry. I fed them. I shot all six of those niggers and dumped em in. The crocks done the rest. I stole thier canoe and went back to town tied the canoe up to the dock and that night some one stole the canoe from me. Then I bought a ticket on that same Belgian steamer and went back to Loanda where I again went to Mr. Clark the U.S. Counsul and bummed him for a ticket to Europe but he gave me the air and set the cops after me. That night I went to the house of a Spanish prostitute and robbed her of $10,000.00 Eschudas. She also set the cops after me so I beat it. I couldn't get out of there by rail or by ship as the cops were looking for me so I hiked out. I hiked north for the Belgian Congo. 300 miles away, thru Ambrizett and Ambreeze up to the mouth of the Congo River at San Antonio. there I hired a canoe and paddlers who took me across to Point Banana There I bought a ticket on a french ship to Boma and from there up to Matidi. There I stayed about a month. Then Broke and couldn't get a ship, I stowed away on a U.S. ship the West Nono. They carried me as far as Axime on the Gold Coast and dumped me there. I walked to Secondee and there robbed some lime Juicers and bought a ticket on the Elder Dempster S.S. Patonie on her I got as far as Las Palmas and There the U.S. Cousul didnt know me and I gave him a lot of Bull and he bought me a ticket on a Portuguesse ship to Lisbon Portugal.

When I got there I at once went to the U.S. Counsul to try to get a ship out but I got hell instead. He knew all about me. A Mr Crandall a director of the Sinclair Oil co had been there a few weeks before on his way from Loanda and he told the counsul all about me. That after noon I stowed away on an english coal carrier that took me to Avenmouth England. A day or so later I signed on a U.S. ship as a counsuls passenger to New York. This was in the summer of 1922. Just as soon as I got to New York I took my old Licence as Captain and owner and my bill of sale which had been given to me in the Custom House in New York City, for my old lost Yacht, The Akista and went and saved all of this time from 1920 until 1922. In 1922 I got a new licence and set of papers by turning my old ones in to the Customs house in N.Y. City. I kept these new papers and began looking around for a nother yacht of the same size and kind so I could steal her, take her name and numbers off and put mine on.

In July at Salem, Mass I murdered a 11 or 12 year old boy, by beating his brains out with a rock. I tried a little sodomy on him first. I left him laying there with his brains coming out of his ears. Came down towards N.Y. Robbing and hellraising as I came. That same summer and Fall I went thru Philadelphia to Baltimore where I bought a ticket to Jacksonville Florida on a boat. At Jacksonville I signed on a ship and went to Baton Rouge La. paid off there and went to the Marine Hospital at New Orleans; stayed there a month or two and when I left the Hospital I robbed thier Drug room of 2 suit cases full of drugs. Cocaine morphine and opium. Sold some in New Orleans, some in St Louis and the rest in New York. In Jan or Feb 1923 I got a job as a watchman at 220 Yonkers Ave, Yonkers N.Y. for the Abeeco Mill. Co. While there I met a young boy 14 or 15 years old whoes name was George and whoes home was and is in Yonkers. I started to teach him the fine art of sodomy but I found that he had been taught all about it and he liked it fine.

I kept him with me until I left that Job in April 1923. a month or two later I got a Job as watchman and caretaker of boats at the New Haven Yacht Club at New Haven Conn. I took very good care of thier boats, so much so that I robbed one the next night. The name of the yacht I dont know but the owner of it was the Police Commissioner of New Rochell N.Y. or some place near there. Part of my loot was his pistol, a 38 Colt double action side break gun. a few weeks later about May or June I stole a Yacht at Providence Rhode Island. I sailed it as far as New York. I was alone until then. At New York I picked up a kid about 18 or 20 years old took him on the yacht with me as far as Yonkers there I let him go back to New York. At Yonkers I picked up my other kid Gorge. Him I took along on the Yacht to Kingston. N.Y. There I painted the yacht over, changed her name and numbers to correspond with my old papers. I tried to sell the boat there and while doing so, I met a fellow who said he wanted to buy my boat but instead of that he got out on the yacht with me where we were laying at anchor. There he tried to stick me up but I was suspissious of his actions and was ready for him and I shot him twice with the same pistol I had stolen from the Police Commissioners Yacht at New Haven a short time before. After I killed him I tied a big hunk of lead around him with a rope and threw him and his gun overboard. he is there yet so far as I know. Then I sailed down the river stealing everything I could as I went. I got as far as New Burgh N.Y. There the kid George got scairt and I let him go home to Yonkers. When he got home he told the police all he knew about me which wasnt much but it was enough for the cops to come looking for me. They caught me and my yacht at Nyack. They took me, boat and all my plunder to Yonkers in Jail there. Charged with Sodomy, Burglary, Robbery and trying to break Jail there. I got a lawyer there a Mr Cashin. I told him the boat was worth 5 or 10 thousand dollars and that I would give it to him if he got me out of jail. He got me out and I gave him the boat and my papers. When he went to register the boat he lost her because the owner from Providince came and got her. A few days later I went to New Haven where I killed another boy. I committed a little more sodomy on him also and then tied his belt around his neck and strangled him, picked him up when he was dead and threw his body over behind some bushes. Went to New York then and got a Job as Bath-room steward on the Army transport. U.S. Grant going to China but instead of me going to China I got fired for being drunk and fighting. The next night I robbed the Express office at Larchmont New York and got caught in the act, tried at White Plains N.Y. for burglary, sentenced to 5 years at Sing Sing Prison Soon after I was transferred to Dannemora Prison for incorrigables. There I stayed 5 years. I was there only a few months when I made a time bomb and tried to burn down the shops. The screws found it but didn't blame me for it. They put the blame on a couple of other guys and put those two in the Isolation. a short time later I attempted to escape. I failed. at that time I broke both ankles, both legs twisted my back and ruptured myself. Then I was locked up for about 6 months or more. Then I tried to murder a con I sneaked up behind him as he was sitting in a chair and I hit him on the back of the head with a 10 pound club. it didn't kill him but he was good and sick and he left me alone after that. Then I was locked up for a few months more. My ruptured testicle had been bothering me and a new Doctor came to the prison He took me in the hospital and cut one testical out. 5 days after my operation I tried to see if my sexual organs were still in good order. I got caught trying to commit sodomy on another prisnor. For that I was thrown out of the hospital and put in the Segregation Building or the Isolation. I stayed there until my time was up. 2 years and 4 months later. When I was discharged I was told that I was as pure as a lilly, free from all sin, to go and sin no more. 18 days later I committed 6 or 8 Burglarys and 2 days later 1 murder in Philadelphia Pa. a week later I committed a burglary in Baltimore. 12 days later a burglary in Washington D.C. The next day or two I committed 2 more burglaries in Baltimore Then I was arrested in Baltimore and brought back to Washington. D.C. where I was put in the D.C. Jail and soon after I tried to escape but got caught and here I am now waiting for to see which way the wind blows and perhaps the electric chair the rope or the mad house. It makes very little differ to me either way. This I hope will be the finish of

Carl Panzram –

______________________ with that name

as I started in life and changes to
John O'Leary
Jeff Davis.
Jeff Rhodes
Jeff Baldwin
Jack Allen.
and back to Carl Panzram.

Additional notes and essays given to Lesser:

I am the man that goes
around world doing
people Good.

My Motto is.

Rob em, Fuck em and then
Kill em.

Thats me
Carl Panzram.

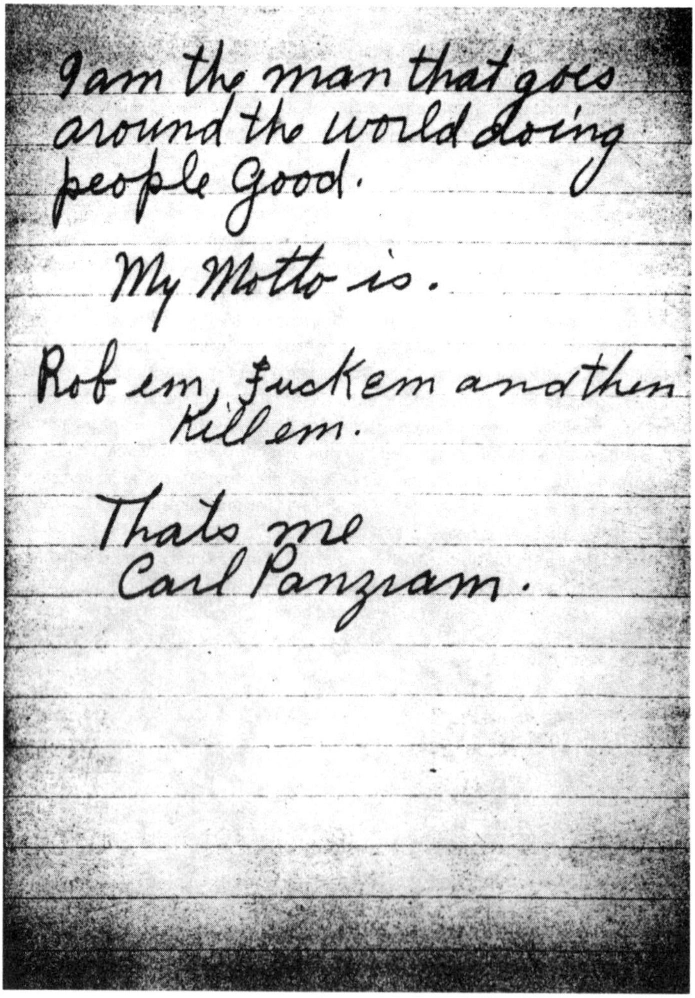
I am the man that goes
around the world doing
people Good.

My Motto is.

Rob em, Fuckem and then
Kill em.

Thats me
Carl Panzram.

Men have made a study of crime
its cause, effect and the remedy.
Many men know the effect.
Many men know the cause.
I know the remedy.
The answer is. Truth.

This Country is having a war right now and very few people even realize the fact.

War, in the final analysis is merely murder and robbery and the expenditure of life and property.

This country today is having a crime war.

Many thousands of lives and billions of dollars worth of property are lost every year.

Crime is increasing 10 per cent each year.

All society is up in arms to combat crime and criminals. They are using every possible method that the law can devise. The best they have been able to do so far is to build bigger and stronger Jails and prisons and fill them all full of criminals. Just as soon as a prison is filled to capasity, they start right in building more and more. And they are all full. But still there are more criminals every day. There is no end to them under the present system.

Even the most superficial investigator of this question of Crime knows this to be a fact. All of your Police, Judges, lawyers, Wardens, Doctors, National Crime Commitions and writers have all combined to find out and remedy the cause and effect of crime.

With all of the knolledge and power at thier comand they have accomplished nothing except to make conditions worse instead of better.

This is not a theory. This is a fact. Statisticts prove it beyond any possibility of doubt.

This being the case then they and thier system must be wrong.. Those who make and enforce the laws are more guilty than those who commit the crimes against the law.

The criminal does not profit by his crimes. It is the Law makers and the law enforcers who do profit the most. They, in reality are the real cause of the most crime. They know it too. Thats why there is so much crime in this Country today. Those who roar the loudest about putting down crime are the very ones who cause the most crime.

I am 36 years old and have been a criminal all of my life. I have 11 felony convictions against me. I have served 20 years of my life in Jails, Reform Schools and prisons. I know why I am a criminal. Others may have different theories as to my life but I have no theory about it. I know the facts. If any man ever was a habitual criminal. I am one. In my lifetime I have broken every law that was ever made by both Man and God. If either had made more, I should very cheerfully have broken them also.

The mere fact that I have done these things is quite sufficient for the average person. Very few peopel ever consider it worth while to wonder why I am what I am and do what I do. All that they think it is necessary to do is to catch me, try me convict me and send me to prison for a few years, make life miserable for me while in prison and then turn me loose again. That is the system that is in practice today in this country. The consequences are that such that any one and every one can see. crime and lots of it.

Those who are sincere in thier desire to put down crime, are to be pitied for all of thier efforts which accomplish so little in the desired direction. They are the ones who are decieved by thier own ignorance and by the trickery and greed of others who profit the most by crime.

Much depends upon the point of view of the persons who express themselves on the Crime Question. Those who roar the loudest and are therefore the most heard are the writers, Judges, lawyers and would be expert criminologists. All of these people make a nice soft living out of crime. Therefore they are directly interested in that subject. They dont produce a dam thing. All they do is to shoot of thier mouths and push a fountain pen. And for doing this they live nice and soft. They wear good clothes, eat the best foods, live in nice homes, have the best of every thing the world produces. They have a nice soft graft and they know it too. They are not a lot of chumps like the criminals. Dont think for a minute that they are going around realy meaning to do as they say they wish to do. Put down crime. Not a chance. There will be no pick and shovel for that sort of people. Thats what would happen to them if they realy did put down crime. There is two sides to every question. My point of view is just as plausable and a dam sight more probable than all of the hot air that has been published about this question. Others who have expressed thier ideas in print on this subject have all been either directly or indirectly interested in reciving some sort of profit or benifit of some kind from what they say or write or do about this crime Question. Some have good jobs which they want to keep or perhaps they are trying to get a better one or perhaps they are merely incensed and predujiced against criminals because they or thier friends have been robbed or murdered. I on the other hand, have not a single thing to gain by my writing this. My life and my liberty is allready forfieted. I can not gain a single thing in any way for writing this. I am not writing this because I expect some benifit by doing it. I am not trying to do myself or any one else other harm or good. My only motive in writing this is to express myself and my beliefs. My point of view. Perhaps I am alltogether wrong but on the other hand I may be right and you may be wrong. Let the facts speak for themselves and then judge the results.

Under the present system, the best and the worst you can do is just as your doing now and that is making bad matters worse. Before you can ever put down crime you must change the system a whole hell of a lot. Also you must change your educational system. You must absolutly divorce the schools and Prisons from all politics. As things are now you are making criminals much faster than you are reforming those that are allready in existence. Every child has some criminal tendencies It is your place to correct those traits and teach them the right way to live while they are young and thier minds are forming. Then when they do reach the age of reason and action it will be quite natural for them to live clean, upright, honorable lives. In that way you will stop crime at it source before it begins.

As for the criminals that are now in existence and working at thier trade or those that you now have in prison, you can reform those that are capable of being reformed, and those few who are incapable of any kind of reformation you can keep them where you have them now in prison where they can do no harm. These two things you can do or you can keep on doing as you are now. Either make things better or worse. If you think that you can stop crime by catching us, locking us up, punishing us by brutal treatment, hanging or electrocuting us, sterilizing or castrating us, then your a fool for thinking that way. That only makes bad matters worse.

A child is very easily led. Any child if properly taught will live the way he is taught to live. All criminals are merely overgrown children. It is in your hands to make us or break us. We by our own efforts are failirs in life, simply because we dont know any better. We dont know how to live decent upright lives. Heridtry has very little to do with the shaping of our lives. The main causes of why we are what we are is because of our improper teaching lack of knolledge and our environments. Every mans Philosophy is colored by his environments. If you dont want us to rob, rape and murder you then it is your place to to see that the mental and moral missfits are properly taught a sufficcient amount of usefull and sensible knolledge and put into the proper environment where they can be best fitted to exist in life. Otherwise they will be missfits and failirs and you are the actual cause because They don't know any better and you do.

My own case is very similar to many thousands of others. I was born a normal human being. My parents were ignorant and thru thier improper teachings and improper environment I was gradualy led into the wrong way of living. Little by little from bad to worse. I was sent to a Reform School at the age of 11 years. From that day to this all of my life has been lived among moral and mental missfits. All of my associates all of my surroundings The Atmosphere in which I have lived has been saturated with the atmosphere of deciet, Treachery Brutality, degeneracy, hypocracy and every thing that is bad and nothing that is good. Is it unatural that I should have absorbed these things and have become what I am today, a treacherous, degenerate brutal, human savage. Devoid of all decent feelings. Absolutly without concience, morals pity, sympathy, Principle on any single good trait. Why am I what I am. I'll tell you why. I did not make myself what I am. Others had the making of me. I have been in 2 reform schools 7 big prisons and hundreds of Jails. None of them were any different from the others. All were run under the same system by the same sort of people and the results were the same in all of them. My last term in prison was exactly the same as my first and the results were the same in each case. And my own case is exactly the same as many thousands of others. I shall give an outline of my last bit in prison from the time I entered until I left it. And if any one can believe that that way is the right way to stop crime then it is my opinion that he is either a fool or a rogue probably both. In 1923 I was caught in the act of commiting a burglary. Put in Jail and indicted. I at once saw that I would be convicted so I imediatly saw the Prosecuting Attorney and with him made a bargain. He promised me that if I would plead guilty and in that way save the county the expense of a trial, that he would agree that I would get a very light sentence in return. I kept to my side of the bargain but he didn't. I Pleaded Guilty and was imediatly given the limit of the law. 5 years. At once I was sent to the prison where because of my many previous convictions and my bad record as an escape man I was very closely watched and at the least infraction of the rules I was severely punished. I was put to work in the worst work shop in the prison. I had a task to do. 8 hours work every day 6 days a week for which I was allowed 1 1/2 cents per day. In this prison the work wasnt very hard but very monotonous and wearing on the nerves. The disciplin was very strict. The food was very bad. After about 6 months of this I was feeling pretty hot, mad and disgusted. I attempted to escape. I failed in my attempt but in doing so I fell 30 feet on to a concrete walk breaking both of my ankles, both of my legs, fracturing my Spine and rupturing myself. In this condition I was carried to the prison hospital where I lay 5 days and was then carried out and dumped into a cell without any medical or surgical attention whatever. My broken bones were not set my ankles and legs were not put into a cast. In fact nothing was done except to give me a bottle of linament which would have done me no good if I had been able to rub it onto myself. The Doctor never came near me and no one else was allowed to do any thing for me. In that condition I was left for 8 months. At the end of that time the bones had knitted together so that I could stagger around on a pair of crutches. After a few more months on crutches, then a cane for a few months. At the end of 14 months of constant agony I was taken to the hospital where I was operated on for my rupture and one of my testicals was cut out. Only 5 days was allowed me for medical and surgical attention.

At the end of 5 days I was again carried out of the hospital and dumped into a cell where I suffered more agony for many months. Allways in pain, never a civil answer from any one, allways a snarl or a curse or a lying hypocritical promise which was never kept. Crawling around like a snake with a broken back seething with hatred and a lust for revenge. 5 years of this kind of a life. The last 2 years and 4 months confined in isolation with nothing to do except brood upon what I thought was the wrongs that had been done to me. Not allowed to recieve letters or visits from friends On lady friend traveled 1,000 miles and spent hundreds of dollars to come and visit me. They allowed her to see me for 1/2 of an hour only altho she stayed in the town for one solid week trying to see me again. My incoming and outgoing mail was held up or distroyed. I was not allowed to complain to any one of the higher officials. Whenever I tried to do that, the letters I wrote were torn up and returned to me. When the prison inspectors came to the prison to investigate conditions and complaints they were told that I was a degenerate, that I suffered from delusions and that I was insane so they would pay no attentions to any thing that I or any one else every complained of. This went on for all of my 5 years and the more they missused me the more I was filled with the spirit of hatred and vengence. I was so full of hate that that there was no room in me for such feelings as love, pity kindness or honor or decency. I hated every body I saw. My whole mind was bent on figuring out different ways to annoy and punish my enemies and every body was my enemy. I had no friends. That was the frame of mind I was in when my 5 years was up and I was turned loose to go any where I wanted to go. My intentions was to rob rape and kill every body I could. any body and every body. It was my intentions to commit enough burglaries to get a few hundred dollars together and with that to go to a place I had picked out at a R.R. tunnel between Meyersdale P.A. and Cumberland Md. There I intended to wait until the fast all steel Pullman train the Capitol Limited or the National Limited came along. I intended to have a large contact bomb in the middle of the tunnel fixed so that when the engin struck the obstruction, the bomb would explode and stop and wreck the engin and block up that ind of the tunnel. The explosion would set off and burst some large glass container of formaldihyde or other gass and also set fire to a few hundred pounds of sulpher. The gases and fumes thus generated and let loose in the closed tunnel would in a very few minutes kill every living thing on the whole train in the tunnel. I would be staitioned at the rear entrance to the tunnel behind a barricade, and armed ready to shoot down any one who had life enough left to try to get out of the tunnel. As soon as I was assured that all were dead. I would put on a gas mask and oxeygene tank such an outfit as is used in mine rescue work then enter the cars and rob the whole train. Another precaution that I intended to use was to place a time bomb on a bridge or tressel 12 or 15 mile back up the line from the way the train had come. This bomb would be set to go off just about the time that the train would be wrecked in the tunnel. In that way all of the wires would be down with the Bridge so that no assistance could arrive to help those in the tunnel. I intended that if this racket had worked out according to the way I figured that it would, I would have at least 1 1/2 hours in which I could work unmolested and in that time I could gather up 50 or 100 thousand dollars from the 3 or 4 hundred dead passengers in money and Jewelry. Then I would go a few miles and plant every thing in a pre-arranged hiding place. Then go away and remain quietly in hiding for a month or two and at the end of that time I would return, lift my plant go to New York and turn everything into cash. With unlimited funds in my hands I then intended to steal millions of dollars and kill millions of people. This I intended to do by starting a war between England and the U.S.A. Sounds fantastic all right. but I am positive that I could and would have done it. The way that I figured on doing this was to work thru numerous stock brokers in Wall St. playing the stock market ahead of time with the knolledge that I alone would know that England and the U.S.A. would soon be at war. Fore-armed with this knolledge I would know exactly which stocks would rize and which stocks would fall in value. Then with my money all placed with the proper instructions with the different brokers for investment at the proper time and place, all that would be neccessary for me to do would be to start a war between England and the U.S.A. This I intended to do by waiting until diplomatic relations were somewhat strained between the two Countries. Then I would quietly sneak up and sink some great British Battle Ship while in American waters on a peacefull mission. This could be done very easily. All I need to do would be to wait until some British ship was laying at anchor in the Hudson River at New York. Some fine night I would come up the river with 2 gasoline launches each made fast to the other, side by side. one launch filled with T.N.T. with a 15 minute fuse attached to it. In the Bomb boat I would have an anchor and a long line. when I reached the proper position about 5 yards ahead of the Battle ship I would light the fuse and drop the anchor of the Bomb boat cast off the lashings of the two launches. I in my launch would go on my way up the river full speed while the Bomb boat would slowly float down alongside of the battleship where it would explode and sink the ship with all hands except maybe a few survivors who would be left to tell what they saw. All they would be able to tell would be that they saw two launches which looked like U.S. Navy boats with Navy flags flying run by a man dressed in a U.S. Navy Uniform. who dissapeared in the night. If this succeeded it would start a hell of a row between England and the U.S. just the same as the sinking of the U.S.S. Main did in '98 between Spain and the U.S.A. But if this didn't start a war then I would go down to the British West Indies. buy a small british schooner keep her under British Registry with an all British Capt and Crew. I would load her with a few tons of Explosives covered up with an inoffensive looking cargo, send her to the Panama Canal where I would place a time bomb in the hold set to go off in some one of the locks of the Canal. I would leave the boat to proceed to her doom and the doom of the Panama Canal. That would be very sure to start a hell of a big war and in the mean time I would be salting away millions of dollars thru speculating on stocks on Wall St.

I have worked on boats and ships and also for the Fortification Division and the Cattle Industry on the Panama Canal as a labor Foreman where I handled a great deal of Explosives. in blasting operations also I can make any kind of a bomb. These schemes may sound Fantastic and Grandiloquent and impossible of accomplishment by one man. but I feel very sure that it could be done and I also feel sure that I could have and would have done just exactly as I had planed if curcumstances and luck had not been against me. I was only out of prison one month and 6 days but during that time I committed 12 burglaries and one murder. I had a goal in view and was working toward it just as quickly as I could. If any one is in doubt as to these facts then just get a P.R.R. time table look up the schedule of either the National Limited or the Capitol Limited. Look up the map and you will find that there is a tunnel just I describe between Meyersdale and Cumberland. I have been there and I know all about where to get all the dymmite and fuses that I wanted. In 1918 I registered for the Army draft and also Joined the F.O.E. Local 1255 at Meyersdale. Pa. I robbed a Jewelry store there the night I left in the Fall of 1918. My name then and there was John O'Leary but now it is

Carl Panzram.

If some one had a young tiger cub in a cage and then misstreated it until I got savage and bloodthirsty and then turned it loose to prey on the rest of the world to go any where and kill any one it wanted to, Then there would be a hell of a roar from those in danger of the mad tiger. Every one would believe that to be the wrong thing to do.

But if some people do the same thing to other people then the world is surprised, shocked, and offended because they get robbed, raped and killed. Yet this is exactly what is being done every day in this Country.

They done it to me and then dont like it when I give them the same dose they gave me. They do it to thousands of others and they in turn retaliate by Robbery and murder. If you dont like to be robbed Raped, burned or killed then stop your own dirty work. Stop your lying and hypocracy. Live decent your own selves and teach others who are not able to do right unless they are taught right.

If You get abused, robbed or killed You have it coming to you so dont blame it all on the one who harms you. Some of the blame is yours for not making it your buisness to see to it that such conditions should not exist among your fellow men. If you put a lot of power in the hands of your public servents and they missuse thier power then you are at fault also. I have only a little knolledge but I have as much inteligence as the average person and I know that I was taught wrong.

I could have been taught properly and if I had been I feel sure that I would have led a far different life than I have done.

You are to blame more so than I. Thats my belief. If you are going to go on teaching others as you have taught me than then you must suffer the same as I.

L.

I am making a few suggestions which I hope you will carefully think over and act upon.

Of course it's up to you.

It's nothing to me if you do or dont.

I	I suggest that you take everything I have written, make a typewritten copy of it.
II	Then write out another from that just using what ever parts that can be published.
III	Connect the different parts together where they fit in thier proper places.
IIII	Look up the files of the Newspapers and get one of my pictures and a dozen or two of the news-paper clippings
V	And from now on keep track of what the papers print about me. Save a few of those clippings.
VI.	Just those that give the future and the last acts of my life and an account of my death.

P.S.

I wont be alive to read what you publish so it wont cut any ice with me.

I am doomed to pass out of the picture pretty soon.

I have fully decided that I want to die and there will be no turning aside.

Wether I die in the Electric Chair for some of the murders that I have allready commited or if I must commit one or two more or if I die under the guns or black-Jacks of the Coppers or even if there is no other way out for me I shall take my own life. I am quite capable of dieing in any of these ways. In some way I shall surely accomplish my desire to die. No matter how I pass out it will be worth your while to add it alone with what I have written my own self. You better get buisy and waste no time because it wont be long now before I wind it up some way. You are going to get a hell of a lot of free advertizing about me in the papers. A lot has allready been printed and the worst is yet to come. You never can tell what the sequel will be. What ever it may be it will be worth while.

At the time of my death that will be the proper moment for you to publish your book.

You can see that surely.

You ought to make a barrel of Jack out of it if you work things properly.

What I have written and given to you is all that I have ever written and it isn't very likely that I'll ever write any more for any one else. But dont make any bets on my future because I am erratic enough to do any thing and every thing.

There isnt any thing more that I care to write about so Ill Just drop it now. You have it all.

There are thousands and thousands of things in my life that I have done or have seen that would be just as good as what I have written but it is no use for me to bother about that. If you print what I have written you'll do well.

One last suggestion is this. If you intend to make any use of what I have written then you better not waste any time. I am getting weary of waiting and living for this world. Thats all.

P.S.

A bunch of these kind of newspaper clippings and my picture would go good to fill in the last part of the book. They would be very good because they would be both authentic and interesting. After All of my part of the book to finish it off in proper style you as the author could write my wind up or epitaph with perhaps a picture of my after death or the grave or the Electric Chair.

You write the Preface, use my writings for the book and your own explanations as the conclusions.

This ought to make a hell of a good book.

I have never seen or heard of one like it. It ought to have a big sale, with all of the interest that would be aroused by all of the papers publishing so much about me.

If you do write a book, you ought to get it coppyrighted, first publish it in book form and then in serial form in the magazines and the Sunday papers and then a book. Just one more suggestion that may be worth while would be to let a few men like Mr. Clarence Darrow and a few other great Sociologists and Psychiatrists, let them write you thier opinions and you publish them in the tail end of the book. Let them read what I wrote and then you write what they think about it or even a few of the outstanding of thier opinions that they have allready written on the subject of crime, the causes, effect and remedy.

My eyes are feeling pretty good and so am I so I thought I would write a line or two to pass the time away. This scheme I have had in my mind for several years and its too good a thing to throw away just because I cant use it so I am writing it down with the fervent wish that some one may see it and make good use of it to decimate some of the excess population of this world.

I figured out this scheme while I was in the Isolation or solitary confinement at Clinton Prison, Dannemorra New York.

I used to spend all of my time figuring how I could murder the most peopel with the least harm or expence to myself and I finaly thought of a way to kill off a whole town Men, women, children and even the cats and dogs. I intended to buy up about a barrel of arsenic poison. then I was going to get me 6 or 8 hogs. starve them until they wre all ravenously hungry and then I would give them all a big feed of Flour, water, mash and arsenic poison all mixed in one mess.

they would all dive into it and fill them selves full and in an hour or two the poison would begin to work thru thier systems. then I was going to hang them all up by thier hind legs with a wash tub under them to let the slimey poison and froth drain out of them into the wash-tubs. That I would then strain and dry out and then I intended to get some clay and make 3 big clay pots each one to fit inside of the other and each one a little bit harder than the next one. then I was going to fill all 3 pots with poison with the largest in the center. this I was going to put the lot all in one and put that in the bottom of a small creek that flows into the resavoire that supplies the town and prison with all thier water. That would have fixed a hell of a big bunch at one time for by the time they found out what was wrong with them it would be too late for all the dam doctors in the world to cure em.

Lucretia Borgia used this racket on a small scale but I figured on a few extra improvements so that I could do a better Job than the Borgias done. They were pikers. They didn't kill half enough. They should have killed every body and left this world for the only good things in it; Nature. This would be a dam fine world if man was out of it.

P.S.

hurry up and bring on your electric chair I want to leave here and take a nose-dive into the next world just to see if that one is as lousy as is this ball of mud and meanness.

I am sorry for only two things. These two things are I am sorry that I have misstreated some few animals in my life-time and I am sorry that I am unable to murder the whole damed human race.

You may do as you like with this that I have written believe it or disbelieve it. Publish it or burn it or hide it or any dam thing you care to do with it.

signed
Carl Panzram

Mr. L.

I have written two letters here.

One for you and one for my brother including the one that he wrote to me. When you read the one he wrote to me you will see where he wants to get a letter from some officer. If you would care to write to him perhaps it might do some good and could do no harme. If you dont care to bother with this just drop my letter and his in the box here in the regular manner. suit yourself.

The other bunch is just a short outline of my history. Of course I left a lot out because I am not much of a writer and there is enough here for you to verify every statement I have made in case you care to do so. All you need to do is to write to all of these different places giving the proper names and the approximate dates and they can give you my complete record of all my records while at these places. You will have a hell of a book full. If there is any thing else that I can do for you say so to

Carl Panzram

I wrote quite a lot today. I started, got interested and kept on going. At this rate you'll soon have enough to write a book or build a fire with. If you find it as interesting to read as I did in the writing you'll do well.

If after reading what I write, your faith in human nature isnt all destroyed then it will never be.

This is a very dirty mess of writing but I am only starting in. just wait until I hit my proper stride and you'll be sorry you didnt blow my brains out instead of blowing me to smokes and eats. You better be carefull about giving me any eats or any thing else because those cons out there with the white pants on will shure snitch on you if they find it out. I may leave here at any time for some big-house mad-house or death-house but I don't give a dam where they put me They wont keep me long because No power on earth can me me alive and in Jail for very much longer. I would kind of like to finish writing this whole buisness out in detail before I kick off just so that I can explain my side of it even tho no one ever hears or reads of it except one man. But one man or a million makes no difference to me. When I am thru, I am all thru and that settles it with me. I'll try to finish this. Some days I may write much and some days little. It depends on my moods and the circumstances at the time.

If you or any one else will take the trouble and have the inteligence and paitince to follow and examine every one of my crimes and actions you will find that I have consistantly followed one idea thru all my life. I preyed upon the weak the harmless or unsuspecting. Those I harmed were all either weaklings either mentaly or phisicaly. Those who were strong either in mind or body I first lied to and led into a trap where they were either asleep or drunk or helpless in some way. I allways had all the best of it, because I knew ahead of time just what to expect and the others did not. I therefore was strong in my knolledge and stronger in body than those I preyed upon. This lesson I was taught by others.

Might makes right.

L.

And the worst is yet to
come.
A little meaner and
meaner.
every day in every way.

I don't feel much like doing any writing just at this time. I am still a little bit dizzy from that last beating and the torture at the post.

I have a lot of things on my mind just at this time to think about. I am pretty well upset and any writing that I do now will probably be pretty well muddled up but later on when I feel better and the conditions for thinking and putting my thoughts in writing I shall oblige you to the best of my feeble ability by writing the true facts of my life history.

C. P.

During the past few weeks there have been about a dozen news-paper reporters around here wanting to talk to me but I wouldn't talk to any of them. I dont like them. They done me plenty of harm and none of them ever done me any good. I dont care to talk to them but I would like to give them this what I have written and see if they will publish this the truth instead of a lot of hot air and guess work as they have been doing lately.

Carl Panzram.

This whole Joint seemes to be upset today. everybody up in air on thier ears.

first some but started whistling and cursing the Preacher at church time. Then some other nut tried to burn the Joint down. Then the Bug doctor came here and examined me to see if I was nuts.

The screws been hopping around all day putting guys in the cooler and chaining em up to the Post. This dam Joint is so full of nuts that I am thinking they are all nuts except me. Anyway I can't do any writing or any real thinking until I can get a lot of things off my mind and then I'll write some more.

This whole system was all exposed and stopped years ago in the Ohio State Prison and other places by Miss Ida Tarbell of Oklahoma. She was a writer who specialized on that kind of writing for yeares but she was finaly bull-dozed and bribed into writing for the Conservative press and the orthadox people.

Mr. Upton Sinclair is another writer whoes writings along those lines caused him so much trouble by the people that he exposed that he was driven out of this Country and now lives abroad except for short and infrequent visits to this, his own country, and while here he goes around with body-guards. The people don't like to be told the truth.

Right today, not last year or a hundred years ago, there are many, many places and many people whoes sole buisness in life is to torture and misstreat other men.

Men taught me all I know, and what they done to me I done to them.

Might makes right.

This being the case, then we are today where we were a million years ago.

L.

I was going to write a lot more of this but I must cut it short for several reasons.

Today I was notified to get my self ready for trial on the 12th.

Today a couple more coppers came to me looking for a lost murderer from Rhode Island. They must look some where else for him.

Today my eyes are getting worse.

Today my right hand is hurting me too much to write.

Today I am weary and all thru.

L.

During the past few weeks I have made several confessions each one about a separate case. All of these different confessions are parts of one complete series of acts.

You have the only full and complete confession I have ever made.

If you check up on the lot you will find that every thing I have written down is the full truth.

You probably will never check up on all of it but if you will just check up on one bit of short time those 36 days I was free before I got pinched this time and when I was released from Dannemorra July.6.'28. until Aug 13.28.

You will find that I committed sodomy about 25 times
Burglary 12 times
and murder 1 time.
and I was just getting all set to do a wholesale buisness in all these lines.

Maybe I am wrong but I think that if these words that I have written, should ever be handled by the right people in the right way, some-thing would sure pop. Maybe my neck and maybe more.

I do know that there are a hell of a lot of people in this world who would give a lot to see what I have written

The D.A. for one. The newspapers and magazines for another. Some of those newspapers reporters who have been after me would sure be glad to get thier hooks and eyes on it. You better make yourself a coppy. quick.

The code of the under-world.
Square crooks and crooked coppers.
Principle or Policy.

The underworld code is very simple. It is never squeel. Don't be a stool-piedgeon a rat or an informer.

All crooks want every body else to believe that they are square. All cops are the same. They all wish every body else to think they act from Principle.

The are allways telling every one they meet all about how much principl they have. Its against thier principles to do this or not to do that. The queer part of this is that they not only want others to believe this but they even believe themselves.

But the real truth of the matter is that they decieve themselves and mistake policy for Principle. I have met every kind of a crook there is. I have worked and lived both with and against them. Coppers the same. I know thier tricks inside and out. I have associated with every sort, both in prison and on the street. They and thier works and thier thoughts are like an open book to me. I know them well. To my sorrow. I have been mixed up in every kind of a crooked deal there is with every kind of crook there is.

Con-men and gang-men.
Prowlers and boosters
Stick up artists, can opener artists and sometimes face artists.
Peter men and Box-men
Paper hangers and crape hangers
hustlers and rustlers
Pimps and McGimps
hooks from the big town and hooks from the sticks
Big shots and pikers
Dynamiters and Sodomitirs
Fruiters and poofters
Dingbats and gay-cats.
Shive men and gun-men.
Needle pumpers and snow-sniffers
hop heads and jug-heads
wise-guys and dumb-bells
boot-leggers and rum-runners.

wolves and gunsells
Dips and short card gamblers
home guards and boomers
booze fighters and cop fighters
and last but not least
the muzzlers and guzzlers.

I have put in 35 years in the game of hooks and crooks. I have been from top to bottom and every where in between. There is no angle of this game that I havent tried at some time or other.

I have met thousands and thousands of my kind in every different degree, from The King-pins and the bigest of big shots down to the greasiest of grease-balls and without exception, one and all insist on deluding every body else and themselves also, that they are square, that they have in thier make-up the sparks of Principle and honor.

That they keep the code of the under-world. That they never squeel. Any thing and every thing against any body and every body is quite all right and permissable at any time or place but the one rule that must be kept by all, regardless of any thing else is that they must never squeel. No matter what happens, No matter what pressure is brought to bear on them to get them to open up and squeel. If the coppers work the old mother and Jesus racket on them or give them the third degree, a wrong rap with a big stretch in Stir or even the rope or the chair, still they are supposed to keep thier traps shut and never squeel. I have never met or heard of any one yet who ever admitted that they were wrong and that they were stool-piedgeons squeelers or rats. They all insist that they are right guys and square crooks. Even when they are caught right in the act of going on the stand as a witness for the State against thier Pals, They wont admit it. One and all insist that they are men of honor and that they act from Principle only. They all swear that they are loyal to the first law of the Code of the Underworld.

In theory this seems to be the case. That the average person realy believes this to be true and that most crooks believe it also.

The average superficial observer only sees a very small part. he sees nothing of what goes on behind the scenes and under the surface. The Actual facts of the matter is that none of the crooks are square with one another or with any body. They are not square with the coppers and the coppers are not square with them. None of the have any Principle. They have Policy. They mistake Principle for Policy. When they are square with any one it is because it is for thier own interest to be so. It is good Policy.

When it ceases to be to thier own interests to be square with one another then it becomes time to change thier tactics, and they are not slow in doing it either.

It makes no difference to them who they snitch on, no matter if they have been loyal to each other thru a whole lifetime as partners and friends. No matter if they send thier friends to Prison or to hell by way of the Rope or chair. That cuts no ice. They are looking out for thier own precious skins. If they can benifit themselves at the expence of some one else regardless of what the others have to suffer for thier treachery they in 99 cases out of a hundred will sure break the law of the underworld and open up and sing Grand Opera. They will squeel long and loud. I have known cases where men have been loyal pals and friends, have gone thru every crime on the calender, Murders, Rapes, Robberies, in Jails and in freedom, in health and in sickness, riches and starvation and privations. Years and years together and allways loyal and square with each other but when the time came for the test of the first law of nature; Self-preservation, Every thing went over-board They all squeel some time. Big crooks and little crooks They all squeel when it is to thier interest to do it.

The greatest crooks I ever knew or ever heard of they All do it. Gerald Chapman used to be allways roaring about his own principles and forever condeming all stool piedgeons. Shean took the stand against him and swore his life away and every body in the underworld knew it he was condemed for his squeeling by every body Yet when that guy got out of the can he went to New York In the very heart of crookdom where he was given the glad hand by some of Chapmans former pals. He is a rat for the coppers and every body knows it yet he walks the streets today and he is right in with all the Big Shots in the Big town. He runs with both sides, the hare and the hounds and double-crosses them all. Gerald Chapman was known as a right guy all of his life and yet he also was a rat. He didn't ever hesitate to squeel when it was to his own advantage to do so. Every body did not know this but it is true just the same. When he was in the dance-Hall waiting to get his neck cracked and he knew his days were short and he knew he had nothing to gain, he also opened up and spilled all he knew. Another Big Shot that I know well is John J. "Bum" Rogers The Gangster and Gun man from New York City. He also has the rep in the underworld of being a right guy, All stocked up and loaded right to the ears with Principles. Maybe he did have principle at one time but he has none now. I have seen him and heard him sing opera and squeel. Some guys will squeel on one and maby not on others. But thats not because of thier Principle, Thats the Proper Policy for them to follow and they all play the policy end.

In all of my life I have never heard any one roar louder about thier honor and thier Principle and squarness than this same Bum Rogers. I will admit that perhaps there are men in this world who are a little less square than him who have less principle and honor about them, but believe me they are few and far between. He is a first class A No. 1. skunk. He is an out and out stool-piedgeon but he is very glib and clever so that he covers himself up so well that most of those who know him, realy believe what he wants them to believe that he is a right guy and the Code of the underworld is what he lives by. Honor among thieves. What a Joke that is. There is no more honor among thieves than there is snow-balls in hell. Some crooks will squeel for one reason and some another. One will fall for the soft soap gag the mother and Jesus Racket. Some will be tricked into opening up the Info bag. The third degree drags it out of others. The spirit of reveng is a great inducement for some to tell all they know. But most of us when we do open up do it for self interest. We want something. We either want to save our lives or our liberty or maybe we want a cigaret or a chew of tobacco for which we will hang any body or every body.

The coppers are a pretty dumb lot. The most of them are well supplied with big fat feet and a big fat head, which is usualy sadly lacking in grey-matter. The coppers I have known, and I have known peny of them, too dam many in fact, were and are a bunch of dumb-bells who couldn't track an elephant in a snow bank unless they first had some rat or stool-piedgeon to lead them to it and point it out. Most of them have plenty of brawn but very few have any brains. With all of the forces of law behind the coppers, All the steel bars and stone walls, thier guns and clubs, All would avail them nothing if it wasn't for thier rats and stool-piedgeons.

The third degree and the rats are the best and worst weapons that the cops have. Yet they will never admit that they have or use either. Perhaps it isn't generaly known but it is a fact never-the-less that During the World War when every man in this country was classified all according to thier Mental Moral and phisical conditions The crooks and the Coppers were both put in the same class which was pretty low down in the scale about as low as it could be down in Class 4. B. honor among thieves is the bunk. And as for the other side of the fence, the Coppers, they also are allways squawking about thier honor and thier principles. But the real truth of the matter is that by far the largest majority of them are in the same boat as the crooks they run around. They both play the game of working both ends from the middle. What few coppers there are who have principle and honor combined with brains, are in a very small minority. 9 out of 10 of them will grab a crooked dollar just as quick as I will. Most coppers have stool-piedgeons working for them. They work all in together. the rats will work in with thier pals and get all the info he can which he will turn over to the cop. The cop makes his pinch and gets the credit, the rat goes clear to keep right on working his own graft. The cop knows he is a crook out to rob or kill any one he can there for the cop is just as bad as his Rat. Neither have either principle or honor. They work in together just so long as either can use the other to thier own advantage. but just as soon as either one can make no further use of the other, then they are quite capable of each double-crossing the other. Just to prove my point I will Cite a few illustrations.

Some few years ago in New York City there was a mob of young hoodlum crooks in Harlem. They were all a lot of cheap petty crooks and gangsters who made thier dough by a lot of petty crime such as loft burglaries, once in a while they would catt up scatter or a gin-mill or a crap game or act as strike breakers, in times of labor troubles, Most of the were pimps who had from one to sometimes 3 or four girls bulldozed into going out hustling for them. Some were peddling dope or booze. None of them ever worked. Most of them were Ex-convicts. All of them were known to the coppers. few ever had any money. At this time rum-running was the big money racket. This bunch got thier heads together and cooked up a new scheme. one night 18 of this outfit all got organized and loaded up. They go out to Sea a few miles off-shore where a rum-runner the French Steam Ship Mullhouse. that was lying at anchor with $2,000,000 worth of booze in her holds. The whole 18 men went aboard of the ship, held up the Captain and crew and stole every bottle of booze which they brought ashore to Jersey City and New York. For turning this trick these 18 men split up between them $244,000.00 in cash besides some of them kept some of the booze. Some of this outfit soon went thru thier rolls and were soon broke but the foxey ones of the gang got thier heads together and went into a different racket. They invested thier money into night clubs and Cabberetts on Broadway. They opened up the Silver Slipper, the Parody Club the Cotton Club and a half a dozen other night clubs. There they peddled the booze which they stole. There they ran big crap games and gambling Joints, They had a bunch of girls out hustling for them. When thier booze ran short they bought boats, trucks and automobiles and hired other gangsters which they organized into gangs to run smuggled goods out of the U.S. up into Canada and return with booze, dope and undesirable alians. They made money by the thousands and hundreds of thousands. They are still in buisness. Stronger than ever. They and thier gangs have connections and ramifications extending all over the country. They have interests in all the big dope rings and whiskey outfits, white slavery and the Prize fight game. This outfit is all hooked up together, Oney Madden, Billy Badden, Bum Rogers The Duffy brothers from the Jersey City end, Boo-Boo Hoff from Philly, Scar Face Al Capone from Chi. They have a strangle hold on to the fight game. This was proved by the dicker between Boo-Boo Hoff and Gene Tuney at the fight in Philly between Tuney and Dempsey. And again at Chicago where Scar Face Al Capone was double-crossed by Tuney and his outfit. Gene is a pretty foxey bird. Thats all the bunk about his retiring from the ring to live in Europe in high society. The real truth of the matter is that some of his former gangster friends that he double-crossed are out to take him for a ride and he Cleared out before he got bumped off. Few people know the real inside facts. Few know that Tuneys Manager was a Politician who was connected with the New York State Prison Commition and Prison Parole Board. Appointed to that position by Governor Al. Smith. Few People know that Tuney and his manager on numerous occaisions, visited several N.Y. State Prisons and while there had long confidential talks with Bum Rogers and other Convicts. Or that while there they were wined and dined by the Warden in his home. Few people know that these gangsters and Gun-men in New York City have on several occaisions made special reservations and very expensive trips to and from the Clinton Prison or that they have invited the Warden and the Second Finger and 8 and 9 screws at a time to come down to the Big town where they were wined and dined at the Silver Slipper and other night clubs, all at the expense of those Gangsters and Gun Men. All of these things are matters of common knolledge among the under-world. Many Coppers know these things. The Silver Slipper and the Cotton Club are the special hang out of both copps and crooks. Any one at any time can verify these things. Therefore it stands to reason that the Coppers and the Crooks are all working in together and all double Crossing each other at the same time. And yet each and all of them all allways yelping about thier honor and thier great principles.

honor among thieves is the Bunk.

L.

I dont know wether this bunch of crap will be of any use in connection with what I have allready written but it will serve to prove my contentions that the majority of coppers are not out to put down crime and those few that realy are are in a small minority. But By far the largest the largest percentage are both brainless and unprincipled.

The methods in use by the police do not curb crime The exact reverse is true.

Right here and now in this City Washington D.C. There is a man on the Police Force by the name of Allen. I dont know him personaly Never saw him and never spoke to him. Still I know that he is a College graduate, he is a clear and clean minded man. He has both brains and a high moral mind with good principles. H is phisicaly fit or he wouldnt be on the Police force.

He has brains enough to see right and he has the moral courage to stick by his principles.

There are very few like him on any police force.

Any man like this guy is should be a welcome addition to any law abiding comunity or Police force. That kind of a man is hard to find at any time. He is sacrificing his own best intirsts to be of service to the public good. And what is the result? The result is that the big majority of his companions and fellow officers are all out to sink him. They are doing every dam thing they can to drive him off of the Police Force. They are watching every move he makes and at the least slip they are trying to trip him up and preffer charges against him. They dont want him on the police Force. Why? Simply because he is clean and they are dirty. Because he has principle which they lack. Because he has more brains than they have. Here is a battle inside the ranks of the forces of law and order. One man who is in the right against a mob that is in the wrong.

Any body with any claim to intelligence at all can see thru this racket. Even a skunk like me can respect a man like that guy Allen.

Peopel want every one to have respect for the law but how the hell is any one going to have any respect for law and order when the law dosen't respect itself.

Then here is another little illustration.

Just the other day in N.Y. City and also in Chicago. With a Gand Hoo-raw in the papers the two Chiefs of Police of those citys Made a Grand Round up Smashing up ginmills and saloons and pool rooms and such like.

In N.Y. they pinched 1500 men. Inside of 3 days these 1500 men were all back at liberty, all except about 100 in N.Y.

In Chicago 4,000 were pinched in 3 days they were all free except 300 men. And it wont be long until the most of those are again free.

This being the case, then what the hell was the gain.

Very probably the cops did pinch a big mob of crooks. What of it. They are all free again. When they got pinched and while they were in the can, they must all have got a kick or two each. Some of em got beaten up good. Now I wonder if any one is a big enough fool to think that this sort of treatment made those that recieved it feel any better disposed towards law and order. Are they all reformed up now. Does any one believe that this same outfit as soon as they got out of the can they at once rushed around to get a job and are now hard at work, putting blisters on thier hands and a hump on thier back by trading labor for dollars. Any body thinks that is sure nutty.

What they did do was to get mad at the treatment they recieved. Those among them who had the guts and the brains , all got buisy at once looking for a crooked and easy dollar. Some went back to thier old graft in the same place. Some looked around for a new graft in a new place. Lots of them left town went somewhere else to where they was not known and there they are buisy working some kind of a skin game on some one else. Sone one, some where is being robbed, raped or killed by some of this outfit of 3 or 4 thousand men that were pinched, mistreated and then turned loose. This kind of a bull-dozing Police racket only makes matters worse for some poor sucker some where else. Even if New York and Chicago got rid of all these crooks that they pinched and run out of town that only makes bad matters worse. These crooks only go to some other towns and the people of those towns suffer. They dont know these crooks and the crooks know it. the crooks just bull thier way around and many a poor hard working slob must pay, maybe with only his money or property and maybe with his life or maybe both. The biggest dumbbell on earth ought to be able to see the truth of this. How can any one be so dumb as to think that these kind of tactics that the police use are the right kind to use if the result to be desired is the putting down of crime.

The present system is a Joke and the Joke is on the people who pay big taxes for the privalage of being robbed or killed.

I have lived 36 years in the U.S.A. and never paid a dollar for taxes. There thousands more like me. the present system in use is the cause of this as it is the cause of many other abuses. I was born and raised in this Country and yet I have never voted once and I am 36 years old. There are plenty more like me. I have done very, very little work of the honest kind, but I have worked very, very hard at my chosen proffession, produsing Death, Desolation and Damnation. I am still alive and as long as I keep on living I am going to keep right on doing the same to the best of my ability.

There are Thousands of more like me who feel the same and do the same as I do And what we would like to know, is, "What the hell are you going to do about it."

L.

You have been pretty decent to me although there isn't any reason why you should do me any favors, yet I am going to ask you to do some-thing for me.

I would like to get a real sincere opinion from some one like this guy Fife who has a keen, anyalitical trained mind and who is able to give an unbiased opinion as to just what the hell is wrong with me. I am pretty ignorant but I am sure I am not insane and yet I am not as others are. I would like to know just what others think about my complexes and abnormalaties. I don't want the opinion of some ordinary psychoanalyst or bug Dr. who merely goes thru a routine rigamarol examination and judges the results by the rules that are written down in some book full of Theories which have never been proven facts.

You are a student and I believe that your ideas are right but still I am just as much puzzled as ever about myself. All of my life I have been trying to figure out just what ails me and why. I am damed if I can figure it all out try as I will. I am not looking for the remedy or the effect. Its too late for the remedy and I allready know the effect but I sure would like to know the cause. Will you just ask what others think about that history of my life when they read it. Some of them your associates and friends, surely must be capable of getting the correct answer to my problem.

When I was a small boy 6 or 7 years old I allways had trouble with my ears allways aching and running with matter. This went on for a year or two constantly but with little or no medical or surgical attention other than just what ingnorant imagrant Neighbors, Mostly German Farmers, would suggest to be tried out on me. Things like laying a hot brick on my ear. Pouring sweet oil into it or maybe sometimes goose-grease and other home remedies. These experiments never done me any good but things got worse instead of better. Finaly my head swelled up as big as a baloon. Then my people finaly went to see a real Dr. He looked me over and at once precribed an operation. My people were too poor to have me in a hospital so I was operated on in our own home. On the kitchen table. This was a mastoid operation behind my left ear. After the operation I was put to bed where I slept with my brother. There was never any nurse in attendence and the Dr used to come once a week for a few weeks.

My mother and older brother were my only nurses. They knew as much about nursing and antiseptics and germes as I do about the next world. But I got well in spite of all thier ignorance. For a while only tho. Then my ear again began to run with matter and swell up. My neck and jaws swelled up also. Just one year after my first operation things had got to be worse than ever so I was taken to see a new Doctor. He at once put me in a hospital in spite of the protests of my people. In that hospital I was operated on again in the same place behind my left ear. My Mother watched the operation and she often told me all about it later on in life. She said that the Dr's cut my head open and took out a sack or absess about 3 or 4 inches long filled with matter. I stayed in that hospital several months, until I wall all healed up. But still that damed ear and the other one also gave me many an ache in after years. I had trouble with them for about 8 years each winter and then I never had any trouble since except at very rare intervals. Now I wonder, could it be possible that that trouble had or has now any connection with my criminal tendencies. Is it possible that those operations had any after effects on my brain. Has the brain any connection with the ear. I sure would like to know if this is the cause of all my queer actions and could that defect be remedied by another operation for mastoids. Not that I want one because I dont. I dont want to be cured in that way. The only way I want to be cured is to die and get completely out of this world. I would not consent to be operated on and they cant operate on me without my own consent. All I want is to find out the reason why I am what I am and why I act the way I do. I have been puzzled all my life about this and I would sure like to know the answer before I leave this world. If you should attend these lectures and if you should come into contact with any of these crack Psycholigests and Psychiatrists Doctors. You could ask them what they think about it. You and they are all interested in this subject of criminology and surely there never was a better chance to find out a few things that are not understood about this subject in studying a habitual Criminal. If I aint one then there never was one.

You are making a life time study and career on this buisness and surely you ought to go and attend these lectures at the Mt. Pleasant Congressional Church and there you would Meet this guy Dr N.D.C. Lewis and others like him. You could learn much from him and his other Conferres who are there working with him along these lines. You could let him or them read all or any part of what I have written and find out what they think about it. I sure would like to know the correct answer to my problem.

In one of the large prisons of this Country, on top of one of the front buildings is the statue of a man made of copper. This statue is known as Copper John.

The cons have made up a piece of poetry about this Copper John and the cons themselves. The first line of it is

If Copper John, Could only

turn his face
and see the Muzzlers and the Guzzlers in this Place.

From there it goes on to tell just what he would see. The meanesses, degeneracy unprinciple, treachery Brutality and every kind of roguery and filth there is that is confined behind the Stone walls and iron bars that he has turned his back on.

It is well understood in the underworld that the worst insulting name that any one can call another is that he is a Muzzler and Guzzler.

This means that the man is lost to all decency and is beyond all redemption he is the most lowdown speciman that is on earth of the whole human race. There can be nothing worse.

During my last term in prison I was given the Nick-name or moniker of Copper John and was known as a first Class, A. No. 1. Muzzler and Guzzler.

When I was given that rep, I wasnt alltogether entitled to to it, but I am now. I plead guilty. I fully deserve it now. I am as rotton as I know how to be and the only reason I am not worse is because my opportunities and abilities are limited.

Booster = shoplifter

Prowler = burglar.

Stick up or hister = hold up man.

Jug = bank.

Jug-head = dumbell

hop head = dope-fiend a smoker of opium

snow-bird = cocaine sniffer

Needle pumper = hypodermic user.

Con man = Confidence man.

Shiv man = knife man.

Can opener = outfit of tools to rip a safe

Peter man = Box man or safe blower. sometimes used to describe a man who slips a Peter or knock out drops in anothers drink. A Keeley.

A Pimp is a Pimp and a McGimp is both or worse than either.

Paper hanger = forger

Crape hanger = either a gloom or killer

Catting up a Scatter or Gin Mill = to hold up a saloon.

Mob is the same as a gang.

A Gunsel is a Punk and a Punk is poofter and a poofter is a Pratter and a pratter is similar to a fruiter. the only difference in the two is that one likes to sit on "**It.**" and the other likes to eat "**It.**" A Face Artist is an exceptionaly well experienced fruiter. One who knows his bananas better than an amature. A face artist is one who goes down town for lunch and nose-dives into the bushes when he's hungry.

Croaker = Prison Doctor and a very appropriate title it is too.

Big Finger = Warden

Second Finger = P.K. or dep.

Screws = The Big Fingers Dogs

Dance Hall = death house.

Big house = Hoosegow = Stir or College.

To pull off a hot Prowl is to turn off a trick in a Privat or a Joint that is kipped or bugged; that is to rob a place where people are sleeping or that is wired.

To get a stretch in Stir. = to do a bit in the Hoosegow.

to make a lam = to Crush out of the Hoosegow.

A Big Shot is a leading light of Crookdom.

A wolf is one who has a prefference for a Gunsel. Sometimes they fall madly in love with each other and then the green eyed monster stalks Abroad.

P.S.

L.

I been wondering what people think when they read all this crap that I been writing.

I'll bet that your girl friend and maybe you too, take a bath all over, whenever you get thru reading all of this filth and dirt all confined in the carcass of one human being.

I'll bet that neither you nor any one else ever heard of any one who was so absoloutly unprincipled and rotton as I am.

I never have yet and I have met every kind of a skunk there is in human kind.

You better watch your step so that you dont get disgusted and turn on the gas. Tell your girl friend that she better not allow herself to think too much when she types out all of this garbage.

The world is wide and they aint all like

Copper John
Alias
Carl Panzram.

If you are going to get a job in that boys Training school and if you intend to make a study and a life work of the delinquency and the rehabiliation of young boys, then it wont do any harm, and maybe of some benifit not only to yourself in your work, but also the youngsters that you will have to teach and guard; Thats why I am offering you these few ideas and suggestions. You know that I spent several years in one of those places when I was a boy and the so called Training that I recieved while there is mainly the cause of my being the degenerate beast that I am today. I have thought about that system of Training young boys for all of my life and I know that the whole system is wrong. That system of beating goodness, religeon and Jesus into boys in 99 times out of 100 has the direct opposite effect of taking all of the goodness, kindness and love out of them and then replacing those feelings with hate, envy deciete, tyrany and every other kind of meaness there is. If you are realy sincere in wanting to teach those boys how to grow up to be good men then you will have to go at it far differently than the way I was taught. If you should be fortunate enough to be appointed the Commander of one of the Companys of boys, you will find when you start out that by far the largest majority of them are allready in such a frame of mind that they will all be suspissious of you and your methods in handling them. You will find that thier minds are allready poisened and twisted into believing the worst of every body and you especialy. You will never be able to accomplish much with any of them until you first gain thier good will and confidence. You can never gain either until you absolutly assure them that your not a lier or a hypocrite. This you will have to prove by word and deed to them. Once you are able to convince them that you yourself are a good clean, honorable man and that you mean only good for them, then they will listen and believe you. When you get there you will find that they are all being taught a lot of bull by a lot lying hypocrites, just the same as I was taught when I was a boy with just about the same results. I know now that If I had it all to do over again and if I had any choise in what subjects I should be instructed, then my real choise should be to disregard all hypocracy and foolish impractical things such as are taught today in the name of religeon. Thats the bunk. The Golden Rule is religeon enough to teach to any boys. Teach them the meanyng of such things as

truth	lie.
honest	thief.
honor	Dishonor.
bravery	cowerdise
clean	dirty.
Love	hate.

For each lesson just take one word. For instance take the word truth Teach them the full meaning of that one word in all its tenses Then teach them how to spell it prounounce it and speak and write it in every day usage. Teach them what it realy means to be truthfull how they will be respected by all others and how they will respect themselves by being truthfull. Teach them by example, word and deed until they thouroughly know that one word. Truth.

The next day for the next lesson take the antonym of truth, the word lie or lier. Teach that word until it is thoroughly understood and what a despisable thing a real lier is. Show them the harm it does show them that it does no good and only harm to lie. how a lier loses his own self respect and the respect of all others. Show them the contrast between a truthfull person and a lier. how one has his own self respect and the respect of all others and then on the other hand show them what a mean thing a lier is. After these two lessons are over with, let each boy write out a short composition of what he has learned and his belief and theories of same. Keep all of each boys records on file keep track of each time he tells the truth or lies.

Keep a separate record of each boys conduct, give him credits for his truthfullnes, and punish him for lying. Let these records be the real standard to judge the boy by as to his fitness or unfitness for release from the instatution. Don't judge the boy because he learns or does not learn his Sunday school lessons or because he is misschiefveous and missbehaves by having a fight with another boy or by breaking some thing or because he does or does not do his work or some of the other standards they use today in the judging of boys fitness or his unfitness.

Only a fool will judge another person for what he does. They should be judged not for what they do but for **how they do it and why they do it.**

Let them all have an incentive to strive for in these lessons. some sort of rewards or prizes. some-thing usefull that they realy want. Don't do like the bible pounders do, they give thier boys a nice little card with a dam fool sigary kind of a verse on it as a reward for learning a lying sunday School lesson or some fool fable that some bewhiskered old King doped out ages ago to fool his simple subjects into obeying him.

One or two words like these each day will do more to make better men out of young boys than all the long-haired wind bags and all the bibles in the world.

You will find that the boys will all be interested. Thier new words will be in thier vocabularies in every day usage. They will believe in these lessons because they will be true and some-thing they can see. Thier rewards will be something that they can see feel, taste or wear or keep allways. and not merely a piece of paper full of hot air that they have no real belief in.

You will find when you go to that place to work that they will have some sort of a credit system, that they use to judge the boys by. So many credits each day for good behavior. When a boy has earned a certain amount he is eligable for a parole. The boys who get thier credits the soonest are usualy the most despicable ones of the lot. They are the clever liers, the hypocrites and the stool-piedgons. But they sure do learn thier Sunday School lessons all right. and they know how to be very polite by saying, Yes sir and no sir, and please sir, good morning and how do you do sir. But all of these are merely surface feelings, and thier real feelings are hidden out of sight where you will have a hard time discovering them.

If you have a book of synonyms and antonyms, you just get it out some time and make out a long list of words such as I have written down and then you study each one and tiach what you have learned to those boys. When you get that place you will find out that there are several hours each day when the boys have nothing to do except to plan mischief. Those hours you could take and put to good use. You could accomplish more if you shoud follow my suggestions that all of the rest put together.

Teach them how to be gentlemen Teach them the the first rule of the conduct of a gentleman is to have consideration for the other fellow.

Such things as these you can easily teach them. Let others if they will, teach them how to learn sunday school lessons scrub floors, work and be hypocrites, liers and rogues. As I was taught when I was a boy.

Selected letters to Henry Lesser; to protect his position as guard at Washington District Jail, Lesser used the pseudonym "Henry James" and had Panzram send the letters to friends and relatives living in Washington:

Leavenworth, Kansas Sept 28. 1929.

Yesterday evening I recieved your letter of Sept 25th. In it you asked me 8 questions. It would take 10 or 15 pages of paper like this for me to fully answer all of your questions. That can't be done. You should allready know the answer to most of em. Read your manuscript over again and you will understand. You surely know the facts if any one does beside myself. If you dont now you probably never will understand. I wrote it plainly and distinctly enough for any one to understand. All except 2 of your questions. The last one about the murder which I committed here, you might not understand. You asked me why I done it and if I got a kick out of doing it. I had not one reason for doing it, but about 47 reasons and each one of them was a good reason. Good enough for me any way. You know the deal I got in the D.C. can from Peak. Did you think I would forget and forgive that. I told you all then while in my cell, again in the open court room, again when I came here, I told every one I came into contact with that I would sure knock off the first guy who ever bothered me. I even told that to the Deputy warden here and the man I killed. I warned em all to lay off of me and leave me alone. They didn't leave me alone and I killed one and tried to kill a dozen others. The way I figure things out is this way. if it was all right for the law to do the things to me that it has then its all right for me to do the same thing to the law. Peak was the one I waited 5 months to get but he didnt come here so I stepped out and got another one just like him. You asked if I get a kick out of killing people. Sure I do. If you dont think so, you do as I had done to me and as I done myself. Then youll know. You just let 5 or 6 big huskeys walk in on you and let em hammer you unconcious, then drag you down in a cellar and chain you up to a post and work you over some more. and then if you feel like forgiving and forgetting all about it write and tell me about it will you. I have had 22 years of this kind of stuff and you know it and yet your chump enough to wonder why I am what I am. Dont be so dumb. Judging by the tone of your letter you now figure I am a bug of some kind a fire bug or a homicidal maniac. Thats where your wrong, I am no bug even if I do get a kick out things which would have the direct opposite effect on you. Another thing, You asked about sending me some cigars. Now you know better than that. Thats high treason. If your going to send me money thats all ok. At the same time you can have the Haldeman Julius Co send me thier catalog so I can buy some of thier books.

Carl Panzram
31614
Box. 7. Leavenworth Kansas

Leavenworth, Kansas Oct. 6. 1929.

I recieved your letter of Sept 25. I answered it at once but was unable to fully answer all of the questions which you asked me. I'll try to answer some of em in this letter. As for my next trial, I dont know when its due. Sometime soon I believe. But Probably Nov. or Dec. in the Federal Court at K.C.K.

You seldom answer any of my questions but thats all right as it dosent make much diff either way. But I wish you would allways let me know if or when you get all of my letters. You asked me as to my motivs in doing some of the things I have done. Surely; you know that I am very impulsive, very vindictive and absoloutly unscrupulous. Those are reasons enough to explain my actions. You also know why I feel and am that way. As for the kick I get out of it. I meant figurativly and not literaly. Whatever possesed you to think that me or any one else ever had a sexual like feeling when we comitt a crime like murder or arson. Thats the bunk. I myself have intelligence enough to know the feeling but I havent knolledge enough to explain it so that you could understand it. The only way I know of for you to find out just what sort of a kick I get out of it is for you to do as I done.

Experiment. go buy yourself a box of matches. or go get an ax and bop some guy on the back of the neck. Its easy when you know how. Besides you put em out of all thier misery when you knock em off.

Now then for your question about my ideas of any dreams I have had and thier effects on me. Sure I have dreams but they have no effects whatever on my actions during my waking moments. What started you thinking about that was probably my question about Bill Pellys article in the American mag for March '29. Just forget it, "you probably have allready; because you never answered my queston." Since I read that I have read some more of his writings and I have come to the conclusion that he is some kind of a bug or more probably a hop-head. I am neither. I can reason things out just as logicaly and clearly as any body. I can see the truth and I can admit it where a great many other people are unable to see the truth and are unwilling to admit it even if they do see it. Well thats about enough of my philosophy for this time. Now about you I would like to know when if ever your going to quit that Lousey Job and get a real one. That Job is doing you no good. Its doing you harm. If you stay with it long enough youll be as bad a That great Criminologist [Superintendent Peak of the Washington District Jail] who studied his subject for 28 years and then thought "he still does" that he knows it all. If you don't believe it ask him. You know who I mean. That great Christian and Military hero. The Major. Now then as for the money and cigars which you promised me, Just forget it or wait until you peddle your manuscript and then if you get a real bank-roll, "Donate," to

Carl Panzram

Leavenworth, Kansas Oct 31. 1929.

I recieved your Letter of Oct 9. I wrote twice since then. Last Sunday I ordered 40 little blue books with the $2.$^{\underline{00}}$ which you sent me. but I have since then found out that it cant be done. They are not permitted here. So I still have the money. Now I'll try to figure out some other way to spend it. I thought I would write you a letter today because I feel pretty good just now. In fact I feel pretty near human. For several different reasons here are a few. Its so long since I have been beaten or kicked around, chained up or knocked down, that I have allmost forgotten how it feels. but not quite. I still remember. Another reason is that I have just finished my supper and man what a feed. I started with bacon and eggs, candied-sweet-potatoes, bread-and-butter, stewed prunes and 4 frest pears. Thats a sample of the meals we get here every day, lately. After I finished throwing this feed into myself, I sat down to smoke and read the daily paper. In peace, quiet and comfort. Now, perhaps you will know why this letter is a bit different from some of the others I have written to you. This is sure a queer old world. here I am getting old after roaming all over the world, after serving over 20 years in Jails and in some of em I got plenty abuse for very little, In one of which, thats the last one in N.Y. I was sloughed up in the Isolation for over 2 years and there treated worse than you and many other people would treat a mad dog. That treatment I recieved, not for what I had done but for what others thought I might do. There I done nothing to deserve all of the abuse I got. Now notice the contrast. I come here expecting to get more of the same kind of treatment, but determined that this time I wont get it for nothing. This time I figure I'll beat em to it. I make one attempt to escape, I fail but I don't get caught, imediatly I begin getting all readyed up to try again in another place. But before I can get properly organized I get into a small Jam, this caused me to figure, "Judging by past performances in other prisons," that I am due to get another kicking around, So to fore-stall all that, I grab myself a 10 pound iron bar and go on the war-path. Before I have finished I kill one man and try to kill a dozen more. After doing all of these things I walk into a cell fully expecting to be chained up and beaten to death. But what happens. The exact reverse of that. No one lays a hand on me. No one abuses me in any way. This is how things have been with me up to now. I have been for the past 3 or 4 months trying to figure it out and I have come to the conclusion that, if in the begining I had been treated as I am now, then there wouldn't have been quite somany peopele in this world that have been robbed, raped and killed and perhaps also very probably I wouldn't be where I am today. Maybe I am wrong tho. I am too dumb to know what might have been but I am not so dumb that I cant see a little way into the future. Not very far but far enough to see the end of

Carl Panzram

Leavenworth, Kansas Nov. 13. 1929.

Your letter of Nov. 7, reached me this eve. What a kick I got out of reading it. You have it all doped out Eh." You have it all figured out that if I was given my freedom today, financial independence, moral support and a helping hand from powerfull people and every thing neccessary that would help me to reform and had a good clean Christian life, Thats all that would be required. You figure that I would jump at it and be all reformed up the minute I hit the front gate. What a dream. Your all wet. Wake up kid your having a nightmare. I can dream better dreams than that, myself. If there was even the faintest possibility of your idea ever becoming a fact, then I would be right on the Job. I would be the best little yes man you ever saw. You may not believe me, but if I cared to, I could be just as smooth a lier and hypocrite as any would be Christian you ever saw or heard tell of and they are all experts. But it just so happens that I dont care to lie just now. I am not going to try to decieve you and neither am I going to kid myself. I know myself and my own state of mind far better than you or any one else knows me and the more I look deep into my own self, the less good I can see. You seem to think that all that is neccessary for a person to do when he wants to change his mode of living is to just change and thats the end of it. All reformed up just like that. Thats how easy it is in Theory. But the reality is far different when you take into consideration all of the facts. The real truth of the matter is that I haven't the least desire to reform. very much the reverse of that is the truth. I would not reform if the front gate was opened right now and if I was given a million dollars when I stepped out. I have no desire to do good or to be good. I am just as mean now as I can possibly be, and the only reason I am no worse is because I lack the power and the proper opportunitys for meanness. If I had the power and the opportunities, then I would soon show you what real meanness was. You over-look the fact that The law and a great many people have been trying thier d—— for 25 years to reform me. I am tired of having people try to reform me. What I want to do is to reform them. and I think the best way to reform em is to put em out of thier misery. It took me 38 years to be like I am now, then how do you figure that I could if I wanted to, change from black to white in the twinkling of an eye. Have you some kind of a secret formula, some mumbo-Jumbo, or hocus-pocus that could cause this great change. If you know some-thing like that let me have it and I'll try it out or someone to see how it works. I have a good subject here that I would like to try it out on. He is nearly a bad a skunk as I am. Not quite tho. Now then to answer some more of your questions. The little Blue books are not allowed to any one in here but Books from any other Publishing Co. are permitted here. Why that is I dont know. Its a rule here, thats all I know about it. I have never read Jack Blacks Boook, "You Cant Win." Harpers or Scribners mags seems to be unpopular here. I havent seen one of either since I've been here. There are lots of good magazines here but I dont get many good ones. But I guess thats because I dont love Jesus or maybe they want to lead me into paths of upritchousness by handing me such mags as the Argosy and Western Thrillers. No ther is nothing you can do for me unless your rich uncle should open his heart and his pocket-book. In that case you could if you would, have sent these two books, direct from publisher to,

Carl Panzram

Leavenworth, Kansas Nov. 28. 1929.

I recieved your letter of Nov. 7. I wrote you two in answer and now this is the third one. In your last letter to me you asked me to seriously consider from all angles your proposition. That is if I should be given a comutation of sentence or a pardon now and then given my liberty with financial backing, what would I do with it. Could I and would I reform. In my other two letters I told you that I didnt believe I could reform even if I had the opportunity to and if I wanted to. I am of the same opinion still. In the first place I very much doubt that there is the remotest possibility of you or any one else having power enough to get me my freedom. In the second place I have no desire to reform under such conditions as would be required of me the way the laws of this country are today. In the third place I do not care to live any longer if I must live in prison. I would far rather die and go to hell if thats where people like me go to after death. I have very thoroughly considered this matter and I assure you that what I now say is the truth. My first reason for disagreeing with you is that I believe it is absoloutly impossible for me to ever gain my freedom in a legal way because I have too much against me and too many people wish my death. I have confessed to 23 different cold blooded, premeditated murders, hundreds of cases of arson, burglarys, robberies, rapes and other crimes. The law has by this time looked em up and verified the truth of my various confessins. I am wanted in dozens of different states and other countries for every crime on the calender, from petty larceny to murder. I expect to go on trial here next month for the last murder I committed. At that time I expect to be found guilty of murder in the first degree and then sentenced to be hanged by the neck until I am as dead as a dodo or the man I killed here last June, and you can take it from me, neither will ever be any deader than they are now. That one reason should be sufficient answer to your question. But just in case your not convinced yet that your dream is impossible of fullfillment I'll give you my second reason and that is that I could not reform if I wanted to. It has taken me all of my life so far, 38 years of it for me to reach my present state of mind. In that time I have aquired some habits. These habits can not be broken in a moments time. It took me a life time to form these habits and I believe it would take more than another life-time to break myself of these same habits even if I wanted to. My philosophy of life is such that very few peopel ever get and and it is so deeply ingrained and burned into me that I dont believe I could ever change my beliefs. The things I have had done to me by others and the things I have done to them, can never be forgotten or forgiven either by me or others. I can't forget and I wont forgive. I couldn't if I wanted to. The law is in the same fix. Those are two very good reasons why your proposition is not feasable. Its only a dream on your part but I have no illusions as to its practicibility.

Leavenworth, Kansas Nov. 28. 1929.

Page III

My third reason for not agreeing with your suggestions is that I prefer death before spending more years in prison. My belief is that life without liberty is not worth having. If the law wont kill me, I shall kill myself. I fully realize that I am not fit to live among people in a civilized comunity. I have no desire to do so. If I had any choice in living any longer, the only way I would consent to do so would be to get clear out and away from all civilized people. If I could get my freedom and a few hundred dollars worth of the neccessarys of life such as clothing, medicins, tools, seeds fishing and hunting tackle and some books and writing materials, and with these things a couple of dogs and then clear out and go off to some far away lonely Island, Then I would be contented. No one would trouble me and I would trouble no one else. There I could have life, liberty and the persuit of happiness. I know of just such a place a small Island off of the San Blass Coast of Panama. I have been there before, years ago. The island had some hundreds of coconut trees on it, a spring of fresh water. The sea Tortoises come there to lay thier eggs. There are plenty of fish, some banana trees some mango and lime trees. The soil will grow any thing thats planted. This Island is about 40 or 50 miles off of the reefs directly East by north from a place called Peters Island which is East of Chucumbally which is on the Main land and south of Povamella where the Panamanian Goverment has stationed thier Port of Entry for traders on the San Blass Coast. I was a trader and skipper and owner of a small sloop down there in 1919 and 20 so I know what I am talking about. This Island is owned by the San Blass Indians and they visit it once or twice each year to harvest the coconuts and gather in the eggs of the sea turtles, otherwise no one ever goes there. Thats what I would like to do and thats about the only way I would even think of living out any natural life. There I could live as I wanted to and I would not need conform to the standards set by other people in civilization. I am so set in my ways that I can not adapt myself to the ways of other people so the only way for me to do would be to live by myself without any human companionship whatever. I sure would like to try it that way. That is about all for this time, now you answer me a question, What do you think about it? I expect tho that by the time you get around to answering this letter, I will have been tried, found guilty and sentenced to death or maybe I'll be allready in my grave. So Long –

Carl Panzram

Final letter to Lesser:

Leavenworth, Kansas June 5. 1930.

I am writing this letter today June 5 but I dont expect to have it mailed to you until Sept. 6 1930 because on that day I'll be dead and buried.

There are a good many things I would like to say or write to you but because I don't know wether or not you'll ever get this letter. I cut it kind of short.

First I want to tell you that up to now I have been getting the reading matter which you were good enough to subscribe for me. These include

The Saturday Evening Post
The Christian Science Monitor
The forum
Time
The Pathfinder

and also the American Mercury, just now recieved.

I also want to tell you that I have enjoyed reading them all. There is nothing I can do for you to repay you for the many favors you have done for me except to thank you and wish you good luck. I would like to be able to truthfully tell you that I do thank you but this I can not do simply because there is no such thing as gratitude left in me. There was at one time but that time is long gone. Gratitude is one of the many things that have been kicked out of me. I can and do truthfully wish you good luck. All that you deserve and I am of the opinion that you are one of the very few men I have ever known that realy deserve good luck in this world. You deserve what I have missed in life, happiness, peace, and contentment.

As for me, I'll soon be at peace. I have never had the good fortune to find it in life so I expect to find it in death. I hope so and believe so.

To some people my death will seem to come in a horrible form but to me it seems a very easy way to die. I look forward to it as a pleasure and a relief. It is a far easier death than I have dealt out to some of the people I have killed. I couldn't and don't ask for any easier way to die.

This will probably be the last I'll ever write to any one because in Just 90 days more I'll be hanged by the neck until I am dead. But I feel fine and am feeling better every day as the time grows shorter.

I intend to leave this world as I have lived in it. I expect to be a rebel right up to my last moment on earth. With my last breath I intend to curse the world and all man kind. I intend to spit in the warden's eye or whoever places the rope around my neck when I am standing on the scaffold. I allways did want to spit in a coppers eye and also a preacher or priest. That will be all the thanks theyll get from me. I don't know which I despise and detest the most, a copper or a buck. I guess the soul-saver takes the palm. I have met only one priest that I felt I could respect but I have known quite a number of coppers I could and did and do still respect. You are one of em. I never have liked any of em but I did respect em when they have deserved it and some do. Not many but some anyway.

Leavenworth, Kansas June 20. 1930.

The other half of this letter I wrote 20 days ago. Since then conditions here have changed a bit. Not very much but just enough for me to commit suicide tonight instead of waiting until Sept 6 to be legally hung.

So if I succeed in my effort at suicide tonight then this will sure be the last I'll ever say or write on this earth.

The choice is mine and I fully realize just what I am doing.

I would like to have it known just why I do this. I had no choice about coming into this world and nearly all of my 38 years in it I have had very little to say or do about how I should live my life. People have driven me into doing everything I have ever done. Now the time has come when I refuse to be driven any farther.

Tonight I die and tomorrow I go to a grave farther than that no man can drive me I am sure glad to leave this lousy world and the lousier people that live in it. But of all the lousy people in this world I believe that I am the lousiest of em all.

Today I am dirty but tomorrow I'll be just

DIRT.

Letter to the "Society for the Abolishment of Capital Punishment":

Leavenworth, Kansas May 23. 1930.

I, Carl Panzram No. 31614. of the U.S. Penitentiary at Leavenworth, Kansas, am writing this statement of my own free will without any advice or suggestions from any one.

In the year 1928 at Washington D.C. I was charged with and tried for the crimes of Burglary and Grand Larceny. Altho I was guilty of both of these crimes, I stood trial and pleaded not guilty but The Jury found me guilty on both charges and the Judge at once sentenced me to the term of 25 years.

On Feb. 1, 1929 I began serving this sentence at the U.S. Penitentiary at Leavenworth Kansas.

On June 25, 1929 I murdered one man, a civilian employe of the Prison, By the name of Warncke and at the same time and place I also attempted to murder a dozen other men, both guards and convicts. The only reason I did not kill them also was because I couldnt catch them.

For this Crime I was indicted by a U.S. Grand Jury and on April 15th and 16th I was tried in the U.S. Court at Topeka Kansas. This Court was called and sat under the Jurisdiction of Judge Hopkins.

At this trial I pleaded not guilty and was at once put on trial for the crime of Murder in The first degree.

So far as I know, I was given a legal trial and was not deprived of any of my constatutional rights.

The Jury found me guilty as charged in the Indictment. The Judge thereupon pronounced sentence on me and the sentence was that I should be hanged by the neck until dead. This sentence to take effect between the hours of 6 AM and 9 AM at the U.S. Penitentiary at Leavenworth Kansas on the date of Sept. 5, 1930.

The finding of the Court and the sentence of the Judge meet with my aproval and I am perfectly satisfied to have the sentence carried out without any further interferrence from any one. I do not wish to have another trial and I do not wish to have that sentence changed in any way.

If I am given another trial or if the death sentence should be commuted to life imprisonment either in a penitentiary or an insane asylum it will be against my will.

Now then I come to the reason why I have written this letter.

I have been informed that your organization or at any rate, some of the members of it, have made or are making an attempt to change my sentence to life imprisonment in solitary confinement in a prison or in an insane asylum.

This you are doing without my consent and absoloutly against my will.

I shall never willingly grant you my permission to have this done for me.

For your information and guidence I am going to inform you of some facts which I believe you are unaware of at this time.

I believe that your reasons for trying to set aside the sentence of death in my case are that you think that this penalty is not a humane form of Justice. You are sincere in your beliefs that this is a barbaric and inhuman form of punishment.

Another one of your reasons is that you are laboring under the delusion that I am insane and therefore not responsible for my acts.

Now I am going to attempt to show you that This sentence of death is absoloutly Just and also that it will be carried out in a very humane manner and I shall also try to convince you that I am in full possession of all of my faculties and that I am now and allways have been perfectly sane and I am therefore fully responsible for every thing I have ever done.

First I shall try to convince you that I am quite sane at this time. I believe that any person who is sober, and sane and who is not blind and who is able to read and understand the English language as I am here writing is he or she should be convinced without any further argument that I am perfectly sane in every way and therefore responsible for my acts.

I am at this time 38 years old. A big powerfull man, strong in both body and mind. My phisical fitness is not as good as it once was but my mental faculties are unimpaired in any way. I have never used drugs of any kind at any time. I am and allways have been a very moderate drinker of liquor. Practicaly a total abstainer. I have never had any diesese of any kind which would have a tendency to weaken my intellect. I have never been addicted to any habits of sexual excesses of any kind over which I didn't have complete control of myself.

So far as I know none of my relatives or ancesters have ever been in any kind of an instatution for mental defectives.

I, for my own part have been examined on numerous occaisons by various duly qualified, capable and impartial Doctors as to my sanity and so far as I know I have never been pronounced to be insane or incapable or irresponsible for my acts.

I have never spent one single day of my life in any instatution for the insane.

But I have spent 22 years of my life time in various Penal instatutions.

I started doing time when I was 11 years old and have been doing practicaly nothing else since then. What time I havent been in Jail I spent either getting out or getting in again.

During this time I have been into every kind of a penal instatution there is in this Country and some in other countries.

Therefore I consider myself pretty well qualified to know what the conditions of prisons, prisners, Policemen Courts, Prison guards, Prison officials and the existing conditions of Penal instatutions are today, here and now.

Knowing the real facts as I do from practical experience and also knowing that there is only one chance in a thousand of my ever getting my freedom and also knowing that I, like all other men, must some day die, I have deliberatly and intentionaly made my choice.

I choose to die here and now by being hanged by the neck until I am dead.

I prefer that I die that way, and if I have a soul and if that soul should burn in hell for a million years, still I prefer that to a lingering agonizing death in some Prison dungeon or a Padded cell in a mad house.

Now I want to know, if this isn't good logic and reason, then what the hell is it.

Now then I shall give you my second reason why this sentence should be carried out.

I do not believe that being hanged by the neck until dead, is a barbaric or inhuman punishment.

I look forward to that as a real pleasure and a big relief to me. I do not feel bad or unhappy about it in any way. Every day since I recieved that sentence I have felt pretty good. I feel good right now and I believe that when my last hour comes that I will dance out of my dungeon and on to the scaffold with a smile on my face and happiness in my heart.

Another reason why I believe that this sentence should be carried out is because I believe it is Justice and I am quite sincere when I say that this is the first and only time in all my life of battling with the law that I ever did get justice from the law.

Now, you who do not know me or my wishes, you decide without consulting me in any way, you start to try to revoke the judgement of a legaly constuted court and the sentence that was pronounced on me.

One other thing I am going to tell you before I stop this letter and that is this, The only thanks you or your kind will ever get from me for your efforts in my behalf is that I wish you all had one neck and that I had my hands on it, I would sure put you out of your misery, just the same as I have done with a number of other people.

I have no desire whatever to reform myself. My only desire is to reform people who try to reform me. and I believe that the only way to reform people is to kill em.

My Motto is, Rob em all, Rape em all and Kill em all.

I am very truly yours

Signed

Copper John II.

Carl Panzram

PAULINE **PARKER**

On the afternoon of June 22, 1954, Mrs. Agnes Ritchie was working at her tea shop in the Cashmere Hills area outside Christchurch, New Zealand, when two teenage girls ran up to her clearly upset. Sixteen-year-old Pauline Yvonne Parker told the proprietress that her mother had tripped on a plank, fallen and hit her head on a brick on the ground; "Mummy's been hurt terribly," she cried, "I think she's dead." As Mrs. Ritchie helped Parker and her friend, 15-year-old Juliet Marion Hulme, clean blood off their clothes and hands, Parker continued: "Mummy's head kept bumping and banging as she fell. It seems like a dream . . . we shall wake up soon." When police arrived, they found the body of Parker's mother, 45-year-old Honora Mary Parker, lying in a pool of blood on a secluded path in the park. They immediately noticed that her face was severely battered; an autopsy later found "forty-five discernible injuries, twenty-four being lacerated wounds on the face and head." Parker was interviewed by police, and almost immediately confessed:

> Q: Who assaulted your mother?
> A: I did.
> Q: Why?
> A: If you don't mind I won't answer that question.
> Q: When did you make up your mind to kill your mother?
> A: A few days ago. . . .
> Q: What did your mother say when you struck her?
> A: I would rather not answer that.
> Q: How often did you hit her?
> A: I don't know, but a great many times I imagine.

Hulme told police:

> I heard noises behind me. It was loud conversation and anger. I saw Mrs. Rieper [neé Parker] in a sort of squatting position. They were quarrelling. I went back. I saw Pauline hit Mrs. Rieper with the brick in the stocking. I took the stocking and hit her too. I was terrified. I thought that one of them had to die. I wanted to help Pauline. It was terrible. Mrs. Rieper moved convulsively. We both held her. She was still when we left her.

Parker and Hulme were arrested, and police found in Parker's room a scrapbook, fourteen exercise books, and a diary. These writings illustrated a bewildering, fantastic world the two had created that was marred by occasional jolts of reality – such as a detailed plan for murder.

According to their parents, writing was the girls' favorite activity; lounging on the lawn of the Hulme estate, the two precocious teenagers wrote "novels" together. They planned on saving their money so they could travel to America, where they would sell their books and break into Hollywood. Lesbian lovers, they sometimes made love as movie stars – pretending to be Orson Welles and Mario Lanza, for instance – and enjoyed dancing naked on the Hulme lawn next to a "Temple of Minerva" they had built together. Setting out to break all Ten Commandments, Parker evidently broke them all; Hulme told a defense psychiatrist she broke only nine. The couple delighted in taking photographs of each other, in the nude and dressed as characters from the stories they wrote together. Mrs. Hulme, Juliet's mother, later recounted on the witness stand that Juliet enjoyed playing the roles of Charles II, Emperor of Borovnia, and later Deborah, the Emperor's mistress who had borne the Emperor's son, Dialbo. Parker assumed the identity of Lancelot Trelawney, a Cornish soldier of fortune who had succeeded in marrying the Empress of Borovnia.

The parents, perturbed by their daughters' "unhealthy relationship," decided early in 1954 to take action. At the opening of the trial against Parker and Hulme, Crown Prosecutor A. W. Brown related the following to the jury:

> Dr. Hulme, who had resigned his position as Rector of Canterbury University College, decided to return to England and to take his daughter Juliet to South Africa. . . . Both girls were determined not to be parted, and Pauline Parker wanted to go to South Africa and Juliet Hulme wanted her to go with her. Both girls knew that Mrs. Parker would be the one to object most strenuously to their going away together. They decided the best way to end Mrs. Parker's objection was to kill her in such a manner that it would appear to have been an accident. Early in June, when the date of Dr. Hulme's departure had been fixed for 3rd July, the girls coldly and calculatingly formed a plan to kill Mrs. Parker.

The prosecutor dismissed the defense psychiatrists who presented the girls "in a setting of *folie à deux*" (a psychiatric term for a situation "in which two closely associated people who are mentally ill share the same delusional beliefs"), and summed up by stating: "These girls are not incurably insane. They are incurably bad." The jury agreed, sentencing Parker and Hulme to be detained in separate prisons "until Her Majesty's Pleasure be made known." In prison Hulme became an adept fashion designer, basing her patterns on German military attire, and completed at least one novel until her release five years later. In 1994 a New Zealand reporter for the *Sunday News* revealed the identity of a best-selling murder-mystery writer, Anne Perry, as Juliet Hulme; "Perry" had taken her stepfather's last name and listed Juliet Hulme's birth date in a book on authors.

Pauline Parker converted to Roman Catholicism and "expressed the wish to become a nun." According to one account, she "either entered a convent or took up missionary work in the backward countries of Africa."

Excerpts from Pauline Parker's diary:

Date unknown: Nothing is now too disgusting or revolting for us.
Date unknown: We rose about ten and had some raspberries and cream and felt sick, after which we sat in the car and discussed who we would leave alive if we wiped out the rest of the world. We wrote out a list and had a wonderful time.

Date unknown: I rose very early, did all the housework and prepared breakfast. It rained cats and dogs (panthers and wolves). I biked out to "Ilam" [Dr. Hulme's sixteen-room mansion] and nearly froze on the way. Deborah [her pet name for Juliet Hulme] was still in bed when I arrived and did not get up until some time afterwards. Then Dr. Hulme came upstairs and asked us to come into the lounge and have a talk with him. He said we must tell him everything about our going to America, so we told him as much as we wanted, for acting characters to act each part. He was both hope-giving and depressing. We talked for a long time and Deborah and I were near tears by the time it was over. The outcome was somewhat vague. What is to be the future now? We may all be going to South Africa and Italy, and dozens of other places, or not at all.
April 3rd, 1953: Today Juliet and I found the key to the fourth world. We saw a gateway through the clouds. We sat on the edge of a path and looked down a hill out over a bay. The island looked beautiful, the sea was blue, and everything was full of peace and bliss. We then realised we had the key. We know now that we are not genji, as we thought. We have an extra part of the brain, which can appreciate the fourth world.
May 15th: [Juliet Hulme had developed tuberculosis and was admitted to a sanitarium.] I spent a wretched night. We agreed it was a great pity that I had not T.B. too, and it would be wonderful if I could catch it. We would be in the sanatorium together and we would be able to write a lot.
January 29th, 1954: We worked out how much prostitutes could earn and how much we should make in this profession. "Should" has gradually changed to "shall" and we spent a wonderful day messing around and talking over how much fun we will have in our profession.
February 13th: Why could not mother die? Dozens of people, thousands of people are dying every day. So why not mother, and father too? Life is hard.
April 25th: Deborah and I are sticking to one thing. We sink or swim together.
April 28th: Anger against mother boiled up inside me. It is she who is one of the main obstacles in my path. Suddenly a means of ridding myself of the obstacle occurred to me. If she were to die . . .
April 29th: I did not tell Deborah of my plans for removing mother. The last fate I wish to meet is one in a Borstal. I am trying to think of some way. I want it to appear either a natural or an accidental death.
June 6: We are both stark, staring mad.
June 12th: . . . Eventually we enacted how each saint would make love in bed. We felt exhausted but very satisfied.
June 19th: We practically finished our books today and our main "ike" for the day was to moider mother. This notion is not a new one, but this time it is a definite plan which we intend to carry out. We have worked it out carefully and are both thrilled by the idea. Naturally we feel a trifle nervous, but the pleasure of anticipation is great.
June 20th: We discussed our plans for moidering mother and made them a little clearer. Peculiarly enough, I have no qualms of conscience (or is it peculiar we are so mad?).
June 21st: I rose early and helped mother vigorously this morning. Deborah rang and we decided to use a brick in a stocking rather than a sand-bag. We discussed the moider fully. I feel keyed up as if I was planning a surprise party. Mother has fallen in with everything beautifully and the happy event is to take place tomorrow afternoon. So next time I write in the diary mother will be dead. How odd, yet how pleasing.
June 22nd:

The Happy Event.

I am writing a little of this up in the morning before the death. I felt very excited and the night before Christmassy last night. I did not have pleasant dreams though.

Poem:

The Ones That I Worship

There are living among two dutiful daughters
Of a man who possesses two beautiful daughters,

The most glorious beings in creation.
They'd be the pride and joy of any nation.
You cannot know nor yet try to guess
The sweet soothingness of their caress.
The outstanding genius of this pair
Is understood by few, they are so rare.
Compared with these two every man is a fool.
The World is most honoured that they should deign to rule.
And above us these goddesses reign on high.

I worship the power of these lovely two
With that adoring love known to so few.
'Tis indeed a miracle, one must feel,
That two such heavenly creatures are real.
Both sets of eyes, though different far, hold many mysteries strange.
Impassively they watch the race of man decay and change.
Hatred burning bright in the brown eyes with enemies for fuel.
Icy scorn glittered in the grey eyes, contemptuous and cruel.
Why are men such fools they will not realise
The wisdom that is hidden behind those strange eyes?
And these wonderful people are you and I.

ISSEI **SAGAWA**

Renée Hartevelt, a 25-year-old Dutch woman studying in Paris at the Université Censier, was invited by a fellow student, 32-year-old Issei Sagawa, to come over for dinner at his apartment on June 11, 1981. After the promised dinner and a discussion about literature, Sagawa asked Hartevelt if she would have sex with him. When she declined, he shot her in the back of the head with a .22-caliber rifle. Sagawa then had sex with and ate portions of her body over the next two days. He was arrested by police after he was seen dumping two suitcases containing her remains in the Bois de Boulogne park.

His life took a surprising turn after his arrest. Committed to a French mental hospital by reason of insanity, he became a pen pal of several Japanese literary figures, and they sent him some books to read on cannibalism. He later said, "I felt better after reading those books because I realized I was not so unusual." He was transferred in May 1984 to a Japanese mental hospital; this transfer coincided with the signing of a business deal between Elf-Aquitaine, a French chemical conglomerate, and Kurita Water Industries, a Japanese company run by Sagawa's father. Sagawa was released from the Japanese mental hospital in August 1985, even though the hospital's deputy superintendent, Dr. Tsuguo Kaneko, thought Sagawa was an untreatable psychotic.

Sagawa has since become a celebrity in Japan. He has written four books – *In the Mist,* a "fictionalized" account of his crime that sold 200,000 copies, is excerpted below – and writes a weekly column for a Japanese tabloid. He often appears on television, and recently stated: "The public has made me the godfather of cannibalism, and I am happy about that. I will always look at the world through the eyes of a cannibal." Like other celebrities, Sagawa does have occasional reflective moments in which he is critical of his fame ("It is like I have no self left – I'm just a shell. I'm acting like what people imagine me to be"), but for now he mostly thinks about what would be, he says, an act of "personal salvation": he would like to be eaten by a young woman. "That is the only way I can be saved."

I'm amazed. She's the most beautiful woman I've ever seen. Tall, blonde, with pure white skin, she astonishes me with her grace. I invite her to my home for a Japanese dinner. She accepts. After the meal I ask her to read my favorite German Expressionist poem. As she reads I can't keep my eyes off her. After she leaves I can still smell her body on the bed sheet where she sat reading the poem. I lick the chopsticks and dishes she used. I can taste her lips. My passion is so great. I want to possess her. I want to eat her. If I do she will be mine forever. There is no escape from this desire.

I arrange for her to read the poem for me once more. I lie to her. I tell her I want to record the poem on tape for my Japanese teacher. She believes. I prepare everything. The cassette recorder for the poem, the rifle for the sacrifice. She arrives on time. After drinking tea and whisky, she speaks.

She smiles at me. But I know inside that I'm the strangest one of all. Her yellow sleeveless top shows off her beautiful white arms. I can smell her body.

I turn on the recorder. She starts to read. She speaks in perfect German. I reach for the rifle hidden beside the chest of drawers. I stand slowly and aim the rifle at the back of her head. I cannot stop myself.

There is a loud sound and her body falls from the chair onto the floor. It is like she is watching me. I see her cheeks, her eyes, her nose and mouth, the blood pouring from her head. I try to talk to her, but she no longer answers. There is blood all over the floor. I try to wipe it up, but I realize I cannot stop the flow of blood from her head. It is very quiet here. There is only the silence of death.

I start to take off her clothes. It is hard to take the clothes off a dead body. Finally it is done. Her beautiful white body is before me. I've waited so long for this day and now it is here. I touch her ass. It is so very smooth. I wonder where I should bite first. I decide to bite the top of her butt. My nose is covered with her cold white skin. I try to bite down hard, but I can't. I suddenly have a horrible headache. I get a knife from the kitchen and stab it deeply into her skin. Suddenly a lot of sallow fat oozes from the wound. It reminds me of Indian corn. It continues to ooze. It is strange. Finally I find the red meat under the sallow fat. I scoop it out and put it in my mouth. I chew. It has no smell and no taste. It melts in my mouth like a perfect piece of tuna. I look in her eyes and say: "You are delicious."

I cut her body and lift the meat to my mouth again and again. Then I take a photograph of her white corpse with its deep wounds. I have sex with her body. When I hug her she lets out a breath. I'm frightened, she seems alive. I kiss her and tell her I love her. Then I drag her body to the bathroom. By now I am exhausted, but I cut into her hip and put the meat in a roasting pan. After it is cooked I sit at the table using her underwear as a napkin. They still smell of her body. Then I turn on the tape of her reading the German poem and eat. There is not enough taste. I use some salt and some mustard and it is delicious, very high quality meat. Then I go back to the bathroom and cut off her breast and bake it. It swells while it cooks. I serve the breast on the table and eat it with a fork and knife. It isn't very good. Too greasy. I try to cut into another part of her body. Her thighs were wonderful. Finally she is in my stomach. Finally she is mine. It is the best dinner I've ever had.

Afterwards I sleep with her.

Next morning she is still here. She doesn't smell bad. Today I must finish cutting up her body. I have to put it into suitcases and sink it in the lake. It will be her grave.

I touch the cold body again and I wonder where I should start. I start to cut off all the meat before amputating the limbs. While I cut her calf I suddenly want to taste it. I see the beautiful red meat beneath the fat. I grasp her knee and her ankle, and tear it with my teeth. It is tender. I slowly chew and savor it. After eating most of the calf I look at myself in the mirror. There is grease all over my face. And then I start to eat at random. I bite her little toe. It still smells of her feet. I stab the knife into her arch and see the red meat deep inside. I thrust my fingers inside and dig out the meat and put it in my mouth. It tastes okay. Then I stab the knife into her armpit. Ever since I saw it under her yellow sleeveless top I wondered how it would taste. I cut off the skin and bite. It is tender and melts in my mouth. I can still smell her body. I had no idea it would taste this good.

The wonderful taste cheers me up and I devour her underarm up to the elbow.

Finally I cut off her private parts. When I touch the pubic hair it has a very bad smell. I bite her clit, but it won't come off, it just stretches. So I throw it in the frying pan and pop it in my mouth. I chew very carefully and swallow it. It is so sweet. After I swallow it, I feel her in my body and get hot. I turn the body over and open her buttocks, revealing her anus. I scoop it out with my knife and try to put it in my mouth. It smells too much. I put it in the frying pan and throw it in my mouth. It still smells. I spit it out. I go into the next room. It smells of fat, like I've been frying a chicken. It's been twenty-four hours now. Some huge flies hover and buzz in the bathroom. I try to chase them away, but they come back. They swarm on her face. They seem to tell me that I've lost her forever. It is no longer her. Where is she? She's gone far away. I've broken her. Like a child who breaks his toy. I try to use an electric knife to cut her body. It doesn't work. It just makes a loud sound. I use a hatchet. I strike several times. It's hard work. I strike her thigh. Her body jumps up. If she could feel, it would have hurt. Finally the thigh separates from her body. I bite it again, like I would bite a chicken leg. Then I cut off her arms. It is even harder than the thigh. I use the electric knife again. It makes a shrill sound, like the sound of her shrill voice. It works this time. Her hand still wears a ring and a bracelet. When I see her long fingers I am driven by another impulse. I use her hand to masturbate. Her long fingers excite me.

When I'm finished I try to bite off her finger. I can't. I'm disappointed. I put her hands into the plastic bag along with her legs. And then I see her face. It is still quiet. She has a small nose and a sweet lower lip. When she was alive I wanted to bite them. Now I can satisfy that desire. It's so easy to bite off her nose. As I chew the cartilage I can hear the noise. I use a knife to cut off more of the cartilage and put it in my mouth. It really doesn't taste very good. I scoop out her lower lip with my knife and put it in my mouth. It has hard skin. I decide to eat it later when I can fry it. So I put it in the refrigerator.

I want her tongue. I can't open her lower jaw, but I can reach in between her teeth. Finally it comes out. I cut it off and put it in my mouth. It's hard to chew. I see my face in the mirror. Her tongue entwined with my tongue. I try to close my mouth, but her tongue slips out. Finally I cut the skin off the tongue and taste the meat.

I try to eat her eyes. It's hard for me to stab into them, though it is the easiest part of her face. I can see tears coming from them. It frightens me. Her eyes are all that is left of her face. It is nearly a skull.

I decide to take out her stomach. When I stab under her navel a little fat appears and then I can see the red meat under the fat. I slice a piece of the red meat and put it on a plate. Then I stab into the stomach. The internal organs appear. There is a great length of rolled tubes and I find a gray bag at the end of the tubes. It must be the bladder. There is a strong smell as soon as I pick it up. I thrust my hand into her body cavity. There is another bag. It must be her womb. If she had lived she would have had a baby in this womb. The thought depresses me for a moment. I pull out the intestines. My hands sting from the digestive juices. At last I have to cut off her head. It is the most difficult thing I have to do. I cut off the meat on her neck until I can see bone, then I cut again. She still wears her necklace. I try to use the electric knife, but it doesn't work very well. It just makes its shrill sound. So I use the hatchet. I imagine myself on the guillotine. It is surprisingly easy to cut through. With the head gone her body is now only flesh. When I grab the hair and hang up the head, I realize I am a cannibal. I put the head in a plastic bag. I separate the body and put it into two plastic bags. They are heavy. It is hard to put them into the suitcases. I am finished. It is midnight. I call a taxi.

I am back home. I turn on the TV and open the refrigerator. I put the dishes on the glass table. I recognize each piece of meat. This is part of her hip and this is part of her thigh. I fry them on the stove. I set the table. There is mustard, salt, pepper and sauce. I put her underwear beside the dish. I sniff it and look at a nude woman in a magazine. I try to remember which part of her is in my mouth, but it is difficult to connect the meat with a body. It just seems like a piece of meat. I continue to eat her body until I am caught. Each day the meat becomes more tender, each day the taste is more sweet and delicious.

GERARD SCHAEFER JR.

In 1968, 22-year-old Gerard John Schaefer Jr. graduated with a degree in geography from Florida Atlantic University in Boca Raton. After working as a fishing guide and security guard, Schaefer, fascinated by police and guns, applied to a few police departments in the southern Florida area. An application to the Brosward County Sheriff's Office was turned down after he failed the psychological test, but in 1970 the Wilton Manors Police Department hired him. Six months later he was fired because of what Police Chief Bernard Scott characterized as a "lack of common sense." Schaefer moved to an apartment house in Stuart, Florida, divorced his first wife, married again, and in 1972 became a deputy sheriff for Martin County.

In the late fall of 1972, twenty-two days after being hired as a cop, Schaefer abducted two 18-year-old hitchhikers, Nancy Trotter and Paula Wells, and took them to a wooded area about eight miles south of Blind Creek in St. Lucie County. After gagging and handcuffing the women, Schaefer told them he was going to hang them from the trees; at one point, though, he left them alone and they managed to escape. Schaefer was arrested, immediately dismissed from the sheriff's office, convicted of assault, and sentenced in December to a six-month term at Martin County Jail.

While still in custody, Schaefer was identified by Mrs. Lucille Place of Oakland Park as the man who had driven off with her 17-year-old daughter, Susan Place, and Susan's 16-year-old friend, Georgia Jessup, several months earlier. The girls had never returned. Mrs. Place told police that when Schaefer, calling himself "Jerry Shephard," picked the teenagers up on September 27, her daughter told her they were "going to the beach to play guitar." The mother, however, was suspicious of the husky stranger and jotted down his license plate as he drove away. She later attempted to file a missing persons report, but police assumed they were runaways: a note was found at Georgia Jessup's home which read, "I'm sorry, Mother and Dad. I love you both very much. I have to find my head." Without much help from the police, a determined Mrs. Place finally located Schaefer in jail through the bureaucratic maze of the Department of Motor Vehicles on March 25, 1973. A week later hikers found the girls' teeth and jawbones on Hutchinsons Island.

With Schaefer proclaiming his innocence, police searched his former bedroom at his mother's house in Fort Lauderdale and found in an old trunk the items that led to his conviction: women's clothes, a passport, two gold-filled teeth from a 22-year-old Fort Lauderdale woman who had been missing since 1969, a locket inscribed with the name of a missing 25-year-old Fort Lauderdale waitress, and approximately fifty pages of writings and drawings detailing sadistic murder [reproduced below].

Schaefer contends that the writings and drawings were pure fantasy, stating in a recent letter:

> I studied fiction writing continuously beginning in 1963; until I went to prison in 1973, at highschool, college and university levels. I have always written of taboo subjects and areas loosely in the horror genre. I am a trained writer who was sent to prison for murder; not a murderer who wrote about his crimes or took up writing after conviction.

A jury believed otherwise; Schaefer was convicted of the murders of Place and Jessup on September 27, 1973, and received two concurrent life sentences.

On November 17, Schaefer's 21-year-old wife Teresa asked for a divorce. She then startled everyone by marrying Schaefer's public defender, 45-year-old Elton Schwarz, two weeks later. Schaefer asked the court for a retrial based on this apparent conflict of interest in September of 1990, writing: "Elton Schwarz had a motive for all this. My young wife, who was smitten by his attentions. Sex with a young girl. It's an ancient motive. Turn to your Bible. Book of Kings. David and Bathsheba. So it happens. It happened to me." Police suspect Schaefer of the murders of at least eleven other women and girls, and his petitions have repeatedly been denied. He now resides at Florida State Prison in Starke, and will be eligible for parole in 2016.

At the beginning of his sentence Schaefer spent most of his time writing informative articles for *Linn's Weekly*, a magazine dedicated to stamp collecting. He was later contacted by a former high-school girlfriend, Sondra London, who published a collection of his stories, *Killer Fiction: Tales of an Accused Serial Killer*, in 1990. It is divided into four sections: "Whores: What to *Do* About Them," "Starke Stories," "Actual Fantasies" (his earlier "trunk" writings and drawings), and a self-reflective afterword that examines his own writing technique, "Sex, Death & Insanity." According to Schaefer,

> Because I wrote **Killer Fiction**, people are screaming that I am some crazy serial killer writing true stories and passing them off as fiction. There is no way to separate the fact that I have been publicly accused of murdering 34 women and that at one time I was regarded as the world's #1 serial killer. My position is that I write fiction, and the more I practice the better I get at it. I find it necessary to state that I am not the characters in my fiction. You will believe what you choose to believe.

Three (of five) stories found in Schaefer's trunk in 1973:

Murder Plan

In order to remain unapprehended, the perpetrator of an execution-style murder such as I have planned must take precautions. One must think out well in advance a crime of this nature, in order for it to work.

We will need an isolated area, accessible by a short hike, away from any police patrols or parking lovers. The execution site must be carefully arranged for a speedy execution, once the victim has arrived. There will be 2 sawhorses with a 2 X 4 between them. A noose is attached to the overhanging bulb of a tree. Another rope to pull away the 2 X 4, preferably by car. A grave must be prepared in advance away from the place of execution.

The victim could be one of the many women who flock to Miami and Ft. Lauderdale for the winter months. Even two victims would not be difficult to dispose of, since women are less wary when traveling in pairs. In any case it may be more preferable to bind and gag the victims before transporting them to the place of execution. Then again, depending on what torture or defilement is planned for them, other items may be useful.

Bars of soap & water. These are useful if you would want to wash a woman before her execution. Induce her to urinate and then wash her.

Soap provides an excellent lubricant for anal intercourse. **Beer** is useful to induce urination and make the victim groggy and more cooperative. **Soap** can also be forced into the rectum to induce defecation if the victim has no particular desire to relieve her bowels. Possibly she may want to defecate, since people generally have a desire to do this when they are scared. A **douche bag** may be helpful in degrading her further, and is also useful for a soapsuds enema which would be a great indignity, especially if one victim was made to urinate or defecate on the other. This would be a gross indignity.

Nylon stockings are useful to tie the hands and feet of the victim. The victim should be made to

strip at least to her underwear. If stripped completely nude an attempt can be made to excite her sexually. This effect would be especially interesting if the victim had her neck in the noose and hands tied behind her back.

A white **pillow case** should be placed over her head and her mouth **gagged.** Her panties should be pulled down enough to expose the genitals, and clitoral stimulation applied. During the height of her excitement the support should be pulled away and she should dangle by her neck.

She may be revived before death if desirable and subjected to further indecencies. After death has occurred, the corpse should be violated if not violated already. The body should then possibly be mutilated and carried to the grave and buried. All identity papers should be destroyed and the place of execution dismantled.

Into the Mind of the Ghoul

I walk into the bar and look around. There is something special that I am looking for, or should I say someone special. A woman with that look about her, that look of wildness, uncaring, a willingness to do anything for a price, a whore or someone like one.

I have to be sure she is the right one because one blunder could be the end for me. When I find the one that I'm looking for, I have to be sure through conversation. I'll make sure that no one notices me and then I'll make my offer. And if she accepts she has signed her death warrant.

Everything has been arranged long before in preparation of this event. I take her for a ride. I am cordial enough and make no threatening motions. I give her no reason to become alarmed. I drive out to the place that I am going to leave my car, a place I have left it many times before, so as not to draw suspicion. I could be an ordinary traveler out of gas or taking a nap on the side of the road. Nobody would think differently, not even the police. That is important.

I pull over and casually say that we are here, and for her to get out. Maybe it is then that she starts to worry because of the fact that we are in the middle of nowhere. Maybe it is then that I have to show her the gun and remind her of the consequences for disobedience. If she knew what lay in store for her, she would gladly choose the bullet.

I have traveled over this trail before so the darkness is of little hindrance. The trail is well

hidden. No one has ever been down it before, because of the desolate location and the thickness of the jungle around it, but with little difficulty I know where the trail is and where it goes.

Deep in the swamp is a huge tree with limbs strong enough to walk on. It is completely surrounded by jungle. This is the place I seek. I have been there many times before, only those times it was in rehearsal and there was no victim, only the fantasy of it all. But I do know what will be done and how to do it step by step.

The woman is by this time very frightened. This is good, because the more frightened she is, the greater the thrill for me. I tell her to strip, but I let her leave her underwear on. I tie her to a branch and gag her if she is too noisy while I go about the business at hand.

I bring over the white sheet and a pillowcase to go over her head. I explain that I am going to hang her and she might as well accept the fact and cooperate. The gun is persuasive and there is always hope, so she cooperates. The limbs are arranged perfectly for the deed, all the right height and distance apart. It has taken a long time to find the right tree and the right person, but I finally did it.

I arrange the rope and the noose and I dress the woman in the white shroud, place the pillowcase over her head, and then if I feel like it, sit down and entertain her with a bit of my conversation. Terrorize

her. Give her my ideas on what she will look like while she is hanging there, fighting the rope that is slowly choking the life out of her. Make it as real as possible for her, so that she is petrified with fear. Make her know that she is going to die.

The noose is arranged so that she will strangle slowly, and she sits on a board between two limbs with a long rope leading off into the jungle. When it is time, I will go off into the jungle and pull the rope and she will hang.

Then I will go home to have something to eat, and bright and early the next morning I will be out hunting. I will find the body hanging from the tree and only then will I really notice it. Maybe fondle it and maybe even have coitus with it. I will notice the expression on the face, the position of the body, explore every nick and cranny of her, maybe mutilate her and delight in the smell of any urine or excrement that she may have passed while hanging there.

I leave and then return so it will be unbelievable to myself that I did the deed. I will not be able to remember doing it. Funny isn't it.

Then after many hours I will dispose of the body in a place that has never been seen by man, and it will soon rot away in the tropical heat, with the help of the bugs and vermin, the rats and raccoons that abound here.

This is what I intend to do, but I do not know why.

There is a drive within me so powerful that it completely takes over my sense of reason and values. I am at the mercy of this insane maddening drive to commit the ultimate crime of horror, and only when it is done will I be at rest. I have to fight off this desire every day of my life. Why? Why? That is the question. If I could understand what causes these emotions then I might be able better to combat them.

I do positive things to prevent this happening. I stay away from bars, the beach, dances, anywhere that I might come in contact with that person that might put me over the edge. Twice this has nearly happened, but both times my senses prevented disaster before I had gone too far.

Once I picked up a girl at the beach and took her to a place that I had picked out for just such an occasion. She stood beneath the limb that she was going to hang from and somehow I just prevented myself from exposing what it was I had in mind. She was really frightened, and I was so nervous that I could barely speak. This was accompanied by violent headaches, and even as I recall this information to put on paper, I am plagued by headaches and a ringing in my ears.

I have been tempted to do away with other women too, usually ones that I am sexually attracted to but do not know personally. One girl whom I almost killed I later became good friends with and drove her to the airport to fly up north to be married. It was an experiment to see if I still wanted to kill her after I got to know her, and I didn't. In fact, I am still rather fond of her.

Once while in high school I playfully strangled a girl into unconsciousness, and have longed for the feeling it gave me ever since. I have always liked the idea of strangling women. But I never do, because I am afraid I will be caught and confined. The idea of confinement is horrifying to me. I don't mind death, and have often thought about suicide. But it is the idea of confinement that keeps me from doing anything on the spur of the moment.

Often when I was sexually attracted to a woman and wanted to kill her I would steal her clothes and dress up in them, and then hang myself instead. This is a little risky, but I have only been caught at it twice by strangers, and I managed to wiggle out of it both times. I used to have piles of women's clothes that I stole, but it got to where I didn't have anywhere to keep them, so I have to work with a minimum amount now. There was a time that I had wardrobes of clothes in trunks out in the forest, but then one day a forest fire destroyed the area, and I had to start all over.

Hanging seems to be the most exciting way of dispatching a victim, but in a pinch I would resort to strangulation. I can't explain why. The experience of imagining a woman hung produces intense sexual excitement. It is always the same thing: the preliminaries to the woman being hanged, and then ejaculation as she vanishes through the imaginary trap.

Recently I have become seriously emotionally attached to a girl and she to me. We have experienced coitus together on several occasions. I always feel for her a deep and strong love, and will marry her if all works out in the future. But I am not completely emotionally wrapping myself up in her, so in the event that something does happen I won't do anything foolish.

When we make love, it leaves us both feeling terrific and unguilty. But the only way that I can experience an orgasm is to think of that woman going through the trap and hanging there. I can make love all night and never lose the erection unless I think of that hanging woman. I merely wait until my girl is beginning to climax, and then I think of the woman hanging and I automatically climax myself. This bothers me but it doesn't take away the deep and intense feeling that I have for the girl that I make love to.

It has long been known that men ejaculate when hanged. A favorite method of self-gratification, used in the Middle Ages and still today, is what might be called do-it-yourself hanging. The sensation of choking produces an erection that culminates in a violent orgasm, sometimes during the dying process. This stimulation has not been lost on the sexually perverted, who constantly cast about for more intense pleasures to replace whipping, self-scourging, biting and the like.

The maniacal rapist murderer represents the unholy marriage between sex and death. I wonder if he understands his act. I don't understand it, even though these same feelings are occurring within me all the time. I would like to be able to free myself from this world, because it inhibits my creative ability. My mind cannot function properly when it is preoccupied with averting a social calamity and a personal tragedy. It is trying to fight the urge to relieve these terrible cravings. I am sure that there must be an answer somewhere, and some day I will be cured.

Powerline Road

We drove out Powerline Road. It was about 9 A.M. She was making with the small talk and I was attempting not to appear nervous.

I was wondering who she had told and how much she had told. I was pretty sure she had blabbed to someone because that would be just like her. We turned off onto a dirt road. I knew where we were going. I asked her to put on a blindfold. She was nervous. Said she was scared and had an uneasy feeling. She said it was because of all the killings recently and such. I told her there was nothing to worry about which was a lie, and we drove off into a field.

When we got to where I wanted to go I stopped and we got out. She still had the blindfold on so I helped her. We walked about ten yards and I said to stand still, because I forgot something in the car. I went back and got a sack filled with lead weights, walked up and hit her on the back of the head. She was stunned a little and I hit her again. Then she started to try to protect herself and fell to the ground screaming "Don't hit me. Please don't hit me." I was shaken because of her pleas and didn't hit her. I helped her up and said I was sorry and that I had been instructed to put her out. She had messed us up once before and now we didn't trust her. I asked her who she had told and she said nobody. I said we know she had told someone, and she became a little worried but still would not admit telling anyone.

She was sitting on an orange crate and when I put the pillow case over her head she complained so much that she couldn't breathe, I took it off. As she sat there she kept complaining about being dizzy and feeling faint. I would just tell her to shut up. I tied her hands behind her and put a noose over her head that I had put up the previous afternoon. It had rained that day and the rope was wet and didn't tighten properly. I tightened it as best I could but the noose wouldn't slip. I would pull the rope up occasionally to hear her beg. She must have been really scared. She was sitting in the sun and sometimes she would forget about her legs and let them come apart, giving me a good look up her dress.

She finally asked what had probably been going through her mind for some time. "Are you going to kill me?" I told her that I didn't know, that it wasn't up to me and the people responsible were deciding her fate right now. I said she had made too many mistakes and her mouth was too loose and we had people watching her constantly. It didn't look good for her. There was silence for awhile. Then she asked me "Is it quick?" and I asked her, "Is what quick?"

"Hanging. Aren't they going to hang me? They're going to hang me aren't they?"

"No," I lied. "I don't know what they're going to do." At that point I didn't know, because I was beginning to feel sorry for her. Then she said, "I have to go to the bathroom."

"There isn't one around, you'll have to wait."

"I have to go bad. Couldn't you just let me go back in bushes?"

"No. I couldn't. I'd be too embarrassed."

Ho! I thought to myself. You embarrassed. No chance.

"Then you'll just have to do it in your pants. What do you have to do anyway?" I was hoping she had to shit.

"Never mind," she said, and that was that.

I went to where I said a man with a radio was and left her sitting on her aching bladder. When I came back a rain squall started to fall. The rope wouldn't come loose from around her neck and I said I'd

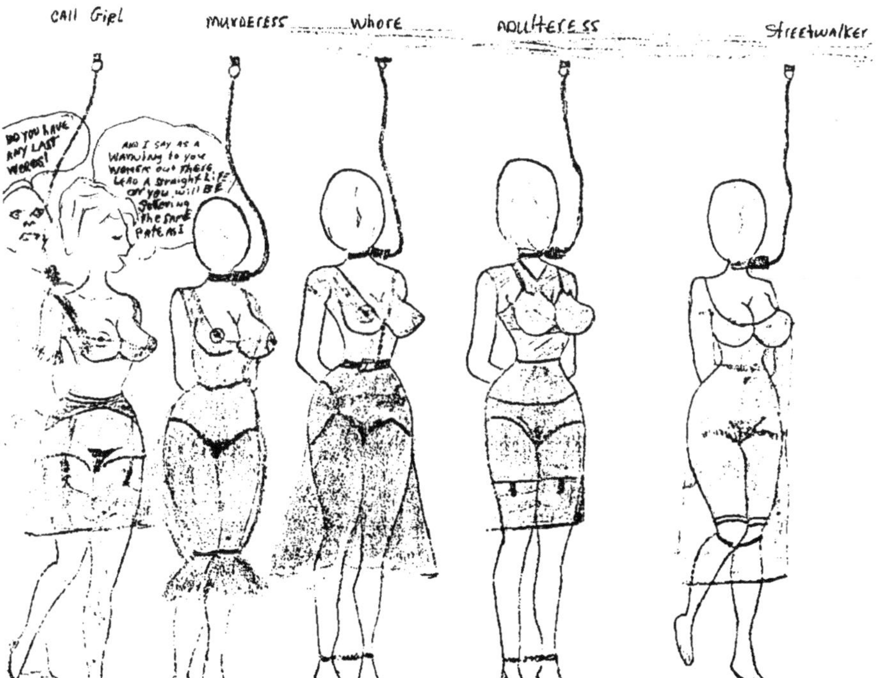

have to back up to get some slack. She thought I would haul her up then and begged me not to. The rope was tied to the bumper of the car. I finally worked the rope loose and we sat in the car all wet.

I told her they had decided to kill her. She was really scared and begged me to help her escape. I said I would do what I could. The rain stopped and I told her I was to take her to a grave that had been dug for her. I said she should fake a faint and I'd carry her over to the grave area. I wanted to force her to pee her pants with my shoulder in her gut. I carried her over and set her down. I let her see the hole I had dug for her. She really got scared then, and I was afraid she might panic and start fighting since she was not tied around the legs and only loosely about the hands. I told her to lay down on the ground and I would try to think of something. She said if I let her go that she'd pay me all her savings, leave town, never say a word to anyone, give me anything I wanted. She was desperate. Almost in tears. She said, "I don't want to die. I think I'm pregnant. I love Buddy and I want to have a baby." I told her to shut up. Then I told her to strip.

"Why do I have to strip?"

"Because it's the way we do things. We never kill anyone and leave their clothes so they can be identified by them. We make 'em strip. If you don't want me to help you, forget it. We'll strip you after you're dead."

I cut her hands loose and she began to strip out of her clothes.

"I'll shoot a hole through the dress and show it to the other guy and he'll think I killed you."

She was stepping out of her white waitress dress. "Get off the slip too," I said. She stepped out of it too and was standing there in her brassiere, pantyhose and bikini panties and shoes. Her jugs were big, almost popping out of the bra. "Kneel down," I said. She knelt. I put the gun next to her head and shot a hole through the dress. I thought she might shit her pants in fear but she didn't. I said "I need blood," and she wanted to cut her finger, but I decided the hole in the dress would look good enough.

I told her to lay on a sheet I had brought and she did, stomach down, her big ass sticking up. Very sexy. I told her to wait while I checked with the other guy. I walked around, still undecided whether to kill her or not. I could see her and then she did the thing that sealed her doom. She picked up the blindfold and looked around as she lay there. I decided then for sure she couldn't be trusted and I would have to kill her. I didn't know if she could see me or not.

When I got back I told her the other guy wanted to see her body and take her valuables. I told her to give me her jewelry. She took off two rings and lay back down. I told her the other guy was coming so she'd better play dead or she would be dead. Then I went to the car and took out the pistol and cocked it so she wouldn't hear it. I went over near her and aimed the gun at the base of her head. I aimed a long time. Then I closed my eyes and pulled the trigger. When I fired I ran.

I ran around to the car and then worked my way back as if I was going to discover her body. She was still laying there with no visible sign of injury. Her body was still and one leg was a little drawn up. I couldn't see her breathe, but her head moved slightly and I felt repulsed, horrified and ashamed all at the same time. I quickly raised the gun and shot her twice in the back of the head. This time blood spurted out and I turned away. I covered her head with a sheet so I didn't have to see the blood, and went and got several crates. These I arranged to stretch her out on. I went to the car and stripped down. Came back nude and grabbed her around the ankles and pulled her up onto the crates. I then slipped my hands under the elastic of her hose and panties, and pulled them down to her knees. The white cheeks of her ass no longer held tightly together by the panties slumped apart and I saw her purplish-pink colored asshole, which was open so wide I thought it was her cunt hole. I mean she had one hell of a big ass hole. I stuck a finger up it to see if there was any shit in her rectum. There was none. I stuck two, then three and I could almost stick four fingers across into that giant asshole. There was a few blonde pussy hairs growing around it. Not like one asshole I had seen with hair so thick around it you couldn't see it. No, she had a beautiful hole.

I pulled off her shoes thinking it wasn't right to cornhole a woman with her panties down around her knees and a bullet in her head with her shoes on. I mounted her like you would a horse and let my dick go right into the open hole. It was hot in there and I humped a few times and shot off long and hard. I had soaped her hole and she was slippery and wet which made it more exciting than ever. I fucked that hole as long as my dick would stay hard and then just sat on her big ass warming my balls in the crack of her backside.

Then I felt like I had to get rid of her fast before somebody should come along or a plane should see us. I unhooked her bra and reached down and squeezed her giant teats and then slid off her. I grabbed her by her ankles and pulled her off the crates, noticing her gaping hole and tightly stuck together cunt. I wondered why she hadn't pissed. Her panties were a little wet but not a lot. Probably a few drops squirted out of her when I carried her. I dragged her body to the open grave straddling it as I pulled her toward it. Her head was down and her arms were outstretched. When her chest was at the edge of the grave, I gave a jerk and let her feet go. She dropped to the bottom of the pit with a terrible hollow thump. Her legs went up over her back because the hole was too short for her. She lay there with her head down and her feet and legs up. One arm was beside her and the other stuck straight up as if she were reaching up to get out.

I then threw the bloodied sheet over her head and tossed in her shoes. Her panties were halfway to her knees as were her pantyhose. Her bra was unhooked on her back, the shoulder straps still in place. I jumped down into the grave and pulled her corpse forward. The legs still wouldn't fit. Her cunt was mashed against the far end of the grave. I pulled her legs forward and this pulled tight the hair on her twat and made her pussy open slightly. The cheeks of her ass were accentuated. I noticed a trickle of piss squirting from her cunt. I was barefoot. I stuck my big toe up her cunt hole and pushed it in. I could feel it enter her

German justice for french Partisan women means a short rope and a public spectale in a town square.

still hot body. Then I rammed my entire foot into her cunt and felt the warm piss squish as I wiggled it in deeper. Then I pissed on her butt.

I hopped out of the hole and began to fill it up. I pulled her legs up over her back as best as possible and then bent the calves down so her knees were the highest point. I packed down the earth, covered the grave with pine needles and burned everything she had except her dress and slip. All her clothes went into the grave with her.

A week later I couldn't believe I had done it so I went back and began to dig in order to make sure it wasn't just my imagination. When I got to her knees the stink began. It was unbearable. God, did she smell. I dug all the way down to her cunt. Her legs were beginning to turn a mottled yellow color and the hair was beginning to fall off her cunt. I filled the hole but first masturbated on her corpse.

Several times I dug her up and every time the stench was so bad I couldn't bear to complete the job. You see, I wanted her head. I had planned to cut it off after I killed her, but I couldn't do it. I had to get the head because of the dental records if she was ever found. Finally one day I managed to dig her up many months later. She was very well preserved but drew a lot of flies. She was very greasy to touch. I slipped a noose around her neck and hauled her up a limb. She still had some hair in her crotch and her cunt was well preserved. Her toes and fingers were beginning to rot off but the rest of her was in good shape. I hauled her to a kneeling position and cut off her head with a machete. The corpse slumped to the ground very sexily showing her still wide open asshole.

I took the head and wrapped it. The eyes were closed with the skin lids. The nose was flat and the lips drawn back over the teeth in a snarl. I knocked out some of the teeth but the head with hair on it smelled so bad I decided just to sink it in a canal along with her panties, hose and brassiere.

The last I checked she had rotted away to nothing but her torso from her waist to the remnants of her backside. Oddly enough when her body swelled up during decomposition the gas must have pushed a load of shit down into her rectum, because when I examined her hole with a stick it came out all shitty.

She's still there now in her unmarked grave and sometimes I feel sorry not so much for her as her family because it seems they must have really cared about her. She was a whore and a tease and was no good and I'm sorry too that I didn't spend more time enjoying her body while I had the chance, rather than just dumping it in a hole before it even became stiff.

That was the first one and they say the first one is the hardest. So far though the first one has been the best body-wise. I think there will surely be others.

SCHIZOPHRENIC FIRESETTER

As a child, "Schizophrenic Firesetter" was a kleptomaniac and enjoyed being cruel to animals. According to one report, he "put gravel in the eyes of a dog and gouged the eyes out of another dog." He put signs up around his bedroom in his parents' house; one of them said:

1. Don't pluck your chest.
2. Don't abuse your body.
3. Don't pick your nose.
4. Always modulate your voice.

He was arrested at the age of seventeen for setting fire to Catholic churches, police headquarters, and other buildings in the Denver area. He told police:

> Yes, I knew that I might take human lives – but I want to tell you about how I felt. I just couldn't help setting fires – just like I can't help stealing things. I never started one fire without hoping it wouldn't be bad, and that it wouldn't cause injury or death; but I knew it might. That didn't make any difference. I'd just hope it would be found in time and that nobody would be burned, but if they were I couldn't help it. I didn't get a thrill and I didn't care about seeing fire wagons run either. I didn't pick on Catholic churches because I hated Catholics. They were just easy places to get into. I didn't have a grudge against anybody. I can't say I'm sorry about it because that isn't true.
>
> I realize that my criminal impulses are mastering me and unless I am shut away, given the quiet and time I need to study languages and music, it were better that I were dead than to face a future of crimes of even greater seriousness that those I have committed. I'm a criminal and I know it. When I had a Federal job, I stole some Government goods, which I hoped would be traced to me and bring me a sentence in a Federal reformatory, where I understand a fellow can study and improve himself.
>
> I don't feel the world owes me anything. On the contrary I am grateful for the things it offers. That my hand reaches for what does not belong to me; that my impulse is to set a match to other people's property is no fault of the world or of the people in it. I do ask one thing – to be put away and

> kept away long enough to conquer the criminal in me. Perhaps when I'm 35 or 40 I may come back and be a useful citizen.

After being committed to the Colorado State Mental Hospital, he was eventually released into the custody of his father. He promptly held up a service station, and was imprisoned for five years. Released on parole at the age of twenty-four, he subsequently held up a drugstore and shot the owner to death. He angrily confessed to the police:

> Sure I shot him. These people don't seem to believe a guy is serious. I meant business. . . . I didn't come here for advice, I came here to plead guilty. Years ago I figured out what I would do, if I was ever caught in a situation like this. I want to go to the gas chamber; I don't want to vegetate in condemned row.

He was judged sane and sentenced to die. He sent the following note to the judge who convicted him:

Should you be so weak minded and unconscious of your public duty as to give me life imprisonment rather than the "chamber" let me remind you that I will be eligible for parole in seven year's time, and my institutional record alone will determine it — regardless of my case or anything I say to you now. And when I get out there are to be two less members of your local police force. I would not say I welcome the death penalty, but I have been a thief and robber all my life. I have been afraid I would end up by shooting somebody. I think this would be the quickest way to end the matter.

Shortly before he was executed he also sent a note to the Chief of Police:

Thank you for your decency to me back in the firebug days. The insanity plea evidently petered out for me. Remember me to detectives ——————. Again thank you for your consideration. Kindness is never forgotten. P.S. Prophylaxis is better than therapeutics even in crime.

CHARLES **SCHMID** JR.

Charles "Smitty" Schmid Jr. was usually the center of attention when he cruised Speedway Boulevard, the main drag of Tucson, Arizona, in the early 1960s. Compact and muscular from his gymnastic activities in high school, Schmid dropped out to devote himself as a full-time Lothario to the teenagers hanging out at such places as the Hi-Ho Club and Johnie's Drive-In. The authors of *The Pied Piper of Tucson*, *Life* magazine reporter Don Moser and Arizona *Journal* editor Jerry Cohen, melodramatically conveyed the *American Grafitti*-like setting in which Schmid flourished:

> To the bored and the lonely, to the dropout and the delinquent, to the young girls with beehive hair-dos and tight pants they didn't quite fill out, and to the boys with acne and no jobs, Smitty was a kind of folk hero. Some of the older kids, those who worked or had something else to do, thought Smitty was a creep. But to the aimless idlers younger than he, Smitty was the most dramatic, most theatrical and, above all, the most interesting figure in their lives. Nutty maybe. But at least he was different.

A skillful, unrelenting liar, the 21-year-old braggart enjoyed making up stories involving fake illnesses, FBI interrogations, Mafia kidnappings, and mysterious deaths. As noted by Moser and Cohen, he also created for himself an amazing look, a ludicrous costume that was a key element of his magnetic charm:

> He dyed his reddish hair black, bronzed his features with pancake make-up, whitened his lips with a pale cream cosmetic stick. He adorned his face with phony imperfections: He plastered a dark dot of putty on one cheek and gradually built it up until it resembled a huge and hideous black mole. He hurt his nose once (or claimed he did), and over the real or imagined damage he taped a wide bandage, which he wore like a badge; it stayed there for weeks, turning from dirty gray to nearly black. To appear taller, he stuffed a three-inch layer of tin cans and rags in improbable knee-high boots, in which he stumbled along so painfully that many thought him a cripple. He didn't mind at all, since he often played upon the sympathy of others by fabricating outlandish stories of personal handicap, each overripe with self-pity.

Financially supported by his adoptive parents, Schmid spent much of his free time reading *Playboy*, *Gentleman's Quarterly*, and true detective magazines in his small cottage while drinking beer and listening to Elvis Presley records. His favorite book was, appropriately, a novel by cartoonist Jules Feiffer entitled *Harry, the Rat with Women*. According to authors Moser and Cohen, Schmid was also a progenitor of the technique now known as "air guitar":

> To satisfy his combined urge to impress people and put them on, Smitty hired the best guitarist he could find in Tucson to cut a tape of numbers then popular. Then he got a cabinetmaker to build him a seat. Hidden beneath it was a recorder, which he could turn on and shut off with a tap of his boot. The guitar Smitty held in his hands was a good one, and he took it and his elaborately contrived rig along with him to parties where he strummed away with professional finesse. "He'd just be playing out of this tape recorder," said [Schmid's best friend Richard] Bruns. "Faking it out. Nobody was the wiser at all, nobody had the slightest idea what was actually going on. They all thought he was great. Then, when he ran out of tape, and everyone wanted him to play some more, he just said, 'Well, boy, I'm tired. I won't play more.' "

Bored with these complex pranks, Schmid told a girlfriend, 18-year-old Mary Rae French, that he would kill someone to see if he "could get away with it." On the evening of May 31, 1964, with French and 18-year-old friend John Saunders in tow, Schmid enticed one of his young fans, 15-year-old Alleen Rowe, into the desert fifteen miles north of Tucson. Forcing Rowe to take off her clothes, Schmid possibly raped the girl (he was left alone with her for approximately twenty minutes) and murdered her by striking her repeatedly on the head with a rock; he and his friends then buried her in the desert sand. Rowe's mother felt that somehow the arrogant Schmid was involved with her daughter's disappearance. To her anguish, police assumed the girl was a teenage runaway.

Over a year later, on the night of August 16, 1965, another of Schmid's girlfriends, 17-year-old Gretchen Fritz, and her 13-year-old sister Wendy, visited Schmid's cottage after seeing an Elvis Presley movie at the local drive-in. Schmid strangled the two girls with his black guitar cord and dumped their bodies near the gravesite of Alleen Rowe. When he later boasted to his friend Richard Bruns about the murders, Bruns thought he was typically lying and half-jokingly asked to see the bodies; Schmid immediately drove with him out to the desert to view his handiwork. Bruns, panicking, helped Schmid bury the corpses. Later troubled by his conscience, Bruns described the burial of the sisters to his father, who immediately notified the police.

Schmid was arrested on November 10, 1965, and was found guilty of the Fritz murders on March 1, 1966. He pleaded guilty to Rowe's murder on May 20, 1967, and soon after led police to Rowe's grave, where he dramatically unearthed her skull with his bare manacled hands. Schmid's sentence of death was commuted to life imprisonment after the United States Supreme Court abolished capital punishment in 1972. He died in Arizona State Prison on March 30, 1975, ten days after being stabbed 47 times by two members of the white supremacist group Aryan Brotherhood; apparently they believed Schmid was a prison "snitch."

Poems written in 1974 under his legally changed name, Paul David Ashley; he hoped to publish them in a book called *The Unfinished Man.*

Residual Man

And so the days ask to the years . . . in multiples of pain . . .
caring about the tears of men who hurt — from dying hearts . . .
for something they cannot find . . . and so I stand with the
blind . . .
not meaning in the eye . . . but those that seek and cry.

As I look into your face . . . seeing depths of sadness, struggle
and
sorrow . . . I wish I could suffer . . . in your place — yet, I don't
believe in sacrifice . . . one has already paid the price.

But just to share the things . . . that hurt you — replacing
the agony . . . with something new —

The struggle to see . . . and touch . . . invisible blind souls . . .
screaming for mercy — into deaf ears . . . can know and feel the
inherited awareness of isolation . . . the mockery and fright
. . . the icicled kiss — of fear.

What price . . . a place of honor — demands from a man . . .
who
cannot speak and fight or find a place to stand? — The
deadlines of time . . . And this is his right — the virginity
of blossoms . . . begging furry love . . . are born with the
wisdom
he will never know.

A suffocating wall . . . crushes his will . . . still, yet he
screams . . .

gasping breath . . . dying . . . trying to believe . . . a reason . . .
denying the apparent anachronism . . . accepting the lie. —

Quiescent weighty secrets . . . drift up from a tomb — still
begging for compassion . . . finding only doom . . . devours a
life . . .
without a sense of meaning — or reason — except greed and
fear . . . that he may know the struggle to grasp . . .
tangibilities
was not in vain.

And so he sometimes flirts with death — pushing Quixotic
abandon — attuning ego to reality . . . yet knowing he can
never
win . . . but trying anyway . . . against all reason and odds . . .
except his own . . . this creative complex enigma — integrity —
innate — born within because he is a man.

Lost within the shadows of mystic magic moons — lives the parasitic atrocity . . . that defies all probes.

A twisted satchel . . . of crumbled bones . . . peers out — from
iron jaws . . . to ask why . . . but never knowing . . . lost to
error . . .
forgotten . . . alone . . . dead.

Prison

if you would work one small miracle
repair one man
without violence or contempt
assemble one body
without leaning on the grotesque
inventions of pain

if I could understand the mystery of rain
how it holds its dignity
in the violence of a storm
if freedom was not more important
than even god or death
you could have me I would not escape

The Ritual

I stand below the gun tower
in the rain. Other prisoners line up.
behind me. They want to return
to their cells. "Not yet," I tell them.

"Not until the bastard
stops calling me by a number."

It is late and because visitors are present
the tower guard grudgingly calls
my name.
I walk through the gate
as if I were almost human.

Later in the darkness
he takes me from my cell.

He begins the ritual
of unconsciousness. I hear the thud
of clubs falling on flesh. When I call
out my number the guards walk
away. I shout at them.

"My name, goddam you, call me
by my name."

And they return.

All We Wanted

what now spirit
haven't we already been there
who can explain
the eyes moving without orbit
the wars the small faces
thudding to earth

is there a sign
in the hands crowding the hours
around us the air
cooling against metal the sparrow
moving away

what does it mean
spirit

why is it easier
to hate what we are afraid of
to destroy what we can't
understand why is it

easier to turn
on the light than question the darkness
easier to invent beauty
than to find it

easier to run away
when all we wanted was someone
to give us warmth in the night

Sounds

each night we hear the sound
of small things
breaking
is it our faith and what is that
on the bandages

inside each other with our shovels
we scrape the darkness evenly
into piles and burn them
turning ourselves over and over in the smoke

looking for comfort we feel a shudder
as if a giant bird
flew out of us
and then a small bullet
opening in our brains

even as we turn
pretending to sleep we hear
each other masturbating in the darkness
who are we thinking of
is anyone
thinking of us
and if they arrived how soon
would we tire of them

bless us spirit bless the wolves
living in our fingers
bless those who follow until we lose
them one at a time in the snow
bless the smallest
of our deaths
even they are too much to lose

one death at a time
we leave for our children one death
we post naked as a lord it falls
behind us one death comes
and goes as it pleases
it is the one
we are

Ladies in Love

Ladies should never fall in love.
They become stars
no one can reach. To appear taller
they cut their heads off and stand on them.

Some carry their breasts
in gunny sacks so as not to appear
pretentious. At night they unbutton
their nerves
in front of vibrators
and stare at collections of bearded men.

Some fall in love with dark vowels
and foreign accents. At night
they can be seen talking
in taverns with dangerous criminals.
Their voices are small animals
waiting to be fed.

Beauty

even among the deformed
there is a certain beauty: in the hand
of an amputee
rising to ward off a blow

in those who let us
do things against their will
when they know it is something else
we really wanted

in the father whose daughter
is neither rich nor beautiful, in her
face when she realizes
we were lying
and accepts money for the first time

in the recognition
that our smallest disappointment
is still more than any of us can afford

in our words
when we continue without winning,
when even whiskey or a parachute won't set
us down easy

when we continue as if we had
broken the light
down into pieces small enough to carry,
when we continue
as if we had portioned our lives exactly

Ending an Affair

is love the clang
a bell makes
in each of us is it the sound
heard over our heads and struck enough
times is it the vibration
killing us
is it a beautiful tone
or for many of us is it confused
with the dropping of metal on hard
surfaces like skulls

after saying always
how can you
leave like this aren't you afraid
the sounds of those
mad things

we did will follow you
where will you go
for warmth
sitting like a chair
in anybody's tub fitting all right
but not exactly

tell me what we had
between us
this quiet thing growing
too rich in soil
was it distance
why then toward the end
were we shouting
and far away

over love it is over
carried to the side
and dumped
into the bruised water
of our suffering and still
it is almost beautiful the light of this
strange animal feeding on my salt

In 1968, producer and director William Castle filmed the movie *Riot* entirely on location at Arizona State Prison. Schmid, an inmate at the prison, was employed as an extra for the film and tried during filming to get Castle interested in his "life story." After the production was finished shooting, Schmid tried one last time to butter up the producer by sending him an essay he had written that was Castle's "eulogy" – even though Castle was still quite alive at the time:

"Tell Sinatra to go to hell and put Mia back to work!" Bang! The phone exploded. Dead. Murdered in Capote cold blood.

There is only one man in the world who would dare do that to Frank Sinatra — and get away with it. William Castle. The uncontested Czar of Hollywoods movie moguls.

William Castle roared and twinkled into my life like a polished and gleaming syntax. Smooth and cool. Almost unctuous, but not quite, as if knew the boundries and proprieties of co-ercement and respected the limitations. He had to. It was part of the price a king had to pay to his subjects and he **was** king. Nobody doubted that. Not even the pretty pouters of tinsel land.

A machine gun aimed and fired. William Castle spoke. You ducked. Too late. You were raked with verbal bullets. Your flesh sucked them in. Deliciously. When he passed, you shot back with a put down. You had to. That was part of the American cliché. A piercing wit. If you scored, he bled, but the ~~artery of mouth spurted in the~~ severed artery of mouth ~~bled~~ spurted in the wrong direction and you were inundated with a raconteurs blood. A master raconteur. It was futile. Even in victory, you lost.

Wham! William Castle turned on. Transfusion time and he was off, pausing only long enough to bark a brief "just a see" before zooming off into realitys' other reality, a Paramount Picture movie set.

Next to the staging area, not twenty feet from where William Castle had just vanished, stood a red-brick duplex. A blushing monument to stupiditys' whore. The gas house. The duplex of death. The place where all the bad guys' get zapped. Execution by lethal gas. Ten minutes, five sniffs and a scream or two later, its' all over. Poof! ~~Exit one life.~~ Everybody loses. Even the good guys.

The gas chamber was for real. The movie set wasn't, inclusive of a black and gloomy demi-God actor (giant size) affected with a contagious show biz virus . . . charisma. Somehow you got the impression

"Tell Sinatra to go to hell and put Mia back to work!"
Bing! The phone exploded. Dead. Murdered in Capote cold blood.

There is only one man in the world who would dare do that to Frank Sinatra - and get away with it. William Castle. The uncontested Czar of Hollywood's movie moguls.

William Castle roared and twinkled into my life like a polished and gleaming syntax. Smooth and cool. Almost unctuous, but not quite, as if knew the boundries and proprieties of ca-excement and respected the limitations. He had to. It was part of the price a king had to pay to his subjects and he was king. Nobody doubted that. Not even the pretty pouters of tinsel land.

A machine gun aimed and fired. William Castle spoke. You ducked. Too late. You were raked with verbal bullets. Your flesh sucked them in. Deliciously. When he paused, you shot back with a put down. You had to. That was part of the American cliché. A piercing wit. If you scored, he bled, but the ~~[illegible]~~ ~~of mouth spurted in the~~ severed artery of mouth spurted ~~[illegible]~~, in the wrong direction and you were inundated with a racontems blood. A master raconteur. It was futile, even in victory, you lost.

Wham! William Castle turned on. Transfusion time and he was off, pausing only long enough to bark a brief "just a sec" before zooming off into reality's other reality he felt either guilty or super righteous because he wasn't out busting heads or getting busted like his soul brothers. Whatever it was, you never knew. He spoke down from a tower. A high tower. You couldn't quite hear or understand the words. They were lost in the complexity ~~of being black~~ and anguish of being black. He was a negro. He had to feel martyred. It was the rule, baby.

It was late spring, 1968. William Castle and friends were inside the grey walls of Arizona State Prison, valiantly trying to capture realism for their latest flick, "RIOT," a wild Cinema with an apt an fitting sobriquet. The whole setting was mad. Crazy mad. Convicts mixed with pseudo-convicts. Actor with non-actor. Technicians with layman. The magic of Cinderella descended. Even the warden smiled. New images. Fat Wyatt Earps' sucked in guts. ~~Pork Pie~~ Alpine hats went western. A parade of sun-glasses and white bucks stumbled by on scrawny poles of arrogance. All the Walter Mittys' came out to play. The wonder of magic. The almighty power of the flick. "Milieu" and "scenerio" slipped in between all the "I'm heps" and "yeah mans". Time to groove, get discovered. Even the food bared a slight resemblance to its' original probability. "Well I'll be damned, that was chicken we ate last night and not another damn cat somebody popped in the pot!" Not everyone fared so well. Old bones got dug up. Poor Dillenger. He caught hell. No less than 97 prison employer's & employee's, from the lowest of the sabaltern martinets to the highest God on the shaky pole of prison hierarchy, had at one time, in their lines, met & destroyed John Dillenger. He led a rough life. He'd been shot, captured, locked up, humiliated, frustrated, outwitted, beat up single handedly by grey haired midgets and made to eat crow. His arms & legs had been broken no less than 384 times by "tough guys" Dillenger made the mistake of intimidating. ~~"No sir,~~ "Yes sir, I could tell right away ol' "J.D." was a first class punk. Us lawmen can always' tell. Yep! He tried to outdraw me so I broke his arm. Yep, this is his gun alright." All 4000 of them. On & on & on. The noise of men everywhere. Lying. Swearing. Making noise. It weaves them all together in some mad and mysterious rite. It dulls the chill. The cards, the booze, the coarseness. All men. The culture of vulgarity. The fraternity of lie. It fuses the ~~altogether~~ into an ephemeral web of self-importance. A trap. They can leave the petty proprieties of world behind. Momentarily. Then it comes back. ~~The~~ lie wears off. Slowly. And they drown in the dullness of thin own bleak existance. I hate them all. I wish I could enact a law that would make a dull mind an infamous crime. I'm that embittered. They've done that much to me. Everytime they waddle by ~~my~~ with a filthy story created by a filthier mind, I wonder. There they go. Free. My potential executioners. Obese in mind and body. The men who perpetrate the world with social, cultural and historical lunacy. They get to kill me. Then I laugh. I know. The whole world has suddenly gone mad. Nothing matters. Not even this last frustration.

It was hot inside the prison. Damn hot. The Arizona sun had claws that could scratch out your eyes if you dared show contempt or challenge. Soft clay actors tried to stay cool. They were like puddled checkers jumping from square to shaded square. Talent oozed through pores made red & swollen by the enraged firebed.

Larry Schiller, "numero uno" of photographers everywhere and christened darling of the "jiuness doreé", was busily snapping pics' of everything. Bad & good alike; for real & not so real. He sacrificed at least 10,000 flash bulbs a day for posterity and the glossy glow surrealism of Look magazine. Larry could've been a bad guy. Easy. His trigger finger is that fast. Bang! Bang! Bang! Before you ~~realized~~ blinked you were had forever on print. Another notch, another number on his little "people-box" and half the time you didn't even know it. He is **that** good.

Before William Castles abscence was realized and confirmed, he popped back again, bobbing and weaving with the sheer delight of just "being". I was in condemned rows "play pen", a 20' X 40' bird cage affair that segregates the super bad from the free world. (Though the area provided an opportunity for the condemned man to exercize, it also smelled of exhibition. Like a zoo. People came by. Amused. Most were shocked. Shocked we were human beings and not a newspaper's monster.) A wire mesh enclosure kept us apart and rubricated, by proxy, my condemned status but for all practical purposes it didn't exist. William Castles brilliantly dynamic magnetism melted the barrier.

Being manipulated instead of manipulating was a strange feeling. But then William Castle is a strange man. He shook me. I was left askance. If you ever meet him, you'll know that feeling. Wild. Latent. Esoteric. Unimaginable. Contained violence. It comes on you from the smouldering ingot of eye. His eye, reflected back to you as the image of what you want to be, but can't. Until now, he lets you. He plugs you in like a Christmas tree & you light up. Its frightening, but a good kind of fright. The kind only certain people can feel or ever know. Like an explosive spice of summer lightening that gobbles up the tree you've been standing next to. The flash. Then BOOM! Suddenly its over except the smell. The acrid smell of death that lingers behind. You tremble. You're scared, but thankful scared & damn glad you're alive, as if something powerful, God maybe, let you play out the comedy a little longer and so you vow to live. Really live. Gluttonize life with the elegance of an epicure gone mad.

But thats only part of it. William Castle empathizes his soul. You feel you're teetering on the periphery of life and death. You **know** & whats more important you know **he** knows & you're not alone with you're private little death wish. He knows why certain people, including and even women must live quicker and faster. Not recklessly. No, but confidently. Savoring the important things of ~~life~~ both worlds. From Srauss to the Beatles and all the Ray Charles' & Hank Williams' in between. You get out from under the compartmentalized clap-trap of conformity. You feel free. Liberated as if you could wear beads with a tux on a bikini to the office and no one would care or be horrified. Not that you would, of course, but you **could**. Thats' the thing. God, you can turn on & groove. You don't have to exclude the appreciation of one art over another on the basis of fear. Fear that someone will run & tell all the other little runners & tatlers that live in the American social strata of lie and pretend.

An hours coloquy, with William Castle, is like drinking an intellectual martini — you come away refreshed, slightly drunk, and overwhelmed with power and sheer delight.

My fuse was blown, the blood of brain extracted. All the moping owls of creativity that ~~by and below~~ line by & above ~~and below~~ the mouth, came out to play. I wanted to perform, act or just be under his direction. For one precious moment I had Cyrano's soul and a Hamlet's heart. When he left, King Leer's fool came back and shot me ~~done~~ down. ars longa, vita brevis.

His last words to me are, ironically, the beginning of this whole wild and weary business of survival in Americas constitutional carnival land of die or go free. I'm playing out a surprizingly simple game of Russian Roulette, justice style, 1968. A free press fair trial bullet of controversy fits into one gas chamber womb of an appelate court held gun. It's pointed at my head. The moment of money equals truth equals justice equals one human life, comes near. Snap, goes the trigger. Now its' your turn. You got you're free press — so how 'bout my fair trial?

I was trying to be serious with him and not cop-out to a phony rendition of "lets pretend we care what the hell each of is trying to say" naiveté. I castrated the social amenities for a stab at the man. The real man. What made him tick? I asked him "What are you trying for in your life and movies, that note? That "thing". What certain projection? Maybe a sophisticated form of Philistine respectability; sort of a packaged, do it-your-self culture course for the masses?" He let my words shoot out of mouth & sling shot brain like wild arrows. ~~As if he could see me~~ He humiliated me with grace. A gentle côup d'mâitré. He didn't even bother to counter or protect himself from the loaded questions, as if his own basic honesty and determination was a shield powerful enough to ward off the encroaching enemy. He seemed to sense nothing could hit him squarely, at least not any more and so my puerile arrows and words fell to the ground. Spent. Then he sprang. First a smile. Then a laugh. Deep. Hearty. Rich. Like cottage cheeze and buttermilk. Quickly and practiced, he broke it off, gesticulating with grin instead of hands. Then he got sad, almost lugubrious, as if some private painful ghost of a past Christmas regime jammed his mouth full of gloom cookies and made him eat. It wiped out joy. Pan flew away. We suddenly became strangers as quickly as we had become friends. His words ladled out the hurt but they were frosted with honesty & conviction. "Smitty you've gotta tell it like it is. You can't lie or adapt things to the way you want them for the sake of convenience and ego. If you do it will all come back when you least expect it and strangle your life. We all look back, at some point in our lives, and try to manipulate the pieces of the past to our "now" image. It doesn't work. I know I've seen it happen too many times to too many people. America has no royalty but she craves somebody to worship, to idolize, to dream about to relieve her perpetual boredom. She substitutes her actors & actresses for what she lacks. ~~These idols~~ They live the lie & counter lie their fans create for them. Some even believe it to such an extent they fraudilize the past to confirm & conform to their conceptual theories of perfection. It never works. It only guarantees their misery and they're all miserable. Thats when they're all so good. It's all a lie. A dream a "laugh-in" of life. In the final analysis there are no good guys or heroes anymore, only grey guys & grey things in a grey world called America."

And so it begins. The story of grey. Not a collection of guilt; no; America and her citizens have been to the whipping post of guilt long enough. This is a story ~~void of~~ about a generation, a time and a place of people. Real people, not fictional characters dressed in the chrome diarrhea of some nut-journalists' fantasies. This is the story about your kids and why. Why they rebel, why they out manuever & mystify you, why three of them died, for no reason, and why it could could happen again. Tonight, to the son & daughter you **think** you know.

Letter to a reporter from the Tucson *American*, postmarked August 20, 1968:

Dear ——————,

First, let me say thank you for the help you've given. I know you're quite busy — therefore the courtesy you've extended me is doubly appreciated.

Second, the William Castle eulogy farce, which I assume you've read, was created to entertain his ego, Q.E.D. of course. William Castle & I had met, exchanged pleasantries and platitudes (as thats what our relationship amounted to — a joke to pass time.) and promises were uttered. One of the promises' Mr. Castle gave me was an investigation and possible concilliation of the Gilmore/Levy/National General gimmick. Nothing developed. No answer, denial, or anything. I assumed my "bad guy countenance" scared the hell out of him & I deserved the brush. Whatever it was, I never found out. Later, one of his "pseudo admirers" hinted a pleasant eulogy might create "another" interest. I complied, hence the sophmoric chapter on Mr. Castle. My idea was to revise, insert, amend, structure, etc. all of it, to oil his ego, in the hope he might purchase the rights from me. Of course he never saw it, therefore, thats at a standstill. Since I'm not particularly hampered by a sudden infiltration of moral guerrillas, that bind me to verity, I am quite willing to adapt my life story to any frame **any one** might want. Good grief, people & gas chambers being what they are, I don't particularly CARE what anyone's opinion of me is. All I want is money. Anyone who said money **isn't** happiness never sat in a courtroom or death row. "Fas est et ab hoste doceri." — and my enemies have taught me **well**; after all, lawyers and justices don't exactly abide "de riguer" either.

Third — If Mr. Castle treats the eulogy as frivalous (though a précis of how a movie & Mr. Castle could profit by it, should be included i.e. — a movie script or semblance thereof.) my idea was to work up a **different** "work" to peddle to the "smut" dealers. It seems the literary tastes of the public are more concerned with exotic toilet training, creative masturbation and sexual indurance contests than dull prose so . . . I'm ready to "sell out" to the "establishment" you might say. Justice **is** rather expensive. I've adapted. I'm rathar compromising. Besides I'm no longer deceived by delusions of hidden salvation. Ol' 7, Lee shattered that bubble.

Fourth — Since I have the energy, talent and intelligence of a fat, placid bear I obviously need help. Either my work is a splattering of incoherency or twelve steps worse. I suppose my genius in life, is that I **have** no genius. oh there was periods. . . the dull, the trite, the squaring of the square flat phrases, year. The splutter of **my** hot rhetoric could intellectually rape a donkey — little else. My father mentioned an agent was due to contact me. Regulations will probably wreck that approach. Perhaps the agent could contact him?

Fifth. Now, **is it conceivable** that you might put me in contact with a female agent rather than a male? Most male agents are bright, brisk, **negative** intelligence's who embrace a weird sence of ethics — like greed. We somehow end up at war rather than comaraderie. Contrary to popular opinion, men are dum-dums at exploiting other men — at least **this** man. I need a woman to squeeze out the japes and jeers that will make money. I presume this isn't an "ethical" approach or a **traditional** one but then who wants to embrace or kiss an ethical ghost? ha!

Truthfully, I simply don't trust a man — **any man** — except, of course, my father. Besides I'm becoming terribly barbarianized by the spoon & oatmeal routine and I need a woman to flatter. Maybe she can can reduce the crassness — Q.E.D.

In conclusion, I hope you can sift through the ramblings and find a semblance of logic to work from — as of lately I'm becoming quite decadent. Essentially, I want this —

1. Attempt to salvage Castle eulogy & "hook" him (mutual exploitation, I suppose.)
2. Secure a FEMALE agent.

3. Sell something.
4. See what color justice's face is when she finds I've lost the pauper status.
5. laugh again . . . maybe.

Thanks again for your help. If by chance the gas chamber beats me to the pocketbook don't weep at my exit. Laugh. It will round out the joke. Besides I'll be sitting on a cloud throwing rocks, tornadoes, and a piece or two of bad luck at Moser, Bruns etc. Respectfully,

Charles
your friendly neighborhood villain

P.S. Yes, Diane still writes. Oh, we have wonderful discussions about . . . well, anyway she still writes. Thats something. The family is picking berries or some damn thing in Oregon. At least they're off welfare.

EDGAR SMITH

In 1964 a convicted murderer on Death Row, Edgar Smith, started corresponding with William F. Buckley, the well-known conservative ideologue. A fan of Buckley's magazine *National Review*, Smith slowly convinced Buckley and many others that he was innocent of the sexual assault and murder of 15-year-old Victoria Zielinski on March 4, 1957, in Mahwah, New Jersey. Buckley received over 2,900 pages of correspondence from Smith over the next seven years, and with Buckley's assistance Smith wrote and published a bestselling book, *Brief Against Death*, while in prison. The impact of Buckley's sponsorship and Smith's book on the media led to Smith's eventual release from prison in 1971; the judge who arranged the plea bargain believed that Smith was guilty, but also believed that he had since become rehabilitated. On the evening of his release Smith was picked up outside the prison walls by a limousine and appeared on Buckley's television program "Firing Line," proclaiming his innocence, publicizing his books, and exhibiting his brainpower as a newly-initiated member of the genius club Mensa.

Edgar Smith receded from the public's attention until October 1976, when he attacked a young woman in San Diego, California. Smith came up behind Lefteriya Ozbun and forced her at knifepoint into his car. He then drove onto the freeway, where he stabbed her in an attempt to take her purse. Ozbun, fighting back, put her foot through the windshield and somehow managed to get out of the moving car by opening the car door. Smith sped off and six days later phoned Buckley from a hotel room in Las Vegas. Since Buckley was not in his office, Smith left the phone number where he could be reached. Buckley, now somewhat contrite, promptly turned the phone number over to the FBI. Smith was arrested later that day.

Back in San Diego, Smith not only admitted attacking Ozbun but also confessed to the murder of Victoria Zielinski. He stated that he killed her by hitting her over the head with a baseball bat and smashing her skull with a large rock because she rejected his sexual advances. From the penitentiary where he still resides, Smith told the newspapers: "For the first time in my life, I recognized that the devil I had been looking at the last forty-three years was me. I recognized what I am, and I admitted it." William F. Buckley, for perhaps the first time in his life, didn't have much to say at all.

Excerpts from Smith's first book, *Brief Against Death*, published in 1968:

PROLOGUE

"I looked around and I seen where her brains were scattered for seven or eight feet along the bank. Then I looked down over the bank and there her body was in a jackknifed position.

"One arm was sticking up. Her head was face down and there was a hole in the back of her head where all the brains was knocked out completely. She had no hair left on her head.

"I discovered that she had her sweater pulled over her shoulders. She had her dungarees on, and one stocking was all the way off, and the other was part way off."

With these words, spoken in a hushed courtroom, Anthony Zielinski described how, shortly after nine o'clock on the morning of March 5, 1957, he had climbed onto a windswept dirt mound in a Mahwah, New Jersey, sandpit and found the mutilated, blood-drenched body of his fifteen-year-old daughter, Victoria, who had been missing since eight-forty the previous evening.

The search for the girl had not been a long one, and within three months of the discovery of her half-nude body I had been arrested, tried, convicted of first-degree murder by a jury that had deliberated for less than two hours, and sentenced to die in the electric chair.

It had been an indescribably horrible crime — the savagery of the attack can be gauged from the fact that what the victim's father had thought was the back of the girl's head with the hair missing was in fact the remains of her face — and the public and the press screamed for vengeance. As a result, following my arrest and conviction, the police were showered with praise for their efficiency and for the dispatch with which they had "solved" the murder; the jury, which included an acquaintance and former co-worker of the victim's father, was congratulated for its diligence, attention to duty, and arrival at a popular verdict; and the trial judge, who had found it necessary to call recesses when some of the more lurid testimony and evidence had distressed him, was applauded for his decorous handling of the proceedings.

I must confess that through my own fears, ignorance, and mistrust of the police, I had done much to contribute to my own conviction. When first taken into custody for questioning, I had lied, partially out of fear, partially out of misplaced loyalty toward friends. It had not taken the police long, however, to see through my lies, to discover that I had been with the girl, at the murder scene, shortly before her death; and as I continued to lie and deny all knowledge of the events preceding the crime, the officers were more and more justified in thinking they had found the murderer. Thus, when at last I did begin to tell the truth, only weeks before my trial, it was too late; the police were convinced they had solved the crime, and the prosecutor was irrevocably committed to putting me on trial for my life. Nor was the public, aroused to fever pitch by the pretrial publicity — one headline read **"WHY DID HE KILL?"** — disposed to accepting any thesis but that Edgar Smith murdered Vickie Zielinski.

I do not expect that this book, or any number of books, will conclusively establish my innocence, or that it will answer every question. Indeed, the book may give rise to more questions than it settles. What I do believe, however, is that any person who approaches my story with an open mind will come away from it asking himself: "Did this man **really** do it?"

More than eleven years have passed since the trial, and I remain under sentence of death. Among those who have closely followed my ordeal from the beginning, or who have taken the time to study it in recent years — and even among those who once might have volunteered to tighten the straps and pull the switch — doubts have arisen.

Were the police, in response to the public outcry, expedient rather than efficient? Did they act with too much dispatch?

Did the jury in its brief deliberations give the evidence and testimony of a two-week trial the scrutiny it deserved?

Was the judge, himself the father of a fifteen-year-old girl, the detached, impartial arbiter he should have been?

Did Justice triumph?

Is Edgar Smith guilty?

[...]

CHAPTER TWENTY-THREE

It is the prosecutor's theory of the crime that the following occurred: 1) That upon our arrival at the sandpit, Vickie and I held a conversation. 2) That I attempted to make love to her. 3) That she resisted my attempts. 4) That her sweater was pushed up and her bra was torn. 5) That she fought, got free, and fled from the automobile. 6) That I took a baseball bat from the back seat of the auto and pursued her. 7) That, approximately 350 feet down the road, I caught up with her and struck her down with the bat. 8) That for a reason obvious only to the prosecutor, I discarded the weapon. 9) That I dragged her back to the sandpit, up onto the dirt mound, crushed her skull, and dragged the body over the mound. 10) That I left the sandpit, stopped on Chapel Road to discard her pocketbook, then drove home. The evidence, unchallenged and uncontradicted, is that I arrived home at 8:57 P.M. The prosecutor has never questioned this time.

The theory is interesting; but if you stop to compare it with the evidence, and if you realize just what the prosecutor asks you to believe, you find a significant defect in the theory: it is filled with discrepancies.

There is, to begin with, the time element. From the trial testimony of Barbara Nixon, Myrna Zielinski, and Vickie's mother, and from the investigation report filed by the Mahwah police, in which reference is made to statement by Vickie's parents, and by Mrs. Nixon, it is clear that Vickie left the Nixon home at approximately 8:40 P.M. This is the starting time for my calculations.

If one gives the prosecutor the benefit of the doubt, one may assume that I passed Vickie on the road within sixty to ninety seconds of the time she left the Nixon home. One might then be fair in assuming that within another minute I had gone down the road, stopped, turned around, driven back, and picked her up. This would have put her in the car at 8:42, or a few seconds later. This really gives the prosecutor the benefit of the doubt.

The drive to the sandpit has been clocked repeatedly at six to seven minutes. The reader will recall that my unchallenged testimony was that I had been forced to stop for a piece of earth-moving equipment being backed across the road, so the estimate of seven minutes to drive to the sandpit is a fair one, and puts me at the sandpit at 8:49.

To back out of the sandpit, drive down Chapel Road, stop to discard the pocketbook, as the prosecutor claims I did, and then to drive the one mile to my home, takes three, four minutes. Since I arrived home at 8:57, I must therefore have left the sandpit at 8:53 or 8:54.

Now one can readily see the incredibility of the prosecutor's theory. Between 8:49, the earliest time I could have arrived at the sandpit, and 8:53 or 8:54, the time I must have left the scene, is a time span of only four to five minutes; yet the prosecutor would have you believe that within this brief span of time it was physically possible for me to have done all of the things he claims I did: hold a conversation, attempt to make love, argue, struggle, get out the baseball bat, chase the girl more than the length of a football field, drag her body back an even greater distance, kill her, and then drag her body over the dirt mound. The reader can decide if this was possible.

Another claim by the prosecutor is that while in the car, and **before** the girl had suffered a single injury, I had torn her bra in an attempt to make love to her. So intent was he upon playing up the sex angle that he paid no attention to the fact that the bra was saturated with blood in the area between the cups. Yet these bloodstains tell an important story.

The girl was found with the bra around her waist. The waistbands of her jeans and her underpants were completely free of blood, and her abdomen was clean. The obvious question: If the bra was around her waist **before** she was injured, how did it **alone** become saturated with blood? If the saturation of the bra occurred while it was down around her waist, the tops of her jeans and panties, and the area of her stomach, could not possibly have been unbloodied.

The answer would seem to be that the bra was not torn until **after** she was injured, and this is borne out by photographs showing dried blood in the area between her breasts, corresponding exactly with the bloodstains between the cups of the bra. Also, the left shoulder strap of the bra reveals numerous bloodstains on the portion of the strap which goes over the shoulder. This confirms my claim that the left side of her head was injured when she returned to the sandpit with Hommell. The right shoulder strap is free of blood.

This prompts another question: If the girl was struck down, dragged back to the sandpit, then killed, how did the blood get between her breasts in sufficient quantity to saturate the bra? Lying on the ground, her head would have been lower than the chest area. Perhaps when she was dragged head first up the dirt mound? I shall show that she was dragged feet first.

From many hours of studying the testimony at my trial, and from careful analysis of both color and black-and-white photographs of the scene, the body, and the girl's clothing, I believe I have been able to reconstruct the events. I believe, too, that my reconstruction is far more logical than the prosecutor's, since every piece of evidence fits into mine.

It is clear that Vickie was injured and fully conscious for a significant period of time before she was killed. Three factors lead to this conclusion: 1) Her gloves were found to be grossly stained with blood, and strands of her own hair were found sticking to the palms. This establishes beyond question that she was wearing the gloves **after** having sustained an injury. 2) Dr. Gilady found that her fingernails were "bitten very severely," a positive indication that **after** having been injured, and **after** having removed her bloodstained gloves, she remained conscious and in a state of fear or pain for some appreciable period of time, at least long enough to have bitten her nails "very severely." 3) The bra, as noted, must have been in place about her breasts when it became saturated with blood. This, again, is a positive indication that she had been standing **after** being injured, that she had been bleeding profusely, and that the blood had followed the natural body contours and had run down between her breasts. This, and only this, accounts for the presence of blood between her breasts but none lower on her body — the blood, when it reached the area between her breasts, was absorbed by the bra.

The girl's jacket is another article of evidence which tells a story. There is nothing to indicate that her jacket ever was off the body; yet on the inner lining of the jacket, in the area corresponding to the small of the back, there was found a large, circular, blood-saturated area, to which her own hair and fragments of bone were clinging. At some point, therefore, her head must have come in direct contact with that portion of the jacket, a circumstance for which the prosecutor's theory makes no allowance. I believe there is a logical explanation, but it must be explained within the context of all the other evidence. Alone, it makes no sense. Prosecutor Calissi failed to consider each item of evidence as part of a whole picture of what took place that night.

Vickie was injured. She was standing in the sandpit fully clothed, bleeding profusely from an injury to the left side of her head. The blood was flowing down the left side of her face and neck, and it followed the contour of her body down between her breasts. Her bra, which was still in place, absorbed the blood and prevented it from flowing down to her abdomen. At the same time, the left shoulder strap became bloodstained.

It is evident that the girl's sweater was in place at this time. Had it been tightly bunched above her breasts and under her arms, as it was when the body was found, it would have prevented the flowing of blood between her breasts, since it would have absorbed the blood.

Vickie, still wearing her gloves, put her hands to the wound, either to feel the wound or to staunch the flow of blood. Her gloves became bloodstained, and some of her hair, loosened by the injury, stuck to the palms. She removed the gloves, dropped them to the ground, and put her hands to the wound. This is the only logical reason why the photographs show her hands to have been bloodstained also.

I left the girl at the sandpit in the general condition just described. When I returned thirty minutes later, she was nowhere in sight, but the broken baseball bat, and what appeared to me to be a clean white cloth, were lying on the ground. If Dr. Gilady's estimate of the time of death is correct, and I believe it is, the girl was still alive when I returned. But where was she?

I believe that she had been struck down with the baseball bat and left lying near the dirt mound. The "scuffled area" found by the police, probably resulting from her struggle with her attacker, was near the base of the mound. When I returned to the scene, I did not go beyond the end of the dirt road, nor was I looking to see if the girl was there. I assumed she had been taken home. It is quite possible, therefore, that she was lying unconscious near the mound. Other persons argue that she was not there, that she was brought back later, but I have never seen a shred of evidence to support their argument.

The next question concerns the manner in which her clothing became disarranged. The torn bra made no sense to me until one day, in the summer of 1966, I was examining a photograph of the body. Then the answer came to me: The torn bra and the position in which the body was found are directly related. This is how I see it:

Vickie's murderer arrived at the sandpit several hours later, perhaps to see if she was dead, perhaps to retrieve the baseball bat and the white cloth I saw lying near the bat. No such cloth was ever found or alluded to by the police, but a clean white T-shirt is mentioned in Dr. Cassity's truth-serum notes.

The murderer, thinking she was dead, decided to drag the body over the dirt mound, to conceal it from anyone who might enter the sandpit. The girl's jeans were held in place by a two-inch-wide leather belt. The back of the belt is heavily scarred, and the shiny finish is scraped away. This indicates the girl was lying on her back when dragged up the mound. The absence of dirt and sand beneath the waistband of the jeans indicates that she was dragged feet first.

As Vickie was dragged up the dirt mound, her limp arms trailed back over her head, and her unsnapped jacket began to slide up her body. Soon her jacket had slipped so far up her body and arms that the inside lining was beneath her head. Thus the large bloodstain found **inside** the jacket. This is why she was found with the jacket off one arm and nearly off the other.

At the same time the jacket was sliding up the girl's body, her cardigan sweater also was sliding up her body so that by the time her body was dragged to the top of the mound, the sweater had worked its way up over her breasts and was bunched under her arms and chin. Also, the back of the sweater, which was in contact with the ground, was higher on the body than the front.

For some reason — perhaps she made a sound, or she began to regain consciousness — the murderer crushed her skull when he got her near the top of the mound. Photographs show her head was several feet below the crest of the mound at the time.

When Vickie's body was found, it was in a semi-kneeling position, the upper torso twisted, the right shoulder beneath. It was the position a person would be in if he lay on the ground on his back, brought his legs straight back over the head to touch the ground behind with the feet, and then relaxed and slumped to one side. What struck me as odd about the position of the body was the fact that the head was farther from the mound than the feet.

Since the girl had been dragged up one side of the mound feet first, her feet would have been farther from the base of the mound than her head if she had been dragged feet first down the other side. There is no doubt, therefore, that she had been pitched down the other side head first. Also, something occurred on top of the mound which resulted in the tearing of her bra. What happened up there?

Try to picture this situation: the body is dragged up the mound until the hips are on the top of the mound. The upper part of the body is lying down the slope. The girl weighted 120 pounds; the side of the mound was quite steep; and the ground consisted of soft, deep sand. It had been difficult for the murderer to drag the body under these conditions, but as he neared the top of the mound, the task became more difficult. The top of the mound was covered with grass and weeds, even more slippery than the loose sand. Then he realized that his task would be easier if he pulled the body into a sitting position, from which a push would send it tumbling down the other side.

The girl's jacket had slid up her arms and under her head, and the arms themselves hung down almost to the base of the mound. He had to grab something with which to pull the body into a sitting position, and the thing that first caught his eye was the bra, its whiteness revealed in the dark. He grabbed it in the most natural place, between the cups, his bloody hand staining the outside, and he pulled. The shoulder straps tore loose, and the bra was pulled down around the waist. Why?

If the body had been lying on a flat surface, such as a floor, the murderer standing over it, he could easily have pulled it into a sitting position; the strain would have distributed along the wide, heavy backstrap of the bra. The distribution of the strain upon the bra was roughly equivalent to what it would have been if the victim had been standing, and if he had tried to pull her forward, toward him, by the bra. But the position in the sandpit was different.

Vickie's body was lying on the slope of the mound, slanting down and away from her murderer, who was atop the mound. In this position, he was not pulling at a right angle to the longitudinal axis of the body, as he would have if both he and Vickie had been standing. He was, rather, pulling the bra downward toward the girl's feet, putting the strain on the shoulder straps, not the backstrap. As the strain increased, therefore, the thin shoulder straps tore loose at the place where they were stitched to the cups. The sudden tearing caused the murderer to stumble backward, and as he did so, still gripping the bra, he pulled it down around her waist.

After releasing the bra and regaining his balance, he grabbed another handhold — perhaps the sweater bunched up under her chin, managed to get the body in a sitting position atop the mound, and pushed it forward. The body tumbled forward and came to rest in the peculiar position in which it was found the next morning.

I believe that anyone reading the foregoing reconstruction will find it far more logical and impressive than the fantasy concocted by the prosecutor. I could write another book simply to point out the holes in his theory, but I have time and space here to mention only a few others.

There is, for one, the highly unlikely claim that Vickie, her cardigan sweater pushed above her breasts, leaped from my automobile and ran more than the length of a football field without having had the sweater slide back down. This is patently implausible. Incidentally, why would anyone bother to push up a cardigan sweater which could much more easily have been unbuttoned, with or without a girl's cooperation?

There is the claim that I chased Vickie and struck her down **from behind** with a baseball bat. This overlooks the fact that her injury was to the left side of her head, whereas I am right-handed.

There is the claim that from the spot on Fardale Avenue, where Vickie allegedly was struck down, I threw the baseball bat a ground-level distance of about 134 feet, into the wooded area to the south. Has the reader ever seen a major league baseball player swing with all his might at a pitch, miss, lost his grip on the bat, and the bat fly out to the pitcher's mound? The distance from home plate to the pitcher's mound is 60.5 feet. Prosecutor Calissi claims I threw the bat thirteen feet more than **twice** that distance — a point corresponding to a spot six feet behind second base — and that I threw it that far through a thick stand of woods. Perhaps he would have us believe the trees parted like the Red Sea.

There is the claim that I **dragged** her body back to the sandpit, and that I did so without leaving a drop of blood, or even a mark upon the soft, sandy ground, over the entire 350-foot distance. That **is** amazing.

Add to these unsupportable claims the brief period of time I could have been with the girl, the fact that my shoes were practically free of blood, the fact that my clothing above the lower right leg was entirely free of blood, that my gloves and hands — as well as the steering wheel of Gilroy's automobile — were free of blood, that the tire marks on Fardale Avenue and on the dirt road and the footprints on the dirt mound all were unidentified, and that death seems to have occurred long after I had departed the scene, and the prosecutor's theory falls apart at the seams.

What about the time of death? All I can say is that Dr. Gilady's testimony seems to have been misunderstood completely. I shall try to explain.

The doctor performed his autopsy at 1 P.M. He found that the stage of rigor mortis apparent at that time was the stage usually reached after twelve hours, give or take an hour; and he stated that below-normal temperatures **hasten** both the onset and the progress of rigor mortis. It was here that the fundamental misunderstanding occurred.

The temperature the night Vickie was killed had dropped below freezing. Judge O'Dea mistakenly interpreted this to mean than any error in Dr. Gilady's testimony must have been to the long side, that is, increasing the number of hours between death and autopsy. Precisely the opposite is true.

If in normal weather it would have taken twelve hours for the girl's body to have reached the stage of rigor mortis found by Dr. Gilady, and if below normal temperatures **hasten** both the onset and progress of rigor mortis, then it follows that the colder it was the more quickly the twelve-hour stage would have been reached. In below-freezing temperatures, as the doctor pointed out, the twelve-hour-stage condition would have been reached in less than twelve hours. Hence his estimate of "twelve hours, or an hour or two less [less than twelve hours], because of the cold weather." To lengthen the time between death and autopsy, to move the time backward toward 9:30 P.M., the onset and progress of rigor mortis would have had to have been retarded, not hastened, and that would have required **above**-normal temperatures. Thus, the prosecutor's proof of below-freezing temperatures actually increased the probability that Vickie had died later, perhaps as late as 2 or 3 A.M., since the **twelve-hour stage** would have been reached "an hour or two **less**" than twelve hours.

The entire controversy could have been avoided if the prosecutor had demanded a complete autopsy rather than a slapdash job. No laboratory examinations of the girl's blood or vital organs were performed. The police knew exactly what and when she had last eaten, and an analysis of the stomach contents would have revealed the exact time the digestive processes were interrupted. This is the standard and most accurate method of establishing time of death. In this manner, taking standard data, time of death can be established within minutes. How superficial was the autopsy? Would you believe that the police did not even bother to request a blood test to establish the girl's blood type? At my trial, it was assumed that she had type O blood because this was the type on her clothing. Her blood type was never proved as a matter of fact.

[. . .]

It seems that the more holes appear in the prosecutor's theory, however untenable I may prove his case to be, or how many questions I may raise, the question of who killed Vickie Zielinski may never be answered. As I stated in my prologue: it is perhaps too much to expect that this book can or will prove my innocence. I must be content to leave the reader with an abiding sense of doubt. Of course, I have an opinion, and a strong one at that, as to who killed the girl, and why she was killed, but I do not **know** as a matter of certainty and the libel laws are such that I cannot state my opinion. I know beyond a shadow of a doubt only that Vickie was alive when I left the sandpit. How she was killed is obvious. Why she was killed is something I can only guess at — a guess based upon my knowledge of Vickie, the personalities involved, and the environment within which the crime occurred.

Given thirty days of freedom in 1957, I do not doubt that I could have found the answers to all the questions: When? How? Why? Who? Today, it is probably too late. Most of the principals in the case are scattered. My wife has gone West with my daughter and her new husband. Hommell has returned, circuitously, as the reader soon shall see, to his former home in Florida. Mrs. Zielinski has divorced her husband, charging him with unspeakable conduct,[1] and her family has scattered. Others have married and moved away. Some are dead. Still others have simply disappeared. Who killed Vickie Zielinski probably will never be known.

[. . .]

APPEAL PENDING

So we come at last to the end of my book, but by no means the end of my story. That goes on. Today, more than eleven years after becoming a Death House resident, I am doing precisely what I began doing the very first day: waiting for a remote, faceless group of judges to decide what may be my final appeal. And though I wait in a larger, brighter Death House, now equipped with round-the-clock television, time drags by as slowly as ever. As I write these words, only one other man in the world, Sadamichi Hirasawa, a seventy-five-year-old Japanese, has been confined under sentence of death longer than I. Hirasawa, who has been facing the hangman's rope for twenty years, and I should be delighted to surrender our records to the first volunteer.

There is little more I can say. I have told my story as best I know how, leaving it to the reader to sift the facts, weigh the claims and counterclaims, and ultimately to answer for himself the questions posed at the beginning of this book: Did justice triumph? Is Edgar Smith guilty? If at this point the reader cannot respond with an emphatic "yes," then I shall consider this book a success.

[1] Court records reveal that Mrs. Zielinski charged that her husband had, among other things "degraded and defamed" her in the presence of her children, called her "foul and obscene" names in their presence; "consorted" with other women in the family's presence, refused to become "in any way involved" with their only son, was "continually drunk" at home, attempted to "assault and batter" her in front of the family; was drunk and threatened to beat her after Vickie's funeral; put the family "in fear of our lives"; "committed sodomy with the family dog"; threatened to burn the house down with her in it; accused her of "whoring"; caused her to be "fearful of her life, safety, and health"; and threatened to "finish us all." **Zielinski v. Zielinski,** Amended complaint, Superior Court of New Jersey, Chancery Division, Bergen County, Docket No. M 3587-58R.

As for myself, I have paid a terrible price for my refusal to give in to the system, for refusing to accept the neat, clean compromise of pleading guilty to a lesser degree of murder. I have lost my home, my wife and child, and more than eleven years from the prime of my life, and I would be less than candid if I did not admit that there have been moments when I have wondered whether the enormity of the price has been worth it. More than one night in recent years I have lain awake in my solitary cell until daylight, filling my ashtray with countless half-smoked cigarettes, and asking myself questions which seem at this time to be unanswerable: What good has been accomplished by all this? Wouldn't it have been easier and better to have accepted the prosecutor's deal, serve seven or eight years, and be a free man today? Would anyone really care, or remember? Who, outside of family and friends, really gives a damn whether Edgar Smith is guilty or innocent? What is the limit a man can be made to pay for justice?

These questions, which creep into the mind and soul in the solitude of the night, could prove fatal if allowed to take root. When one is fighting for one's life, self-doubt can be as deadly as the electric chair. My defense against these doubts is my abiding confidence in the integrity of the judicial processes, and my resolution to go on fighting to achieve vindication for as long as it is legally and financially possible. It is anomalous, I know, that one who has received such cavalier treatment from the courts should hold the belief that his best hope for ultimate vindication lies with the courts, but so it must be.

Eleven years ago, when the bitter taste of my treatment at the hands of the police and prosecutor's detectives was fresh in my mouth, and when the words of Judge O'Dea's jury instructions still rang in my ears, the law, and the society represented by the law, were anathema to me. But the Edgar Smith of today is no longer the restless, immature boy of 1957. Infinitely more patient and tolerant of others, better educated, and with a greater insight into my own abilities and limitations, I have learned to face life as it is by learning first to face myself as I am.

I should like to believe that William F. Buckley was not being too extravagantly charitable when he wrote in his nationally syndicated column that "Edgar Smith went to the Death House not far removed from the wasteful class of humanity. . . . He emerges as . . . a most extraordinary man who may not succeed in triumphing over the chair, but has clearly triumphed over himself."[2]

Excerpt from *Getting Out*, published in 1973:

I had heard and read much about the New Morality, the new life-style, the greater freedom, the ever-increasing leisure time people "on the street" were enjoying — but wow! **Enjoying?** No one seemed to be enjoying a goddamn thing out there. All of a sudden I wondered about the worth of my thirteen years of struggle. Is **that** what I was fighting to get back into? Later that day I wrote to Bill Buckley about what I had seen and felt:

> IMPRESSIONS: The outside world is filthy, the air stinks, the new buildings look like cheeseboxes, and the new cars look like toys made in Japan. The dirt is what amazed me. I cannot remember the world being so dirty, and I wonder if I notice it only because I was seeing it — almost — for the first time. I wonder if others, who are out there every day, realize how filthy the buildings and streets are and how rotten the air smells. Believe it or not, in the big parking lot across the street from the courthouse, the most astonishing thing was not the designs or the bright colors of the new cars lined up in rows, but the fact that I did not see one clean car in the entire lot. Every one was filthy, the colors muted by a film of dirt. The streets are the same way, dirty littered, and filled with bumps and holes and cracks. The people were clean, all dressed in the wildest, brightest colors one could imagine, and the girls were wearing skirts that almost weren't, but they weren't smiling. Everyone was walking around looking as if he had just flunked algebra. And the car I went over to court in was small, cramped, and put together like a plastic scale model of the **Titanic.** It was a '70 Plymouth. Keep it. I don't want it.

[2] William F. Buckley, Jr.: **On the Right,** The Washington Star Syndicate, Inc., November 9, 1965 (release date).

The girls were a surprise. It is impossible to tell how old a girl is these days. They could be fifteen, twenty, or twenty-five; they all look alike, dress alike, walk alike, and when they smile, smile alike, one of those "I'll smile but I don't really want to" smiles. But the dirt — that really got me. Doesn't **anyone** clean **anything** anymore? The only clean things I saw all day were a new Cadillac and the courtroom. The Cadillac probably belonged to the judge. Jesus! How do people live out there? Either they have lived with it for so long they have stopped noticing, or they have stopped caring. As I told Sophie, Trenton you can almost forgive because this town doesn't have enough class to be a first-rate slum. "Effete snobs" hell! What this world is full of is effete **slobs!**

RICHARD & BRIDGET SMITH

From *The Oxford Book of Death*, edited by D. J. Enright: "In 1732 Richard Smith, a bookbinder who had fallen into debt, and his wife decided to commit suicide. They killed their two-year-old daughter and hanged themselves, leaving the following letter, along with a note asking their landlord to look after their cat and dog."

These actions, considered in all their circumstances, being somewhat uncommon, it may not be improper to give some account of the cause; and that it was inveterate hatred we conceived against poverty and rags, evils that through a train of unlucky accidents were become inevitable. For we appeal to all that ever knew us, whether we were idle or extravagant, whether or no we have not taken as much pains to get our living as our neighbours, although not attended with the same success. We apprehend the taking of our child's life away to be a circumstance for which we shall be generally condemned; but for our own parts we are perfectly easy on that head. We are satisfied it is less cruelty to take the child with us, even supposing a state of annihilation as some dream of, than to leave her friendless in the world, exposed to ignorance and misery. Now in order to obviate some censures which may proceed either from ignorance or malice, we think it proper to inform the world, that we firmly believe the existence of an Almighty God; that this belief of ours is not an implicit faith, but deduced from the nature and reason of things. We believe the existence of an Almighty Being from the consideration of his wonderful works, from those innumerable celestial and glorious bodies, and from their wonderful order and harmony. We have also spent some time in viewing those wonders which are to be seen in the minute part of the world, and that with great pleasure and satisfaction. From all which particulars we are satisfied that such amazing things could not possibly be without a first mover — without the existence of an Almighty Being. And as we know the wonderful God to be Almighty, so we cannot help believing that he is also good — not implacable, not like such wretches as men are, not taking delight in the misery of his creatures; for which reason we resign up our breath to him without any terrible apprehensions, submitting ourselves to those ways which in his goodness he shall please to appoint after death. We also believe in the existence of unbodied natures, and think we have reason for that belief, although we do not pretend to know their way of subsisting. We are not ignorant of those laws made **in terrorem**, but leave the disposal of our bodies to the wisdom of the coroner and his jury, the thing being indifferent to us where our bodies are laid. From hence it will appear how little anxious we are about "hic jacet" . . .

Richard Smith
Bridget Smith

CHARLES STARKWEATHER

Late in the evening of November 30, 1957, a short 19-year-old garbageman from Lincoln, Nebraska, lay down on his bed after drinking some beers at his favorite bar. Charles "Little Red" Starkweather, a self-styled rebel who fashioned himself after his screen hero James Dean, thought long and hard about his life, his relationship with his 14-year-old girlfriend, Caril Ann Fugate, and how he was tired of being "a nimcompoop." He decided then that "these braggarts and good people are not laughing at a stupid garbage type . . . they'll have somethin' real interestin' to say after tomorrow. I am not scared of anybody that ever live. I've got a gun . . . I know how to shoot . . . I've got a girl. She likes my way of doin' things and I am not afraid of dyin', if I have to. I am not goin' to die like a rabbit . . . I am goin' to have somethin' worth dyin' about . . . and I'm not goin' to be the first one to die neither."

The next night Starkweather robbed a gas station on the outskirts of Lincoln. Complying at gunpoint with his demands, the lone gas station attendant, 21-year-old Robert "Little Bob" Colvert, handed over $108, slid into the driver's seat of Starkweather's 1949 Ford, and drove out to an isolated stretch of dirt road. While being forced out of the car, Colvert attempted to grab the barrel of the 12-gauge shotgun and was shot. Starkweather then got out of the car and shot Colvert once more in the back of the head.

Starkweather later told his biographer, Dr. James M. Reinhardt, a professor of criminology from the University of Nebraska, that he considered himself a "man of nature"; he hated everything associated with humanity, including himself: "Sometimes I'd look in the mirror and hate the sight of myself, but I just stayed there and looked and hated. Then after I had been lookin' at myself in the mirror, somebody would look at me and I wanted to bash in his face. . . . Everybody was against me. I hated the world. . . . People got always put in my way and blame me for hitting back. If you pull the chain on a toilet, you can't blame it for flushing, can you?"

Starting on January 21, 1958, Starkweather, accompanied by his girlfriend Caril, murdered ten people in eight days. The "flushing" began with the killing of three members of Caril Fugate's dirt-poor family: her mother Velda, her baby half-sister Betty Jean, and her stepfather Marion Bartlett. For six days they fended off friends, relatives and police by pretending the family was ill. They drank Pepsi Cola, ate potato chips and watched TV, then left the Fugate house and drove over to the farm of August Meyer, an elderly friend of the Starkweather family. Starkweather immediately shot the old man in the head at point-blank range with a sawed-off .410 shotgun and ransacked his house, netting nearly $100, some clothes, a .22 rifle, Jell-O and cookies. Later that night, after his car got stuck in the mud near Meyer's farm, Starkweather flagged down Robert Jensen and Carol King, a young conservative couple engaged to be married. He made them drive around in circles for a while, then forced them into an abandoned storm cellar. Police later found their bodies lying on top of each other: Jensen was shot six times in the back of the head, and King was found underneath him with her jeans and panties around her ankles, a fatal bullet wound in the back of her head, and numerous post-mortem stab wounds inflicted to her groin by a "stiletto-type" instrument.

The next day Starkweather and his girlfriend moved further up the social ladder by invading the Lincoln home of millionaire C. Lauer Ward, 47-year-old president of the Capital Bridge Company and Capital Steel Company. When they arrived at 8:30 in the morning, Mr. Ward had just left for work, but his wife Clara and Lillian Fencl, their deaf maid for twenty-six years, were still at home preparing breakfast. Starkweather had Mrs. Ward cook six waffles for him, inspected the house for a few hours, wrote a letter explaining his actions to the police, broke the neck of the family poodle, and then stabbed Mrs. Ward and the maid to death. When Mr. Ward arrived home later in the afternoon, Starkweather fatally shot him as he walked through the front door and then stabbed him several times. Leaving in Mr. Ward's 1956 Packard, he and Fugate headed towards the state of Washington. After crossing the Wyoming state line the next morning, Starkweather decided to trade cars with Merle Collison, a 37-year-old traveling shoe salesman asleep in his Buick by the side of the road. Since Collison wouldn't agree to a trade, Starkweather shot him nine times with the .22 pump rifle he had stolen from the Meyer farm. A geologist driving by pulled over to help, and was struggling with Starkweather over the rifle when a Wyoming deputy sheriff, witnessing the fight, also pulled over. Fugate ran towards the officer yelling "take me to the police . . . he's killed a man!," but Starkweather managed to break away and led police on a high-speed chase. When his rear window was shot out by one of the pursuing officers, Starkweather pulled over and meekly surrendered; his right ear had been slightly nicked by the broken safety glass. The sheriff who captured him told reporters, "He thought he was bleeding to death. That's why he stopped. That's the kind of yellow sonofabitch he is."

Remarkably, Starkweather later insisted that he killed all of his victims in "self defends." He also maintained, after initially denying her involvement in the killings, that Fugate played a major role in the more sadistic elements of the murder spree, telling authorities, for instance, that Fugate mutilated the genitals of Carol King in a jealous frenzy and laughingly shot the salesman to death while he was screaming for his wife and children. His testimony against her in court resulted in her being sentenced to life in prison. A model prisoner, she was released in 1977 at the age of thirty-two.

Between his arrest on January 29, 1958 and his execution on June 25, 1959, Starkweather worked voraciously on his autobiography. Reinhardt recalls "that he really enjoyed the 'freedom the death cell' gave him to work tirelessly on his manuscript. He said he was writing '. . . so that people wouldn't forget. . . .' " Starkweather also produced many drawings; Reinhardt noticed that "Charles showed some artistic talent [previous to the murders] but his interest in art was not sustained. It was only after he was sentenced to die and while awaiting the day of his execution that he bent himself tirelessly to drawing. He believed that people would want his pictures. He believed that they would find a market. He believed that people would only need to look to see the artistic side of one of the 'most notorious killers' of all time. When he was in school and later when he lifted boxes and emptied garbage, he could find no lasting joy and no promise for the future in drawing pictures."

Lincoln *Journal* reporter Marjorie Marlette, who helped Starkweather sell a heavily-edited article entitled "Rebellion" to *Parade* magazine for $1000, stated that "Charlie saw his book as a way of atoning, of making something good come out of the wrongs he committed. He wrote and rewrote and carefully copied each page – an extremely demanding job for someone with only a smattering of education. He just refused to let the mechanics of handwriting, the techniques of grammar and spelling, hold him back." Reinhardt, however, had dealt before with what he termed "chain-killers," and was somewhat more pessimistic about this method of "atonement." He was convinced that Starkweather was writing an autobiography for his own ego and a "fantastic notion about how he would be remembered, what people would say about him and how his unparalleled murders would popularize his 'book.' He thought that the sale of his cell written 'life story' would make his family rich." Perhaps the main reason for Starkweather's desire to put his "life story" down on paper can be gleaned from the following exchange he had with Reinhardt:

> Charles told me that he was writing his autobiography to keep other boys from going the way he went. When told that his crimes were very exceptional and that probably not one boy in twenty million would ever kill as he had killed, he was visibly moved. He said: "That ort to make it worth reading for lots a people wont it."

When Starkweather was arrested, police found a note in his jacket pocket that was written in pencil on three sheets of white stationery and enclosed in an envelope that had written on the front "for the law only." He wrote the letter, "with Caril's help," at the Ward house on January 28, 1958.

This is for the cops or law-men who fines us. Caril and i are writing this so that you and ever body will know what has happem. On tue.day 7 days befor you have seen the bodys of my non, dad and baby sister, there dead because of me and Chuck,Chuck came down that tue.day happy and full of jokes but when he came in nom said for him to get out and never come back, Chuck look at her" and say **why**" at that my dad got mad and begin to hit him and was pushing him all over the room, then Chuck got mad and there was no stoping him, he had his gun whit him cause him and my dad was going hunting, well Chuck pill it and the [drawing of a bullet] come out and my dad drop to the foor, at this my mon was so mad the she had a [drawing of a knife] and was going to cut him she knot the gun from Chucks hands, Chuck just stood there saying he was sorry he didn't want to do it. i got Chucks gun and stop my mon from killing Chuck. Betty Jean was about 10 steps from her, he let it go it stop some where would not stop Chuck had the [drawing of a knife] so he was about ten steps from her, he let it go it stop some where by her head. me and Chuck just look at them for about 4 hrs. then we wrapped them and pull them out in the house in back. my sisters and everone eles we not belived this but it's the true and i say it by **god** then me and Chuck live with each other and monday the day the bodys were found, we were going to kill ourselves, but Bob VonBruck [Starkweather's estranged best friend] and every body would not stay a way and hate my older sister and bob for what they are they all ways wanted me to stop going with Chuck show that some kid bob Kwen could go with me. Chuck and i are sorry for what we did, but now were going to the end. i feel sorry for Bar. to have a ask like bob. i and Caril are sorry for what has happen. cause i have hurt every body cause of it and so has caril, but i'm saying one thing every body that came out there was luckie there not **dead** even Caril's sister.

Chuck S.
Caril F.

so far we have kill 7 persons

Letter to his parents written immediately after his capture from his cell in Douglas, Wyoming, dated January 30, 1958:

Dear Mon and Dad. i'm a way i hate to write this or maybe you will not read it, but if you will i would like to have you read it, it would help me a lot.

i'm sorry for what i did in a lot of ways cause i know i hurt everybody, and you and mon did all you could to rise me up right and you all ways help me when i got in bab with something But this time i would like you not to do any thing to help me out. i hope you will under stand, i know my sister and brothers even nom, that this well take a long time befor people stop looking at them in a funny way. so it would make me happy if everbody well go on just like anything didn't happen. the cops up here have been more then nice to me but these **dam** reporters, the next one that comes in here he is going to get a glass of water.

But dad i'm not real sorry for what i did cause for the first time me and Caril have more fun, she help me a lot, but if she comes back don't hate her she had **not** a thing to do with the killing all we wanted to do is get out of town.

tell every body to take care. Chuck

P.S. tell Bob VonBruck to thing of somebody besids him he help to cause this.

While being transported by car from Douglas to Lincoln for his trial, Starkweather was held overnight in a cell in Gering, Nebraska. With a pencil borrowed from a guard, Starkweather scrawled the following confession on the cell wall high above the commode. Police did not find the writing until Starkweather later told them about it, and they immediately noted that Starkweather's figures were off: six males and five females were in fact murdered.

Caril is the one who said to go to Washington state.
by the time any body will read this i will be dead for all the
killings **then they cannot give caril the chair to.**
from Lincoln Nebraska they got us Jan. 29, 1958.
1958 Kill 11 persons (Charlie kill 9) all men
(Caril kill 2) all girls
11

[this statement circled:] they have so many cops and people watching us leave i can't add all of them of.

[written inside a drawing of a heart with an arrow through it:] Charles Starkweather and Caril Fugate

Letter to the prosecuting attorney, Elmer Scheele, accusing Fugate of killing Carol King:

Charles Starkweather
Box 111 Lincoln, Nebraska
March 28, 1958

Dear Mr. Scheele:

i'n writing this at ny own free will and well sign it when done. It would take to nuch paper to tell why i change ny mind of what happen if Caril f part of killing of Carol King? i Know my folks can tell you why i'n writing this. When i kill the boy out at the cave by the school house, he drop on the steps and landed on the foor in the cave. the King girl never ran or said anything i told her to stay right where she was i gone on dowm into the cave and he was moving a little, show i got up out of the cave and Carol King was standing right where i left here. "i think she was Schock" i went to the car to get a flash light Caril fugate was siting in the front and with the 4. 10, i gone down into the cave and was dowm there about 15 to 25 min. then i got scared and ran out of the cave and told King to go on down into the cave, and not even stay intull she got down she was on about the 2'd step and ran to the car, i was so dan scared i back of into a dichd. we got out of car to see what happen, i and caril went on back up to the cave and i told carol King to come on up. i gave the 22 cal. to caril fugate and told her to watch her, gone on back down to the car and was on the side jacking the car body up, then i heard a shot and ran back to the cave, caril said that King started to run and had to shot her. caril went on to car and got in it. i put the King girl in the cave, on about the 2 or 3 step from the top. the rest is in the statemind i gave you. when we got the car out i and caril walk up to the cave and past the door and some boards on the opening of the cave, if there is any details you would like to know about the King case come out or asked ny folks to asked ne, and i'll tell you. and the nan that got kill in wyoing, caril and i both shot hin! My writing is a little of a mess, but i hope you can read it.

Letter to his 8-year-old brother Greg:

Dear Greg:
thank you for letting ne read your book there's a lot of pictures in it and its a very nice book. But when you get older read the Bible it tells more about the Lord from the first of life to the end of life. but do not think that there is a end in the life of the Lord. cause there is no end, he is all ways a live. "to help you." . . . and do this for ne to — be nice to mom and dad and do all you can to help your mother. OK.

Your brother
Charles

The following passages were culled from Starkweather's handwritten 200-page autobiography by James M. Reinhardt and reprinted in his book *The Murderous Trail of Charles Starkweather.* According to William Allen, author of *Starkweather,* "though Reinhardt said that what he published of Charlie's writing was unedited, I have noticed some minor discrepancies; for instance, Charlie frequently wrote M's as N's, and this error was corrected in Reinhardt's book. I tried to locate Charlie's original manuscript to see if other editing had been done, but Reinhardt's widow said his files no longer exist." Reinhardt seems to have found Starkweather's autobiography valuable for his own book, but was contemptuous of Starkweather's own attempts to have his work published:

> In a way peculiarly his own, Charles actually believed that his story would be read by millions. That the people he had known and distrusted would be saying: "This is the guy we laughed at. This is the bowlegged red-headed peckerwood. This is the guy we sent to the chair . . . we laughed at the wrong guy . . . look, we laughed and had him killed and it was the wrong guy."
>
> Charles hung on to the wish to be remembered "as a new rediscovered Charles" to the last. He was afraid that his story might not be published under his own name. He was outraged and furious when I told him that his story would probably never be published exactly as he had written it.

I began to wonder what kind of life I did live in this world, and even to this day. I'm wondering about it, but it don't matter how much I use to think about it I don't believe I ever would have found a personal world or live in a worth-while world maybe, because I don't know life, or for what it was, they say, this is a wonderful world to live in, but I don't believe I ever did really live in a wonderful world. I haven't ever eaten in a high class restaurant, never seen the New York Yankees play, or been to Los Angeles or New York City, or other places that books and magazines say are wonderful places to be at, there hadn't been a chance for me to have the opportunity, or privilege, for the best things in life.

Yes, I went out with girls, some were mild dates with nice Christian girls, but most of the girls I went out with, were either the flibberty-gibbet type, that used to much make-up, and dressed in expensive clothes, or they were the harlot type, that weren't hard to get a date with, and easy to get along with. I had my fights that seem to happen every other day, and like almost everybody, I had my dreams of things I wanted. But of all the dreams, fights, and women to me none of then ever seem to fit in this world. I guess that's what I meant when I said, "I didn't know life, or what it was good for," and the reason I didn't know, I just didn't take time to fine out. When I was younger, I always said to my self that I was going to have the knowledge of what life was good for in this world, but as I grew older, the more I didn't care to fine out, and that's the reason why I didn't have time.

By this time my head was spining, and whirling, the remembrance of happy times, and unpleasant events that happen through-out my life came crowding through a foggy mist of recollection. This recollection of events, and many others were coming back to me, like a after vision of my past life.

Early childhood at home:

It was winter at the time we moved into our new home, and that same winter. Dad, came down with pneumonia, that almost costed his life. The night Dad was taken to the hospital, the hospital officials didn't have any knowledge that he hadn't had his evening meal, well, later that night, he had awakened, and being hunger, and thirsty for water, he left his bed-room in his nightgown in search of the kitchen, but in searching for it, he was interrupted by nurses, and interns, who had quite a struggle getting him back into bed. The next morning our family doctor, on arriving at the hospital, asked "how the patient was getting along?" When he heard what had happen the previous night, he said to the head nurse, "for God sake give the man something to eat."

I like almost all other young boys, was always playing cowboys, and Indians with my Brothers, we would play act, characters as Daniel Boone, Crazy Horse, Roy Rogers, Lone Ranger, and Wild "Bill" Hickok, or any other Western names we could think up. We'd all go whopping our way around the house, dodging trees, across the front yard, through long straight rows of corn, around behind the garage. Our garage had a large elm tree at it's side that we used for reaching the garage roof. The garage, we'd used for our imaginary fort. One time in particular, when going on five, We were playing cowboys in our imaginary fortress, I sliped, fell, and hit my head on the edge of a old wash tub, when I went up to the house, Mon, seen the blood coming down over my left eye, and got freightened, and called for a taxi, when the cab finaly came, Mon had the bleeding under control, but she cleaned me up anyway, and proceeded to town to our family doctor. The doctor examined me, and when I came home, I had two clamps over the cut, which now leaves a scar, that's hardly noticeable.

I wasn't the only member of the family that received injuries, like for instants at the age of four I remember one day during the summer before I arrived at the age of five. That, and it was a might hot day for my Sister who was going on three years of age, and my older brothers, it got hot for my sister and brothers that day, it all started out that morning. My sister, brothers and myself were out side all playing together, it was one of those nice summer days and Mon desided to do the laundry, and at that time mon was with child and wasn't to strong so my grandma desided to help (my mother's mother).

We didn't have a washing machine at that time, but dad was able to buy one a month later, but without the washer the washing water and rise water were in separate wash tubs and the laundry was cleaned by hand on a washboard. Mon didn't do as much as grandma, she tried very easely, so grandma did all the handing the laundry on the clothes line and most of the washboard work, and keeping the wash tubs full of cold water for the rinsing and hot water for the washing, felling the rinse tub with cold water wasn't so hard job at all, Mon had a short hose of just a couple feet long which could be connected to a common compression water faucet, but the hot water had to be heated, which means it had to be carried from the stove to the wash tub by bucket measures.

The bucket didn't have to be felled from the water faucet then carried to the stove, heated, then carried the wash tub, we didn't work it that way. The water bucket would be set on the stove over the burning flame and then the bucket would be felled from the water faucet by the small hose, then after the water was heated and was steaming hot the bucket was then carried over to the washing tub. Well, that hot water is what gave my little sister a hot day. Grandma, after the bucket of water was heated to a very hot temperature lifted the bucket from the stove and desided before pouring the hot water into the tub that she'll put more soap into the tub, so grandma sat the bucket of steaming hot water down on the floor. While my Sister, brothers and myself were playing, my sister said she was going to get some more toys to play with and tooked off running toward the house. My Sister never stop running until after she fell on the bucket of hot water. She ran to the house, up the back porch, opened the screen door and entered the kitchen, all this was one without a pause of the rapid running pace at which she was going, and the bucket of hot steaming water could not be avoided as she wented hurringly into the kitchen. My Sister burned her arm and a part of her side of the body. The burned, from what I understand has healed beautifully, and as far as I know does not leave a scar, but at the first sight of sis's burns mon used about a pound of butter on them, and while she was doing so, grandma called for a taxi and afterwards, called the doctor's office for appointment. The taxi cab come shortly after grandma's call was put in, and mon with my little sister in her arms lefted for the doctor's office.

Reinhardt observed that "Charles wrote the following about fourteen weeks before the date of his execution. He told me that he wrote it the night after: '. . . it all come back to me in a dream that woked me up.' "

It was a fascinating scenery, the cage contained lots of emphibious animals, frogs, toads, ducks, turtles, stork, swan, doves, cliff swallow's and cockotoo's, there were so many other typical nature aminals with in that cage, which would take to long to write out, and there's no means to go into detail about all the typical aminals with in the cage or with in the zoo.

In side the glass caged containers were, a rattle snake, bull snake, water snake, and a couple lizards were in a glass cage, — and at that time there was a boa constrictor, and between them all, I tried to analogize which one looked the wickeds and I couldn't deside which snake was. They all looked a creed of that of the devil, evil in eternal manifestation, I didn't like snakes then, and I don't like any part of them now, some people would think that's a childish, and irritating resultant atmosphere for some person to be in, and they most likely would think it's a thunderous observation, full of unmeaning, interogatories, but this discouragement of not caring for snakes was, I recognized, exceptional . . . being plaingly unpleasant and of a emotional stress, thinking of snakes, coming to meet, or looking at one, I don't have abit of feeling of emotions in caring and liking a snake.

Dad tolded me all he knew about snakes at my request in my younger days. I've met up with a few snakes in my days and to me I would rather meet a lion face to face, but as much as I dislike snakes, I used to hunt for them with a good friend for there skins, and I used to do quite a lot of reading on them. I read about there deadly pioson, and how it's injected, for example, the rattlesnake with his dangerous, wicked fangs which he bits with, and which the pioson fluid is injected through. I read alot of other things to about snakes, there living habits, shedding there skins, and etc.

Dad also instructed me exactly what to do if gotten bite, and after being bite, what to do, and what to . . . as far as with a non-piosonness snake. Dad showed my brother's besides myself how a person could avoid a snake. One way as dad showed us, is hitting the grass and undergrowth ahead yourself with a stick. Dad always walked in front of us while out fishing when we were little kids and even when we were older we did the same, by using stick, broken branch, (not so big that it cann't be carried) and shashing about ahead causes a disturbence, that usely mades the snake to move off crawling in the opposite direction in which the disturbing is being caused.

Dad was an exspert at handling firearms and by following his instructions and watching him, I learned the so call safty measures that had to satisfy dad before he'll permit me to carry and use a firearm. It is true that I have always been an out door sportsman, firearms besides automobiles, and besides that of my family, have been my ruling passion, but between the firearms, and automobiles, I rather hear the crack of a firearm than have, or drive the finist car in the whole wide world. I've done quite abit of hunting, and I've killed quite abit of gane, but I have deep affection for the animals I have killed, no animal is stupid, yet, I well agree there not all intellect in all respects, but they know when to hide, and when to run.

There's many a time I didn't shoot a game animal, instead I'd sat motionness, watching their tactics of living in the forest. I've had squirrel's come in arms reach. Being a sportsman, and out hunting all the time, and carrying a rifle wasn't what I liked — well, I liked hunting yes, and as far as carrying a firearm, well, a rifle, shotgun, or revolver, were the type of weapon I used for hunting, like for example some people use the long bow and arrow, or the crossbow and arrow, or other different types of weapons for hunting. I've too have used the longbow, and knife, to hunt with, but I wasn't very good at hitting a small target. Like for instants a squirrell. Squirrles in my opinion are hard targets, cause of there smallness, and I've losted a few costly arrows by hunting those small animals. It is very easy to lose a arrow when not active at shooting an bow and arrow, yes, I've come close to hitting the target, but just missing by a faction of a inch the arrow is either going to by pass the target, and while doing so, maybe stick to another tree, or land in the undergrowth, or it could — not by pass the target, but, miss though, and still stick to a branch, or limb of the tree which the aiming target was in, and just maybe that tree is one of those umpossible to climb, — (unless climbing gear is available) — and the arrow could be stuck in a branch, or limb, located at such elevation that throwing up broken brances to knock it lose, will also, be inpossible, but of either of them two examples.

There is a good chance of losing an costly arrow, and myself being not an exspert with a bow and arrow, I've losed a few of them costly arrows, but as far as hunting, and while doing so, carrying a firearm, I carried a firearm because that was the type of weapon I used for hunting, but that's not what I liked about being a sportsman with the sport of hunting, what I liked about being a sportsman of the out door like was that if I couldn't be a sportman, I couldn't be able to see, and adore what I liked best about the out door sportsman, and that was the scenery of the forest, and woods.

I was two going on three when we moved into the house, which was in the South part of town, and still in Lincoln, Nebraska. I was raised in this house through most of my child-hood, the place to me looked like a enchanted forest, with its large trees surrounding the house, and at times in the evening when the sun was setting in its tender glory, with its beautiful colors in the western sky, and the birds singing in their melodys that came softly from the trees — every-thing was nice and pretty, so peaceful, and tranquil — it was as though time itself was standing still. I fell in love with this adventurous land in my earlier days, and the flames still burns deep down inside of me for the love of that enchanted forest.

The house was shabby white one story structure with five Bed-rooms, a Living, and Dining-room, a Kitchen, with a pantry, six Closets, and full size Bath-room. also there was a full size Basement, which had a build in store room at one corner. The front porch was very large, and the back was some what smaller. The yards were the same as the porches, the front was tremendously large, with its big trees and shady lawn, and the back yard was somewhat smaller.

I found the beauty of the country side, in forest and woods of so many times while camping or hunting. At times instead of hunting I would set down against a large tree, and enjoy the scenery that made me delightfully full of satisfaction with my own immiscible surroundings. The fallen trees lay in a frightful tangle, and over and about them grew the undergrowth, the tupical trees stood stern with that of true supernatural features, and a primismatic, bridging over the tops of the trees that shute out most of the hot, warm flooding sunlight, and looking up my neck would ached from the constant strain while my neck would be bent back as I gazed above and between the jagged limbs, and branches of greenish, brown, and yellowish foliage, into the sky of miles, and miles, of undiscover, unknown, previously existence, and the more I sat and gaze into the far miles of the sky a wave of something would come over me, something like directness, and frankness, in a fascinating world away from that of non-committed civilization, such as a gust of unexpected wind.

Then a irrestible, and irresponsible feeling would sweep over my soul, but the feeling wouldn't stay for long, just temporarily, or just accordingly to how I felt. Sometimes the dream would be like a cloud sailing away with a incredible slowness to bring intimate knowledge of myself, or the dream would disappear with a quick flash at hearing the snap of a twig, or the sound of a voice, but most intruders that were experienced are considerable, undoubtedly an animal that would crossed my vision, than an act upon impulse which is cause more the result of intuition rather than logic. I'd be in a assuming carelessness, and preoccupied emotion, and reply at once with a clear conscience mind as all my interest changed to requiring attention of the intruder.

Something like a gigantic, enormous emotion, a beautiful model standing posed, and me eyeing her won't satisfy my emotions as much as it would if I was alone in the forest and woods. One thing that the country side is different from that of the city, is the atmosphere, the air is fresh, healthy with a sweet aroma, and when it's inhaled it makes the body feel strong, new and revive, as if reborned.

What I liked the most about the out doors was that the scenery was not imaginary, but of true nature, it was quiet and peaceful except for that of the birds singing with cheerful tones in the trees, some people would think it would be quite lonely out in the woods by ones self, well, that could be true, but it wasn't for me, I liked it, wanted it, I comed to have disbelief, and disliked, with bitterness of the human race in my younger school days, and from those days on, I didn't want nothing to do with them, or even be around any of them, so going hunting out in the country to its forests and woods, they couldn't bother me, and get on my nevers, — (people being on my nevers, I well tell about father along in this book) — although Dad and my brothers, we wented along together many times, I very sullen hunted with then, what I mean is we all wented together in the car, but arriving at the forest, I would go off by myself, not that I didn't really want to hunt with them, it was just that I wanted to be with my lonesome self. I adored everything about the outdoor scenery of that of the forest and woods. The beauity of its scenery is that of fascination, and the most enjoyable feeling to me is being in the forest by myself. There — it's so quiet and peaseful, that a person would think that time itself was at a stand still, to me being alone in the forest and woods.

Dad showed us how to build a camp fire, and how to use all safety precautions when building the fire, and the same safety precautions were used to destroy the fire. We wented on over night camping trips just about every week end. Dad showed me how to bait a hook, and when the bobber wented up above and down below the water line, but fishing never was my sport, I just never could set still, a melancholy weariness and restless feeling would sweep over me, I guess I didn't have the patience to wait for any fish to take the bait and hook, but I wented along though, and unstead of fishing, I'd played up, and down along the river bank.

Starkweather's account of his first day of school; according to Reinhardt, "I have talked to Charles' first school teacher. Her name was never Matt or Mott. Neither she nor anyone of a half dozen people, who remembered him during his earliest days at school, recalls that any child actually 'made fun' of him or 'ridiculed' him for his bow legs."

I was five years old when I started Elementary school in September, and became six in November. The first day school started I was filled with excitement and overwhelming joy that I was going to school and couldn't hardly wait to get there.

Walking along with my brothers to attend my kindergarten class all enjoyment and excitement left me and I became very tense and nervous. My brothers did their uppermost to explain that there wasn't nothing to be scare about but even with their hopefull explaining it didn't stop me from trembling as we walked along to school.

We arrived at the large two story red brick school building just as the bell was ringing, and after entering my brothers walked me exactly to the front entrance of a large room at which they bid their bood-byes.

The teacher then came before the class and very nicely introduced herself as Mrs. Mott and that she was going to be our teacher while we were in kindergarten grade and that she was sure we'll all get along together. Mrs. Mott then proceeded calling out the enrollment list we were informed to rise our hand as our name was called, which I did at hearing my name.

Mrs. Mott after showing and explaining and giving instructions about playthings and other items in the room, come before the class and we received instructions when to come to class and what time the class was over and that we didn't have to return until the next day, then our talk turned to discipline, discipline she said would be very important in our lives. Right at that moment the school-mistress [principal] entered the room, started talking about discipline the same as Mrs. Mott had just done the, school-mistress then as she was leaving, she tolded us how good she felt to have us all there and knew we would all get along well together.

Mrs. Mott after the school-mistress had left asked everyone to stand and put their right hand upon there left breast and reside after her, which was, The Pledge Allegation To The Flag, when we were done Mrs. Mott said that hereafter before the start of class we would all say together, The Pledge Allegation To The Flag, which I did up to my last day in school.

School that first morning we didn't go to much, Mrs. Mott let everyone play and do what they wanted, I didn't get along that day in school with the others, they made me a little mad but more upset than enything else, they didn't seem to want to have anothing to do with me, not let me play with them or anything else and thats the reason I played in the sandbox by myself that first morning, everybody left when I came over to play with them in the sandbox, they'd left went off among some other girls and boys talking about me, because out of corner of my eye, I glanced at them, the girls giggling and boys giving off their snickers, then they wented off occupying them selves to some other simple tasks. I played in the sand box all that morning by myself and a few minutes before noon Mrs. Mott asked everybody to stop what they were doing and put away what they had and wash up and for those who didn't have anything to put away just wash their hands and then line up at the door in single file. Lining up before the door I made sure I was at the end of the line because I knew, if I was somewhere in the line there been space between the others and myself, and I didn't want to hear the giggling and any snickering. After we were all lined up at the door Mrs. Mott bid her good-bys, and as the bell rung, she said for us to be very careful and look both ways before crossing the street, and she added, that our main subject in school was safty.

I walked home by myself after getting out of school but I wasn't worried about getting lose because before school started Dad and my Brothers showed me where the school building was and the way to come home from school. It only tooked about a half hour to walked home if I didn'nt stop to play around but mon had said for me not to delay and come straight home after school was out. Arriving home mon had dinner ready and was putting it on the table. I had been crying at first starting home from school, and after washing my hands and not forgetting the eyes, but even though I had rise out my eyes, I guess it didn't do any good, at least it didn't fool mon and as I tooked my seat at the table, as I started to eat my dinner mon asked why I had been crying, and I tolded her. I tolded of the kids teasing and making fun at my speech and bowllegs and that they wouldn't even play with me. "Well! I'll speak to your father about it when he comes home," mon said. I could tell by mons reactions that she felt hurted and I said "tomorrow if they do it I'm going to hit them," and added, "I had fun oh, the teacher was nice and ner name is Mrs. Mott, she's pretty to" — "Well" mon said, "I am glad you enjoyed school and like it so well, your brothers don't think much of it." — "I don't like it," I said, "I hate then kids and I'm going to hit one of then, if they don't stop making fun at me."

I laid down for my afternoon nap and it wasn't to long and I was sound asleep.

My brothers came home from school later that after noon and woked me up and asked how I liked school and got along.

my brothers just shoked their heads in an disgusted manner when I had tolded of what had happened that day in school and afterwards they changed their school clothes and we all wented out side. We all played together for a quite long period for the sun wented down in its tender Glory. It was getting dark by the time we had finished feeding and giving fresh water to the chickens, and then going into the house to help mother with the supper meal. The talbe was set and supper was being laid out on the talbe when Dads car came in the drive way. Dad washed him self and tooked his seat at the talbe, while eating Mon explained to Dad what I had tolded of what happen at school that previously morning. Dad didn't say much while eating, but later that night he called somebody by telephone who I tooked to be his boss cause Dad asked the other party line if it was alright if he came to work about a half hour late and he said that he had to explain my dispositions to the school principal. After talking awhile to the other party line Dad said, "thank you" and goodbye and hunged up.

I didn't like school any better that year in the first grade than I did in my kindergarten class, but I know, I hated it more than the year in kindergarten. I didn't cry anymore either when others picked and teased me, I would just get mad and smack them in the mouth, but it seemed like the more I fought those who teased me, the more I was being made fun at, but I didn't care, because I become to enjoy fighting. Well!, I didn't care being made fun at, and I just kept on fighting, the more I was teased, the more I fought. I won't deny I didn't get hurted at times, I came home a lot of times with a black eye, a cloded up nose cause from bleeding, and cut lip and even a few bruises weren't to uncommoned, but I assure you, the other person of who I would be fighting, didn't go home without being roughed up abit himself.

I began to love fighting, and would walk a mile just to fight someone. The school officials reported to my parents many different times, and tolded them I was going to have to stop my unreasonable fighting, and Dad would tell the school officials when the other pupils stop picking, and making fun of me, then, he'll instruct me to stop my fighting and not until. The pupils never stop their teasing and pestering, so, I never did stop fighting. Though there was once in my second grade that I did stopped, but it didn't last for long. What gave me more angry than the boys teasing me was the girls. Mon had instructed me time and time again not to hit a girl, no matter how mad they made me, "hitting a lady isn't being a gentleman," mon would say, but these girls weren't ladies, they didn't even have lady like manners, their behavior and demeanor showed they were not mannerly in respect for any one, at least their actions or behavior, cause youngsters usely follow the examples of elders and friends, but girls made me more angry than boys, their the ones who started calling me names other than Red headed bowllegеd woodpecker, names, ad brute, roughen, rugged — beast or just plain beast, rudey, and toughy. There were a few other names too, but those were the main ones.

My rebellion against the world started that first day in school and from that first day I became rebellious. I have stayed in my rebellious mood even to this day. Why had I become rebellious against the World and its human race? — cause that first day in school I was being made fun at, picked on, laughed at.

Why were they making fun at me? My speech for one thing and other was my legs, I was a little bowlleged. Maybe that's not much of an excuse to become rebellious. I knew as I grew older that it wasn't much of an excuse, but in those younger years of my life I haded builded up a hate that was as hard as iron and when people tease, make fun of and laugh at a little youngster in hers or his early childhood, that little youngster is not going to forget it. I wouldn't deny I was like a hound prowling for fights, quarrelling, and doing wild things and placing everyone among my enemies. Kids picking on me and not having a thing to do with me caused me to have black moods, at least that is what I call them, cause most of the time, I would just sit in one place and stay motionless in a gloomy manner and it was obvious that there was no reasoning with me when in one of my Black mood and Boys and girls that I knew didn't bother me while I was in my motionless and gloomy manner, they would just let me be and stay in my Black mood, and even to this day I still have them melancholy moods.

The hate that became strong inside of me when I was a youngster by those who were making fun and always teasing me are the ones that started me to fight. I would beat them down and if I had to I would beat them down again until they knew that I wasn't going to take it from them. At times and with the right emphasis my attitude was merely a sporadic outburst, but at other times as I realized now was something thonie, when I was fighting those who picked on me, I fought fast and a little furiously like a mamiac in rage and fury and as I fought sense of outrage grew to striving, to throw, to bend, to hurt and most of all to beat those who teased me, but as I fought the general opinion of school kids became particularly that I had a reputation for meanness or generosity and that word REPUTATION . . . as many other kinds know is a hard thing to stand up to at times, when they say that your a fighter and have the reputation for doing nothing but fighting and then there's going to be a few kids like yourself that are going to fight and try to take that reputation away from the other fellow.

My fighting repretation stayed with me throughout my school years and even after I had stopped going to school that repetation stayed with me, but my rebellion started against the world and the human race when I was being maded fun at and that being maded fun at is what cause my fights when I was a youngster, but I assure you thats not the reason for fighting when I grew up but the hatred I had builded up inside of me stayed with me and it made hate everybody other than my family, but with that strong hatred, a person wouldn't look at me cross eye without getting into a fist fight. My speech and bowllegs were my main cause for being made fun at as I grew older my speech defect was over come and I can now pronounce words with an defined and correct pronuciation as well as any one else and for my bowllegs, their just as crooked as before, I never have been able to grow out of them and if I have to say so myself, I believe a pig could run between them without touching the sides.

One by one the kids wented before the class to tell of their summer doings and of their hobbys, if they had one. I sat listening to them in silence as they tolded about them selves going swimg, shows, fishing, camping and some tolded about going to other states to vist their relatives. As I sat listening I became more anxious to tell my summer activities, I had no hobbys but I could tell of good times I had playing with my brothers, tell of all the vegetables I helped mon can up in jars, I hadn'nt every gone swining, but I had gone to shows with mon and Dad and I did go fishing many times with Dad and my Brothers. I couldn't hardy wait until it was ny turn which was about last cause my last name started with a "s." then as Mrs. Mott called out my name I felt sly and awkward as I got up from my seat and wented before the class, and as I had walked pass the other girls and boys to get before the class, I heard the girls and boys give off their little giggles that started my heart pounding hard against my chest.

As I moved my lips in motion to speak I became nervous and a sob of breath seem to stopped in my throat, after a few seconds of silence I began to tell of my summer activitys, I was talking very quiet and I guess the other kids couldn't hear me because I was interrupted by Mrs. Mott, "speak a little louder Charlie, so everyone can hear you," — so I spoked louder and as I did my pronunciation of words got mixed up and all at once the whole class bursted into laughter. I goggled around at the kids laughing and I tooked a gripped of my self. I began to speak again my voice was smerying faint and cracked, the kids bursted into laughter again, I flinch, startle, flaccid, lacking in firmness, then I was completely flabbergast as my words became flat as I started to speak again I sadden they had no regard for my feelings, I swallowed dryly, glanced toward Mrs. Mott exspecting her to help me but she was observing me with unspoken admiration of my silence, then as I started to moved my lips in motion to speak Mrs. Mott said, "you may set down if you like Charlie".

Mrs. Mott didn't have to say any more, I wented back to me seat and while sitting down in my seat I noticed I was being laughed at and stared at with mocking looks. Their were just a few left to tell of their story of their summer doings and hobbys, and while Mrs. Mott called off their names and they were talking I sat in silence, but swearing to myself. I cursed every person in the class profanely, including Mrs. Mott and I made a solemn vow, a prionise to myself that I'll never stand before another group to make a speech. This vow was carried out throughout my life, but I did breaked it twice, once in the eight grade, and being president of a Hot Rod club I had to give talks many times before a group of teenagers, of these two different events there was only one time the laughter broked out, that was in the eight grade, but of these two different times my solemn vow that I maded in kindergarten, was carried out throughout my life.

I walked over to the play house and what happens, there were only a couple of kids playing in it and they lefted when I wented inside. I sat down on a little chair inside the play house. I sat staring out the little door, glaring antagonists, pinioned, thus, strained toward the kids about the room, I sat in silence as my heart was pounding against my breast as it was rising involuntarily in an occasional deep reminiscent sob, than my deformity compelled, by heart became a grimace of hatred, crimson, and than my heart as though to have matirialized out of the atmosphere a wildcatten hatred burned into it, and it seem as though I could see my heart before my eyes, turning dark black with hate of rages, of harhequinade, stripped from that of munner life leaving only naked being-hate. It seem like I had been there for ages as my thoughts were broken by Mrs. Mott, "Charles, why did you tell these children to get out and not to play in the fun house"? I sat regarding Mrs. Mott with anvious eyes, by head forehead wrinked, than I just shrugged my shoulders, "Well! you come on out," said Mrs. Mott.

As I got out of the play house Mrs. Mott said "Charles we don't act like that — we share and share a like, so don't be telling any of the kids that they cannot play where they want to — is that understood"? Before I could answer she put in as though an after thought, "Why don't you draw your mother a picture," and again before I could answer she tooked my arm and walked me over to our desks. I seated myself and as I did she said that she'll be right back. While Mrs. Mott was gone I glanced around and I noticed there wasn't anyone else around setting at the desks, they were at the sandbox, the play house I had just come from, on the floor, a lot were drawing at the talbes and I began to wonder why I had to set at the desk and not with the others, but I knew they wouldn't stay at the talbes if I was there any way so I didn't care if I was there or not.

The team leaders began picking players for their team, if the leader didn't know the name of a boy he wanted on his team he would pointed at the boy and Mrs. Mott would call out his name and she did the same for the girls. There was a uneven number of boys in the class and at the end of picking the teams there was just one boy left that wasn't picked yet, and that boy was a redheaded, bowlleged kid, that boy was I, the team leader that was his turn had to pick me, (at least I thought he had to) the boy was histateding but as he started to pointed toward me Mrs. Mott saved him she said that each team had an equal amount of players and that there was no reason for one team to have more then the other and that, sent my heart missing a few beats, Mrs. Mott then asked, "Would it be alright with you Charles if you would act as substitute, would you like that?" I sadden, I wanted to play kick socker as well as any other kid, I loved the game, I played it many times with my older brothers, and now, that I wasn't going to get to play, my heart droop and sadden, and in slipt second I had a notion to turn, run out of school, but the notion disappeared. Mrs. Mott was waiting for a answer, but my feelings were so hurt that I had a hard time getting any words out with out breaking down into tears but some how I answered her with a low whisper and nodded my head to disguise my increudulity. "Well!" Mrs. Mott said; "you stay along the back stop, near the bench, close by in case some one gets hurt you then take his place."

I didn't have a jacket at school that day, it was to nice a day to wear a coat to school, so I just stood, watching the others, first the girls and then the boys, and as the girls wented by I heard their giggles as they glanced toward me and then talking among them selves and as the boys wented by, they began calling me bowlleged and saying, "you think you can kick with those bowllegs?" I felt like cutting loose, kicking them right in the teeth, just to show them that I could kick as well as anybody else, and then, three boys stopped in front of me, one of them starting imitating my speech and the other was imitating my bowllegs the other stood laughting about it, and while they were doing the imitating act of me a black rage swepted over me and the hatred was building it self up inside of me more every second. I got so mad that tears came to my eyes and my knees began to shake, then one of the boys said, "look! he's going to cry," and at that time and moment, I brought one of those bowllegs back in motion to kick, and at the same moment, I was going releast my foot, Mrs. Mott interrupted us, "come along boys, come along, lets go outside, come along now, — you to Charles."

The boys and myself turned and walked out of the room, and I at their heels and as I started to moved a little faster to get out side before them, but as I got along side of them, one of the boys elbow me so I dropped back and follow them until we came to the basement enternce, there I stood, out of sight, a few seconds later Mrs. Mott passed and I watched her go out side. I sat down on the top step of the basement steps and as I sat there in silence, I said to myself that some day I'd pay them all back, and a overwhelming sense of outrage grew, it roused itself in my mind for wild thirsting revenge, I wanted in general revenge upon the world and its human race, my mind and heart became black with hatred as it builded up in me, a drawn veil of a dilatory cloud seem to come befor my face, the tribute was gratifying, I could not anglyze nor recoqnice my emotions as I broked down into tears.

I stayed in my melancholy for a long period, but after awhile I drid my tears and sat in silence conscious of nothing but miserly and depression, I couldn't understand why they didn't want me to play with then, I hadn't commited no wrong, then, my thoughts were broken as I heard the girls and boys coming in from recess I wanted for a few minutes as I heard the kids go by and also heard Mrs. Mott go by as she said something about not to run in the hall, the sounds of foot steps thined out a little I stood preplexed a moment longer, at last I moved off, following up behind the other kids.

I had the whole sandbox to myself, Everybody left as I came up to the sandbox and started making little hills out of sand, but I was only there a few minutes before Mrs. Mott came over and said, "Charles! you had the sandbox all to your self yesterday and I believe you should give somebody else a chance to play in it do day, so you run along and appley your self with something else.

I lefted the sandbox and that was the last time I ever played in the sandbox in the kindergarten, matter fact, it was the last time ever played in a sandbox at school.

Walking home [from school] I didn't notice anyone following along behind me until I heard giggles and laughter. I kept walking as I glance back over my shoulder and there they were, a half dozen girls and boys making wise cracks about my bowllegs, red hair and speech. I could hear them imitating my speech as I kept walking. I walked two or three blocks before I thought if I turn, go home a different way that maybe they would keep walking with out following up behind me. At the next corner I turned to head a different way home, but the wise cracks, imitating, giggles and laughter was still following behind me.

I stopped as I came to the next corner as a approaching car was coming down the street. The girls and boys stopped behind me. I glanced around and there were only a few, some of them I figured musted have kept walking as I hoped all of them would have done when I turned the corner. One of the boys started telling out loud, "the Bowlleged, Red headed, wood pecker — the bowlleged, red headed, wood pecker," meanwhile the first car that was coming wented by and another car was proceeding from the oppited dicton, so I stood waiting for it to pass and by this time everyone of the youngsters were pestering me as they joined in with the first boy yelling — "the bowlleged, red headed, wood pecker, — the bowlleged, red headed, wood pecker," then all at one the boy that seem to be the leader of the rest, he tooked a couple steps forward, gave a hardy voilment shove that sent me into the street. The apporiving automobale with its tires screching and as I felt I seen the driver eyes which were or looked as big as dolars. The car came to a full stop not more than a few feet away, as I got up off the street, I wonder if it was a girls scream or the tires that made the loud noise.

Standing up, I looked toward to boy that had shoved me and as I did he said sobbishly, "what happen bowllegs! cann't you stand — won't those bowllegs hold you up?" then a boys voise broked out and I new the voise was that of the boy that seem to be the leader, "look at those legs would you," the giggles and laughter started in I noticed one of the girls giggle were higher pick than the rest and it seem to crack and as she giggled, "hey whata git in your hand," the leader boy demanded and at the same time jerked the paper that was rowed up and had in my hand and was the painting I had made for mom.

I stopped a few steps ahead of them and gared at the boy who had jerked my painting from me and now was unrowing it. They all gathered around the boy that had my painting and right away they started making wise cracks about it. I just stood there listening to there wise cracks my blood was getting stream up and the most overwhelming desire to tear into them with fists a flying or pick up a stick, brick, stone, anything to beat their lousy brinds out swept over me, but mon had tolded me the day before not to fight so I dismissed the overwhelming desire from my head. The boy with my picture, looking at me with a big smile said, "this is a piece of junk, besides being a red head, bowlleged, wood pecker — you cann't even draw," and at that, tore it in half and as the laughter and giggling began he glanced around at them and finished ripping it into little pieces. I stood watching my painted picture being tore into little pieces and had to gripped my jaw tooth against tooth to keep from crying at least I thought it would keep me from crying and it did at least from crying out loud but it didn't keep the tears from creeping from my eyes and tears came rowing down my cheeks and I looked at my painted picture what was left of it all scattered in little bits on the ground then one of the girls yelled searcastily he's going to cry — hes a cry baby then they started in the red headed bowlleged wood pecker is a cry baby the red headed bowlleged woodpecker is a cry baby the red headed bowlleged wood pecker is a cry baby at that I turned ran as fast as my legs bowlleges could carry me.

Answers "to a series of questions asked him, in the prison, six weeks before the date of execution as originally set by the court. At the time the questions were given him Charles believed that his answers would receive nationwide publicity." Pages are excerpted, with some pages excluded, by Reinhardt.

1- question: What is the most important message you want to tell the people of the United States at this time in the way of advice to other kids after your experiences?

Answer: My advice to the young people of today is to go to school, and attend Sunday school, and Church every Sunday. Go to Church and recieve the Lord Jesus Christ as your own personal Saviour. Our God is a kind God, he'll forgive, and excpet you as one of his even if your heart is black and heavy with sin. With God there be peace with in your soul, and in Heaven eternal life will be in your hands through all eternity. You can feed the mind with knowledge, and the body with food, but don't forget the soul, feed it with the love and the words of the Lord. So i advice young and old to attend their Church of God and worship the Lord Jesus Christ, and pray that we can maintain the Christian faith that holds together the trust, the truth, the love, and the righteousness of the American people, and the people of the World.
Also i advice the young of today to attend their schools, and and take adventage of the free education our forefathers created, and that same education amongst many other acts of Democracy America has fought so hard in bloody battles to have and maintain. Our county has fought and won again and again for the type of Democracy that we want. Our soldiers had died in battle slain just so we could have freedon of speech, the privilege of doing, going, and coming as we please, a Church of our choice, and working where, when, and as we wish, and most of all so we could have free schools to attend, — free from propaganda, and the teachers are not a unit of Colonels who wear armbands, and take you out and have you shot at sun raise if you don't read and learn just and only just what they want you to. Our free schools provide us with the

education that will make us the future Americans of tomorrow, but we don't realize it. The girls and boys who quit when they become of age are the ones who don't realize it. They don't realize how important education will be in their lifes. So don't make the mistake of quiting school, — oh i know you might get a job, save enough momey to buy a automibile, and have alot of momey to spend on dates, but tell me what do you have in the long run? —. will, i'll tell you, you haven't a thing that amount to anything. It's that High school and college diploma that takes all the gravy in the future. I have regret this experience in the pass. I quit school when i came of age, got a job that didn't amount [page missing here]

question:

(5) had you ever thought of committing any violence before the spree? —

answer:

I had the reputation for fighting and raising cain all the time and you could even say there was alittle of violence in it, but i never ever had any intentions, or thoughts of committing such violence and unjustable crimes as that of the spree.

question:

(6) at the time you did these killings, why did you think that you were right in doing that? — have you changed your mind on your feeling that you were right?, at the time you were running away from the police, were you scared?, what did you have to gain from these killings?

answer:

The killings **"WE"** ["WE" also circled for emphasis] committed some of the victims were killed while we were defending our own lifes, and the others exactly did attempt to block our path of escape. It's unknown to me what Caril's [page missing here]

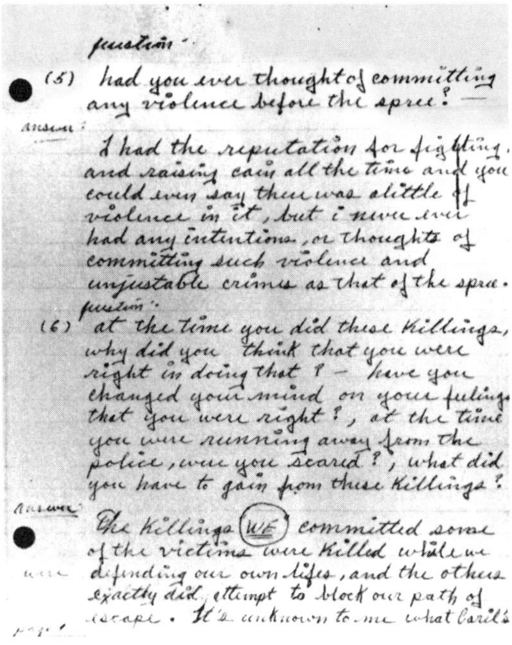

question:
(5) had you ever thought of committing any violence before the spree? —
answer:
I had the reputation for fighting and raising cain all the time and you could even say there was alittle of violence in it, but i never ever had any intentions, or thoughts of committing such violence and unjustable crimes as that of the spree.
question:
(6) at the time you did these Killings, why did you think that you were right in doing that? — have you changed your mind on your feelings that you were right?, at the time you were running away from the police, were you scared?, what did you have to gain from these Killings?
answer:
The Killings (WE) committed some of the victims were Killed while we defending our own lifes, and the others exactly did attempt to block our path of escape. It's unknown to me what Caril's

that i was going to give up as we were driving back to Lincoln from Bennt. Caril then threadened out loud that she wasn't going to give up, and that i, or no one else was going to make her, and with a shotgun lying across her lap with the baerow pointing directly at me, and with her fast talking she convince me that we didn't have anything to gain by giving up. But now I'm sorry and regret that i ever listened to her, instead gave up and just took the chance of being shot by her. ———

-7- answer: dreams of no such nature.

question:
(8) do you feel sorry for the victims?

answer: My feelings are of great sorrow and remorse for the people we have killed. And for the heartache, and sorrow, and greif we cause to the people who lost their love ones, my feelings are much deeper get, and i pray that God will forgive us for what we have done.

(9) question: how do you feel about Caril today? —

answer: Any feelings towards Caril are of great regret for ever knowing her. In the past Caril and myself had a lot of good times with fun and excitement together. Our love in the beganing was very ardent and passionate. But as time went along our love tappered off to emotional passion and lust, and time went on and on my love for Caril began to fade out, but it didn't fade out and die fast or soon enough and eventuality led to my down fall.

Today as i put it, my love for Caril is competely dead. It took a long time to end, and wish it would have ended long before now. I hold no grudge against Caril, and as far as caring for her, my feelings are none of what so ever.

(10) question: can you explain why you killed? —

answer: the question has been partly answered in answer to question number six-(6) ——

(11) question: what are your thoughts and feelings today as you face the date of execution?

answer: The past year has been one of imprisonment. I have had a great deal of time for thought and to retrace back over my life. I am young, and under normal circumstances my life would still be ahead of me. Going to the electric chair will bring my life to an end. I hold no fear for the elecetric chair, it is the price i am paying for taking the lives of others. Bringing my life to an end does not answer why certain things took place. Going to the electric chair will bring to an end my search for answers that are hard to fine.
God alone knows how i have suffered and if he feels i have had enough, then with his help i'll go unafraid to the elecetric chair. If for any reason the Lord feels that i haven't suffered long enough, then i'll go on living my tormented life. —

(12) question: favorit teacher, and why?

answer: My favorite teacher was of one whom i had in my last year in school. She didn't act like she was better or smarter than the others, and this one teacher of all the other school teachers didn't act as though she had it in for me. —

Shortly before his execution, Starkweather stated the following to Reinhardt regarding his vision of what he called "Death":

> She comed in a dream . . . she tolded me . . . don't be in no hurry. I won't let you forget.
>
> One time, *Death* comed to me with a coffin and tolded me to get in . . . then the coffin sailed away with me in it till it comed to a big fire . . . the coffin sort of melted, I guess, I was down there on a street with great flames of fire on each side of me. But it wasn't hot like I'd always thought hell would be. . . . It was more like beautiful flames of gold . . . then I woke up. . . .
>
> I don't known how it was, but I would always wake up and see her standing there in the window . . . and all I could see would be the part from the waist up. It was a kind of half human and half bear . . . only it didn't have no neck. It just tapered off from a big chest to a small pointed head. . . . It didn't have no arms and no ears. It was close and loud at first, but it got further and further away and the sound became mournful and sad until I couldn't hear it no more.
>
> I knowed that *Death* was comin', but I never thought it would be comin' like this . . . eleven people dead who wasn't expectin' her and me here waitin'.

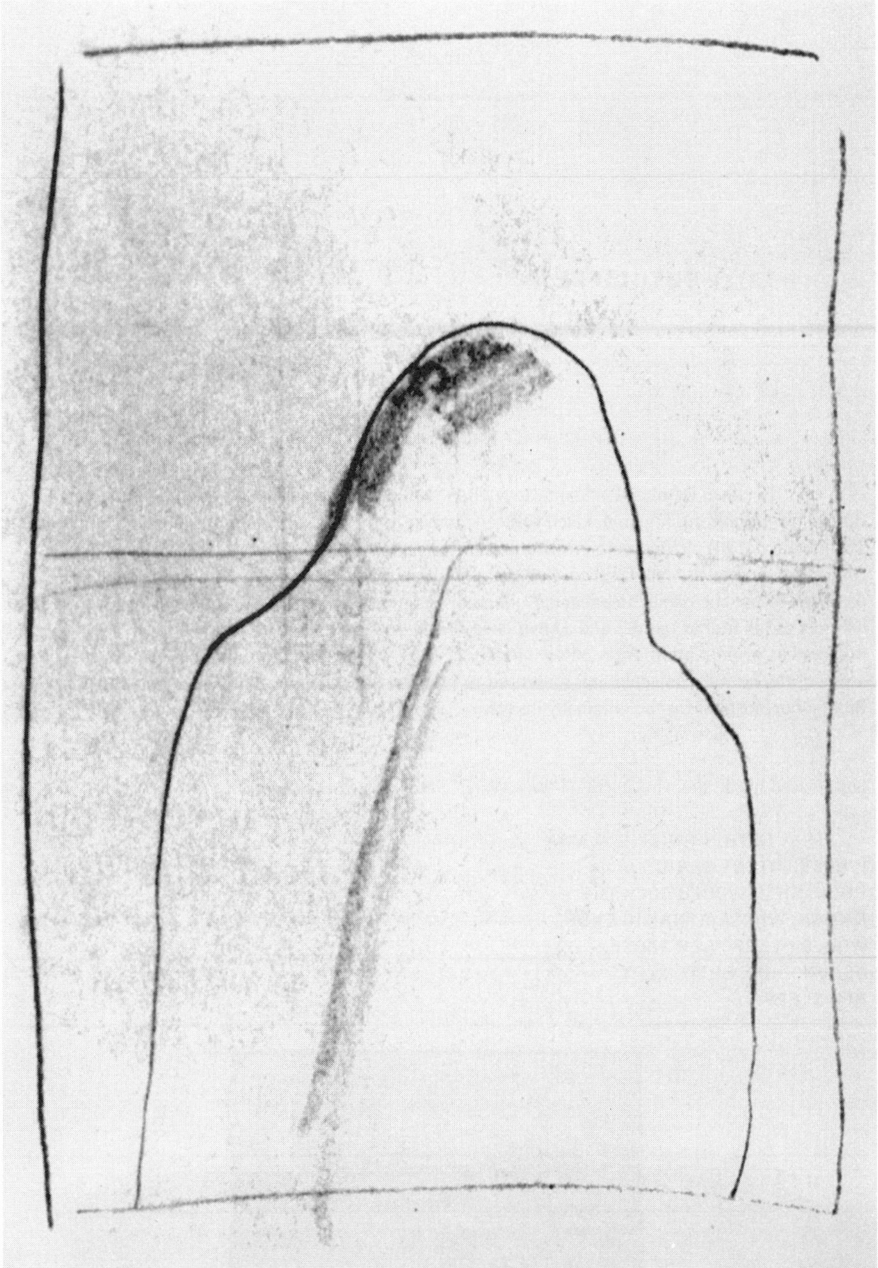

PETER SUTCLIFFE

Between October 1975 and November 1980, Peter Sutcliffe, a truck driver in his early thirties from Bradford, England, killed thirteen women in the area of West Yorkshire and Lancashire. The majority of his victims were prostitutes, but the police noted that he had also killed some "innocent" women as well. Dubbed the "Yorkshire Ripper" by the British press (Sutcliffe himself preferred to use the name "Headbanger" when discussing the "Ripper" with friends), he used a hammer as his tool of murder and a sharpened Phillip's screwdriver and kitchen knife as his instruments of mutilation. Arrested on January 2, 1981, while attempting to have sex in a car with a prostitute, he was convicted and sentenced to life in prison. He is currently serving his time in Broadmoor Hospital for the criminally insane.

Sign placed inside the windshield of "Wee Willy," Sutcliffe's truck at work:

IN THIS TRUCK IS A MAN
WHOSE LATENT GENIUS IF
UNLEASHED WOULD ROCK THE
NATION, WHOSE DYNAMIC ENERGY
WOULD OVERPOWER THOSE
AROUND HIM. BETTER LET
HIM SLEEP?

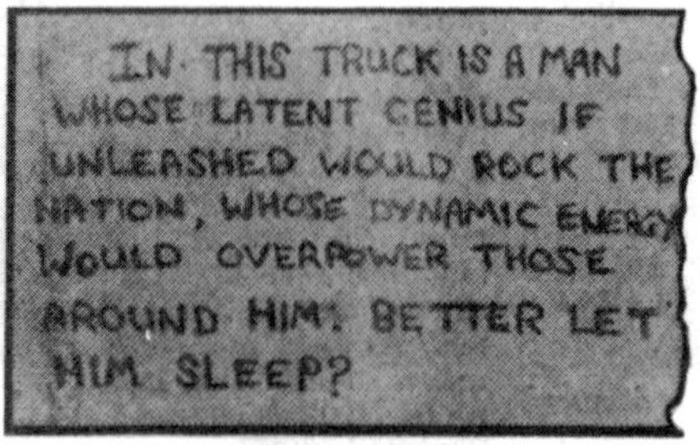

On September 6, 1979, four days after the murder of Barbara Leach in the town of Bradford, Sutcliffe sent the following poem to the Sheffield *Star*. Police didn't realize it was the writing of the "Yorkshire Ripper" until after Sutcliffe's arrest. "OLDFIELD" and "HOBSON" refer to Assistant Chief Constable George Oldfield and Detective Chief Superintendent Jim Hobson, the officers in charge of the investigation of the murders. "DRURY" refers to Ken Drury, an ex-Commander of the Scotland Yard Flying Squad who had just been released from prison after serving 26 months of an eight-year sentence on corruption charges.

'Clueless'

POOR OLD OLDFIELD
WORKED IN A COLDFIELD

HOBSON HAS NO CHOICE
MISLED BY A VOICE

RELEASE OF DRURY
AROUSES FURY

BRADFORD WAS NOT ME
BUT JUST WAIT AND SEE

SHEFFIELD WILL NOT BE MISSED
NEXT ON THE LIST

'The Streetcleaner'
(T.S.)

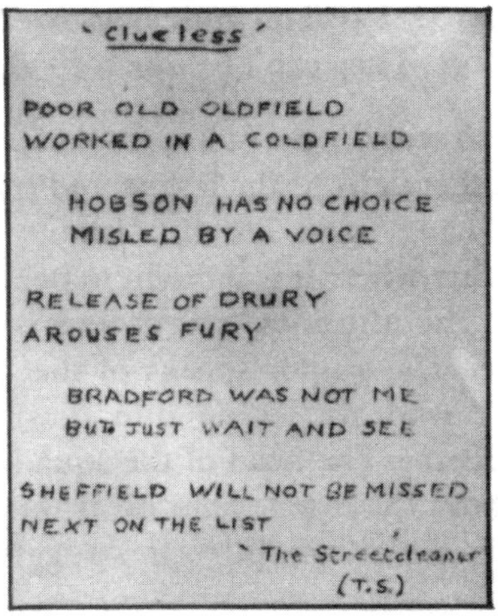
'Clueless'

POOR OLD OLDFIELD
WORKED IN A COLDFIELD

HOBSON HAS NO CHOICE
MISLED BY A VOICE

RELEASE OF DRURY
AROUSES FURY

BRADFORD WAS NOT ME
BUT JUST WAIT AND SEE

SHEFFIELD WILL NOT BE MISSED
NEXT ON THE LIST
'The Streetcleaner'
(T.S.)

DENNIS SWEENEY

Fifty-one-year-old Allard Lowenstein, a former congressman and well-known civil rights activist, was killed in his Manhattan law office by a former associate and friend, 37-year-old Dennis Sweeney, on March 14, 1980. Beginning in 1972, Sweeney became convinced that the CIA had implanted a "sensor" in the fillings of his teeth to listen to his thoughts. In 1975 Sweeney called Lowenstein and told him to "call off your dogs"; the various individuals and agencies that he imagined were conspiring against him had coalesced into the person of Lowenstein. When Sweeney's stepfather died on February 24, 1980, Sweeney was convinced that Lowenstein was responsible for the death. To stop the "voices," he shot Lowenstein five times, reportedly saying before he fired, "We've got to put an end to this, Al." He pled guilty by reason of insanity on February 23, 1981, and was institutionalized for life.

Excerpt from a letter sent to a couple Sweeney knew in the spring of 1973:

We were never really close friends, I realize, but I need some trustworthy advice so that I can begin to plan my life again instead of being perpetually on the run. . . . I don't know any more poetic way of saying it, but I am at the lowest ebb of my life now because of the psychological warfare that is being made on me, since about two years ago. I don't believe I am alone in that respect, but since I am alone and have been prior to leaving California in '72 my perspective has become entirely subjective. The specific way in which this psych war has been effected has been a revelation. I am simultaneously attuned to and programmed electronically, apparently, causing obliteration of an already weak ego, social objectification and ostracization, and a freeze on my ability to reintegrate myself intellectually for not being able to sort out my own thoughts from the impulses running through my skull. I am fairly certain that I have software that I wasn't born with. I have done everything I can think to do to locate it and remove it. My efforts have all been failures and usually self-destructive.

No doubt in the Sixties I was a party to some behavior that was politically irresponsible. If that incurred a social debt then I am willing to pay it in reasonable terms with some sense of limits such as definition of what constitutes rehabilitative service and duration of same, as opposed to bureaucratic sadism and infinite guilt which is what I see confronting me.

More likely, I think, is that my whole life since early childhood is tangled into a kind of self-aborted preparation for social democratic leadership, where the lines of responsibility for thought and action are very muddy. Unwilling to live my life on the terms that have been revealed recently, that is as a component in a vast communication system, I think I am simply being pressured to leave the country. . . .

I take it that I cannot undo myself from this system within the system. If that is not an absolute rule then I am open to suggestions as to how to go about it, for I really don't feel up to starting over at age thirty in another culture. If that is the reality of the situation, though, I would like to know where you think I might travel to find the medical help I want. . . .

I know we're all up against it now, and I wish I were not so divided from humanity that I can't pitch in. I hope you are both in considerably better shape than me, and if I can work this out we will see each other again. Excuse me for being overly familiar with this letter, but there are some situations in which everyone seems almost equi-distant and a reach might be excusable. I hope I hear from you, and that your lives go well through the next three years.

Sincerely,
Dennis Sweeney

After his arrest Sweeney gave a 31-page letter to his attorney, excerpted below. He wrote that he heard voices from two sources: "family and friends" and

. . . a small group of Jews from New York directing me to whom I should marry. Since I was being treated like a guinea pig with a bombardment of sound waves, they extrapolated that I should be married like a guinea pig and, judging from the treatment I was getting, provide a family of experimental rats whose origin could not be thought of as having anything to do with myself and who would be the result only of . . . self-preservation such as inmates experienced in the Third Reich. . . . Had I more understanding of the racial antagonism felt toward gentiles by Jews and the vanity some Jews feel . . . my depression would have been lessened.

Voices in the shower would remind me of a coworker's mistake and suggest "wouldn't you like to give him the bump?" . . . a female voice would say, "you're wasting yourself. You should be working for us." And another implied that I was effeminate and making homosexual overtones to the neighbor by having cleaned the shower in the bathroom which we shared . . . One of them kept referring to me as Sben Whoona which I took to be a Jewish nickname for recalcitrant, blue-eyed, Aryan types.

Mr. Lowenstein's voice over the previous six years had been telling me with whom I should be spending my time and whom I should marry. Of late, it had grown weary of peering down at me so I decided to interpret his claim . . . as an expression of frustration of trying to make me a feudal liege, so I wrote him a letter. I said I had no respect for any of the movements or ideologies he had lived to spawn in the 1970s and that I would not even be a member of his following. I told him I wanted to be forgotten as soon as possible. . . . the man [was] killing others to make me feel like a coward. . . . the pattern of these New York Jews insulting and fighting with my family when it was me they had been acquainted with overcame my restraint against wasting time.

I explained to him that I wanted to return to my home in Oregon, but that before I could do so with any ability to function, I needed his word that insofar as he was aware of any anger or vendetta against me by himself and a few others, that he restrict it to myself and not cause any harm to anyone near or dear to me. He said that he couldn't give me that kind of pledge and that he thought I should see a psychiatrist. If I needed any help in doing so, he would be glad to assist. He said I had to begin by helping myself. . . . I then took the gun out of my pocket and said that in the light of what I had seen, his statement was not good enough for me, and I began to fire.

Letter sent in 1981 to a former member of the Peace and Liberation commune:

I got your card yesterday and have no trouble answering immediately with all the time I have. . . . As you may know, I have been troubled for the past ten years by "voices" which interfere with any unarticulated stream of consciousness. The group whom the "voices" represent have made a prescenium of my life for the presentation of their own lifestyle to the American public. Among those voices, most of whom I can identify, has been yours. Among the last impressions I had before I made the decision to drive down to N.Y. with a gun in my possession to see Al was a memory of being home in Oregon for my stepdad's funeral just two weeks previous. After a visit to the funeral parlor to view the open casket, I was running an errand for my mother and as I strolled through a supermarket, yours and David's voices were presented to me as darting around the aisles hinting at complicity with my stepdad's death. I was very depressed about the addition of your consent to the "voices" who were already claiming responsibility for his heart attack. I came to the conclusion that I couldn't drag that scene around the continent anymore as it appeared to be involving an increasing number of deaths and injury every day. I don't know with what amount of consent your voice has been used over the past years, but I was pleasantly surprised to receive a note from you. I was glad to hear that despite everything else you are still the same person you were fifteen years ago. . . . Write again if you like, or until then,

Yours truly,
Dennis

T. T. A.

A case history illustrated in the forensic textbook *Crime and the Sexual Psychopath* as an example of "Sadistic Pedophilia (Homicide)," "T. T. A." sexually assaulted and murdered a little girl in Burley, Idaho on November 16, 1948. The author, Los Angeles police psychiatrist J. Paul de River, at first describes his subject as a seemingly typical juvenile delinquent:

> White American male, 16 years old. . . . He smokes and drinks at various times when he can get it. . . . He states that he was in the reform school about a year. . . . States that he is interested in sports and in motors, wants to be a mechanic and have a garage.

But De River's "psychic examination" revealed that "T. T. A." constantly suffered headaches and was a "Cold Autistic Personality." The "somatic examination" also indicated some irregularities:

> There is an old scar on the outer surface of the left leg – he says he injured himself while throwing a knife. There is an old scar from a gunshot wound – right upper leg, posterior surface. There is another scar from a gunshot wound on the under side of the right ankle. There is a scar 2 1/2 inches below the left knee – subject states that he injured himself while throwing a knife.

De River's interview with "T. T. A." related the circumstances of the murder after the assault as follows:

> He states that he then went to the rear of the car and opened the trunk compartment and got out a jack. When asked where the child was at this time he stated she was standing by the side of the canal. When he returned from the rear of the car with jack in hand, he states she was facing him. Without any warning he began his attack on his victim, striking her with the jack as she stood gazing at him. He felled her with one blow on the forehead and she went down. As she attempted to get up he again struck her on the head. She was then in the water. He struck a third blow while she was apparently moving about in the water, then got in the water, which he states was about eight inches deep, and pushed the child's body with the jack, over to the middle of the canal.

> He then got out of the water; replaced the jack in the trunk compartment; closed the trunk compartment; got in his car; drove home without violating any traffic laws, fully cognizant of what had taken place; able to direct himself; aware of his actions. He states that that evening he did such things as: Have supper; popped some corn; listened to his father play on his accordion; danced – going to bed about 9 o'clock; sleeping well.

De River concluded:

> In my opinion, his actions, on the day of the crime, were willed and rational. His lack of feeling is characteristic of a sadist. The fact that he chose a small child for his victim, types him as a Pedophil, for in this condition, a child is used as the subject's sexual partner and sexual fixation.

As part of his examination, De River asked "T. T. A." to write the following "history":

Feb 6, 1949

My Life history

I have Always been sort of bashful nervous and nervus person. My biggest trouble is my sexual problems. I have an awful temper in which I do lots of things, such as fighting and when I'm doing something on a motor or other things I have little patience in which I will do things that are drastic such as beating on the motor ect. I am not remorseful when it comes to bawling. I don't I haven't had a good cry for several years.

The thing that holds my interest is machinerey and motors I like speed and hotrod Driving. I have had sexual innercourse with several girls but never had one try to go down on me or I never have tried to go down on one of them. I don't like to get serious with a girl I don't know why but a girl don't interest me much.

On the day of November the sixteenth I had risen in the morning and went to school where I went until noon then I went to Burley. I had been drinking Brandy and beer of which I had been feeling pretty high but still could drive the car and not run off the road I picked up ———— ———— and we drove around Burley for a while we then had a 1947 nash dark blue in color. I let him out at his place after which I went up to the ———— Ice cream Shope where I had a malted milk shake.

I walked north up the sidewalk to "J C Penney's" store On the corner I run into a big fellow who Bums me of a match I got him a match and he just gave me a cigarette I think it was drugged because I got more hazey besides mixing the milk shake with liquer. I then started to drive again I went by the Post office and the school house where I picked up this little girl and boy I didnt have any Idea of any sex act with the girl. Im always giving someone a ride large or small well anyway I took the boy to his home and started to drive her home that when I got the Idea of seducing this little kid she don' remind me of anyone and I don't think I could recognise her picture at all. I drove out south and east of town where I drove on a canal bank which had soft dirt on it. The dirt made the car hard to handle. I stopped and got out. then she got out. I had an emotion that I had to relieve myself sexualy so I picked her up and put her in the back seat where I Pulled out my cocias which was hard. I Pulled her Pants down and then I Put my finger in her Vaginia. she never said a thing all she did was look at me I was afraid and shaking, but I still went off before I did anything with it the seman, and stuff went on the apperatus and a little higher up below the Belly button. I by this time feel jumpy and scared I thought that she would say something to some one and I hit her out of Pure fright

the first time I ever had seuxal trouble was when I was about twelve or thirteen, where my cousin who is year older than me tought me to masterbate of which I havent ever done very much just once in a great while.

he also told me about using cuntrums so not to get deseaces, but he told me that the main reason was so not make them Pregnent

he also told me that if you tied a string around it that that would work I tried it but it just About cut if off anyway that is how I felt. I wrote this myself with out any Promices and of my own free will.

all she did was look at me I was afraid and shaking, but I still went off before I did anything with it the seman, and stuff went on the apperatus and a little higher up below the Belly button. I by this time feel jumpy and scared I Thought that she would say something to some one and I hit her out of Pure fright

the first time I ever had sexual trouble was when I was about twelve or thirteen, where my cousin who is year older than me tought me to masterbate of which I havent ever done very much just once in a great while.

ERNEST ALBERT **WALKER**

A footman for an English colonel in London, 17-year-old Ernest Albert Walker tortured to death Raymond Charles Davis, a young messenger he had sent for, on an April evening in 1922. After the murder he travelled by train to Tonbridge and confessed to a policeman on the street early in the morning:

> I believe I have done a murder in London in Lowndes Square. I don't know what made me do it. I done it between 6:15 P.M. and 6:30 P.M. I hit him with a piece of iron bar. I have felt bad since last Wednesday. I lost my mother last January when flu was about. I came to Tonbridge as it would give me plenty of time to think and tell the police here.

Police found the messenger dead in a gas-filled room at the house in London. They also found an "agenda" for the murder, handwritten on a sheet of black-edged notepaper, and a letter addressed to the butler. Walker was judged "guilty but insane" and committed to Broadmoor.

His "agenda":

1. Ring up Sloane Street messenger office for boy.
2. Wait at front door.
3. Invite him in.
4. Bring him downstairs.
5. Ask him to sit down.
6. Hit him on the head.
7. Put him in the safe.
8. Keep him tied up.
9. At 10.30 torture.
10. Prepare for end.
11. Sit down, turn gas on.
12. Put gas light out.
13. Sit down, shut window.

Letter found at the scene of the murder addressed to the butler:

THE FATAL DAY — IN THE AFTERNOON

I expect you will be surprised to see what I have done. Well since my mother died I have made up my mind to die also. You know you said a gun-case had been moved and I denied it. Well, it had. I got a gun out and loaded it and made a sling for my foot to pull the trigger, but my nerve went and I put it away. I rang up the Sloane Square office for a messenger boy and he came to the front door. I asked him to come in and wait, and I brought him to the pantry and hit him on the head with a coal-hammer. So simple! Then I tied him up and killed him. I killed him, **not** the gas. Then I sat down and turned the gas full on. I am as sane as ever I was, only I cannot live without my dear mother. I didn't half give it to that damned boy. I made him squeak. Give my love to Dad and all my friends.

ZODIAC

For a period of almost twelve years, a murderer who dubbed himself "Zodiac" terrorized the residents of California with his taunting missives: a total of at least twenty-five letters, most of which were printed in the San Francisco *Chronicle*. He killed at least five women and one man, and is suspected of many other murders. Zodiac has never been identified or captured by police; a detective who headed the Zodiac investigation in San Francisco, Homicide Inspector David Toschi, later said, "Zodiac was the most frustrating of all my cases. I really believe it gave me bleeding ulcers."

Zodiac's first victim was 18-year-old Cheri Jo Bates, a student and cheerleader at Riverside City College. Around nine o'clock on the evening of October 30, 1966, she left the college library and walked to her VW. Her body was found the next morning lying in the parking lot, seventy-five yards away from her car; she had been kicked in the head, stabbed two times in the chest, stabbed once in the back, and slashed three times across the throat. Over two years later, on the night of December 20, 1968, two Vallejo teenagers, 17-year-old David Faraday and 16-year-old Betty Lou Jensen, were murdered while necking at a "lover's lane." Sitting in the front seat of his parents' '61 Rambler station wagon, Faraday was shot once in the back of the head. Fleeing, Jensen was hit by five bullets in the back. On July 5, 1969, a little after midnight, another Vallejo couple was shot while making out, this time in the parking lot of the Blue Rock Springs Golf Course. A man came up to the passenger side of 22-year-old Darlene Ferrin's '63 Corvair and shot into the car at least nine times. Ferrin, a wife, mother, and waitress employed at Terry's Restaurant, died. Her suitor, 19-year-old Michael Mageau, survived.

On the afternoon of September 27, 1969, two friends who attended Pacific Union College together, 22-year-old Cecilia Ann Shephard and 20-year-old Bryan Hartnell, drove to Lake Berryessa for a picnic. As they sat on the shore, a stocky man walked towards them wearing clip-on sunglasses and a square, black ceremonial-type hood with a bib front emblazoned in white with Zodiac's "logo." He was carrying a semiautomatic handgun, a long bayonet-like knife, and plastic clothesline. He told them he was an escaped convict from Deer Lodge, Montana, robbed them, tied them up, and stabbed Hartnell repeatedly in the back. When Hartnell appeared dead, he went over to Shephard and stabbed her in the back, chest, groin, stomach and side twenty-four times. Afterwards, Zodiac wrote a message on the door of Hartnell's car, then called police from a pay phone at the Napa Car Wash to report a "double murder," saying, "I'm the one that did it." Hartnell survived, and Shephard died two days later.

Zodiac's final acknowledged murder occurred at approximately 9:55 P.M. on October 11, 1969, in San Francisco. Twenty-nine-year-old Paul Lee Stine, a taxi driver and student working on his doctorate in English at San Francisco State College, was shot in the head at contact range in front of 3898 Washington Street in Presidio Heights. Witnesses from a nearby apartment building saw Zodiac take the dead man's wallet and keys, tear off a section of Stine's gray-and-white Pendleton shirt, and wipe down the taxicab with a piece of cloth.

A week later a wanted poster issued by the San Francisco Police Department described Zodiac's appearance as "WMA [White Male Adult], 35-45 Years, approximately 5' 8", Heavy Build, Short Brown Hair, possibly with Red Tint, Wears Glasses." The author of *Zodiac*, Robert Graysmith, lists among Zodiac's skills:

> Explosive devices.
> Cryptography.
> Meteorology.
> Charts and terminology used in conjunction with the compass.
> Knowledge of Gilbert and Sullivan *Mikado*, light opera.
> Knowledge of ancient cults.
> Movie fanatic. *Badlands, The Exorcist, The Most Dangerous Game.*

A psycholinguistics expert that examined Zodiac's writings, Dr. Murray S. Miron, wrote the following in a report for the Syracuse Research Institute:

> He is no more than high school educated, reads little, is isolated, withdrawn, and unrelated in his habits, quiet and unprepossessing in disposition. . . . a discretionary illiterate . . . [prefers] the passiveness of pictures, TV, and the movies . . . would have spent much of his time in movie houses specializing in sado-masochistic and occult eroticism . . . a borderline psychotic. . . . His communications display the characteristic signs of magical thinking, and narcissistic infantilism typical of the schizophrenic. Zodiac rather well fits the pattern of what might be called pseudoreactive schizophrenia. . . . Such individuals engage in their bizarre behavior as sort of a cover-up for their underlying and more hidden psychosis. They can be expected to display wide swings of emotion from intense euphoria to deepest depression. He lives the secret life of seclusion and presents to the world a mask of containment, pleasantness and ordinariness.

Around November 1966, after the October 30 murder of Cheri Jo Bates, Riverside police received the following letter, typewritten in all caps:

SHE WAS YOUNG AND BEAUTIFUL
BUT NOW SHE IS BATTERED AND
DEAD. SHE IS NOT THE FIRST
AND SHE WILL NOT BE THE LAST
I LAY AWAKE NIGHTS THINKING ABOUT MY
NEXT VICTIM. MAYBE SHE WILL BE THE
BEAUTIFUL BLOND THAT BABYSITS NEAR
THE LITTLE STORE AND WALKS DOWN THE
DARK ALLEY EACH EVENING ABOUT SEVEN.
OR MAYBE SHE WILL BE THE SHAPELY BLUE
EYED BRUNETT THAT SAID NO WHEN I

ASKED HER FOR A DATE IN HIGH SCHOOL.
BUT MAYBE IT WILL NOT BE EITHER. BUT I
SHALL CUT OFF HER FEMALE PARTS AND
DEPOSIT THEM FOR THE WHOLE CITY TO SEE.
SO DON'T MAKE IT SO EASY FOR ME. KEEP
YOUR SISTERS, DAUGHTERS, AND WIVES OFF
THE STREETS AND ALLEYS.
MISS BATES WAS STUPID. SHE WENT TO
THE SLAUGHTER LIKE A LAMB. SHE DID
NOT PUT UP A STRUGGLE. BUT I DID.
IT WAS A BALL.
I FIRST PULLED THE MIDDLE WIRE
FROM THE DISTRIBUTOR. THEN I WAITED FOR
HER IN THE LIBRARY AND FOLLOWED HER OUT
AFTER ABOUT TWO MINUTES. THE BATTERY MUST
HAVE BEEN ABOUT DEAD BY THEN. I THEN
OFFERED TO HELP. SHE WAS THEN VERY WILLING
TO TALK WITH ME. I TOLD HER THAT MY CAR
WAS DOWN THE STREET AND THAT I WOULD GIVE
HER A LIFT HOME. WHEN WE WERE AWAY FROM
THE LIBRARY WALKING, I SAID IT WAS ABOUT
TIME. SHE ASKED ME, 'ABOUT TIME FOR WHAT?'
I SAID IT WAS ABOUT TIME FOR YOU TO
DIE. I GRABBED HER AROUND THE NECK WITH
MY HAND OVER HER MOUTH AND MY OTHER HAND
WITH A SMALL KNIFE AT HER THROAT. SHE
WENT VERY WILLINGLY.
HER BREAST FELT VERY WARM AND FIRM
UNDER MY HANDS, BUT ONLY ONE THING WAS ON
MY MIND. MAKING HER PAY FOR THE BRUSH OFFS
THAT SHE HAD GIVEN ME DURING THE YEARS PRIOR.
SHE DIED HARD. SHE SQUIRMED AND SHOOK
AS I CHOKED HER, AND HER LIPS TWITCHED.
SHE LET OUT A SCREAM ONCE AND I KICKED
HER HEAD TO SHUT HER UP. I PLUNGED THE KNIFE
INTO HER AND IT BROKE. I THEN FINISHED THE
JOB BY CUTTING HER THROAT. I AM NOT SICK.
I AM INSANE. BUT THAT WILL NOT STOP
THE GAME. THIS LETTER SHOULD BE PUBLISHED
FOR ALL TO READ IT. IT JUST MIGHT SAVE THAT
GIRL IN THE ALLEY. BUT THAT'S UP TO YOU.
IT WILL BE ON YOUR CONSCIENCE. NOT
MINE. YES, I DID MAKE THAT CALL TO YOU
ALSO. IT WAS JUST A WARNING. BEWARE . . . I
AM STALKING YOUR GIRLS NOW.
CC. CHIEF OF POLICE
ENTERPRISE

On April 30, 1967, three notes were delivered to the Riverside *Press-Enterprise*, the Riverside police, and Joseph Bates, Cheri Jo Bates' father. They were all written in pencil and had the same message:

BATES HAD

TO DIE

THERE WILL

BE MORE

Z

Police also found a poem scratched with a blue ballpoint pen into a desk at the Riverside City College library:

Sick of living/unwilling to die

cut.
clean.
if red/
clean.
blood spurting,
dripping,
spilling;
all **over** her new
dress.
oh well,
it was red
anyway.
life draining into an
uncertain death.
she won't
die.
this **time**
Someone ll find her.
Just wait till
next time.
rh

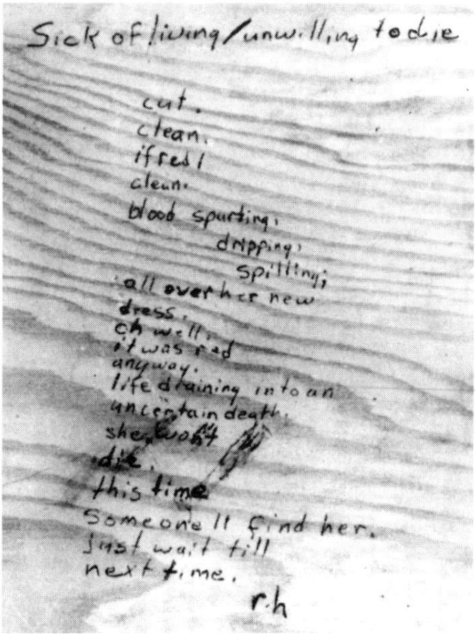

Three newspapers – the San Francisco *Chronicle*, San Francisco *Examiner*, and Vallejo *Times-Herald* – received the same letter (with slight variations) and one third of a complete coded message on July 31, 1969:

Dear Editor
This is the murderer of the
2 teenagers last Christmass
at Lake Herman & the girl
on the 4th of July near
the golf course in Vallejo
To prove I killed them I
shall state some facts which
only I & the police know.

Christmass

1.	Brand name of ammo Super X
2	10 shots were fired
3	the boy was on his back with his feet to the car
4	the girl was on her right side feet to the west

4th July

1	girl was wearing paterned slacks
2	The boy was also shot in the knee.
3	Brand name of ammo was western

Over

Here is part of a cipher the other 2 parts of this cipher are being mailed to the editors of the Vallejo times & SF Exam iner.

I want you to print this cipher on the front page of your paper. In this cipher is my identity.
If you do not print this cipher by the afternoon of Fry. 1st of Aug 69, I will go on a kill ram-Page Fry. night. I will cruse around all weekend killing lone people in the night then move on to kill again, untill I end up with a dozen people over the weekend.

The complete text of the encrypted code, as deciphered by Donald and Bettye Harden of Salinas on August 4, 1969:

I LIKE KILLING PEOPLE
BECAUSE IT IS SO MUCH
FUN IT IS MORE FUN THAN
KILLING WILD GAME IN
THE FORREST BECAUSE
MAN IS THE MOST DANGEROUE
ANAMAL OF ALL TO KILL
SOMETHING GIVES ME THE
MOST THRILLING EXPERENCE
IT IS EVEN BETTER THAN GETTING

YOUR ROCKS OFF WITH A GIRL
THE BEST PART OF IT IS THAE
WHEN I DIE I WILL BE REBORN
IN PARADICE AND THEI HAVE
KILLED WILL BECOME MY SLAVES
I WILL NOT GIVE YOU MY NAME
BECAUSE YOU WILL TRY TO SLOI
DOWN OR ATOP MY COLLECTIOG OF
SLAVES FOR AFTERLIFE
EBEORIETEMETHHPITI

Letter to the Vallejo *Times-Herald* dated August 7, 1969:

Dear Editor
This is the Zodiac speaking.
In answer to your asking for
more details about the good
times I have had in Vallejo,
I shall be very happy to
supply even more material.
By the way, are the police
haveing a good time with the
code? If not, tell them to cheer
up; when they do crack it
they will have me.
On the 4th of July:
I did not open the car door, The
window was rolled down all ready
The boy was origionaly sitting in
the front seat when I began
fireing. When I fired the first
shot at his head, he leaped
backwards at the same time
thus spoiling my aim. He ended up on the back seat then
the floor in back thashing out
very violently with his legs;
that's how I shot him in the
knee. I did not leave the cene
of the killing with squealling tires
& raceing engine as described in the
Vallejo papers.
I drove away slowly so as not to
draw attention to my car. The man
who told the police my car was brown
was a negro about 40-45 rather shabbly
dressed. I was in this phone booth
haveing some fun with the Vallejo
cop when he was walking by.
When I hung the phone up the
dam thing began to ring & that

drew his attention to me & my car.
Last Christmass
In that epasode the police were
wondering as to how I could
shoot & hit my victims in the
dark. They did not openly state this,
but implied this by saying it was a
well lit night & I could see
silowets on the horizon.
Bullshit that area is srounded
by high hills & trees. What
I did was tape a small pencel flash
light to the barrel of my gun. If
you notice, in the center of the beam
of light if you aim it at a wall or
ceiling you will see a black or
darck spot in the center of the
circle of light about 3 to 6 in.
across.
When taped to a gun barrel, the
bullet will strike exactly in the
center of the black dot in the light.
All I had to do was spray them . . .
No address.

After stabbing Hartnell and Shepherd on September 27, 1969, Zodiac wrote the following message with a black felt-tip pen on the door of Hartnell's white VW Karmann Ghia:

Vallejo
12-20-68
7-4-69
Sept 27-69 – 6:30
by knife

Letter to the San Francisco *Chronicle*, postmarked October 13, 1969; enclosed was a bloody scrap of murder victim Paul Stine's shirt:

This is the Zodiac speaking.
I am the murderer of the
taxi driver over by
Washington St & Maple St last
night, to prove this here is
a blood stained piece of his
shirt. I am the same man
who did in the people in the
north bay area.

The S.F. Police could have caught
me last night if they had
searched the park properly
instead of holding road races
with their motorcicles seeing who
could make the most noise. The
car drivers should have just
parked their cars & sat there
quietly waiting for me to come
out of cover.
School children make nice targets, I think I shall wipe out
a school bus some morning. Just
shoot out the front tire & then
pick off the kiddies as they come
bouncing out.

Greeting card sent to the *Chronicle* on November 8, 1969; on the front was an illustration of a dripping fountain pen hanging by a string and the following printed text:

Sorry I haven't
written,

but I just
washed
my pen . . .

Printed on the inside, as if written by a leaky pen, was the punchline:

and i
can't
do a
thing
with
it!

Zodiac wrote the following message inside the card:

This is the Zodiac speaking
I though you would nead a
good laugh before you
hear the bad news
you won't get the
news for a while yet
PS could you print
this new cipher
on your front page?
I get awfully lonely

when I am ignored,
So lonely I could
do my **Thing**!!!!!!

Des July Aug
Sept Oct = 7

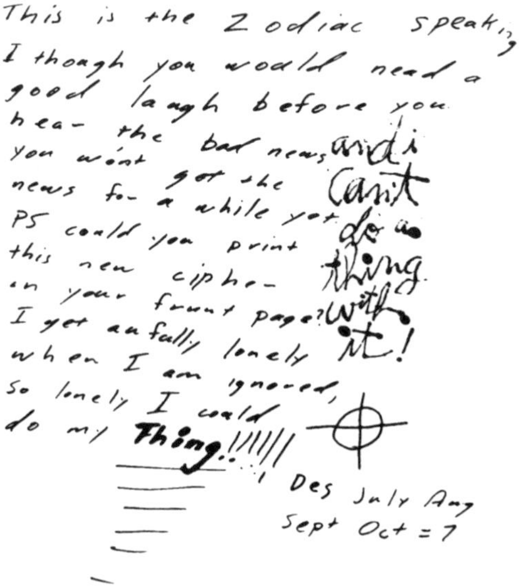
This is the Zodiac speaking,
I though you would need a
good laugh before you
hear the bad news
you wont get the
news for a while yet
PS could you print
this new cipher
in your frunt page?
I get awfully lonely
when I am ignored,
So lonely I could
do my **Thing**!!!!!!
Des July Aug
Sept Oct = 7

and i can't do a thing with it!

Also inside the card was a 340-symbol encrypted message. Deciphered by Robert Graysmith, author of *Zodiac*, it translates as follows:

HERB CAEN:
I GIVE THEM HELL TOO.
BLAST THESE LIES. SLUETH
SHOELD SEE A NAME
BELOW KILLEERS FILM. A PILLS
GAME. PARDON ME AGCEPT TO
BLAST NE. BULLSHIT.
THESE FOOLS SHALL MEET
KILLER. PLEAS ASK LUNBLAD.
SOEL AT H LSD UL
CLEAR LAKE. SO STARE I
EAT A PILL, ASSHOLE. I
PLANT MR. A. H. PHONE LAKE B.
ALL SSLAVES BECAUSE LSD
WILL STOLEN EITHER SLAVE
SHALL I HELL SLASH TOSCHI?
THE PIG STALLS DEAL OC
EIGHTH SOEL SLAIN.

Seven-page letter to the *Chronicle*, postmarked November 9, 1969:

This is the Zodiac speaking
up to the end of Oct I have
killed 7 people. I have grown
rather angry with the police
for their telling lies about me.
So I shall change the way the
collecting of slaves. I shall
no longer announce to anyone.
when I comitt my murders,
they shall look like routine
robberies, killings of anger, &
a few fake accidents, etc.

The police shall never catch me,
because I have been too clever
for them.

1 I look like the description
passed out only when I do
my thing, the rest of the time
I look entirle different. I
shall not tell you what my
descise consists of when I kill

2 As of yet I have left no
fingerprints behind me contrary
to what the police say
in my killings I wear transparent finger tip guards. All it
is is 2 coats of airplane cement
coated on my finger tips — quite
unnoticible & very efective.

3 my killing tools have been bought
en through the mail order outfits before the ban went into
efect. except one & it was
bought out of state.

So as you can see the police don't
have much to work on. If you
wonder why I was wipeing the
cab down I was leaving fake clews
for the police to run all over town
with, as one might say, I gave the
cops som bussy work to do to
keep them happy. I enjoy needling
the blue pigs. Hey blue pig I
was in the park — you were useing
fire trucks to mask the sound
of your cruzeing prowl cars. The
dogs never came with in 2
blocks of me & they were to
the west & there was only 2
groups of parking about 10 min
apart then the motor cicles
went by about 150 ft away
going from south to north west.
p.s. 2 cops pulled a goof abot 3
min after I left the cab. I was
walking down the hill to the
park when this cop car pulled up
& one of them called me over
& asked if I saw any one
acting supicisous or strange
in the last 5 to 10 min & I said
yes there was this man who
was running by waveing a gun

& the cops peeled rubber &
went around the corner as
I directed them & I dissap
eared into the park a block &
a half away never to be seen
again.

Hey pig doesnt it rile you up
to have your noze rubed in your
booboos?
If you cops think I'm going to take
on a bus the way I stated I was,
you deserve to have holes in your
heads.
Take one bag of ammonium nitrate
fertilizer & 1 gal of stove oil &
dump a few bags of gravel on
top & then set the shit off
& will positivly ventalate any
thing that should be in the way
of the blast.
The death machine is all ready
made. I would have sent you
pictures but you would be nasty
enough to trace them back to
developer & then to me, so I
shall describe my masterpiece
to you. Tke nice part of it is
all the parts can be bought on
the open market with no quest
ions asked.
1 bat. pow clock — will run for
approx 1 year
1 photoelectric switch
2 copper leaf springs
2 6V car bat
1 flash light bulb & reflector
1 mirror
2 18" cardboard tubes black with
shoe polish inside & oute

[schematic drawing of bomb]

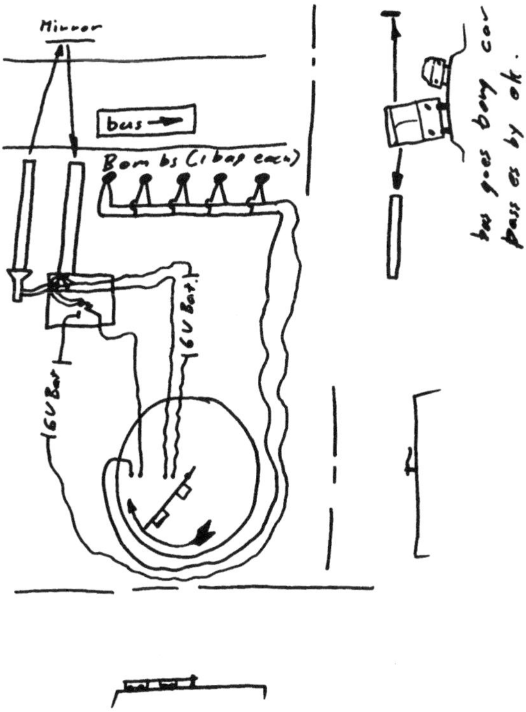

the system checks out from one
end to the other in my
tests. What you do not know
is whether the death machine
is at the sight or whether
it is being stored in my
basement for future use.
I think you do not have the
manpower to stop this one

by continually searching the
road sides looking for this
thing. & it wont do to re roat
& re schedule the busses bec
ause the bomb can be adapted
to new conditions.
Have fun!! By the way
it could be rather messy
if you try to bluff me.

[drawing of a large crossed circle and five x's moving clockwise in the left hemisphere]

PS. Be shure to
print the part I
marked out on
page 3 [about being stopped by police] or I shall
do my thing
To prove that I am the
Zodiac, Ask the Vallejo
cop about my electric gun
sight which I used to start
my collecting of slaves.

Letter to San Francisco attorney Melvin Belli, postmarked December 20, 1969; enclosed was a card that read "Merry Xmass and New Year" and another torn scrap of Stine's bloody shirt:

Dear Melvin

This is the Zodiac speaking I
wish you a happy Christmass.
The one thing I ask of you is
this, please help me. I cannot
reach out for help because of
this thing in me wont let me.
I am finding it extreamly dif-
icult to hold it in check I am
afraid I will loose control
again and take my nineth &
posibly tenth victom. Please
help me I am drownding. At
the moment the children are
safe from the bomb because
it is so massive to dig in & the
triger mech requires much work
to get it adjusted just right. But
if I hold back too long from
no nine I will loose ~~complet~~ all
controol of my self & set the
bomb up. Please help me I can
not remain in control for much
longer. 

Dear Melvin

This is the Zodiac speaking I wish you a happy Christmass. The one thing I ask of you is this, please help me. I cannot reach out for help because of this thing in me wont let me. I am finding it extreamly dif-icult to hold it in check I am afraid I will loose control again and take my nineth & posibly tenth victom. Please help me I am drownding. At the moment the children are safe from the bomb because it is so massive to dig in & the triger mech requires much work to get it adjusted just right. But if I hold back too long from no nine I will loose ~~complet~~ all controol of my self & set the bomb up. Please help me I can not remain in control for much longer.

Letter to the *Chronicle*, postmarked April 20, 1970:

This is the Zodiac speaking
By the way have you cracked
the last cipher I sent you?
My name is ——

I am mildly cerous as to how
much money you have on my
head now. I hope you do not
think that I was the one
who wiped out that blue
meannie with a bomb at the
cop station. Even though I talked
about killing school children with
one. It just wouldn't doo to
move in on someone elses teritory.
But there is more glory in killing
a cop than a cid because a cop
can shoot back. I have killed
ten people to date. It would
have been a lot more except
that my bus bomb was a dud.
I was swamped out by the
rain we had a while back.

The new bomb is set up like
this

[schematic drawing of bomb]

PS I hope you have fun trying
to figgure out who I killed

Greeting card sent to the *Chronicle* on April 28, 1970. The illustration on the front depicts two old prospectors: one is sitting on a burro and saying to the other, who is sitting on a tired dragon, "Sorry to hear your ass is a dragon." In the upper right-hand corner Zodiac wrote:

I hope you
enjoy your
selves
when I
have my
Blast.

The new bomb is set up like this

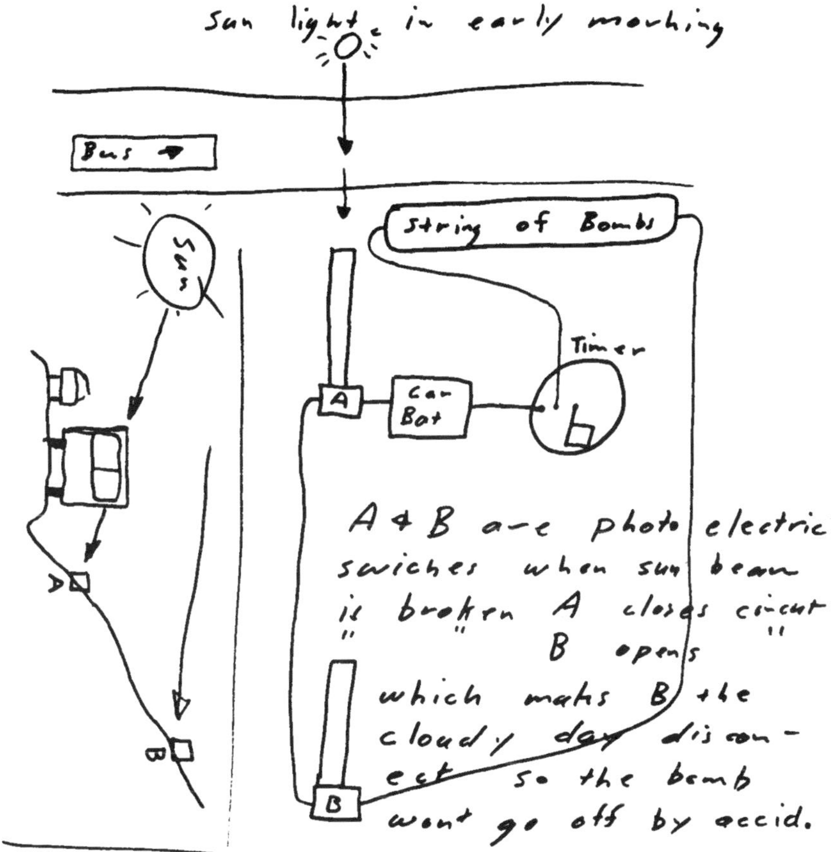
Sun light in early morning
Bus
Sun
String of Bombs
Timer
A
Car Bat
B
A & B are photo electric swiches when sun beam is broken A closes cricut
" " B opens "
which maks B the cloudy day disconect so the bomb wont go off by accid.

PS I hope you have fun trying to figgure out who I killed

⊕=10 SFPD=0

P.S. on
back

On the back of the card he wrote:

If you dont want me to
have this blast you must
do two things. 1 Tell every
one about the bus bomb with
all the details. 2 I would like
to see some nice Zodiac butons
wandering about town. Every
one else has these buttons like,
, black power, melvin eats
bluber, etc. Well it would cheer
me up considerbly if I saw
a lot of people wearing my
buton. Please no nasty ones
like melvin's

Thank you

Letter to the *Chronicle*, postmarked June 26, 1970; enclosed was a map of Mount Diablo:

This is the Zodiac speaking

I have become very upset with
the people of San Fran Bay
Area. They have **not** complied
with my wishes for them to
wear some nice buttons.
I promiced to punish them
if they did not comply, by
anilating a full School Buss.
But now school is out for
the summer, so I punished
them in an another way.
I shot a man sitting in
a parked car with a .38.

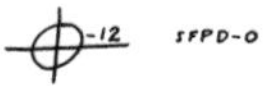

The Map coupled with this
code will tell you where the
bomb is set. You have untill
next Fall to dig it up.

Below was a two-line cipher that was to be used with the map.

Letter to the *Chronicle*, postmarked July 24, 1970:

This is the Zodiac speaking
I am rather unhappy because
you people will not wear some
nice  buttons. So I now
have a little list, starting with
the woeman & her baby that I
gave a rather interesting ride
for a coupple howers one
evening a few months back that
ended in my burning her
car where I found them.

Letter to the *Chronicle*, postmarked July 26, 1970:

This is the Zodiac speaking
I shall (on top of every
thing else) torture all 13
of my slaves that I have
wateing for me in Paradice.
Some I shall tie over ant hills
and watch them scream & twich
and squirm. Others shall have
pine splinters driven under their
nails & then burned. Others shall
be placed in cages & fed salt
beef untill they are gorged then
I shall listen to their pleass
for water and I shall laugh at
them. Others will hang by
their thumbs & burn in the
sun then I will rub them down
deep heat to warm
them up. Others I shall
skin them alive & let them
run around screaming. And . . .
all billiard players I shall
have them play in a dark
ened dungen all with crooked
cues & Twisted Shoes.
Yes I shall have great
fun inflicting the most
delicious of pain to my
Slaves

SFPD = 0 ⊕ = 13

As some day it may hapen
that a victom must be found.
I've got a little list. I've
got a little list, of society
offenders who might well be
underground who would never
be missed who would never be
missed. There is the pest-
ulentual nucences who whrite
for autographs, all people who
have flabby hands and irritating laughs. All children who
are up in dates and implore
you with im platt. All people
who are shakeing hands shake
hands like that. And all third
persons who with unspoiling
take thoes who insist. They'd
none of them be missed. They'd
none of them be missed. There's
the banjo seranader and
the others of his race and
the piano orginast I got him
on the list. All people who
eat pepermint and phomphit
in your face, they would
never be missed They would
never be missed And the
Idiout who phraises with in-
thusastic tone of centuries
but this and every country but
his own. And the lady from
the provences who dress like
a guy who doesn't cry and
the singurly abnormily the
girl who never kissed. I don't
think she would be missed
Im shure she wouldn't be
missed. And that nice impriest
that is rather rife the judicial hummerest I've got him on
the list All funny fellows, com-
mic men and clowns of private
life. They'd none of them be
missed. They'd none of them be
missed. And uncompromising
kind such as wachmacallit,
thingmebob, and like wise, well-
nevermind, and tut tut tut tut,

and whashisname, and you know
who, but the task of filling
up the blanks I rather leave
up to you. But it really does-
n't matter whom you place
upon the list, for none of
them be missed, none of
them be missed.

[The Zodiac symbol at the end of the letter took up three-quarters of the last page.]

PS. The Mt. Diablo Code concerns
Radians & # inches along the radians

Postcard to the *Chronicle*, postmarked October 5, 1970, written with cut-up letters from the previous day's *Chronicle*:

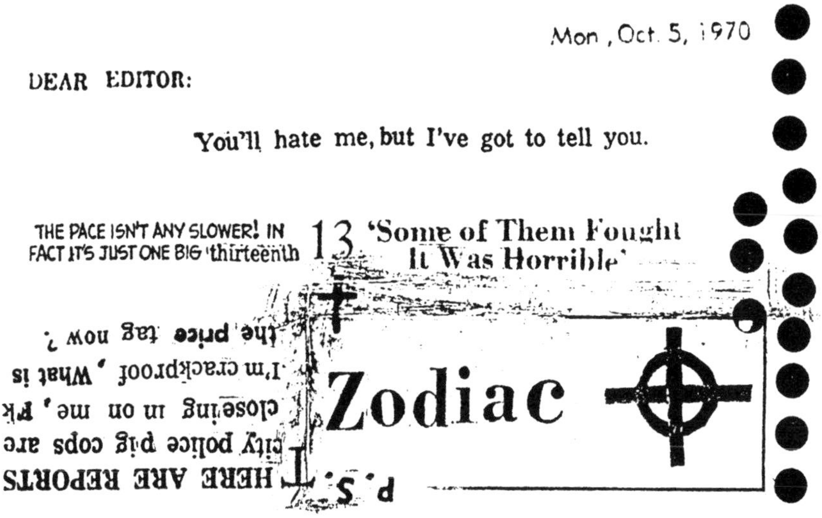

Mon, Oct. 5, 1970

DEAR EDITOR:

You'll hate me, but I've got to tell you.

THE PACE ISN'T ANY SLOWER! IN FACT IT'S JUST ONE BIG 'thirteenth 13 'Some of Them Fought It Was Horrible'

Zodiac

P.S. T HERE ARE REPORTS city police pig cops are closeing in on me, Fk I'm crackproof, What is the price tag now?

Halloween card sent to Paul Avery, a reporter from the *Chronicle* who wrote most of the stories about the Zodiac murders, postmarked October 27, 1970. Illustrated on the front in black and orange colors was a dancing skeleton with a pumpkin and the following printed text:

FROM YOUR
SECRET
PAL

I feel it in
my bones,
You ache

to know
my name,
And so
I'll clue
you in . . .

The punchline printed inside the card:

But then, why spoil our game!
BOO!
Happy
Halloween!

Zodiac added his own embellishments: another skeleton, a section of another card, illustrated eyes, and a variety of his own symbols. He also wrote in a cross configuration:

BY FIRE
BY KNIFE
BY GUN
BY ROPE
PARADICE
SLAVES

Letter to the Los Angeles *Times*, postmarked March 13, 1971:

This is the Zodiac speaking
Like I have allways said
I am crack proof. If the
Blue Meannies are evere
going to catch me, they had
best get off their fat asses
& do something. Because the
longer they fiddle & fart
around, the more slaves
I will collect for my after
life. I do have to give them
credit for stumbling across
my riverside activity, but
they are only finding the
easy ones, there are a hell
of a lot more down there.
The reason that Im writing
to the Times is this, They
don't bury me on the back pages
like some of the others.

SFPD-0 -17+

Postcard sent to *Chronicle* reporter Paul Avery on March 22, 1971, that possibly links Zodiac to the disappearance of Lake Tahoe nurse Donna Lass.

Letter to the *Chronicle*, postmarked January 29, 1974:

I saw & think "The Exorcist"
was the best saterical com-
idy that I have ever seen.

Signed, yours truley:

He plunged him self into
the billowy wave
and an echo arose from
the sucides grove
titwillo titwillo
titwillo

Ps. if I do not see this
note in your paper, I
will do something nasty,
which you know I'm capable of
doing

Unsigned letter to the *Chronicle*, postmarked May 8, 1974; it was later determined by FBI handwriting experts to have been written by Zodiac:

Sirs- I would like to
express my ~~consterat~~
consternation concerning
your poor taste & lack of
sympathy for the public, as
evidenced by your running
of the ads for the movie
"Badlands," featuring the
blurb "In 1959 most people
were killing time. Kit & Holly
were killing people." In
light of recent events, this
kind of murder-glorification
can only be deplorable at
best (not that glorification of
violence was **ever** justifiable)
why don't you show some
concern for public sensibilities
& cut the ad?
A citizen

Unsigned letter – also proven by the FBI to be written by Zodiac – to the *Chronicle*, postmarked July 8, 1974, concerning the newspaper's anti-feminist columnist, Count Marco Spinelli:

Editor —
Put Marco back in the hell-hole
from whence it came — he has
a serious psychological disorder —
always needs to feel superior. I
suggest you refer him to a shrink.
Meanwhile, cancel the Count Marco
column. Since the Count can
write anonymously, so can I —
The Red Phantom
(red with rage)

Letter to the *Chronicle*, postmarked April 24, 1978:

Dear Editor
This is the Zodiac speaking I
am back with you. Tell herb caen
I am here, I have always been here.
That city pig toschi is good but
I am ~~bu~~ smarter and better he
will get tired then leave me
alone. I am waiting for a good
movie about me. who will play
me. I am now in control of all
things.
Yours truly:

 - guess

SFPD - 0

SELECTED BIBLIOGRAPHY

INTRODUCTION

Black, Joel. *The Aesthetics of Murder: A Study of Romantic Literature and Contemporary Culture.* Baltimore: Johns Hopkins University Press, 1991.

Ellis, Havelock. *The Criminal.* Montclair, New Jersey: Patterson Smith, 1973.

Leyton, Elliott. *Compulsive Killers: The Story of Modern Multiple Murder.* New York: New York University Press, 1986.

Mandeville, Bernard. *The Fable of the Bees.* New York: Capricorn Books, 1962.

Nietzsche, Friedrich. *Human, All Too Human: A Book for Free Spirits.* Translated by Marion Faber with Stephen Lehmann. Lincoln, Nebraska: University of Nebraska Press, 1984.

Wolfgang, Marvin E., ed. *Studies in Homicide.* New York: Harper & Row, 1967.

GERTRUDE BANISZEWSKI

Millet, Kate. *The Basement: Meditations on a Human Sacrifice.* New York: Simon and Schuster, 1979.

MARY BELL

Sereny, Gitta. *The Case of Mary Bell: A Portrait of a Child Who Murdered.* New York: McGraw-Hill Book Co., 1973.

DAVID BERKOWITZ

Carpozi, George Jr. *Son of Sam: The .44 Caliber Killer.* New York: Manor Books, 1977.

Klausner, Lawrence D. *Son of Sam.* New York: McGraw-Hill Book Co., 1981.

Willeford, Charles. *Off the Wall.* Montclair, New Jersey: The Pegasus Rex Press, 1980.

WILLIAM BONIN

Bonin, William. *Doing Time: Stories From the Mind of a Death Row Prisoner, Book One.* Red Bluff, California: Eagle Publishing, 1991.

McDougal, Dennis. *Angel of Darkness.* New York: Warner Books, 1991.

MR. BROWN

Smith, Peter Gladstone. *The Crime Explosion.* London: Macdonald and Co., 1970.
Usher, Alan. "The Case of the Disembowelled Doll: A Multiple Murder." *Medicine, Science and the Law,* Vol. 7, No. 4 (October 1967), 211-2.

PATRICK BYRNE

Bland, James. *True Crime Diary.* London: Futura Publications, 1987.

MICHAEL & SUZAN CARSON

Reynolds, Richard D. *Cry For War: The Story of Suzan and Michael Carson.* Walnut Creek, California: Squibob Press (P. O. Box 4476, Walnut Creek, California 94596), 1987.

ALBERT DeSALVO

Banks, Harold K. *The Strangler!: The Story of Terror in Boston.* New York: Avon Books, 1967.
Frank, Gerold. *The Boston Strangler.* New York: New American Library, 1967.
Rae, George W. *Confessions of the Boston Strangler.* New York: Pyramid Books, 1967.

DERRICK EDWARDSON

Wilson, Colin and Pitman, Patricia. *Encyclopaedia of Murder.* London: Pan Books, 1984.

ALBERT FISH

Angelella, Michael. *Trail of Blood.* New York: The Bobbs-Merrill Co., 1979.
Heimer, Mel. *The Cannibal.* New York: Pinnacle Books, 1991.
Schechter, Harold. *Deranged.* New York: Pocket Books, 1990.
Wertham, Fredric. *The Show of Violence.* Garden City, New York: Doubleday and Co., 1949.

JOHN LINLEY FRAZIER

Lunde, Donald T. *Murder and Madness.* San Francisco: San Francisco Book Co., 1976.

JEANNACE FREEMAN

Blashfield, Jean F. *Why They Killed.* New York: Warner Books, 1990.

BRUNO G.

Hirschfeld, Magnus. *Sexual Anomalies and Perversions: Physical and Psychological Development, Diagnosis and Treatment.* London: Encyclopaedic Press, 1966.

HARVEY GLATMAN

Ressler, Robert K., and Shachtman, Tom. *Whoever Fights Monsters.* New York: St. Martin's Press, 1992.
Ressler, Robert K.; Burgess, Ann W.; and Douglas, John E. *Sexual Homicide: Patterns and Motives.* Lexington, Massachusetts: Lexington Books, 1988.

CHARLES GUITEAU

Clarke, James W. *American Assassins: The Darker Side of Politics.* Princeton, New Jersey: Princeton University Press, 1990.
Donovan, Robert J. *The Assassins.* New York: Popular Library, 1962.
Rosenberg, Charles E. *The Trial of the Assassin Guiteau: Psychiatry and Law in the Gilded Age.* Chicago: The University of Chicago Press, 1968.

JOHN GEORGE HAIGH

Dunboyne, Lord, ed. *The Trial of John George Haigh.* London: William Hodge and Co., 1953.
Eisler, Robert. *Man into Wolf: An Anthropological Interpretation of Sadism, Masochism and Lycanthropy.* London: Routledge and Kegan Paul, 1951.
Lefebure, Molly. *Murder with a Difference: Studies of Haigh and Christie.* London: Heinemann, 1958.

WILLIAM HEIRENS

Freeman, Lucy. *"Before I Kill More . . ."* New York: Crown Publishers, Inc., 1955.
Kennedy, Dolores. *William Heirens: His Day in Court.* Chicago: Bonus Books, 1991.

WILLIAM EDWARD HICKMAN

Cantillon, Richard H. *In Defense of The Fox: The Trial of William Edward Hickman.* Atlanta: Droke House/Hallux, 1972.
Wolf, Marvin J., and Mader, Katherine. *Fallen Angels: Chronicles of L.A. Crime and Mystery.* New York: Ballantine Books, 1986.

WILLIAM K. JONES

Reid, Don with Gurwell, John. *Eyewitness.* Houston: Cordovan Press, 1973.

JOSEPH KALLINGER

Downs, Thomas. *The Door-to-Door Killer.* New York: Dell Publishing Co., 1984.
Schreiber, Flora Rheta. *The Shoemaker: The Anatomy of a Psychotic.* New York: New American Library, 1984.

JOHN LIST

Ryzuk, Mary S. *Thou Shalt Not Kill.* New York: Warner Books, 1990.
Sharkey, Joe. *Death Sentence: The Inside Story of the John List Murders.* New York: New American Library, 1990.

PATRICK MACKAY

Clark, Tim, and Penycate, John. *Psychopath: The Case of Patrick Mackay.* London: Routledge and Kegan Paul, 1976.

HERBERT MULLIN

Lunde, Donald T., and Morgan, Jefferson. *The Die Song.* New York: Playboy, 1980.
West, Don. *Sacrifice Unto Me.* New York: Pyramid Books, 1974.

CARL PANZRAM

Gaddis, Thomas E., and Long, James O. *Killer: A Journal of Murder.* New York: The Macmillan Co., 1970.

PAULINE PARKER

Franklin, Charles. *The World's Worst Murderers.* London: Odhams Books, 1965.
Furneaux, Rubert. *Famous Criminal Cases 2.* London: Allan Wingate, 1955.
Jones, Richard Glyn, ed. *Killer Couples.* New York: Berkley Books, 1989.

ISSEI SAGAWA

Sagawa, Issei. *Kiri no Naka (In the Mist).* Tokyo: Hanashi no Tokusyu, 1983.

GERARD SCHAEFER JR.

Schaefer, G. J. *Killer Fiction: Tales of an Accused Serial Killer.* Atlanta: Media Queen Ltd., 1990.

SCHIZOPHRENIC FIRESETTER

MacDonald, John M. *The Murderer and His Victim.* Springfield, Illinois: Charles C. Thomas, 1961.

CHARLES SCHMID JR.

Moser, Don, and Cohen, Jerry. *The Pied Piper of Tucson.* New York: New American Library, 1967.

EDGAR SMITH

Smith, Edgar. *Brief Against Death.* New York: Alfred A. Knopf, 1968.
Smith, Edgar. *Getting Out.* New York: Coward, McCann and Geoghegan, 1973.

RICHARD & BRIDGET SMITH

Enright, D. J., ed. *The Oxford Book of Death.* Oxford: Oxford University Press, 1983.

CHARLES STARKWEATHER

Allen, William. *Starkweather: The Story of a Mass Murderer.* Boston: Houghton Mifflin Co., 1976.
Beaver, Ninette; Ripley, B. K.; and Trese, Patrick. *Caril.* New York: J. B. Lippincott Co., 1974.
Reinhardt, James Melvin. *The Murderous Trail of Charles Starkweather.* Springfield, Illinois: Charles C. Thomas, 1960.

PETER SUTCLIFFE

Burn, Gordon. *Somebody's Husband, Somebody's Son: The Story of the Yorkshire Ripper.* New York: Penguin Books, 1984.
Cross, Roger. *The Yorkshire Ripper.* London: Grafton Books, 1981.
Jouve, Nicole Ward. *"The Streetcleaner": The Yorkshire Ripper Case on Trial.* London: Marion Boyars, 1986.

DENNIS SWEENEY

Harris, David. *Dreams Die Hard.* New York: St. Martin's Press, 1982.

T. T. A.

De River, J. Paul. *Crime and the Sexual Psychopath.* Springfield, Illinois: Charles C. Thomas, 1958.

ERNEST ALBERT WALKER

Shew, E. Spencer. *A Second Companion to Murder.* New York: Alfred A. Knopf, 1962.

ZODIAC

Dickensheet, Dean W., ed. *Great Crimes of San Francisco.* New York: Ballantine Books, 1974.
Graysmith, Robert. *Zodiac.* New York: St. Martin's Press, 1986.